MAJ. GEN. SAMUEL GIBBS FRENCH, C. S. A.

TWO WARS:

AN

AUTOBIOGRAPHY

OF

GEN. SAMUEL G. FRENCH,

An Officer in the Armies of the United States and the Confederate States,
A Graduate from the U. S. Military Academy, West Point, 1843.

MEXICAN WAR;
WAR BETWEEN THE STATES, A DIARY;
RECONSTRUCTION PERIOD, HIS EXPERIENCE;
INCIDENTS, REMINISCENCES, ETC.

NASHVILLE, TENN.:
CONFEDERATE VETERAN.
1901.

New Edition
Published in 1999 by
BLUE ACORN PRESS
P.O. Box 2684
Huntington, W.Va. 25726

ISBN 1-885033-22-2

THIS VOLUME IS DEDICATED

TO

MY WIFE AND CHILDREN,

AND TO

THE CONFEDERATE SOLDIERS

WHO BATTLED WITH THE INVAD-
ING FOE TO PROTECT OUR HOMES
AND MAINTAIN THE CAUSE FOR
WHICH OLIVER CROMWELL AND
GEORGE WASHINGTON FOUGHT.

PREFACE.

Some years ago, when living on an orange grove at Winter Park, it occurred to me that my idle time might be usefully employed in transcribing from memoranda and my diary many incidents of my life for preservation in one manuscript for my children. This was continued at intervals until it became as here presented. It was mainly discontinued after my children became old enough to observe passing events for themselves.

But inasmuch as a few books have been published containing errors in describing some military operations in which I participated, justice to the troops under my command induces me to publish my account of them as recorded when they occurred.

This volume, then, is a simple narrative of passing events, without discussing their importance and bearing politically in shaping the destiny of the nation.

Although my lot was cast with the South, and whatever may be my opinion of the action of the North before, during, and after the war as expressed in these pages, I am as loyal to the Constitution and as ready to uphold and maintain the rights and dignity of the United States as any man within its boundary; and this was evidenced when I tendered my services, as a soldier, to the President before war was declared against Spain.

I do not know that I am indebted to any person, except Joseph M. Brown, of Marietta, Ga., a son of Gov. Joseph E. Brown, for what I have written, and to him I make acknowledgment for obligations. THE AUTHOR.

Pensacola, Fla., May 1, 1899.

INTRODUCTION.

OF all forms of history, a good autobiography is the most pleasing and attractive. If the writer has been a prominent and responsible participant in great events, if high character warrants his faithfulness to truth, and if the events of which he writes are in themselves of great historic value, his autobiography will possess a peculiar charm and interest for every intelligent reader.

The generation that recalls from memory the events of our history connected with the admission of the great State of Texas into the American Union and the war with Mexico which followed has nearly all gone. Here and there a strong man survives whose memory is clear and whose conscience is true. To hear him talk of these events, or to read after him as he writes of the universal excitement in the country—the angry debates in Congress, the opposition to the admission of Texas, and to the war with Mexico, the brilliant campaign of Taylor, the battles of Palo Alto, Resaca de la Palma, Monterey, and Buena Vista—is to enjoy history in its most attractive form. The historian who has been an active participant in the events of which he writes, whose passions have been cooled by age, and whose judgment has been disciplined by long years of experience and reflection enjoys an immense advantage. However we may disagree with him in his criticisms upon the conduct of men or upon their motives, if he be a man of high and true character, we enjoy the greatest satisfaction in accepting his positive statements as to facts which represent his own actions and experiences.

Gen. French is such a historian. The clear, natural, dispassionate style of his book—its freedom from bitterness, the tenderness with which he dwells upon the history of his classmates at West Point, several of whom became distinguished generals in the Federal army (Grant, Franklin, Ingalls, and Quinby)—all these characteristics of his autobiography soon win the confidence of the reader.

INTRODUCTION.

For the general reader of to-day, and especially for the survivors of the Confederate Army, Gen. French's autobiography will possess peculiar interest. The writer has enjoyed the opportunity of reading the advance sheets of the book only through the account of the battle of Allatoona, which was fought October 5, 1864, but as Gen. French participated in the campaign of Gen. Hood up to its predestined disaster at Nashville, the autobiography will be read with more than usual interest by students of the ill-starred march into Tennessee and the battles of Franklin and Nashville.

The venerable author of "Two Wars" has been an able and gallant soldier of his country, and the simple and graphic manner in which he writes of his distinguished services, and relates the great events in which he bore a faithful part, entitle his book to the confidence of his countrymen. It is a most valuable addition to our country's history, and a book which will be of permanent use in the study of our great Confederate struggle.

ELLISON CAPERS.

Columbia, S. C., July 1, 1901.

CONTENTS.

CHAPTER I.

CHAPTER II.

CHAPTER III.

CHAPTER IV.

Contents.

CHAPTER V.

CHAPTER VI.

CHAPTER VII.

CONTENTS.

CHAPTER VIII.

CHAPTER IX.

CHAPTER X.

CHAPTER XI.

CONTENTS.

CONTENTS.

CONTENTS.

CHAPTER XVIII.

CHAPTER XIX.

CHAPTER XX.

CONTENTS.

APPENDIX.

ERRATA.

The name of Joseph H. French, a brother of the writer, was inadvertently omitted on page 3.

On page 323, eleventh line, Edward Cooper should be Louis Cooper.

On page 334, last line, H. N. Hood should be W. N. Hood.

On page 358, First Missouri should be First Minnesota.

TWO WARS.

CHAPTER I.

Ancestry—Thomas Ffrench—Military Aspiration—Important Document —Appointment to West Point—New Jersey Farm Life—Great Changes— A Real Yankee—Pennsylvania Hall—The Fashions—Capture of a Hessian Soldier—Rufus Choate and Bishop Wainwright—West Point— Cadet Life—Senator Wall—John F. Reynolds—The Boycott—Rufus Ingalls—Requisites of a Commander.

INASMUCH as the government of this country cannot grant any title to nobility, nor can it be conferred by any foreign power, the people of the United States have, to gratify a natural pride, been obliged to obtain distinction in various ways. Among them may be mentioned the accumulation of money, political preferment, the pride of ancestry, and professional attainments.

The pride of ancestry is a very laudable one, and no doubt it has a guiding influence in shaping the destiny of our lives. We discover it in the honor felt by the members of such societies as those of the Colonial wars, the Cincinnati, Sons of the Revolution, Aztec Club, Sons of Veterans, and many others. And it is true: "Those will not look forward to their posterity who never look backward to their ancestors."

Of the countless millions of human beings who in successive generations have passed over the stage of life, most of them, on their exit, have sunk into oblivion. The names of twenty-seven are all that are known of the human family from man's creation down to the days of Noah.

From the deluge to the present time a few men of great genius as poets, historians, warriors, conquerors, and criminals claim *general recognition* from mankind. All others are relegated or consigned to the special history of a people, and thereby rescued from an otherwise oblivion. As individuals they perish.

I am quite sure we are more indebted to Boswell for a true insight into the life and character of Samuel Johnson than we are to his writings, and there is the utmost interest attached to the home life of all the world's great actors. Even as late as our revolutionary war we find much interest in the part played by the fashionable ladies during the war, and gossip of the Wistar parties, and card parties of New York and Philadelphia. From the "Mischianza" * we have a clear insight to the true and gentle character of Major André and his accomplishments; and the beauty of some of the Quaker City belles.

Now in consideration of the desire of every gentleman to have a knowledge of his ancestry, and some knowledge of the times in which they lived, I purpose for the benefit of my children to write down somewhat of things I have seen and a part of which I was, and to make mention of some of the famous men with whom I have been acquainted during the eventful years between 1839 and the present time (1895).

As I was an officer in the United States army from 1843 to 1856, and a major general in the Confederate army, I purpose to relate some of the events of the Mexican and Confederate wars in the course of this narrative.

I was born in the county of Gloucester, State of New Jersey, on November 22, 1818. My father's name was Samuel French, whose ancestry in this country runs back to Thomas French, who descended from one of the oldest and most honorable of English families. The Ffrenches were Normans and went to England with William the Conqueror. In after days some of the family went with Strongbow, the Earl of Pembroke, when he invaded Ireland and "laid waste the country, reducing everything to subjection," whereby they gained great possessions. Thomas Ffrench, who was a descendant of the Norman Ffrenchs, was, as the register shows, baptized in the church now standing in Nether Hayford, North Hamptonshire, in the year 1537. The painting of that church you have.

A direct descendant of the aforesaid Thomas Ffrench, also named Thomas Ffrench, an adherent of the Church of England, for some reason abandoned it and became a member of the Society of Friends (Quakers), and for this apostasy was persecuted and imprisoned. To escape the persecution he sailed to the colonies, and when he returned to England he became "one of the landed proprietors of West New Jersey in America."

---

*A fête given by Maj. André in Philadelphia, May, 1778, in honor of Sir William Howe.

Taking passage for himself, wife, and nine children, he landed in Burlington, West New Jersey, on the 23d of July, 1680, O. S.

In 1664 Charles II. granted to his brother, the Duke of York, the territory along our coast north of the mouth of the Delaware river. The duke sold the land lying between the Delaware and Hudson rivers to the forty-first degree of north latitude to Lord John Berkeley and Sir John Cartaret, who named it New Cæsarea, or New Jersey. They divided it into East and West Jersey; but later, the grant being unsatisfactory to the king, owing to conflicting claims of the proprietors and their heirs, James in 1689 compelled them to surrender or sell their claims to the crown, and all were embodied in one province, New Jersey. Thomas French, under these proceedings, signed the articles relinquishing to the king his proprietary privileges to the one-ninetieth of the one-eighth of West Jersey. Thus New Jersey became a royal colony after the king bought the rights of the proprietors. Sir John Carteret named the land purchased New Jersey because he had been governor of the Isle of Jersey off the coast of France in the English Channel.

My mother's name was Rebecca Clark. She was born January 1, 1790, at Billingsport, on the banks of the Delaware river, in New Jersey. She was married to my father on the 3d day of October, 1816. The names of their children were: Garret, Samuel G., Charles C., John C., Sallie C., and George W.

Passing from family records, I will now revert to myself, and will endeavor to show what creatures of circumstances most men are. One day, when a boy (aged about eight years), my father left me at a store in Market Street, near Water Street, Philadelphia, Pa., where he usually obtained his family groceries. Over the door of that store was a modest signboard, and on it was painted the names, Hamilton and Hood. Mr. Hood was always kind to me, and usually gave me a paper of candy or other sweetmeats. On this particular occasion, it being a rainy day, I was left there alone with Mr. Hood, and I remember now— although near seventy years have passed—what there and then occurred. Eating candies and playing about in the store, I discovered hanging in the office a picture of a young person (full-size bust) clad in a gray coat, with three rows of round brass buttons thereon, braided horizontally. From some cause it riveted my boyish attention. After looking at it for some time,

I exclaimed: "Who is that?" Mr. Hood replied: "That is my son." "What is he dressed so fine for?" I asked. Mr. Hood then told me his son was a cadet at the United States military academy at West Point; that he was at school there. Dancing around, I said: "I want to go to that school too." The response was, "Only a few boys can go to that school; to get there the boy's father must have influence with the President, and get an appointment from him," etc. I still looked at the picture, and I can see it to-day as I did then. It will never be effaced. As years rolled on, and I knew nothing about West Point, except that it was not open to all applicants, it was fading away in my mind, until one day when passing along Chestnut Street I saw in the window of a clothing house a large picture of the cadets of the United States military academy on dress parade. I gazed on it a very long time, oblivious to all around me, calling to mind only the remarks made to me by Mr. Hood; on these I pondered long, and made some inquiries, and finally resolved to make an effort to get an appointment to the academy. On entering school, kept by the Rev. Samuel Aaron in Burlington, N. J., my roommate was a boy named Duer, who was from Pennsylvania. One day he opened his trunk and showed me his appointment as a cadet to the United States Military Academy. I told him I wanted to go there also, and questioned him about how he obtained the appointment. It was the same story that Mr. Hood had told me when I was almost a child. But, undaunted by the requirements, I resolved to act for myself, for up to this time I had not mentioned the subject to either my father or mother, because the former belonged to the Society of Friends, or Quakers; save only that, marrying "out of meeting," he was no longer regarded as an orthodox member, and they were not considered as warlike people in any respect. Accordingly, when at home one day, I wrote to the President of the United States asking in the name of my father the appointment. As his name was the same as mine, I supposed I would get the reply myself from the post office.

I was on the lookout for the answer, when one day in walked, to our house, my Quaker Uncle Charles, and handed to my father a letter that looked to me a foot long, and as it had on the envelope "War Department, Engineer's Office" in large letters, he said he was "anxious to know the contents of the document."

As father replied he did not understand why such a letter was sent to him, I rose "to explain."

My father said but little, but my uncle created some confusion by telling the family I was going to the "bowwows" and the "bad place." Without waiting to first ascertain whether I was "going to the war" or not, several of my Quaker aunts called soon after to say good-by before I got shot, as they were sure the British would kill me, so filled were their minds with "war's alarums" caused by the war of 1812.

When peace was restored and my uncle gone, my father told me that if I really desired the position he would aid me in getting it. So one day he took me with him and called on Charles C. Stratton, a relation of ours living near by, and then a Whig Member of Congress. New Jersey was not at that time divided into congressional districts, and a Whig delegation was seated in Congress under "the broad seal of New Jersey," and had no influence with a Democratic administration; and so no appointment came.

But, nothing discouraged, the following winter, being still at the Burlington Academy, I called one day on Gen. Garret D Wall, then one of our United States Senators, a resident of Burlington. I made known to him the object of my calling. He listened attentively to my request, said that he knew my father and many of my relatives very well, and that he would aid me. The winter passed, Congress had adjourned, and no appointment came.

About this time my father, passing through the town of Woodbury, N. J., happened to stop at the courthouse, and meeting Senator Wall there, asked him about my cadetship, who, on being told the appointment had not been received, sat down in the court room, wrote a few lines to the President, handed them to father, and told him to mail them. In a few days the appointment came, the reward of diligent perseverance and waiting.

Good Mr. Hood! I suppose I often stopped at his store in after years, and yet I can only call to mind one allusion made to West Point. He told me once that his son, Lieut. Washington Hood, was in Cuba surveying a route for a railroad—for Tacon, Governor-General of Cuba—from Havana to Matanzas.

As there may be a desire in long after years to have a knowl-

edge of how the "well-to-do" farmers lived in the early part of
the present century in New Jersey, I will describe the condition
of the people at my father's. New Jersey was a slave State
when I was born. In 1820 slavery was abolished; but there
were two hundred and thirty-six slaves for life in 1850 in the
State, because it did not emancipate a slave then in being. It
only set free the *unborn babes.* You see the difference between
abolition and *emancipation?* The superabundance of the neces-
saries of life at that period can scarcely be realized now, and every one fared sumptuously, and nearly all alike. Under the
house there were four cellars. As winter approached, perhaps
forty cords of oak and hickory wood, four feet in length, were
hauled to the wood pile. Some twenty or more fat hogs were
killed, the hams and shoulders sugar-cured and smoked in a large
stone smokehouse. The sides, etc., were salted down in great
cedar tanks. The beeves were killed, the rounds dried, not
smoked, and the rest "corned." Minced meat and sausage, in
linked chains by the hundreds of pounds, cider boiled down in
great copper kettles, and apple butter and pear sauce made without stint. Shad from the fishery were bought for salting down
for six dollars per hundred. Oysters by the wagon load were
in winter put in the cellar and kept fat by sprinkling them with
brine and corn meal. In bins the choice apples were stored,
each variety by itself, for daily use, while large quantities were
buried in the earthen pits for spring. On the swinging shelves
was the product of the dairy, cheese and butter. Four hogs-
heads were kept full of cider vinegar; and "apple jack" (apple
brandy) in barrels in a row, according to age; great old-fash-
ioned demijohns were kept full of cherries, wild and cultivated,
covered with brandy. Apples, peaches, pears, huckleberries,
currants, plums, etc., were dried on scaffolds in the sun for pies
and other purposes: and the children forgot not their ample
supply of chestnuts, shellbarks, hazelnuts, etc. Turkeys, geese,
and barnyard fowls were raised largely, but they were considered produce for sale. There was no stint to these superabundant supplies, and they were yearly consumed. Rabbits, pheas-
ants, partridges, and woodcock were abundant, and often were
secured by trapping; and the ponds and streams were filled with
fish. I might perhaps convey to you a better idea of the abundance of fruit and its cheapness by stating that I have seen wag-

ons come to the farm for peaches, and they were told to go into the orchard and get as many as they wanted, and on coming out an estimate would be made of the number of bushels gathered, and they were charged ten cents per bushel. Apples, the finest of varieties, were unsalable, and were hauled to the great public cider mill, ground up for cider, and that distilled into brandy on shares—that is, the mills allowed the farmer a certain number of gallons of brandy for every hundred bushels of apples delivered. And as numerous as were these great cider mills, I have seen the gates locked and teams turned away because of the supply exceeding the capacity of the presses.

There were Germans who wove carpets, and mills that converted the wool into cloth. All along the king's highway, which was marked with granite shafts for milestones, each one denoting, in carved letters, how many miles it was to Camden (Cooper's Ferry), there were smith's shops, wheelwrights, cabinet-makers, and country shoemakers, and taverns for entertainment of "man and beasts."

Daily, four-horse stagecoaches, carrying the mail and passengers, passed over the road, and, by common consent, I suppose, they were granted the right of way, or it may have been the last lingering observance of respect to kingly prerogative.

Now somewhere in this part of the country there lived an old and very polite Frenchman. He possessed a pony and a little wagon, and in that wagon he carried a bench, his lasts, and his tools, for he was a shoemaker, and went the rounds of the neighborhood to make, yearly, the family shoes. Out of morocco imported from Barbary, calfskin from France, and leather from the village tannery he fashioned most beautiful boots and shoes for male and female; yes, neat and befitting they were; and how long they lasted! Wonder not that I have introduced you to this polite and kind old Frenchman. He belonged to the Emperor's old guard, and after Waterloo he came to this country. Young as I was, many times and oft would I persuade him to tell me of "the battles, sieges, fortunes he had passed, of moving incidents of flood and field, of hairbreadth escapes," and grand charges he had made under the eye of the Emperor, how he detested England and loved the vine-clad hills and pleasant fields of France. At our house he would fix himself up in the loft over the carriage house, and then while at work he would tell us boys so much about the "Little Corporal" and the grand marshals of France.

His abiding faith in and admiration for the Emperor passed all bounds. When it was known to all the world that Napoleon was dead, sleeping in a lone grave in a far distant island, guarded by English bayonets, as though he might "awake to glory again" and make the little monarchs tremble once more even at his name, this devoted soldier of the old guard would not believe it, and swore it was an English lie.

I have given these minute details of the manner in which the people lived in New Jersey and adjoining States in the olden times, "when the richest were poor and the poorest had abundance," to show you how well they lived, how comfortably clad, and how content they were in the days when trusts, combines, and protective tariffs were unknown, and no great corporations existed. To-day (1895) these great combines have destroyed individual competition, and impoverished more than half the entire population of the country and reduced it to rigidity of hours and the *slavery* of *wages*. They control legislation, corrupt the courts, subsidize the press, maintain advocates in the pulpits, and this will estrange the poor from the rich more widely than the peasant from the prince; and, continued, may implant an unkindly feeling, which, if not placated, may have to be settled by a resort to arms.

What a change has sixty-five years wrought! The stage-coach has disappeared on the advent of railroads, steam will be displaced by electricity as the candle and lamp have been, and as the friction match has banished the flint and steel and tinder box, the scythe and sickle have been superseded by the mower, the magnificent sailing ships have given way to the ocean racers. Ere long we will see the wind pass by as we see the streams of water now. "The cloud of witnesses around that hold us in full survey" may themselves be seen, for we are discovering the secrets of Arcana every day; the source of life and the mystery of death will soon be discovered.

When I was a boy the habitat of the Yankee did not extend south of Connecticut, as bounded by that elegant writer, Washington Irving, in his *veritable* history of New York. In that Knickerbocker history you will find the southern limit of the Yankee. Is it possible to conceive that Wouter van Twiller,

Rip van Winkle, William the Testy, or Peter the Headstrong, and the drowsy, dreamy Dutch people of New Amsterdam were Yankees? No! they dwelt farther north; yet they might have overrun and subdued New Amsterdam had not their minds been diverted by a sudden outbreak of witchcraft, that afforded these saints infinite amusement in a pious way, which saved New Amsterdam. When I was young it was not considered complimentary or prudent to call a boy of your own size a "Yankee."

My first recollection of seeing a real Yankee was connected with a clock. At home there stood in the hall an eight-day clock, nearly eight feet high, and it is to-day in the city of Woodbury, N. J., in possession of my sister, Mrs. John G. Whitall. On its face are the words, "Hollingshead, Woodstown, N. J., 1776." I infer that it might have commenced recording time about the hour that the liberty bell in Independence Hall, Philadelphia, on a certain fourth of July rang out the Bible proclamation of liberty to all the land, and the "inhabitants thereof."* It is a clock of some repute. It has Arabic numerals to express the hours. The pendulum was adjusted in length to the latitude, and vibrated every second and recorded it. It marked the day of the month, and the month itself, and a picture of a round-faced female would peep up from behind the scenes just as the moon rose, and veiled her face when she set. In the absence of the moon a ship sailed slowly on.

It had another accomplishment: an alarm that was worse than a Chinese gong. I should think that handsome clock, which has been recording time now for one hundred and nineteen years, would have sufficed; but no! One bright May morning, when all the fruit trees were in bloom, and the white-faced bumblebees were buzzing around, and the air was redolent with perfume, a wagon stopped at the gate, and a tall, lean individual came to the door and wished to see the mistress of the house. Said he was "a stranger in these parts, that his load was too heavy for his horse, and that he had clocks and other notions." Father was not in, so my mother gave him permission to leave a clock until such time as he would call for it. So he brought in an eight-day clock about three feet high and adjusted it on

---

* "Proclaim liberty throughout all the land unto all the inhabitants thereof." (Lev. xxv. 10.)

the mantel in the dining room.   It was rather ornamental, and
instead of the common, everyday figures such as were in the
multiplication table, it had an I for one, and II for two, and so
on, which was the Roman style; and then when it struck the
hours, instead of ringing a bell, the hammer fell on a coil of
wire, producing a cathedral sound that died away far off.

We all soon got used to the clock, and some three months
after when the man called to take his clock away mother said
she was attached to it and would keep it.   It was all a Yankee
trick to sell the clock, for he disposed of many others in the
same way.   The Yankee clock has ticked its last tick, but the
old eight-day clock may outlive the nation whose hours from its
birth it has, by seconds, recorded.   All *your life* you have heard
the people of this country north of the slave States called Yankees, and the people south Confederates, which is not true, but
only an incident of the war.

In Philadelphia I was present at the dedication of Pennsylvania Hall, May 15, 1838, an abolition edifice.   It was announced
that David Paul Brown would officiate at the dedication.   His
reputation as a lawyer and an orator was well known, and on
this occasion he did some stage acting with fine effect.   He was
hidden away from the surging audience in some manner, and
after the chairman had stated the object of the meeting he closed
his remarks by saying that David Paul Brown *had promised* to
be present to deliver the address.   Presto!   From concealment
he rose to his full height and exclaimed: "And I am here to
fulfill that promise, a promise as freely given as it shall be fear-
lessly performed, and as high priest of this day's sacrifice I ded-
icate this hall to freedom," etc.   A short time after, in the presence of some *ten thousand spectators*, I saw about twenty persons, unmolested, batter down the doors and destroy the building by fire; and from its ashes sprung up the free soil party.

As fashion plates of dress worn sixty years ago are not plen-
tiful, I will briefly refer to the tyrant, Fashion.   Men wore tight
pants, two inches longer behind than before.   In front they
were cut away so as to expose the instep, and were fastened
down under the boot with a pantaloon strap, and it was no small
job to get the pants off.   The coat had a collar quilted to give it
stiffness, and was, behind, about four inches broad, and one
could not throw his head back and well enjoy a merry laugh.

Then in front they wore as neck gear a *stock*, yes a *stock* about as comfortable as those public ones used for punishing criminals. These stocks were nearly four inches wide, consisting of a pad of bristles of the hog, fashioned to fit the neck, and were covered with dark silks or satin. The lower part rested on the collar bone, and the upper supported the head aloft while the shirt collar cut the ears. It was "heads up, eyes to the front," and one seldom saw his boots. Young men could not cross their legs when sitting in a chair without accident. John Pope, better known as Gen. Pope, when on furlough returned to West Point with nice linen pants, with straps at the bottom and open down the front, which was found very convenient for a soldier who had to wear a waist belt; and although it shocked the sense of propriety of some maidenly ladies, it caught the eye of Maj. Richard Delafield, Superintendent of the Academy. His hobbies were economy and practical utility. He saw the advantage of Pope's breeches over the broad flap buttoned at the side, and notwithstanding the protest of Mrs. Delafield—who was reported to have said "the cadets thus dressed should not come in person to the house with their account books for orders"—and other ladies, that stern old soldier gave the tailor permission to make the cadet pants open in front, and that consigned to oblivion the broad flap pants. West Point then, as the Prince of Wales now, set the fashions; Pope's pattern of breeches are now worn by all Christian men, and some that are not of that religion.

Out of all the students that were at the academy in Burlington, I know of but one living now, Gen. W. W. H. Davis, of Doylestown, Pa. He was aid to Gen. Cushing during the Mexican war, and a general in the Union army during the late war between the States.

After my appointment as a cadet I made no preparation for the examination for admission to the Academy, because I had no doubt of being able to meet the mental examination, for I had mastered nearly every elementary branch of mathematics, including navigation and Hutton's recreations in mathematics. I never understood or realized the "recreation" concealed in that volume. Recreation, however, is very often a matter of taste. There was a young officer on my staff, W. T. Freeman, who found recreation in going on every expedition, demonstration, or fight that was on hand; and that good soldier, Gen. Richard S. Ewell, often would seek recreation by a visit to the picket line to see what the "Yanks" were doing. Taste will differ, you observe.

When the time was near at hand for me to report at West Point, some of my Quaker aunts came to see me. They had gotten pretty well over the belief that the British would kill me, or that we would soon have another war with England. Our relatives were numerous about Trenton, Evesham, Red Bank, Billings-port, and all the region around, and stories of the old war were common. I will relate but one: When Count Donop, with his six battalions of Hessians, came down through Haddonfield to cap-ture the fortifications on the Delaware river at Red Bank, a Hessian soldier strayed away from the ranks, and, entering the back yard, came up to the back porch of a farmer's dwelling. There was a churn (in form a truncated cone—that is, it was big at the bottom and small at the top); and moreover, it contained fresh buttermilk. The poor fellow took up the churn and was enjoying a drink when a stout servant girl, coming to the door, took in the situation at a glance, and, instead of crying "Mur-der," she took hold of the bottom of the churn, raised it up, and thrust it down quickly over his head. It was a tight fit, and as he could not remove the churn he was captured, hid away, and delivered to the garrison after the defeat of Donop's troops. Donop was killed. Often and often I wandered over Red Bank and Billingsport when a boy, sitting down on the great iron can-non strewn all around, meditating on war.

I now bade adieu to good Quaker uncles and aunts (I say good —yes, more deserving, truthful, honest people than the Quakers cannot be found, for they are all good) and father and mother, and took the stage for Philadelphia, thence by the Camden and Amboy railroad went to New York. The two great hotels in New York then were the Astor House and the American.

I felt lonely in the city crowd, and, strolling "down Broad-way," heard the noise of voices in a hall, or perhaps it was in a church, so I went in, and soon the orator exclaimed, "It present-ed to the world the first instance of a Church without a bishop," upon which great applause followed, which I did not compre-hend, and at the same time an elderly gentleman rose up and left the stage, causing some commotion. By the papers I learned that they were celebrating their New England dinner, that the orator was Rufus Choate, and the indignant gentleman was Bishop Wainwright, all of which led to a long and bitter newspaper controversy. Leaving New York City, I went by steamer up the Hudson river to my place of destination at the foot of the Catskill Mountains, then robed in purple from the setting sun.

I shall never forget my voyage on the Hudson when life was young and all was bright and fair, and hope imparted a feeling of joy and gladness to all my environments. There were several candidates for admission to the Academy at the hotel. In the morning when I came down to breakfast I chanced to take a seat beside a smart-looking, black-eyed boy, and, finding him *not* inquisitive, I remarked to him, "I suppose you have a cadet appointment;" and in the twinkle of an eye he answered my question by exclaiming, "May I ask you the same question?" I was amazed, but reverting to his reply, I calmly and deliberately told him that his inquiry would be responded to first, and then he could answer mine at his leisure. That boy was from Connecticut. He graduated second in his class; his name is George Deshon; he is a Jesuit father, Redemptorist, and Paulist, and resides in New York City, spending his life for the good of a fallen race.

I was having a pleasant rest at the hotel, and had been there two or three days when an orderly made his appearance with an order for all the candidates for admission to report at headquarters. Frederick Steele, J. J. Booker, and I were assigned to a room in the south barracks.

I cannot recall to mind much about the examination; I only remember Capt. W. W. S. Bliss asking us some questions in a polite manner, and then dismissing us. In due time we went into camp. J. J. Peck, Vandergrift, and I were assigned to Company D, and occupied the same tent.

As the State of New Jersey was not divided into congressional districts at that time, it did not matter in what part of the State an applicant resided. There were four vacancies in the State, and they were filled by appointing Isaac F. Quinby, Shotwell, Vandergrift, and myself. Shotwell and Vandergrift left the Academy.

During the encampment Senator G. W. Wall came to the

Point on a visit, and had all four of us call to see him. He expressed much interest in us, and gave us good advice, as he was personally interested in our success and welfare.

I carried with me to West Point a letter of introduction to John F. Reynolds, of Pennsylvania, who, as general in the Union Army, was killed the first day at Gettysburg. In his death the Federal army sustained an almost irreparable loss. He was a soldier of marked ability; kind, and, above all, was well loved, and the highest position in the service awaited him without his seeking it. He was ever kind to me, and later on, during the Mexican war, I was intimately associated with him. The officers of Bragg's Battery of Monterey were G. H. Thomas, J. F. Reynolds, and myself, and Reynolds and I occupied the same tent, and I never knew him to speak an unkind word.

Cadet life at the Academy has often been described, and it is so well known that I shall pass it by save with a few remarks. In the first squad of cavalry Grant, when a cadet at West Point, rode the horse that could jump a pole, one end against the wall about seven feet high while the other end was held by a soldier over the top of his head. In the second squad of our class Cave J. Couts rode the same animal. I never envied them their enjoyment, yet I rode a horse (properly named Vixen) that would go around the ring at a speed that would have distanced Tam O'Shanter's mare when she crossed the bridge of Doon and lost her tail.

One day as our section in mathematics was marching to recitation hall Frank Gardner produced an old silver-cased watch about four inches in diameter. It, as a curiosity, was passed along from one boy to another to examine; it chanced to be in Grant's hands as we reached the door of the recitation room, and he slipped it under his coat bosom and buttoned it up. The regular professor was absent, and cadet Zealous B. Tower occupied his chair. He sent four cadets to the blackboards, Grant being one. Grant had solved his problem and begun his demonstration, when all of a sudden the room was filled with a sound not unlike a Chinese gong. All looked amazed, and Tower, thinking the noise was in the hall, ordered the door closed, and that only made the matter worse. Grant, with a sober countenance, had the floor to demonstrate. When the racket ceased the recitation proceeded. Tower had no idea whence the noise came.

Gardner had set the alarm in that antique piece of furniture concealed in Grant's bosom, and it went off. Tower's bewilderment and Grant's sobriety afforded us much amusement, which we could not manifest until we got outdoors, and roared with laughter.

Of all the cadets in our class, I believe I. F. Quinby possessed the most profound and the brightest intellect. It was scarcely necessary for him to study a mathematical proposition. One day, thinking he would not be "called up," he had not opened the text-book. However, Prof. Mahan sent him to the blackboard, and announced a proposition for him to demonstrate. In due time he faced the Professor ready to begin. He demonstrated the proposition in an original manner, frequently interrupted by the Professor, who failed to follow his reasoning, and would not admit the proof to be conclusive. Then cadet William F. Raynolds said: "Mr. Mahan, Mr. Quinby is right; I was attentive, and followed him all through." The result was Quinby wrote out his mode of demonstration and Raynolds handed it to the Professor next day, and the proof was conclusive. Professors are not inclined to have students deviate from the text-books. One day Grant failed to name the signs of the Zodiac, aries, taurus, gemini, etc., so I was asked, some time after, to repeat them, which I did as follows:

The Ram, the Bull, the Heavenly Twins, next the Crab the Lion shines,
    the Virgin and the Scales,
The Scorpion, Archer, and the Goat, the Man who carries the watering
    pot, and Fish with glittering tails.

and was told to translate it into the language of the text-book. Professors were not dependent on patronage, and there was no marked degrees of partiality shown any cadets. Prof. Wier kept one of my paintings in water colors that I regretted very much. One day, years after, I asked President Grant if he would not have the War Department issue an order to have it returned to me, and he said: "Certainly, and you may have any of *mine* that are there." He knew I well understood the humor in the remark about his paintings. However, I neglected to write to him and thus secure my picture. When I visited the Academy in 1881 I saw it hanging on the walls (and it is there now). Those that I left at my mother's in Woodbury, N. J., were confiscated and sold by the United States marshal, and this would have shared the same fate had it been there. After the Confederate war ended some of these paintings were returned to me. Such acts of kindness I appreciated.

When we entered the first class, as usual, we had accorded us the privilege of purchasing of the sutler, Mr. John DeWitt, many articles that were denied the junior classes. Owing to some of the class not being properly treated, the following document was drawn up, to wit:

We, the undersigned, do hereby agree that we will purchase nothing from John DeWitt after this date, except what we have already ordered, or whatever is absolutely necessary, the reason being supposed manifest to every one.

John H. Greland,	J. Jones Reynolds,
C. J. Couts,	L. Neill,
Isaac F. Quinby,	John Preston Johnston,
N. Etting,	J. J. Peck,
R. S. Ripley,	H. R. Seldon,
George Stevens,	A. Crozet,
G. Deshon,	F. Gardner,
F. T. Dent,	L. B. Woods,
Henry F. Clark,	T. L. Chadbourne,
J. H. Potter,	E. Howe,
R. Hazlett,	S. G. French,
Henry M. Judah,	J. C. McFerren,
W. K. Van Bokkelen,	Rufus Ingalls,
George C. McClelland,	W. B. Franklin,
U. H. Grant,	Joseph Asfordd.
C. G. Merchant,	

West Point, April 15, 1843.

To explain this *boycott* I copy a letter from Gen Rufus Ingalls to Gen. Isaac F. Quinby, sent to me by the latter when he received it. Quinby's familiar name was "Nykin."

Portland, Oregon, September 16, 1889.

My Dear "Nykin:" Your letter surprised me most joyously. I was thinking of you constantly and lovingly. Do not give up. Let us *live* to the last possible hour. I hope to meet you this fall—late perhaps. I came here two years ago to stay three months, and here I am! I have had a "monkey and parrot time of it," as these slips * will only partially disclose. Read them at leisure. But I am now booming in luck, . . . and I expect to save some money out of the wreck for myself and pretty wards. But what a fight all alone for it!

I am robust, never better. Habits perfect; fact. Why not at 70? Did

---

* Newspaper cuttings.

we not cut old DeWitt because he caused some of us to be reported? How is Hamilton? Write me, dear "Nykin." Nail your flag high up, and don't regard dark clouds.

Very affectionately, Rufus.

Gen. Quinby, Rochester, N. Y.

My dear, good Rufus! How I recall the many happy days we have passed together! My love for you was like unto Jonathan's for David, and you have gone and left me, gone to your long home. Yet I can see you now. I can see you at the card table having "fun" even though the "time be 4 a.m." There always was mirth when Ingalls was present. He was the prince of good fellows; ever cheerful, never selfish, full of quaint humor, and was wont to "set the table in a roar."

There is a story related of him that runs in this way: One night in the spring of 1865 at City Point Grant and staff were sitting around their camp fire. Conversation had lapsed into silence, which after a while was suddenly broken by Grant exclaiming: "Ingalls, do you expect to take that yellow dog of yours into Richmond with you?" "O yes, General, he belongs to a *long life* breed," was Ingall's sober reply. Silence returned, but there were sides ready to burst with suppressed laughter.

Ingalls possessed a brilliant mind. Grant states that, had it become necessary to change the commander of the Army of the Potomac, he would have given it to Ingalls. When at last Lee's weak lines were broken at Petersburg, and certain corps commanders said they could not pursue Lee, Ingalls whispered to Grant, "If you do not order an immediate pursuit, you will be a ruined man; I will have supplies on hand;" and the army was ordered to move at once in pursuit. This was told me by Gen. Frederick Steele in 1865.

But to return to the boycott, I find this matter in the newspapers of the day, and it is termed the oldest boycott known. I have copied the signatures from a newspaper article to correct some of the errors it contained; and I would observe that I cannot recall any member of our class named Joseph Asfordd. About the signature of Gen. Grant having been written U. H. Grant, we all knew that Gen. Harmer obtained him the appointment, and that his real name was U. H. Grant, but the appointment called for U. S. Grant, and he entered the Academy as U. S. Grant, and was usually called "Uncle Sam Grant." Poor

2

Stevens, who it appears had this document in his possession, I saw drowned in the waters of the Rio Grande when at
the head of a squad of dragoons he attempted to swim the river.
The paper was, I presume as stated, sent home with his effects,
and the original, or facsimile, is now hung up in the War Department in Washington City. Of those who signed it, there
are now living only four, Father Deshon, J. J. Reynolds, W.
B. Franklin, and your father, who is now writing this; and if I
write two other names, Gens. C. C. Auger and W. F. Raynolds,
you have the names of the six surviving members of our class
in 1893.*

The class of 1843 is remarkable in one respect. So far as my
investigations have extended, every one of the class living in
1861 entered the military service, except Father Deshon; all obtained the rank of general save one. In no class did all the grad-
uates enter the service, nor did those in the armies obtain uni-
formly such high rank as the class of 1843.

When the encampment ends, and the cadets go into quarters
and study commences, the fourth class is formed into sections,
taking their names alphabetically. If they desire twelve cadets
in the first section, commencing at the A's and B's they go on
down until twelve are obtained; the second and other sections
are formed in the same way; study and recitation begins, and
the struggle commences. At the end of a week some are trans-
ferred up to the first and second sections, and others down; and
this continues until every one settles to the rank he merits, or
at least to the rank his studies entitle him to.

High class standing is not conclusive evidence of preëminent
ability as a commander. Of all the positions that mortal man
has occupied on earth, that of a great captain requires a combination of *more* of the rare gifts that God occasionally bestows
on man, each differing in character and quality, than any other
profession. In him they must *all* be balanced and in harmony.
He must be a great organizer, and a skilled administrator; possessed of courage, untiring energy, and keep the one great purpose in view, crushing every obstacle in the way to its accomplishment. His powers of combination must be made with
mathematical precision; his knowledge of the country correct,

---

*August 31, 1898. Raynolds and Auger are now at rest, and four re-
main. April, 1899, Gen. J. J. Reynolds has passed over the river.

and at a glance comprehend the field of action; instant to detect an error made by his antagonist, and prompt to avail himself of it; intuitive knowledge of character, acute in discovering men's motives, faultless in reasoning to enable him to fathom the designs of the enemy, and maneuver so as to defeat them. Then comes the prestige of victory, confidence in his success, love for his person; and the army in his hands is as obedient to him as the ship to her helm, and will breast the tempest, be it never so high. From Moses down history does not mention the names of as many great soldiers, for whom "the stars in their courses fought," as there are fingers on a man's hand, and the star of Austerlitz, I think, guided the greatest of them all.

> "He who ascends to mountain tops shall find
> The loftiest peaks most wrapped in clouds and snow:
> He who surpasses or subdues mankind
> Must look down on the hate of those below."

I make no reference to heartlessness or selfishness, I speak only of great intellects and boundless ambition that impels the man on, on, upward, till crowns become baubles, and kings who wear them are moved on the world's stage, and traded off like those on the chessboard, who would subjugate the earth, and then sigh for other worlds to conquer.

There is a moral in the lives of some of the most renowned captains. Joshua had trouble with his tribes; Alexander died from excess of drinking in Babylon; Hannibal, living in exile, took poison to escape being surrendered to the Romans; Pompey, thrice a consul, thrice honored with a triumph, master of the world, was assassinated on Egypt's barren strand and left without a handful of the earth (of all the world he once possessed) to cover his remains; Cæsar was murdered in the senate chamber; Cortez died in poverty in Seville, neglected by his sovereign; Napoleon ended his days a prisoner in exile on a desert island; "Stonewall" Jackson, in the zenith of his glory, was accidentally killed by his own troops; R. E. Lee died, after declining many honors, the president of a university in Virginia; Grant, more fortunate, became President of the United States. Yet his life in after years was embittered by his confidence in dishonest bankers, which trouble, preying on his mind, shortened his days.

CHAPTER II.

I BELIEVE it was on the 9th day of June, 1843, the examinations ended, we bade adieu to old Fort Putnam, the Crow's Nest, the Dunderburg, the halls, the lovers' walk, the professors, in short to West Point and all that it contained, and took passage on a steamer on the ever-beautiful Hudson for New York City. A new life was opened to us, the wide world was before us, and we believed we were equal to all environments, and anxious for the strife; and, if I possess a correct power of retrospection, we generally had a higher opinion of ourselves *then* than we have had *since* in the battle of life, amid joy and sorrow, hopes and disappointment, praise and detraction, sordid avarice and the little trust in the sincerity of man. In the course of time we comprehended that "all is not gold that glitters."

In a day or two we began to separate for our homes, and I bade farewell to some whose faces I never saw again. When the assignments to the army were made, in July following, I was notified that I had been commissioned a brevet second lieutenant in the United States army and assigned to Company —, Third Regiment of Artillery, then stationed at Fort Macon, N. C.

I was ordered to report for duty by the first day of October. Bidding good-by to all at home, I started for Beaufort, N. C., Fort Macon being on an island opposite to the town. I traveled by way of Baltimore, Washington, Richmond, and Petersburg to Goldsboro; thence by stagecoach to New Berne and Beaufort.

The journey was made without incident of note. On the train there was a spruce individual from New York City on his way to Charleston. Some one had alarmed him very much about "malaria," and he cautioned me against rising in the morning until after the sun had dissipated the poisonous vapors of the night. The consequence was I remained in bed at the hotel in Goldsboro, waiting for the mist to rise before I did, until I heard the stage horn calling for passengers, and I came near getting no breakfast. But the driver was one of those happy-go-easy fellows, who said: "I am in no haste; go and get your breakfast."

That New York man had alarmed me to such a degree that when a courtly old gentleman came to the stage door with a large basket of scuppernong grapes and requested me to take charge of them to Beaufort, bidding me partake of them bountifully by the way, I thought death was concealed in that basket as the asp was in the one given to Cleopatra. I was the only passenger. After a while I consulted the driver, who was on the box outside, as to the danger of eating grapes in that bilious country, and he assured me there was none. So timidly I took one and found it "was good for food" like the apple in the garden of Eden, and in spite of fears I partook of them freely.

When I arrived in Beaufort I found there to meet me Lieut. C. Q. Tompkins, and I sailed with him over to the fort. One company constituted the garrison. The officers were Capt. W. Wall, Lieuts. Tompkins and E. O. C. Ord, Dr. Glenn, and Capt. J. H. Trapier, engineer officer. The company was composed of old soldiers and required but little drilling, and so our duties were light. I spent most of my time sailing on the sound and fishing. The waters teemed with fish, and both game and oysters were abundant.

There had been a report that the company would soon be ordered to Fort McHenry, Baltimore, and all were anxious to leave the place, for they had been stationed there over two years.

As time passed on they expected by every mail the order for them to leave, but it came not. However, one evening toward the close of November when we were enjoying a good supper, Mingo, the best of old colored servants, announced the arrival of the day's mail, and placed all the letters before Capt. Wall. Opening a ten-inch buff envelope from the War Department, he took therefrom a letter, and as he glanced over it a smile played over his countenance, observed by all. Ord exclaimed: "That is the order for Fort McHenry!" Dr. Glenn bet wine with Ord that it was not; and while the bets were being arranged Capt. Wall handed the letter to me. I read it with surprise; it was an order for me to proceed to Washington City and report to the Board preparing the artillery tactics, composed of Maj. John Munroe, Capts. Francis Taylor and Robert Anderson. There was dejection of spirits on the faces of all present; but Ord rose with the occasion, and ordered Mingo to have three bushels of oysters in the shell prepared, and to bring on the accompaniments. I left them late at the table and retired to my casemate room, and I avow to this day that some invisible spirit seemed to move my cot around the room. Round and round it went. I leaned against the table in the middle of the room and enjoyed the circus for a while, but the cot would not grow weary. After some vain attempts I caught it as it passed by, threw myself on it, the light burned dim, and I fell asleep.

But O the vivid recollections of the wild, incoherent dreams of that night, the aching head and quickened pulse. Childish scenes arose. I was at the home of my childhood. I was crossing the Delaware river on the ice, as in days of yore, and was carried away on a floating cake. It was dark, and no one heard me cry for help. Then I was at a hotel, and a girl, once so lovely, on whom I lavished all the love of a child, came in to dine. She was old, ugly, and changed, and I gazed on her in horror. Next I was in command of a fort on the banks of a river, and British ships of war were coming up; they opened fire, and I ordered our guns to reply, and not one could be fired; in vain the gunners worked while the fleet passed by, and I cried in agony of mind. Like a kaleidoscope the vision changed. I became an essence of the Creator of the universe, and the universe was heaven. A spirit robed in white was with me. Gravitation was destroyed, and we moved with the rapidity of thought, past the moon, past the sun, past the stars. Whither I wished we went. Bright suns were on all sides, above and below, rolling in silence in the infinite ethereal spaces which had no center and were without bounds. When I asked what power held all these worlds in a relative position no answer came. I was alone! Phantoms of a burning brain! I was at West Point again, in Kosciusko's garden, walking on the banks of the Hudson. I saw a cave and entered it, and immediately a rock weighing tons dropped down and closed the entrance. A passage led to another chamber, and again came a vast rock and closed it. I was now in darkness in a vaulted cave, shut in from the world and all the worlds that were shown me. As I sat down on a rock in despair, a ray of light was seen through a crevice in the rocks. Hope came to my relief. The passage was small. After I had got partly through, my body, in fright, began to swell, and I could neither go on nor get back. Breathing had nearly ceased, and I could not cry for help, or move hand or foot.

From this condition I was awakened. The vision bore away, and I found myself lying on my cot, and an old hag that had assumed the form of a peculiar cat was standing on me holding me down on my back. Her body was a part of a broomstick; her legs were rounds of a chair with wire hinges at the joints; her head was like three sticks forming a triangle, with ends projecting for ears. Her countenance was like a cat's. Her forefeet were on my chest pressing it down so that I could scarcely breathe, while her savage eyes glowed with rage in my face. I was awake and remembered that circulation of the blood would relieve me from this horrible nightmare. I gave my body a sudden turn, the blood rushed through my veins, the witch flew through the window, and the day was dawning. My head was swimming like a buoy on the water.

The elixirs of Cagliostro, the preparations of Paracelsus, the use of *hashish* of the Mohammedans, never produced visions or dreams more strange and painful than did that, my first and unwilling trial of old "Monongahela."

I drew a moral from my experience on that occasion, and have never forgotten it. May you draw a good one from it also!

The next morning the officers accompanied me to the landing. Bidding them good-by, I got in the boat and sailed over to Beaufort. My stay at Fort Macon was pleasant, and I was not overjoyed to leave the place. I could lie on that treacherous cot and be lulled to sleep by the ever-murmuring sea, or awakened by the thundering waves of the stormy Atlantic that seemed to make the island tremble at the shock; and I could tell at night by the lightning's "red glare" and the breaker's roar when a storm was moving on over the Gulf Stream.

The casemate used for a magazine adjoined mine, and in it were stored many thousand pounds of powder, and the lightning rods did not quiet all my fears when those violent thunderstorms passed over the island.   Along the shore near Cape Lookout these violent winds had buried large pine forests in sand ridges.

Well, I journeyed back to New Berne alone in the same Concord stagecoach I came in, and remained there all night.

I now began to observe the difference in manners, customs, and deportment of the Southern people from the people in the North.   I shall refer to this, perhaps, farther on.   I noticed that the outer door to the general lounging room was never shut. The weather was cold; servants piled on the hearth pine wood in abundance, till the flames roared up the chimney; men came in and men went out, and never a door was closed.

After supper the landlord drew up a chair near mine, close by the bright fire, and we entered into a conversation about the people and the surrounding country.

A negro servant came in to replace the fuel and departed, and I availed myself of the occasion to ask the landlord for what purpose doors were made, and he was amazed at my want of information on such common affairs.   I think I demonstrated to him that to keep the doors closed would be economy in fuel and comfort to his guests.   He must have been convinced, for in the morning I found the servants closed the doors when passing in and out.   This custom of open doors prevailed generally in the South.   When I boarded the train at Goldsboro, among the passengers were two officers that were at the Academy whilst I was there, George H. Thomas and John Pope.   As Thomas was on a visit to his home in Southampton County, Va., on the line of the Weldon and Norfolk railroad, he persuaded Pope and myself to go on with him and take the steamer from Portsmouth to Baltimore instead of the route by Richmond; and so we remained all night in Weldon.   The weather was cold and the ground covered with snow, and the accommodations miserable.   I little thought then that I would be destined, nineteen years after, to sleep there again with snow on the ground and a tent for shelter, but so it was.   On the way to Norfolk the rails were covered with frost and the driving wheels slipped so that we all had to get out the cars and help push the train over a slight ascent to a bridge.   There was not much comfort on the trains in those days.

On reaching Washington I reported to the Board of Artillery.

They handed to me the manuscript of work to be published, and directed me to prepare drawings of horses, harness, guns, gun carriages, and all the maneuvers of the battery to be illustrated by plates.

I was engaged in the performance of this duty from the early part of December, 1843, to November 12, 1844. When the drawings were all finished, there were added drawings of all heavy guns, their carriages, implements, etc., and I am pleased to state that the Board, after comparing them with the manuscript, accepted them without the alteration of a line, letter, or dot.

I went to West Point to make the drawings for the horse artillery. During the latter part of my stay there I occupied a room at Mrs. Kinsley's. Lieut. John Newton, W. S. Rosecrans, William Gilham, and W. R. Johnston also had quarters there. They were on duty as assistant professors in the Academy. From West Point I returned to Washington and made the plates of the heavy artillery. Thence in September I went to meet the Board at Old Point Comfort. Gen. John B. Walbach was in command of the post, a gallant old German who entered our army in 1799. A large number of officers were on duty there. The hotel was filled with beauty and fashion; and, as I had nothing special to do, I was free to join in the amusements the locality afforded. From Old Point Comfort I returned to Washington early in November, 1844. During the summer of this year, and whilst the Democratic convention was in session in Baltimore, Prof. Morse invited Lieut. I. F. Quinby and me to ride with him to the capital to test the telegraph line built from Washington to Baltimore by act of Congress. On arriving at the capital the Professor signaled to the operator in Baltimore, and in a short time the following message was received by him:

Convention not in session now. Polk stock in the ascendency. Douglass now addressing the people.

Or words to that effect; and this was the first telegram ever sent in the United States. I have seen it stated that the first message *announced the nomination.* That must be an error, because the one he received was before the nomination had been made.*

---

* It is also reported that the first message over the line, sent by a young lady, was: "What hath God wrought!" The Professor did not mention this, and this dispatch was sent over the ocean cable years later.

From Washington I was ordered to join my company at Fort McHenry. That order to leave Fort Macon, and about which so much anxiety was manifested when I left there, was afterwards received and the company moved accordingly. Maj. Samuel Ringgold was in command of the post, and among the officers were Randolph Ridgely, W. H. Shover, Abner Doubleday, E. O. C. Ord, and G. W. Ayers, and P. G. T. Beauregard was the engineer officer.

Fort McHenry, at this time, was considered one of the most desirable posts to be stationed at in the whole country.

During the autumn and winter there was a great deal of gayety in Baltimore, and some of the officers of the post were generally at the balls and parties given. The ladies of Baltimore from their ancestors inherited beauty; and from their environments naturally acquired retiring manners, low and sweet voices, gentleness, attractive grace; and, conscious from childhood of their social position, they were sprightly, exhibited hauteur to none, and moved in the mazy dance so courtly, so slow, and "courtesied with a grace that belonged to an age in the long, long ago."

On one occasion a masked and fancy dress ball was given by a gentleman with whom I was not acquainted, to which many of the élite of the city were invited. A description of that ball which was promptly published in the New York *Herald* created much excitement. The writer, not content with describing dresses and characters represented, touched truthfully some tender points peculiar to each individual. There were many accused of the authorship, and all denied it. Rewards were offered for the discovery of the writer. No one thought it could have been done by any person not present at the ball, but so it was. Only two persons could name the writer.

I went with him, about two days after the publication, the round of morning calls, and we had much enjoyment at the criticisms made by the ladies. Many were indignant; others enjoyed it. Some equivocal expressions had been used in reference to one young lady. She first shed tears; then, smiling, said: "Well, I would rather be described as it was written than not to be mentioned at all." The writer was a promising young lawyer, long since in his grave. I have not seen the other confidant since the war. He was in the Confederate army.

One of the most accomplished young ladies in Baltimore was Miss Charlotte R.   She belonged to no "circle," but was beloved by all.   Among her admirers at that time were Chevalier Hulseman, *Charge d'Affairs* for Austria, Lieut. Ord, and myself.   Two years after, on the banks of the Rio Grande, before a battle that was inevitable, I sat by a fire and committed to the flames letters that I did not intend should be read by any one, and, being alone, perchance some were moistened by a tear.

My father was in politics a Whig, and firmly believed Gen. Jackson deserved to be shot for hanging Arburthnot and Ambriester when he took possession of Florida; and he thought Roger B. Taney no better than a robber because he removed the government deposits from the United States Bank.   Now among the pleasant families that I visited at this time in Baltimore was that of Chief Justice Taney, a man so kind, gentle in manner, so plain and unpretending at his home, that I wondered to what extent a venal party press would villify a pure and honest man who faithfully interpreted the law.*

---

* In the celebrated Dred-Scott case (see Howard's "Supreme Court Reports," Vol. XIX., page 404) you will find that Justice Taney, in describing the *condition* of the negro more than a hundred years *before* the Declaration of Independence, said: "It is difficult at *this day* (1856) to realize the state of public opinion in relation to that unfortunate race which prevailed in the civilized portions of the world at the time of the Declaration of Independence, and when the Constitution of the United States was framed and adopted. . . . They had, for more than a century before, been regarded as a being of an inferior order, and altogether unfit to associate with the white race, either in social or political relations; and so far inferior that they had no rights which the white man was bound to respect; and that the negro might justly and lawfully be reduced to slavery for his benefit. He was bought and sold, and treated as an ordinary article of merchandise and traffic whenever a profit could be made by it. The opinion was, *at that time*, fixed and universal in the civilized portions of the white race."

The above is merely a historical fact as regards the status of the negro about *two hundred years before* the judge rendered his decision. And now behold! For political party purposes: by the abolitionists; from the pulpit; by college professors; by *all* who have hated the South, it is to this day tortured into a *decision* made by Chief Justice Roger B. Taney, which is not true. Furthermore, and before this case was in court, Judge Taney had manumitted his own, inherited, slaves; and as a lawyer had defended a man in court for publicly uttering abolition sentiments. In fact he regarded slavery as an evil, and proclaimed it by deeds. (See "American Authors' Guild Bulletin" for April, 1898.)

While in Washington in 1843 I made my home at the "Hope Club," a club composed mainly of unmarried army officers permanently stationed, or at least on duty there. Gen. George Gibson, Commissary General, was the president of the club. He was one of the best men I ever met; kind and considerate of the feelings of every one, a gentleman of the olden time, a man of patience and unruffled temper. He and Judge Bibb, Secretary of the Treasury, would go to the long bridge and fish all day for a minnow, or even a nibble. Capt. J. C. Casey was the Treasurer. He was a very entertaining man, and had more influence with the Seminole Indians than any one connected with the government. He was a commissary, and they had abiding faith in him because, as they said, "he told them no lies."

One day on taking my seat at dinner I turned up my plate and found under it a note from Surgeon General Thomas Lawton inviting me in the evening to dine with him. As I saw no one else had an invitation, and I was only a lieutenant, I was not inclined to go alone, but Gen. Gibson, Casey, and others told me to go by all means. At this time Lieut. Thomas Williams came in and found an invitation also, and it was decided we would go.

The Doctor had a dinner of thirteen courses, provided by the prince of restaurant caterers. The wines were old and rare. The guests were Gen. Scott, Commander in Chief of the Army; Col. Sylvester Churchill, Inspector General; Lieut. Williams, and myself. Scott, Churchill, and the Doctor discussed the war of 1812 on the Canadian line, and the battles fought there; told how once they had so many prisoners and so few to guard them that they cut the suspenders of the prisoners to prevent their escape so easily, as it required one hand to hold their breeches up. I remember another that shows there must have been a good feeling between the officers on either side. Maj. Lomax, for some purpose, was sent to the British camp; and when he returned he was eagerly asked what news he had. "News! why there is British gold, yes, British gold in this camp." That seemed to imply treason, and an explanation was demanded, and it was given when Lomax from his pockets covered the table with English sovereigns. He had been entertained cordially by the British officers. The dinner did not end until midnight. Gen. Scott drank sherry only, except when sampling some choice wines that the Doctor bid the butler open. Col. Churchill was in fine humor, and partly

O'er a' the ills o' life victorious.

At last the hour arrived to leave; then Gen. Scott, raising himself to his full height, and either impressed with the importance of the occasion, or thinking perhaps he was again at Lundy's Lane, "ordered his own aid, Lieut. Williams, to conduct Col. Churchill to his home, declaring it was not prudent for him to venture in the streets unprotected." Then turning to me with much dignity, he announced: "And I appoint Lieut. French a special aid to accompany me to my residence."

The streets were deserted and silent, and the walk short. Taking his arm, I went with him to his home, rang the bell, and his servant met him at the door, and there my services as aid terminated. In after days and after years he was ever considerate and kind to me. The conqueror lives, but the man is dead. But O how pleasant the recollection of the times when those pure and knightly men with generous hearts, untouched by avarice, never closed the " door of mercy on mankind." Such men were Gens. Scott, Jesup, Gibson, Towson, Lawson, Totten, Abert, Cooper, and others. Then men served God and their country rather than mammon. The maddening, wild, and frantic rush for wealth was unknown, and life was one of enjoyment without extravagance.

CHAPTER III.

A T this time there was being discussed by the public a matter that was destined soon to put an end to the pleasant
life we were leading here.

After the death of Abel P. Upshur, Secretary of State, John
C. Calhoun was appointed to fill the vacancy, and the question
of the admission of Texas as a State was discussed, and on the
12th of April a treaty of annexation was signed by him; and it
was rejected by the Senate of the United States. So bitter was
the feeling that, notwithstanding the purchase of Louisiana
and Florida [and Alaska since], Massachusetts, through her Legislature, declared that Congress had no right or power to admit
a foreign State or Territory into the Union; and that if Texas
was admitted it *would not be binding on her*. By this Massachusetts made a declaration which the State could not carry out
without *seceding* from the Union, yet she seceded not.

Soon after the inauguration of Mr. Polk as President a resolution for annexation was passed by Congress, and on June 23,
1845, Texas accepted the resolution, and became a State in the
Union December 29.

It became evident now, when Texas accepted the resolution,
that the government would be obliged to defend the new State
from invasion by Mexico, and the army officers were anxious to
go to the frontier to defend the boundary of the country. To
meet the threats of Mexico, an army of occupation was gradually formed at Corpus Christi. When the order came for Maj.
Ringgold's battery of horse artillery to be in readiness to move,
and the Adjutant General came over to Fort McHenry to trans-

fer some of Capt. Wall's men to Ringgold's company, I asked Ringgold if he wished me to go with him. Taking me by the hand, he exclaimed, "My dear fellow, yes;" and, turning to the Adjutant General, he asked him to make the transfer and 'twas done, and I made preparations to leave.

The ship Hermann was chartered, and the horses, to the number of one hundred and fifty, were put on board the ship between decks, in temporary stalls, secured by broad canvas bands under their bodies to prevent them from being thrown from their feet by the motion of the vessel. The company officers were Ringgold, Ridgely, Shover, Fremont, and myself. The officers left in the fort were Wall, Tompkins, and Ord. After we left, this company was ordered to California. W. T. Sherman was with it; and they were quiet on the shore of the Pacific during the war. I met Ord once after the war in Washington. His hobby then was the Australian boomerang. He took me to a room, about sixty by forty, to show me how he could throw them to the end of the room and make them come back and fall at his feet. He was studying out some machine to discharge them rapidly and thereby fill the air with scythe blades to cut off the heads of an enemy, and every boomerang that did not strike an enemy was to return to the fort. I could not see why this boomerang, when it returned, would not injure the person that sent it. And thus it is; we all have some hobby on hand, but fortunately most of them are as harmless as Ord's boomerang, except we cannot get off this kind of a horse and rest and sleep as we do from a real horse.

The day came when the cry was heard: "All on board." "Farewell," the parting word of friends, was spoken, the lines cast off, and the ship passed down the Patapsco river to Chesapeake Bay, to the Atlantic. The voyage to Aransas Pass was tedious and not particularly eventful. The captain was a scoundrel and a sinner. I found amusement in going aloft and sitting in the foretop surveying the ocean's wide expanse without intrusion. When we neared the Bahamas we were becalmed nine days, and the wicked captain would lie on his back and curse even his Creator.

I had, as well as the captain, made all the observations for latitude and time, to compare with his. We reached the "Hole in the Wall" about sunset, and I made a sketch of it: passed

Great Stirrup-cay light about 10 p.m. At 2 a.m. the captain and
mate came into our cabin, where his chart was on the table, and
he tried to impress on the mate that the light ahead was the
Florida light; that he had crossed the Gulf Stream and was nearing the Florida coast; and that the ship's course should be
changed southerly.   I heard this with alarm, for I could not believe it possible that we had passed the "Great Isaacs" and the
Straits of Florida.   I went on deck at the dawn of day, and saw
white sand and rocks that did not appear more than a dozen feet
beneath the water.   I went forward, found the captain, and asked
him if he was not on the Bahama Banks.   He denied it.   I went
immediately and made known the situation to Maj. Ringgold.
He appeared to take but little interest in the matter, supposed
the ship was all right, etc.

About sunrise he came out, and I called his attention to the
shoal water and rocks and the lighthouse on our *starboard* bow.
He spoke to the captain about what I told him, and was informed
that I was a boy and did not know what I was talking about.
The blue line of the deep water was in front of us, and a bark
under full sail on the other side of the lighthouse heading south;
and as we neared each other our captain took his trumpet and
asked, "What ship is that?" and the reply was prompt, "What
in h–ll are you doing there?"   I turned to the Major and asked
him if that answer did not explain the situation.   The bark was
the Caleb Cushing, bound to New Orleans laden with ice.   I
believe to-day it was an attempt to wreck the ship, where life
was safe, to get the insurance.

As we were nearly out of drinking water, there was a necessity to run into the nearest port for a fresh supply, and the ship
put into Key West.   What a relief!   That miserable captain had
fed us on junk meat, boiled dried-apple pudding, and hardtack
with weak coffee.   I have never eaten any of these dishes since.
We remained in Key West one day and night, and sailed the
next morning.   There we got some West Indies fruit and plenty of limes.

The ship was now provisioned with green turtle, the only meat
I saw in the market in the town, and now turtle was substituted
for salt beef; and henceforth it was turtle steak, turtle soup (in
name only), and turtle at every meal until it became as unpal-
atable as junk beef.   Some days after leaving Key West clouds

from the south-east began to fly over, extremely low, driven by a current just above us. The captain took in sail, leaving only spread the jib, fore-topsail, main topsail, and spanker, and I believe the mainsail. I was sitting in the cabin when all at once tables, chairs, trunks, and everything moveable were shot to the starboard side in a heap. I caught hold of some fixtures, got out the cabin, which was on deck, and clung to the weather shrouds. The ship was nearly on her side. The captain jumped for the halyards, sailors slid down the deck, feet foremost, to let them go. I had been anxious to be in a storm on the ocean, and here was one quite unexpected.

What riveted my attention mainly was the roaring of the tempest through the rigging. The great shrouds vibrated with a sound that made the ship tremble, and every rope and cord shrieked aloud in a different tone according to size, creating a thundering, howling, shrieking roar that impressed me with awe not unlike that I felt *under* the falls of Niagara. I was so fascinated with the music of the tempest that I was oblivious to the thought of danger, until the ship began to rise from her side, and when she rose well on her keel I thought the horses would kick the vessel to pieces.

When we arrived at Aransas Pass the sea was high and the wind strong, and no lighters would venture outside to come to us. The discharging the cargo was tedious, as the horses had to be swung to the yardarms and lowered into the pitching tugs alongside. I had been forty-six days on board ship, and joyous was it to be landed on St. Joseph's Island.

I will make a small digression here, because it will shed some light on matters hereafter, and show that a camp may have some attractions as well as a palace.

Maj. Ringgold carried with him a middle-aged colored servant who had much experience in arranging dinner and supper parties in Baltimore. He cared for nothing save to surprise us with dishes that would have delighted Lucullus. Such pompano, baked red snappers, boiled red fish, delicate soups, turkeys, geese, ducks, and game birds on toast. In pastry he had no superior. Never could we, by money or otherwise, discover how he prepared his sauces. In taste in arranging a table he resembled Ward McAllister, and he was fitted for a "chef" at Delmonico's or the Waldorf.

3

Ridgely had an old slave servant, and Shover and I colored men hired. They were all true and faithful servants, yet in disregard of instructions they would ride down and find us on the battlefield with a good luncheon. They always wished to go with us when there was a prospect of a fight. So now you can understand how much I rejoiced to leave that villainous captain and ship, and enjoy again the luxury of a clean table.

The terms of annexation proposed by the United States were accepted July 4, 1845, and Gen. Taylor was already at Corpus Christi with a considerable force when we landed on St. Joseph's Island. Consequently our stay on the island was soon terminated by our embarking on a light draft steamer for Corpus Christi. As the water is shoal in front of this place, the steamer was anchored near a mile from shore, and the horses thrown overboard and made to swim to land. Corpus Christi is on the westerly side of the Nueces River, and consequently the United States troops were occupying the disputed territory. I have no date to guide me now, but it must have been about the last of October when we landed on the barren sands of the Bay of Nueces. Here a permanent camp and depot were established, and discipline in the troops commenced.

There was but *one* house in this *town* at that time. It was a canvas town. It was not an unpleasant place to be in. Lieut. John B. Magruder was a good theatrical manager, and under his charge a theater was constructed, and a fair company of actors enlisted. This attracted some professional of the boards, and thus nightly entertainments were provided. The disciples of Isaac Walton had rare sport in the bay and streams; and sportsmen a field for all kind of game. During the winter a cold "norther" prevailed, and thousands of green turtle, pompano, red fish, red snappers, and other of the finny tribe were benumbed and cast on the shores on every side. The number of wild geese that nightly came from the prairies to rest on the waters of the bay was beyond estimate. A few miles up the bay, at sunset, the geese would obscure the sky from zenith to the verge of the horizon, and bewilder the young sportsman, who would always want two or three at a shot instead of one. Ten minutes, usually, would suffice to get as many geese as our horses could carry.

Deer and turkeys were abundant, but on the open prairie would provokingly move along in front of the hunter just out of range of shot. Jack or English snipe would rise from the marshy places in flocks instead of a brace. There was a bird frequently seen in the roads and paths near camp, always alone, shaped like a game cock, that excited curiosity. Finally it was shot, and is now known as the chaparral cock.

Soldiers found amusement in betting on Mexican ponies trained to stop instantly on the slightest touch of the reins. A line would be marked in the sand on the seashore, and the rider of the pony would take all bets that he could run his pony a hundred yards at full speed and stop him instantly (say) within a foot of the line, and not pass over it; and they generally won the bets.

Many fleet ponies were brought there, and racing was a daily occurrence. On one occasion the officers got up a grand race. Capt. May and Lieut. Randolph Ridgely were to ride the respective horses. When mounted, May's feet nearly reached the ground; and they rode "bareback." It was an exciting race. On they came under whip and spur amidst the crowd shouting wild hurrah. As they crossed the goal, May thoughtlessly checked his pony, and instantly the animal straightened his forelegs and stopped; but May, not having braced himself, went on. Seizing the pony by the neck with both hands, his legs rose in the air, and he made a complete somersault, landing on the ground some twelve or more feet in front of the pony. As he was not injured, the crowd went wild with joy.

A great number of Mexicans would daily visit our camp with horses, or rather ponies, saddles, bridles, blankets, and other horse equipments for sale. I have had a horse and saddle offered for seventy-five dollars, or seventy for the saddle and five for the horse. I bought the best trained hunting pony that I have ever known for fifteen dollars. The owner protested that he was "mucho bueno" for hunting, and so he proved. At full speed he had been trained to stop instantly the moment a motion was made to fire the gun. I once had this pony to go up and rub the side of his head on the wheel of a piece of artillery when being fired rapidly in battle. He loved the smell of gunpowder better than I did. Nearly all the officers bought ponies for themselves or servants to ride. We heard so much about the great snow-white horse of the prairies, with a long flowing tail that

swept the green grass, and a mane below his knees, that I thought
it was a phantom horse on the land like the flying Dutchman on
the sea.   I was mistaken.   I heard one day he had been lassoed
and sold to the quartermaster of the post, so I went "for to see"
him.   There he was, chained to the pole of an army wagon.   He
would kick at every person and animal that ventured near him.
I left him kicking at the man who fed him on hay tied on the
end of a twenty-foot pole.   What became of this emblematic
horse I cannot tell.

The desire "to know the world by sight and not by books"
was increased.   I had seen the Atlantic's deep heaving swells,
the tempest in its might on the gulf, the calms on the borders
of the tropics, with those never-to-be-forgotten beauties caused
by the setting sun behind those wonderful clouds.   Every evening as the sun declined, great banks of blue and purple clouds
would form, presenting to the eye, without the aid of imagination, the most lovely plains, bold mountain ranges, whose tops
were draped in fantastic clouds.   Temples that were as gloomy
as Egypt's; castles as enchanting as those on the Rhine; chariots
with horses; human faces and animals in silhouette; lions in repose and lions rampant; phantasms woven out of clouds by rays
of the setting sun; all, all changing in expression and form by the
gentle movements of the clouds, fading away in outline into one
vast glow of crimson twilight that dissolved into air;

"And like the baseless fabric of a vision, left not track behind."

And now learning that a small train of wagons would soon
leave for San Antonio, I obtained a month's leave to visit that
city, made memorable by the defense of the Alamo and other
tragic events.   When the time came to start I met Lieut. W. L.
Crittenden, who told me he had a leave and was also going with
the train.   The expedition was in charge of Capt. N. B. Rossell.   When we came to the San Patricio crossing of the Nueces
river the train could not cross by reason of the rains.   Impatient of delay, I proposed to Crittenden and two gentlemen from
Kentucky that we "cut loose" from the train and proceed on
our journey.   There was with the train a Mr. Campbell, who
lived in San Antonio, and he was willing to undertake to pilot
us over this unknown, untrodden, pathless country.

At the close of the first day, the guide and I being in advance, we came to a small, clear, bubbling brook, and he said: "Here we will encamp for the night." So, dismounting, I hitched my pony and went up the stream in quest of turkeys that I heard gobbling. I found them going to roost, and covetous of numbers, I would not shoot one and return as I should have done. I heard the party shouting for me. So, waiting till a number of turkeys were in the tree, I fired both barrels, and only two of the birds fell when I expected double that number. When I went to get the birds, alas! they were on an island and I had to leave them. It was now dark, and as I had crossed to the left bank of the stream I went on down until I supposed I was near the camp, and made a soft halloo! No answer. I then shouted louder and louder; then all was silence. I felt a peculiar crawling sensation running over me, and I think my hair objected to my wearing my hat. I took a survey of the situation. I was alone in an Indian country; it was very dark, and I must not pass over the trail where we crossed the stream. Aided with the light of matches and burning grass I discovered the trail and found my pony hitched where I left him. Mounting him, I followed the trail. After a while I heard far away some one halloo. It was Crittenden returning for me. We met, and I reached camp in no pleasant mood. It was an experience I have only once since undergone, and the sensations of the mind when lost are bewildering.

It was the average estimate of the party that the number of deer that moved to the right and left of our trail was not less than twelve hundred, besides numerous antelope. Out of all this number we never killed one, for we had no rifle, and they would walk off or keep provokingly just out of gunshot. We killed all the turkeys we wanted for food. In four days we reached San Antonio. There were but *four white families* living in the town at that date: Volney Howard, Tom Howard, our guide Campbell, and Mrs. Bradley. Lands were offered us at six cents per acre that commands now over a thousand dollars per acre, and the population is at present fifty thousand.

At the San Pedro Springs, the source of the San Antonio river, where the river in its strength gushes up from the earth, we found Col. Harney encamped with a squadron of dragoons. He had built an observatory from which to obtain a view of the sur-

rounding country.   From the top hundreds of deer could be seen
quietly grazing on the prairies near by.*

Wild hogs and large wolves infested the chaparral around the
hills, and were caught in traps.   The country is beautiful to the
eye, and the city sleeps in what may be termed a valley, by reason of the low hills on the north and east.   To the west the plain
extends to the Medina river.   Western Texas in the months of
March and April is lovely beyond comparison.   The green grass

---

*Col. Harney was annoyed by the number of blackbirds that would
feed with the horses, eating the grain; so while the horses were out grazing I asked an officer for a gun to kill some of the birds.   He handed me a
long single-barreled one with a bore about the size of a half dollar.   From
the powder flask I put in two charges of powder and shot.   The ground
was covered with birds.   I fired and killed none; the charge was too
small.   The doctor (I think he was a doctor) said he would load it for me,
so I took another shot.   This time I thought my arm dislocated at the
shoulder.   I did not count the number of birds, but the ground was covered with the dead and wounded.   I played indifference while meditating
revenge for a sore shoulder.   Going to the top of the observatory, I saw
perhaps a hundred deer grazing close by; so I was taken with a desire to
kill one, and again asked the doctor for his gun.   He proposed loading it
for me.   I told him I preferred doing it myself.   I put in three charges of
powder, or three drams, and about forty small buckshot, and off I went
for a deer.   The herd grazed along before me up the slope of a ridge, and
passed over it.   I crawled on my hands and knees to the crest, and such
a sight!   A number of single deer were within twenty yards of me.   At
once I became covetous.   Shoot a single deer?   No.   I wanted four or
five (remembering "all things come to those who wait"), so presently five
or six were nearly in a line, but more distant; and when I pulled the trig-
ger the gun said "fush," and the smoke came in my face.   As I looked
over the field I was amazed.   There were all the deer standing facing me,
their heads high, ears spread out wide, and their large, soft, mild eyes
looking at me imploringly; and not alarmed.   Probably they had never
heard a gun (and I am quite sure they did not hear this one), for the Indians then were armed only with bows and arrows.

I sat down on the green grass and looked at the deer, and felt that experience must be a good teacher.   But the days came when I did kill
many; but the first one fell dead from a shot from my pistol.

I make mention of these little events that belong to the past to show
how great is the change made in a few passing years.   Where now is all
this game, and where are the Indians?   Alike they have disappeared before the advance of avaricious civilization.   From San Antonio to Corpus
Christi and to El Paso the country was as God made it, unchanged by Indians, and over the plains and on a thousand hills roamed deer, wild turkey, partridges, and the waters swarmed with swan, geese, and ducks unmolested by sportsmen.

is hidden beneath flowers of every color; not flowers here and there, but one unbroken mass, presenting a richness of coloring beyond the art of man; as we ride along there are acres of solid blue, then of white, now of yellow, then pink and purple; then all mixed up of every hue, as I once saw petunias on the lawn at Capo di Monti, in Naples.

My stay in San Antonio depended on the departure of the train. There were a number of army officers waiting the convenience and protection of the wagons. The evening of our departure was notable for an incident illustrating the power of imagination over bodily feeling. Most of the officers had arrived at the camping ground in advance of the wagons, and were sitting under the trees when they came. As the train was passing by Crittenden got up and took from his pocket what was called a pepper box pistol and fired at a tree in a line parallel to the road. Just at that time Lieut. Lafayette McLaws left the train to come where we were, and shouted: "Quit firing, I am shot." As he was not in range, no one regarded what he said, and Crittenden kept on firing the revolver.

When McLaws rode up he had a wild look, and the bosom of his shirt was red with blood. A ball hitting the tree had glanced off at an angle and struck him. He was taken from his horse and the wound examined. There was the hole where the bullet entered the breast, and he was spitting blood; and no surgeon being present he was put in a wagon to be taken back to San Antonio. He was resting on his back on straw and I was by his side. Again he spit some blood. He said: "My days are numbered. My whole chest is filled with blood, and I can feel the blood shaking inside as though I were filled with water." He was satisfied that he would soon die from internal hemorrhage; and perhaps he would, but fortunately it was discovered that the ball had also *hit his index finger*, that he had unknowingly sucked it in his mouth, and this was the blood he was spitting up. I therefore got out the wagon and left him. On arrival in San Antonio the wound was probed by a surgeon and the ball discovered near the spine. It was a glancing shot that pressing against the skin followed the line of least resistance until arrested by the spine. He soon recovered and came back to Corpus Christi.

On the way back, when we struck the Nueces river we discovered that the timber was a *turkey roost*. As the train was going only three miles farther on to camp, a young man, son of Col. McIntosh, and I agreed to remain there until dark and kill some turkeys.   McIntosh selected a tree under the bank near the river; I fastened my pony to a bush on the plain and sat under the bank in the woods on the second bottom.   About sunset great flocks of turkeys began to appear until the plains were alive with them.   They were disturbed by my pony being tied there.   As it grew dark they came into the trees or woods, flock after flock, in such numbers that they bent the limbs and fell to the ground all around me.   I made seven shots, shooting only at the head as they were so near me.   I picked up six fine gobblers (I would shoot no hens), and, staggering under the load, reached my pony. I threw the turkeys down and mounting my pony rode to McIntosh.   McIntosh had fired both barrels, and had one turkey.   He had stopped without any other ammunition.   Accompanying me back to where my game was, we tied the turkeys and put them over the necks of our horses and went into camp.   I have no doubt that more than a thousand turkeys flew into that timber to roost; they were on the ground all around me, and they could have been killed with a walking stick.   I do not believe they had ever heard a gun fired before.   By the stupidity of not protecting game by proper laws it has all disappeared long since.   Indians obtained rifles and ammunition from traders, and the deer were killed solely for their skins; and the wild members of the Legislature looked on and said: "Let the boys hunt whenever they please; the country and all it contains belongs to them." It is now justly held that all game belongs to the State and becomes the property of the individual only as permitted by law, and after it is killed.

CHAPTER IV.

President of Mexico Resigns, and Paredes Is Elected—Mexican Troops
Concentrating at Matamoras—Taylor Marches to the Rio Grande—Rat-
tlesnakes—Mirage—Wild Horses—Taylor Concentrates His Troops at
Arroyo, Colo.—Bull Fight—Mexicans Flee—Taylor Goes to Point Isabel
—Join Gen. Worth—Field Works—Arrival of Gen. Ampudia—Orders
Taylor to Leave—Taylor Declines—Col. Cross Murdered—Lieut. Por-
ter Killed—Gen. Arista Arrives—Declares Hostilities Commenced—
Capts. Thornton and Hardee Captured.

DURING the winter the friendly Mexicans who came to the
camp would tell us of the preparations their government
was making for war.

At the close of December, 1845, Herrera was forced to resign
the presidency of Mexico, and Paredes was elected in his place; and
detachments of troops began to move north, concentrating at
Matamoras, on the Rio Grande, and the aspect of affairs looked
quite belligerent. On the 22d of February, 1846, a depot of
supplies was established by our troops at Santa Gertrudes, some
forty miles in advance on the route to Matamoras. On the 7th
of March the tents of our company were struck preparatory to
a move, and the day following the line of march for the Rio
Grande commenced.

The advance troops were a brigade of cavalry and Ringgold's
battery of horse artillery. To be more minute, the order of
march was: a company of cavalry, then our battery, then the
main body of cavalry. As you can get all important matters
from history, I shall allude only to what history generally omits,
and relate minor affairs or scenes behind history, like that unknown behind the stage. The first night out we encamped at a
beautiful place covered with blue flowers like the hyacinth. It
was pleasant to look at, an enchanting scene that would have
been drowsy and dreamlike from the fragrance of the flowers
had we not discovered nearly every man grazing his horse carrying a small pole with which he was killing rattlesnakes. That
night I slept on the ground and dreamed a great centipede was
crawling over me, and I awoke with a great scream, like Dudu,
from her sleep.

We had breakfast at daylight, and while we were sitting by

the camp fire waiting for the bugle to call, and watching the wild
geese flying around overhead bewildered by the fires, I held my
gun pointing at them, and by some mishap it went off and alarmed
the camp; but a goose fell down, nevertheless, near me. The
guide, Pedro, said we had sixteen miles to march that day to the
next camp. Our line was diverging somewhat inland from the
gulf shore, and all the prairie was one green carpet of grass and
flowers as far as the eye could reach, when all at once there was
a great ocean on our left and not far distant. Officers galloped
to Pedro to learn what was the matter, and ere an explanation
was had the *mirage* was gone, the ocean was gone, and we were
on the lone prairie as before.

The third day we were marching quietly along when an alarm
was sounded. To our right and a little to the rear in the horizon
was what appeared to be a column of cavalry bearing down on
us. As it came nearer and nearer the cry arose: "Wild horses,
wild horses!" Our battery was closed up, the advanced company of cavalry moved on, leaving a large opening; the dragoons
massed, making an interval for the herd to pass through. On,
and on they came and, at full speed, with their long flowing
manes and tails, passed through the open space made by the battery and dragoons. There were between two and three hundred.
As soon as they passed Capt. May, Lieut. Ridgely, and some
other officers were after them on their fine horses with lariat in
hand, and after a ride of a mile or more came back each with a
young colt. They stayed with our horses several days and then
disappeared. When we encamped a pony that I had bought for
my servant to ride was bitten on the face by a rattlesnake near
the door of our tent. The animal was treated with ammonia and
whisky. The next morning his head was so swollen that I left
him behind. A servant of the paymaster, when the infantry
came along, found the pony and brought it on to the Rio Grande
and returned it to my boy.

The infantry marched by brigades at a day's interval. The
officers and men being in uniform, wearing caps, had their lips
and noses nearly raw from the sun and winds, and could not put
a cup of coffee to their lips until it was cold. I wore an immense sombrero, or Mexican straw hat. On the route I was
often told: "When Gen. Taylor comes up you will be put in arrest for wearing that hat." The army concentrated near the

Arroyo Colorado, where the general commanding overtook us. I went over to call on him the next morning, and found him in front of his tent sitting on a camp stool eating breakfast. His table was the lid of the mess chest. His nose was white from the peeling off of the skin, and his lips raw. As I came up he saluted me with: "Good morning, lieutenant, good morning; sensible man to wear a hat." So I was commended instead of being censured for making myself comfortable. His coffee was in a tin cup, and his lips so sore that the heat of the tin was painful.

A day or so after this the advance pickets encountered a herd of wild cattle that all ran away except an old bull that showed fight. Hearing shots in advance I galloped, on and found four or five cavalrymen around this animal, that looked as if he might be the grandsire of the herd. Every shot fired from the carbines had failed to penetrate the skin. I was armed with my shotgun and a brace of old pistols made in Marseilles, France, that Lieut. U. S. Grant gave me to carry along for him. I fired both these pistols at the enraged animal, and the balls only made the skin red by removing the hair. We now persuaded a dragoon to put himself in front of the beast while I approached within twenty feet of his side, and from my gun fired a ball that penetrated the lungs. Still he pawed the earth and charged the horses, some of which were injured, and inspired new life to all around him while his own was ebbing. At last a dragoon dismounted, cautiously approached, shot him in the forehead, and the already weakened bull fell on his knees and rolled on his side—dead.

This fight was not conducted according to all the rules of the ring at Madrid. We had, however, a dozen picadors and a matadore, and they performed feats of valor without the approving smiles of black-eyed señoras or the applause of the grandees, which in Spain nerves the actors to daring deeds; but there was a compensation, for there were no hisses when one fled from the bull to save his horse, or sought a raking position in the rear to encourage those in front. The lesson I drew from this kind of recreation was that at the next bullfight I would be found among the spectators and not in the arena.

This continued firing by the advance guard caused troops to hasten to the front to ascertain the reason of the tumult, and when it was reported to Gen. Taylor that according to the rules of Texas, Mexico, and Spain a bull had been found, an amphitheater marked out, and that a real bull fight had taken place; that the noble animal had been slain for amusement, and that his cavalry was not well trained and had been tossed by the bull, he grew irate, and alas! to spoil our little game of recreations away in front, caused an order to be issued forbidding all firing on the march, unless necessitated by the presence of the enemy. Henceforth the bulls, deer, and jack rabbits became friendly with us, and we passed them by in silence.

Nearly every day small armed parties of Mexicans were seen away in advance, and once when we rode to a small pond to water our horses we found a party of Mexican lancers watering theirs also. A few words of salutation passed, when they moved on and disappeared. Once they set the prairie on fire, and we had to drive through the leaping flames with our guns and caissons filled with ammunition.

On the 19th the head of the column was halted and went into camp about three or four miles off the stream called Arroyo Colorado, to wait the arrival or concentration of all the troops, about four thousand in number, and preparation to cross was made by the engineers. On the morning of the 20th, our battery was put in position on the banks of the river where the earth had been cut down for it to cross, and where its fire could command the opposite shore and cover the landing of the infantry. Notice had been given the engineer officer by the Mexicans that the forces on the Mexican shore were under positive orders to fire on any of our troops attempting to cross. Again a like notice was sent to Gen. Taylor, and a proclamation that had been issued by Gen. Mejia a day or two past was handed to him. During this time an awful din was made on the Mexican side by bugle calls away down, and far up the river, and kettle-drums and fife in the woods in front. Our guns were loaded and matches lit when the old General gave the command for the infantry to cross. The head of the columns plunged into the water, holding their cartridge boxes and muskets high, and, landing, deployed at once right and left. Other troops crossed above on the right, and when all moved forward not a Mexican was seen.

On the 24th we arrived at a point on the main road running

from Point Isabel to Matamoras which was ten miles from Point Isabel and a like distance from Matamoras. Gen. Worth was directed to move on toward the Rio Grande near Matamoras with the infantry, while Gen. Taylor, with our battery and the dragoons, went down to meet Maj. Munroe at Point Isabel, where he had established a depot of supplies for the army. On the 26th Gen. Taylor, with his escort of cavalry and artillery, joined the main body under Worth, and on the 28th the army encamped on the river bank opposite Matamoras.

The arrival of Gen. Taylor with his army, quietly taking the position he did, no doubt produced some consternation. Mexican infantry was seen in motion in the city. They had the river picketed and batteries placed to bear on our camp.

The Mexican commander insisted that all was lovely, and that there was no war; that the acts of hostility were little events — little incidents—to make our arrival interesting and pleasant. That the Consul for the United States in Matamoras was free, and a gentleman of leisure, but that Gen. Taylor could not interview him without permission from the Commandante.

Notwithstanding "the distinguished consideration" and affectionate regard expressed in the communications for the Americanos, Gen. Taylor concluded to put up some field works or fortifications out of courtesy to those being constructed by the Mexicans. We were in the land of Moab, and the promised land was on the other side. There was the city embowered in green foliage, with tropical plants around the white houses, and there, when the sun was declining, would assemble the female population to see and to be seen, and listen to the music of the various bands. "Dixie" was not then born, the "Bonnie Blue Flag" had not then been waved; and we played "Yankee Doodle" because it made a loud noise, the "Star-Spangled Banner" because it waved over us, "Hail, Columbia" because it was inspiriting, and the sweetest airs from the operas for the beautiful senoritas with the rebosas that disclosed the sweet faces they were designed to hide. The music from the other side I cannot recall now, only it rose with a "voluptuous swell" that floated over the water and died away softly in the distance with the breath that made it. And all the while on our side the shore was lined with officers and soldiers enjoying the scene before them—that had a short existence.

"Ampudia has come! Ampudia has come!" was heralded by every Mexican that came into our camp vending the products of the farms. And so it was. He came clothed in modesty, and made a display of it immediately by sending a dispatch on the 12th ordering Gen. Taylor to get out of his camp in twenty-four hours, and not to stop on this side of the Nueces. I do not believe Taylor was much acquainted with fear, because, instead of "folding his tents like the Arabs, and silently stealing away," he had the audacity to remain just where he was until the twenty-four hours had expired, and long after.

About this time Col. Cross, of the quartermaster's department, was murdered by some one and his body thrown in the chaparral. I was with a party of officers that was riding up the river, not expressly in search of Col. Cross's body, some seven or eight days after he was missed, and we observed some vultures resting in an old tree top. I rode in toward them, and saw a blue coat on the ground. It was Col. Cross's, and some of his remains were there. They were afterwards gathered up and cared for properly. One of the parties, a detachment of dragoons, sent in search of Cross's body got into a fight with the Mexicans and Lieut. Porter was killed; and yet there was no war?

And now a greater than Ampudia had arrived, and on the 24th of April Gen. Arista assumed command of the Mexican army now encamped in and around the city, and he informed Taylor that he considered hostilities commenced, and had "let slip the dogs of war." The enemy was now reported to have crossed to our side in large numbers, and parties were sent out to make reconnoissances, one of which was captured by the Mexicans; and Capts. Thornton and Hardee were now prisoners of war.

CHAPTER V.

Arista and His Cavalry—United States Excited—Two Hundred Thousand
Men Offer Their Services—Congress Declares "War Existed by the
Acts of the Mexican Republic"—Taylor Marches to Point Isabel—Bom-
bardment of Fort Brown—Capts. May and Walker—Taylor Marches
for Matamoras—Battle of Palo Alto—Victory—Arista Falls Back to Re-
saca—Battle of Resaca—Capture of Enemies' Batteries—Capts. May and
Ridgely—Gen. La Vega Captured—His Sword Presented to Taylor—
Duncan and Ridgely Pursue the Enemy—I Capture La Vega's Aid—
Col. McIntosh—Ride over the Field of Palo Alto—Death of Lieuts.
Chadburne and Stevens—We take possession of Matamoras—Gen.
Twiggs appointed Governor—Twiggs and Jesus Maria—Arrival of
Gens. W. O. Butler, Robert Patterson, Pillow, and others—Promoted to
Second Lieutenant—Officers of the Company—March to Camargo—
Thence to Monterey—Seralvo—Arrival at Monterey.

A ND now Arista, on the part of the Mexican government,
having declared that war existed; and some of our forces,
both men and officers, having been killed or captured, the pony express carried this news to the city of New Orleans; and as there
was no telegraph, it spread all over the country and became mag-
nified like "the three black crows." The apprehension that we
were cut off from communicating with home by Arista's army
occupying a position between us and Point Isabel was widespread, and impromptu meetings held for volunteers to go to the
relief of our army, and thousands responded to the call. Congress was in session, and it promptly declared that "war existed by
the acts of the Mexican Republic," and authorized the President
to accept into service fifty thousand volunteers. As over two
hundred thousand men offered their services, it may be, as Mark
Twain once observed, that many persons "persuaded their wives'
relations" to avail themselves of this unique occasion to visit the
land of the Aztecs, and enjoy balmy breezes under the shade of
the acacia, the bamboo, and the pomegranate, with transportation free. In the meantime we were in blissful ignorance that
we were in such danger, and did not know it until our friends
came to our relief.

When Arista landed a part of his force on our side of the
river, it was put in the field under the command of Gen. Torre-
jon, and, being cavalry, had gained possession of the road lead-

ing to Point Isabel, thus cutting off all the creature comforts that we daily enjoyed. If it did not affect our pockets, it curtailed the duties of our *chef de cuisine*, and diminished the pleasures of the table. In plain English, rations were getting short, and the less we had to eat the harder we worked on the fort and other defenses.

May Day, when our friends were inhaling the fragrance of the bloom of the peach and cherry, the rose and the violet, and children were dancing around the maypole, we were striking our tents, packing up "traps," burning letters, preparatory to leaving for Point Isabel. A mocking bird that would sit on the ridgepole of my tent and sing to me daily, and warble sweet notes by moonlight, now sat on the fence adjoining and sung a parting song, for I never saw him again, and it filled my heart with sadness. Sing on, dear bird; I hear thee now!

The Seventh Regiment of Infantry, Bragg's company, or battery, and a company of foot artillery were left in the fort under Maj. Brown, and Gen. Taylor started for Point Isabel, where our supplies were in store. The day following we arrived, and I was delighted to see old ocean again. Our departure should not have been made an occasion for sensible persons to rejoice, for did we not trust about six hundred men to entertain the Mexicans during our absence? and thus notify them that we purposed to return, and did we not do so?

"And I have loved thee, ocean," and I love thee still, and I was content to hear thy voice again and be near thee; but life is a dream, and from that dream I was awakened at dawn on the morning of the 3d. I was sleeping on the ground. A dull distant sound broke on my ear. I rested my head on my elbow, and heard nothing; putting my ear again to the earth, I heard the boom! boom! of distant cannon. It was heard by others, and soon the camp was astir. It was now certain from the continuous sounds that Fort Brown was being bombarded. Gen. Taylor sent out Capts. May and Walker to communicate with Maj. Brown, and Walker succeeded in getting into the fort and returning. The defense of Point Isabel was to be intrusted to Maj. Munroe, assisted by the navy in command of Commodore Connor; and the army, now reduced to two thousand four hundred men, was to move to the relief of the garrison in Fort Brown.

About noon on the 7th this little force started to meet Arista, who was between us and Fort Brown, without a question or doubt of getting there, although it was known the enemy's force numbered about eight thousand men. It was near noon on the 8th of May when far away over the broad prairie, dimly outlined, was seen a dark line directly in front of us. It was the Mexican army drawn up in battle array across our road to Matamoras. When we arrived where there was water Gen. Taylor halted to give the men time to fill their canteens and to have a little rest.

Soon the long roll sounded, hearts beat, pulses kept time, and knees trembled and would not be still. Our line was formed as follows: the fifth infantry (Col. McIntosh), Ringgold's battery, third infantry, two long, heavy iron eighteen pounders, fourth infantry, and two squadrons of dragoons posted on our right, all commanded by Col. Twiggs, formed the right wing; the left was a battalion of foot artillery, Duncan's battery, and eighth infantry. In some respects it was a laughable thing to see the deployment of our line, of which the Mexicans were quiet spectators. Looking back from where we came into battery, which was executed in a half minute and in advance of the infantry, I could see the two great, long, heavy iron eighteen pounders, and the white-topped ammunition wagons lumbering along to get into line, drawn by a team of twenty oxen each. They came into line by words of command not laid down in the work on tactics; they described a great semicircle at the commands, "Haw, Buck! haw, Brindle! whoa, Brandy!" and finally got their muzzles pointed to the front. If we had had elephants in place of the oxen, it would have been more picturesque, and presented a fine panorama.

Arista must have thought he had performed his whole duty when he barred the road with his troops to prevent Taylor from advancing. He had been in line of battle all the morning awaiting our coming, yet he *permitted us to deploy undisturbed*, although we were in easy range of his guns, instead of assuming the offensive as he should have done. With a courtesy becoming a knight of the Middle Ages he permitted Lieut. Blake, in the presence of the armies, to ride down to within musket shot of his line, to dismount and survey his troops through his glass, then to remount and ride along down his front without allowing

4

a shot to be fired at him.   As this reconnoissance had unmasked
his artillery, he ran his guns to the front, and the artillery on
both sides commenced firing.   My rank assigned me to the duty
of sitting on my horse to look at the fight and watch the caissons.   Presently a small shell came along and struck the driver
of the lead horses.   The shell entered his body after carrying
away the pommel of his saddle, and exploded the moment it left
his body, as fragments of it wounded his horse in the hip, split
the lip and tongue, and knocked out some teeth of a second horse
and broke the jaw of Lieut. Ridgely's blooded mare.   That was
the first man I saw killed in battle.   It was war, but it was not
pleasant, and I thought it was no place for me to sit on my horse
idle; so, dismounting, I gave my horse to a horse holder, and
walked to the howitzer on the right, took command of it, and
helped work it.   As no one demurred at what I was doing, I remained in charge of it all day.   I would prefer to take my rod
and line and go fishing, even if I got only a nibble, than to sit
still on a horse offering myself as a target for cannon balls.   To
have a hand in the fray is quite another matter.

I shall not describe this battle.   It was almost and altogether
an artillery fight.   Once the Mexican cavalry with two pieces
of artillery under Torrajon made a detour to our right with a
view of turning it, or capturing our wagon train.   This movement was defeated by the Fifth Infantry and two pieces of artillery being sent to meet it.   The infantry formed in square, and
when the Mexican cannon were being loaded to fire on the square,
Ridgely and I came up, and so *quickly* did we bring our guns
into action that we unlimbered, loaded, and fired before the Mexicans could; in fact they did not fire a cannon shot, but retreated
slowly back whence they came.   Why they moved so doggedly
slow under fire I could not tell; perhaps it was Mexican pride.
Not long after this Maj. Ringgold, while sitting on his horse,
was struck with a cannon shot, from the effects of which he died.
Maj. Ringgold was an accomplished officer and an elegant gentleman, and his loss was a source of universal regret.   Lieut.
Ridgely succeeded to the command of the battery.   The firing
ceased about dusk.   Our loss was only ten killed and forty-four
wounded.   Arista stated that his loss was two hundred and fifty-
three.   They turned their guns on our batteries; we fired at their
infantry as instructed.   During the night Arista fell back to a

strong position on the banks of a dry bed of a stream about thirty yards wide called Resaca de la Palma. It runs through a wood with a dense undergrowth of chaparral, the woods on either side being perhaps a mile wide. From the prairie on which the battle of Palo Alto had been fought the road enters the woods that border the Resaca, crosses it, and leads on to Matamoras.

Early on the morning of the 9th Taylor sent Capt. McCall with about two hundred men in advance to discover the position of the enemy. He found them in force at Resaca, returned, and so reported to the general commanding.

There have been men who *create occasions* and avail themselves of the circumstances arising therefrom; but man generally is the creature of circumstance, and I mention this because it has an application to persons who were engaged in this day's battle. From Gen. Taylor down no one in this army had had much practical experience in the *art* of war, and from practice knew but little of the peculiar province of each arm of the service.

Because the artillery rendered such signal service on the field yesterday Gen. Taylor was impressed with the idea that it was available for pursuit of cavalry in mountain passes, for storming entrenchments, or charging a line of battle. Having discovered the position of the enemy, the General had the trains parked on the prairie and left in charge of a battalion of foot artillery and the two eighteen pounders. May's dragoons were held in reserve on the prairie near where the road enters the woods.

These arrangements completed, our battery, now under the command of Ridgely, was ordered to advance, take the road through the woods and chaparral, and attack the enemy. Here then was the singular tactics of a battery of horse artillery all alone, leaving the entire army behind, moving down the road through the woods without any support whatever. Capt. Walker was our guide. He and I and Ridgely were in advance. We had gone half a mile or more when crash through the tree tops came a shot from the unseen batteries in front. "At a gallop, march," was the order, and on we went until the road turned to the left about forty-five degrees. At the turn we halted, and this gave us a battery front (in part) to their guns near the bank of the dry river. We could not see their guns, nor they see ours, owing to undergrowth, but the guns were discharged at the smoke that each other made. We kept advancing "by hand"

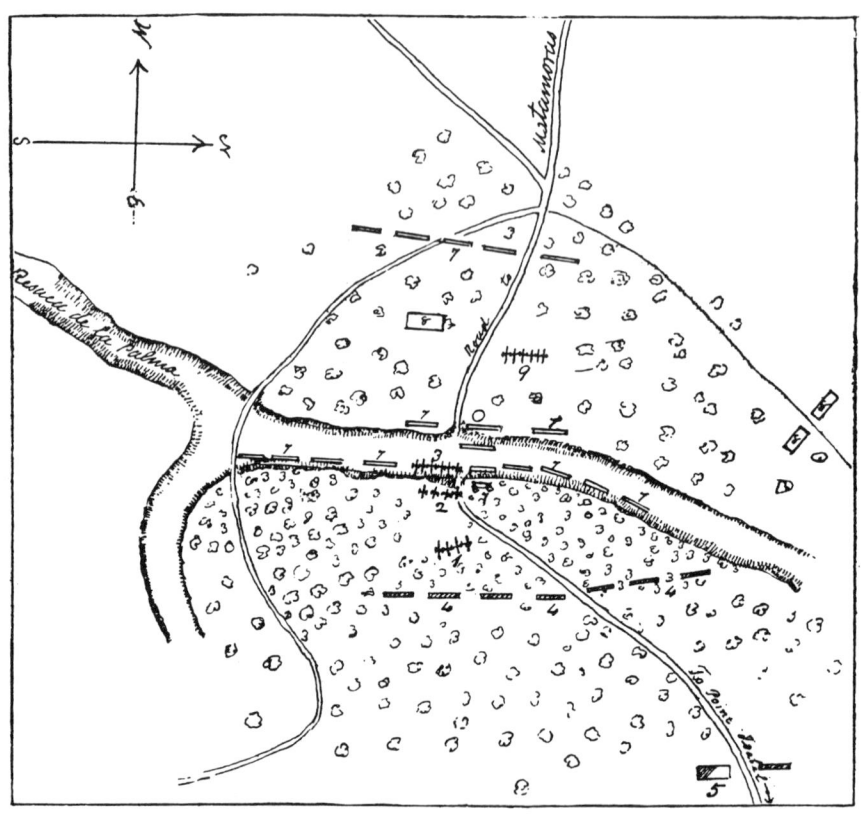

PLAN OF BATTLE OF RESACA, MEX.

Fought May 9, 1846.

1. Ridgely's guns when he called for May's dragoons to capture Mexican Battery.
2. Position of Ridgely after the charge.
3. Position of Mexican battery when captured.
4. United States infantry moving to attack.
5. May's dragoons previous to the charge.
6. Reserve.
7. Mexican infantry.
8. Mexican cavalry.
9. Mexican artillery.

down the road. Their skirmishers now began to annoy us. Ridgely came to me and said: "Go to Gen. Taylor and ask him to send some infantry supports." I got on my horse and galloped back up the road at full speed, met Gen. Taylor, Maj. Bliss, and other staff officers in the road, and delivered the message. The reply was: "The infantry has been deployed and will soon be there." I returned at a run. No one was to be seen anywhere. We had now been fighting the enemy's guns alone for more than a half hour, and had driven them from off the plain into the ravine or dry bed of the river, and had obtained possession of an open camping ground directly in front of their pieces and not over a hundred yards distant. Again Ridgely came and said: "Go to Gen. Taylor as quick as possible, and tell him to *send me* assistance to capture the Mexican batteries in front of us." The road and also the woods on both sides were now full of our infantry moving forward. I soon met Gen. Taylor, delivered the message, adding: "General, their guns are just in our front and can be taken." His only answer was: "*My! my! G—d, where is May? I can't get him up!*"* Nothing more was said, and I returned. By this time our infantry was engaged with the enemy on the right of the road. The firing was very heavy. I had been back with my gun about ten minutes, when down the road came May, in column of fours; he halted and exclaimed: "Hello! Ridgely, where is that battery? I am ordered to charge it." Ridgely said: "Hold on, Charley, till I draw their fire, and you will soon see where they are." Our guns fired, and theirs replied. Away went May toward the Mexican guns, and our guns after him at a run. We came up to them muzzle to muzzle, only theirs were below the banks of the ravine and ours above. May had swept the gunners away and was out of sight on the other side in the chaparral. I was in command of the twelve-pound howitzer, and as I gave the order in battery, "Fire to the front!" a Mexican regiment behind some earthworks in the ravine and on the other side, with their right directly in front, fired a volley. Two drivers fell, the wheel locked the gun in turning, a horse fell, and it was with difficulty we could unlimber. I said to the sergeant, "Run for a canis-

*The inference is that Gen. Taylor ordered May up on the receipt of Ridgely's first message.

ter;" but before he got back a gunner slipped in a shell, and on
top of that in went the canister. I could not prevent it, so great
was the din of muskets. I fired the gun myself. The wheels were
lifted from the ground. Two more canisters were fired before
the regiment broke; but at that moment our infantry opened on
them, and all was over in our immediate front. The second gun
had horses killed, drivers and men shot, and it locked a wheel
in the same way. Ridgely sprang from his horse and leaped into
the dead driver's saddle, straightened the team, and that gun
came into action. What the other two did I know not. Just as
our firing ceased up rode Gen. Taylor with his staff, and complimented us. As he sat there on his horse May's men began to
come back. A sergeant came up first and reported that he had
captured Gen. La Vega; next an infantry officer came and reported La Vega was his prisoner; and then May returned and,
riding up to Gen. Taylor, drew from a scabbard a sword. Taking it by the point, he presented it to the General with these
words: "General, I have the honor to present to you the sword
of Gen. La Vega. He is a prisoner." It was gracefully done.
Taylor looked at it a moment and returned it to May. While
we were all there in a group down the road came Duncan's battery and crossed the ravine. Ridgely could not stand that, and
said to me: "French ask the General if we cannot cross over
too." The reply was: "No, you have done enough to-day."
Ridgely laughed, saying, "I can't receive orders from you;" and
away he went with the guns after Duncan, leaving me to follow
as soon as I repaired the damage to my gun. In a few minutes
I crossed. No one halted me. I found Duncan firing away to
the left and front, where it was reported troops were retreating. We soon moved on. At this time I saw a man hiding behind some bushes about twenty yards from the roadside. I went
to him, and as my knowledge of Spanish had not been cultivated, I undertook to ask him his rank (seeing he was an officer),
and tried to say to him: "¿Teniente o capitan?" It must have
been badly pronounced, for he replied, "Si, senor," and, suiting
action to the word, he put his hand in his pocket and handed me
a biscuit. At that moment up rode Dr. Barnes and Capt. Kerr,
and Barnes exclaimed: "Great heavens! French asked this gen
tleman for bread." No doubt the officer, who was an aid to Gen.
La Vega, understood me to say: "¿Tiene usted pan?" ("have you

any bread?"). Barnes, who afterwards became surgeon genera
of the United States army, declared to the end I asked that gentleman for bread, and never failed to tell the story on me in
company.

Well, on we went for over four miles to Fort Brown. What
a welcome we received! They had heard the sound of battle on
the 8th, and again on the 9th, and had seen the Mexicans crossing the river in great haste and confusion. Great was the commotion in Matamoras that night. Now when darkness came,
Ridgely remembered that he had come on without orders—in
fact, pretty nearly against orders—and he told me to ride back
and see Gen. Taylor and ask for orders. So I rode back over
the road alone. Gen. Taylor was glad to hear from the garrison; said Ridgely could remain on the Rio Grande until further
orders. J. Bankhead Magruder * was at headquarters, and de-

---

*Gen. John Bankhead Magruder was known in earlier days as "Prince
John." When stationed on the Canadian frontier the British officers and
ours were on good social terms. John was indeed a princely fellow, and
the officers at his mess dined always in a rich, gay dinner jacket. His servant was Irish and a jewel, and knew well "Prince John's" foibles. One
day at dinner, to which some English officers were guests, there was a considerable display of taste, and one of them had the temerity to ask his host
what was the pay of a lieutenant of artillery, and obtained for an answer:
"Well, bless you, my dear fellow, I do not remember; my servant always
gets it. What is it, Patrick?" And Pat, well knowing the ways of Magruder, replied: "Your honor must perceive the captain is a gintleman,
and too ginerous to ask me for it."

When the city of Mexico was captured by Gen. Scott "Prince John"
obtained quarters in the bishop's palace. Sending for the butler, he asked
him: "At what hour does the bishop dine?" Answer: "Four P.M." "How
many courses does he have?" Answer: "Four." "How many bottles
of wine does he order?" Answer: "Two." To impress the butler that he
was an officer of high dignity, he gave orders that he would dine at 8 P.M.
and require eight courses and four bottles of wine, doubling the courses,
etc.

And here is another story I will relate as I heard it:

After the battles around Richmond had been fought Gen. J. B. Magruder was sent to command the Department of Texas. As I have formerly
related, he was a *bon vivant* and rejoiced in the pleasures of the table, and
dined with much ceremony. To keep this up, as far as he could, he would
send, like the popes of Rome, a courier in advance to arrange for his comfort. On one occasion a staff officer was sent ahead as usual. Coming to
a good residence, he arranged for comfortable quarters and a sumptuous
supper. When the General arrived and the usual preliminaries were over

clared it was very imprudent for me to return by myself, and
insisted that he should send me under the protection of an escort.   I accepted two men, but as they were not mounted, the
progress was too slow.   I dismissed them and galloped back
safely.   Duncan, who was an ambitious man, was much disappointed that he never got sight of the enemy on the 9th; but it
is true, history to the contrary notwithstanding.

You now have the true history of the circumstances that led
May to be sent to charge that battery; it originated in the brain
of Ridgely.   Duncan, who was not in the action, was made a
brevet major for Palo Alto, and lieutenant colonel *for Resaca.*
Ridgely, who was distinguished for his gallant conduct in both
battles, was rewarded only with a brevet captaincy, which he
declined, for the two battles.   Capt. May was, if I remember
aright, rewarded with two brevets without any distinguished
service, or special service at all in the first battle.   There is
nothing like blowing a horn and having friends at court.   I
mention this without any reflection on those two good soldiers,
and reference is thus made to point out that true service and just
merit does not always meet with its proper reward.   Such is the
way of the world.

The conduct of our troops in this battle was courageous in the
extreme.   Banners were captured by gallant old officers from the
hands of the enemy and held aloft in the front during the conflict that was in some instances hand to hand.   And yet the loss
would not indicate such resistance, for our killed were only thirty-nine, and the wounded about eighty.*   It certainly shows less

---

he was ushered into the dining hall, and there sat at the table a ragged
"Reb" helping himself to the supper all alone.   Magruder, however, took
his seat at the table, and, eying the "Reb" demolishing the viands, he exclaimed: "Do you, sir, know with whom you are eating supper?"   "Reb"
replied: "No, I don't know, and I don't care a d—mn; before I went into
the army I was very particular as to whom I ate with, but it makes no
difference now; just help yourself, do.

*Riding over the battlefield the day after the fight we came to the
camp where the surgeons were attending to the wounded.   A *German*
prisoner was there *standing up*, holding on to the limb of a tree resting
himself.   he had been shot crosswise in the rear, the ball tearing away
the seat of his breeches, that were very bloody.   One of our *Irish* soldiers
was passing by with canteens filled with water, and the German asked
for a drink.   Pat surveyed him, and replied: "Never a drop of wather

stubborn resistance on the part of the Mexicans than was found in the civil war. Col. McIntosh was pinned to the earth with bayonets, one entering his mouth and passing through his neck; he was rescued, and lived only to give his life for his country at Molino del Rey. The day following was spent in burying the dead and caring for the wounded, and in an exchange of prison ers. Our battery, with some infantry, constituted an escort for the prisoners to Point Isabel. On the way there I rode over the field of Palo Alto. I saw a number of the dead that had not been buried. The flesh of the Americans was decayed and gone, or eaten by wolves and vultures; that of the Mexicans was dried and uncorrupted, which I attribute to the nature of their food, it being antiseptic. I observed this also at Monterey.

Again I was where I could see the wild waves of ocean play and come tumbling on the shore; but like most pleasures it was short, for we were soon on the march back to Fort Brown.

If we remember that Taylor had been given twenty-four hours, out of distinguished consideration for his character, to get away from before Matamoras, or take the consequences, and was so impolite in not obeying; and if we consider that when we did leave it was regarded as a flight; and if we call to mind the re joicings of the people that we had fled, we can in a measure real ize the sudden change from high hopes to despondency, from expected joy to overwhelming sorrow when they saw their sol diers returning, not with captured flags and the spoils of war, not with waving banners and triumphant shouts of victory, but fleeing when no one pursued, and madly plunging into the river to gain the shore which they lately left with expectations not realized.

On the 10th we stood on our bank of the river, the other shore so near and yet so far! An army with no pontoon train! no bridge whereon to cross a deep, narrow river! Where was the great organizer that makes war successful? For one week the troops remained in front of the city unable to cross for the want of adequate means.

On the 18th, when the advanced squadron of dragoons was swimming across the river, Lieut. George Stevens was drowned.

will ye get from me, ye bloody hathen. If ye had stayed in your own counthry, where you belong, ye would now be well and have a sound seat to sit down on."

Balance such a man's life with the cost of a pontoon bridge! Two of my classmates, brave men, were now released from war. T. L. Chadbourn was killed at Resaca, and now Stevens drowned! both men dear to me.   I saw poor Stevens

"Beat the surges under him, and ride upon their back,"

then sink and rise no more.

We crossed the river unmolested, and took possession of the town.   Gen. Twiggs was appointed governor of the place, and under his police system perfect order was maintained.   Many pleasant families remained and to some of us a cordial welcome was given at all times.

My time was passed pleasantly in the city during the months of June, July, and part of August.   Our battery was in camp near the headquarters of Gen. Twiggs.   A path leading to the city passed close in front of his office tent, and many persons went to and fro.

One day I was sitting with the General.   It was a beautiful afternoon.   We were under the shade of some trees, and soldiers and strangers passing by so near would salute or otherwise recognize the General.   However, at this time a Mexican came along with a tall sombrero on his head and passed without noticing the General.   He was hailed by the General, came back, and was asked: "What is your name?"   He took off his sombrero politely, and answered: "Jesus Maria."   Twiggs raised both hands above his head and exclaimed: "Go away! go away from me! go away!" and the surprised Mexican passed on.   I inferred from the great excitement the General exhibited at the name of the Mexican that his ancestors may have worshiped in the Temple of Jerusalem, or fought with the Maccabees in defense of their religion.

Whilst the forces under Taylor were resting in camp at Matamoras, the quartermaster's department was busy in procuring light-draft boats to navigate the Rio Grande, it having been determined to establish a depot of supplies at Camargo, a town on the river nearly a hundred miles above Matamoras, preparatory to an advance on Monterey.

Under the act calling for volunteers there were appointed to command them two major generals, W. O. Butler, of Kentucky, and Robert Patterson, of Pennsylvania; and G. J. Pillow, of Tennessee, T. L. Hamer, of Ohio, John A. Quitman, of Mississippi, Thomas Marshall, of Kentucky, Joseph Lane, of Indiana, James Shields, of Illinois, were commissioned brigadier generals, and men to the number of near six thousand were, as volunteers, added to Taylor's force, increasing it to nine thousand.

This force was organized into three divisions: the first under Gen. Twiggs, the second under Gen. Worth, and the third under Gen. W. O. Butler, who was with Gen. Jackson at New Orleans when he defeated the English under Pakenham. Nearly fifty years after, another Butler, Gen. Benjamin F. Butler, figured at New Orleans, and I would not that you mistake them, for they were one to the other as "Hyperion to a satyr."

In June I was promoted to the high rank of second lieutenant of the Third Artillery, and sometime during the summer was assigned to Bragg's company of artillery, whose lieutenants were George H. Thomas, John F. Reynolds, and myself. They were all agreeable officers, but even to this day I recall, like a woman, my first loves, Ringgold, Ridgely, and Shover.

Early in August the first division started for Camargo. It was an uninteresting march, hot and dusty beyond conception. By the middle of August the forces started for Monterey. We now left the alluvial lands of the Rio Grande, and the country was free from dust. From Seralvo we obtained the first view of the lofty peaks of the Sierra Madre range of mountains, seventy odd miles distant, and they created much discussion as to whether they were mountains or clouds. From Seralvo to Monterey the country was beautiful, rich, and fertile. We passed groves of ebony, Brazil wood, oak, pecan, mesquite, etc. The fields of corn were in silk, melons and vegetables of every variety were ripe; and later on in the season we had oranges, lemons, limes, pomegranates, bananas, and grapes.

One morning when we were between Seralvo and Marin I received an order to remain and assist Lieut. D. B. Sacket in having the mule train loaded. I thought it strange that an artillery officer should be put on that duty, and felt indignant; but I was repaid in a measure by what took place, for I sometimes enjoy a little "fun." After the muleteers had packed the old trained mules and started them one after another on their way, there remained a number of wild mules to have their packs put on, I believe for the first time. One was lassoed and thrown and the pack saddle put on.   Then, for his load, two barrels of crackers were securely put on.   All being ready, the blind was removed from his eyes.   He looked slowly around, showed the white of his eyes, took one step, humped himself, and kicked so high that the load overbalanced him and he fell on his back unable to rise, and brayed aloud.   Soon a blind was removed from another; he surveyed the load from right to left with rolling eyes, squatted low, humped himself, sprang forward, stood on his forefeet and commenced high kicking, exploded the barrels of "hardtack" with his heels, threw the biscuit in the air with the force of a dynamite bomb, and ran away with the empty barrels dangling behind, as badly scared as a dog with tin buckets tied to his tail. A third, when his blind was removed, stepped lightly to the front, but casting his eyes on either side, made a loud bray, closed down his tail, and disappeared through the chaparral as quick as a jack rabbit, followed with loud Mexican denunciations that I cannot translate.   In this manner four or five cargoes were lost, and the pack train moved on.   I was sorry for the poor Mexicans, but I could not but laugh at the mules.   My duty ended when the train started; so leaving it in the charge of Lieut. Sacket with his dragoons, I rode on alone and did not overtake my company until it had encamped.

We arrived at Monterey on the 19th.   The dragoons and the two batteries of field artillery encamped with Gen. Taylor at his headquarters at Walnut Springs, three miles from the city.

CHAPTER VI.

MONTEREY, an old city, the capital of the State of Nuevo
Leon, contained about forty thousand inhabitants. It is
situated on the left bank of the San Juan, a small stream that
empties into a larger one of the same name.

It had three forts. The main one, called the Black Fort, was
out on the plain north of the city. Fort Tanaria was in the suburbs, in the northeast part of the city; and about two hundred yards distant south of it was a third fort, the guns of which
commanded the interior of the Tanaria. The hill on the slope
of which was the bishop's palace was also fortified; and strong
earthworks surrounded the city on the north and east sides,
with isolated works to the south and west.

Gen. Ampudia was in command, with a force of seven thousand regular troops, and a large volunteer force. A reconnoissance of the place by the engineer officers, having been completed, dispositions to capture the city were made by detaching
Gen. Worth, with his division, and Col. Hays, with his Texas
regiment, to gain the road to Saltillo, by storming its defenses,
and thereby cutting off the supplies of the enemy and holding
his line of retreat. To accomplish this part of Gen. Taylor's
plan, Worth started late on the 20th, and on the 21st made the
attack, and was successful in carrying the detached works and
securing the road to Saltillo. By way of *divertisement*, or at
most a diversion in favor of Worth, Gen. Taylor moved Gar-
land's division of regulars and a division of volunteers, some

cavalry, and our battery, down to the northeast part of the city. As is often the case, this demonstration terminated in a fight, and the capture of the fort or redoubt called Tanaria and buildings adjacent. Our battery penetrated by a street some distance into the city. The houses were mainly built of soft stone or adobe, and the shot from the batteries in the town passed through the buildings, covering the men, horses, and guns with lime and dust, blinding us so that we could see nothing. From this situation we were ordered out. In passing an opening in the works a shot killed the two wheel horses to one of the caissons, and Lieut. Reynolds and I with the men threw, or pushed, the horses and harness into the ditches on either side, and after we had done this and gone some distance, another shot passed through two horses of one of the guns. These horses were loosed, and with their entrails dragging, in agony of pain, I suppose, commenced eating the grass.

Having gotten out, Bragg ordered me back alone to the ditch in the edge of the town to save the harness that was on the horses. I met Gen. Taylor, who inquired where I was going. When told, he said, "That is nonsense," and ordered me to go to camp, where the battery had been sent. My ride back was rather exciting. For the distance of a half mile or more I was on the plain in open sight of the Black Fort, or the citadel. The gunners must have become quite vindictive, for they opened fire on me, a lone horseman. I had to watch the smoke of each gun, check my horse, and as the shot would cross ahead push on, stopping to allow each shot to pass in front. I think the smoke prevented the gunners from discovering that I halted at every discharge of a gun. At any rate, every shot passed in front of me. I never forgave Bragg for that picayune order, and it was supplemented on the 23d by another equally as wild. As we were withdrawing from the city, we had to go up a straight road leading from a four-gun battery. A shot struck a driver on the elbow, carrying away his forearm. He fell *dead* from his horse, singular but true, and Bragg directed me to dismount and take off the man's sword. I did so; and took from his pocket a knife, for I thought I might be sent back if I did not save that too. I presented the sword to Bragg, and desired him to take charge of the knife, but he declined, as it was not *public* property. I write down these little things, for they give in-

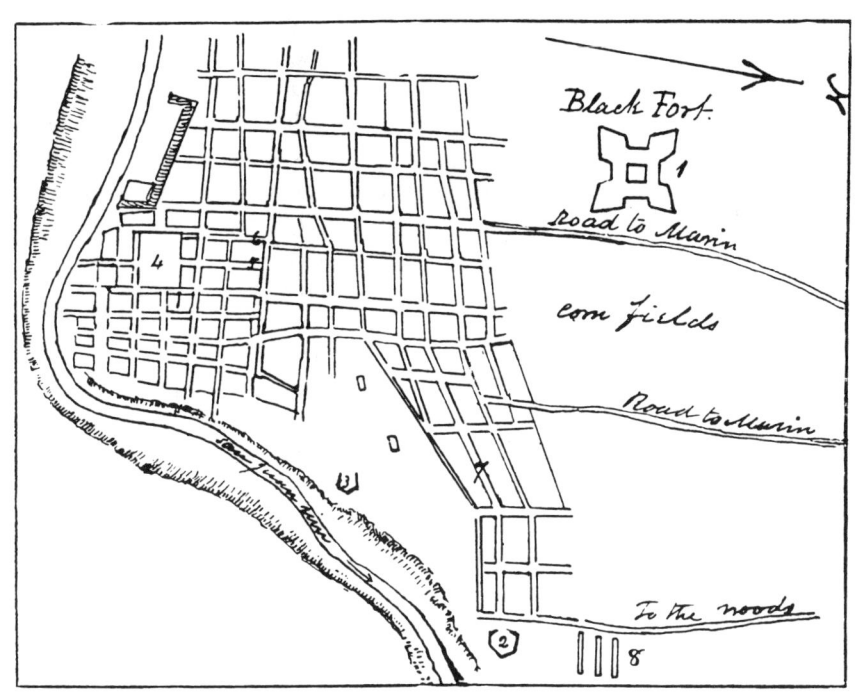

PLAN OF MONTEREY, MEX.

1. Black Fort.
2. Fort Tanaria.
3. Redoubt.
4. Main Plaza.

5. French's gun.
6. Thomas's gun.
7. Bragg's battery—first day.
8. United States troops advancing on Fort Tanaria.

stances of the observance of details, characteristic of this officer, not obtained from history.

The day following, the 22d, our battery was ordered to occupy, in reserve, a depression in a plain north of the citadel.
But they knew we were there, and searched for us with shot.
As I have observed already, the garrison of the citadel was vindictive, and fired at any one in sight and range. Sure enough,
soon two long-haired Texans, on ponies, rode down and halted
near each other, on the plain, and we watched events. Bang!
went one of the heavy guns in the citadel; the ball passed over
us and went between the two Texans. One wheeled his horse
back for camp, and the other galloped down to our guns and remarked: "Them darned fool Mexicans shoot mighty wild; they
came near hitting me." He thought the shot was directed at us,
and not at him.

But, to return to more important proceedings. Behold, now
a glorious sight!

To the northwest of Monterey, and in the suburbs of the city,
there is a very high hill called Independencia, that swells abruptly from the plain, except on the southern slope, which
is more gentle. On this slope, about halfway up, there is a
massy palace, known as the bishop's palace. It was fortified
and garrisoned, and the summit was crowned with a fort. The
capture of this hill was necessary because it commanded the
Saltillo road and prevented Gen. Worth from entering the city.
As I have observed, our battery was put in reserve, and we were
in open sight of the hill Independencia.

Early in the morning when the fog rose, the battery on Independencia hill opened, and a solitary gun responded from a distant one, which our troops had captured the day previous. And
now the base of Independencia hill was encircled in smoke, and
almost simultaneously a wreath of smoke above it burst into
view. The attack on the hill with infantry had begun. Our
men could be seen climbing up from rock to rock, and the smoke
from every musket indicated whether it was fired *up* or fired
down the hill. Gradually the circles of smoke moved higher
and nearer, as our men ascended, and when, near the top, they
commingled into one the excitement was intense. Troops on
both sides looked on in silence, with hearts throbbing, now with
hope, and now stilled with fear, as the line of battle advanced or

receded. But soon it was seen that higher up the hill the combatants struggled, until with one wild shout and rush the lines closed, and the top smoked like a volcano. And then through the rifts of smoke we saw our men leaping over the parapets, and the Mexicans retreating down the slope. We clap our hands with joy, and wave our caps! Now, the scene changes. From out the bishop's palace swarms of men issue and rush up the hill to retake the fallen fort. They are met halfway. Our hearts are hushed as we look on. The enemy recede, break and run for the palace, where foe and friends commingled, enter together, and all is still. A heavy gun flashes, and a shell bursts *over* the city from a captured cannon. The flag descends, the stars and stripes go up and wave over the bishop's palace, and the battle is won; and then arose a shout of joy so loud, so long, it seemed to echo from the sky.

There was not much progress made on the 22d, in the eastern part of the city, except to gain a firm footing on the edge of it, by troops under Gen. Quitman. On the morning of the 23d our battery was ordered to the eastern end, and remained inactive while the infantry steadily advanced from house to house. The dwelling houses all had flat roofs, surrounded by walls about three feet high forming so many small fortresses. The house tops were filled with the enemy, and they commanded the streets; besides, the streets leading to the main plaza had been barricaded, and they crossed others at right angles. Gen. Quitman, about noon, ordered Bragg to send a piece of artillery to drive the enemy from a main street running the whole length of the city. To my surprise, instead of sending Lieut. George H. Thomas, a second in command, he ordered me with the twelve-pound howitzer to report to Gen. Quitman, who instructed me to clear the street.

I could see no troops in this street, except those on the house tops two or three squares in advance: so I moved on down until the musket balls began to clip and rattle along the stone pavement rather lively. To avoid this fire, I turned my gun to the left, into a street leading into the plaza. To my astonishment, one block distant was a stone barricade behind which were troops, and the houses on either side covered with armed men. They were evidently surprised, and did not fire at us. We were permitted to unlimber the gun, and move the horses back into

5

the main street. I politely waved my hand at the men at the barricade, which should read I shook my fist at them, and gave the command to load. Instantly the muskets were leveled over the barricade and pointed down from the house tops, and a volley fired at us that rattled like hail on the stones. My pony received a ricochet musket ball that struck the shoulder blade, ran up over the withers, and was stopped by the girth on the other side. I dismounted, and turned back to the gun. The two men at the muzzle were shot. One poor fellow put his hands to his side and quietly said, "Lieutenant, I am shot," and tried to stop the flow of blood. I had the gun run back into the street by which we entered the city. I now resorted to a device once practiced by a mob in the city of Philadelphia; two long ropes were made fast to the end of the trail, one rope was held by men on the lower side of the barricaded street, and the other by the men above. The gun was now loaded, and leveled in safety, then pushed out, and pulled by the ropes until it pointed at the barricade, and then fired. The recoil sent the gun back, and the rope brought it around the corner to be reloaded. In this manner the gun was worked for two hours, and with all this protection, four out of the five gunners were killed or wounded.

We had not been at this cross street very long before Texans, Mississippians, and regulars began to arrive and cross under cover of the smoke of the gun to the other side, and gain possession of the house tops. Next Gen. Taylor and staff came down the street on foot, and very imprudently he passed the cross street, escaping the many shots fired at him. There he was, almost alone. He tried to enter the store on the corner. The door being locked, he and the Mexican within had a confab, but, not understanding what was said, he called to Col. Kinney, the interpreter: "Come over here." The Colonel said ——, and went over at double-quick, and made the owner open the door. The store was empty. Here Gen. Quitman joined him with some troops and a gun in charge of Lieut. G. H. Thomas. Quitman directed me to take my howitzer down to the next cross street, but to save my men and horses. I suggested that Thomas should put his gun in position first, and let us pass over through the smoke. Comprehending the matter at once, he said: "No, you remain here, and let Thomas pass over when you fire." Thomas moved to the next street, and turned his gun into it. His street was barricaded also, and defended by a piece of artillery. The infantry and riflemen now made good progress in gaining possession of the houses, and driving the enemy toward the plaza.

The command of Gen. Worth was all day working toward the plaza from another direction, by breaking through the walls from house to house, so that when night came, the Mexican troops were pent up in the main plaza. Before dusk, the Mexicans being driven back, our two pieces of artillery were withdrawn and ordered to camp at Walnut Springs.

I have gone into these details to show the simplicity of character and coolness of Gen. Taylor which endeared him to his soldiers. No one discussed depots of supplies, base of communications, lines of retreat, or strategic positions; but every one knew that the brave old soldier would fight the enemy, wherever he found them, to the end. During the night some pieces of artillery, and a large mortar were put in position and opened fire on the heart of the city, now so very crowded with people.

Early on the 24th Gen. Ampudia sent a communication to Gen. Taylor, asking permission to leave the city, with his troops and arms unmolested. Of course this was refused, and finally resulted in the appointment of Gen. Worth, Gen. Henderson, and Col. Jefferson Davis commissioners to meet Gens. Requena and Ortega, and M. M. Llano, commissioners on the part of the Mexican army, who arranged the terms of the capitulation. I went to see the poor fellows depart. As they marched by, the soldiers each carried his musket in one hand, and a long stalk of sugar cane in the other, off of which they were regaling themselves.

They were permitted to retain their arms. In connection with the capitulation, an armistice for two months was agreed to, subject to ratification by the respective governments; and now came rest. Our loss was nearly five hundred, and among the killed was another classmate, Lieut. Robert Hazlitt. I should have mentioned that when the expedition for the capture of Monterey started Gen. Robert Patterson was left in command of the district of the Rio Grande.

After the departure of the Mexican troops, a friendly intercourse was established between our officers and the most respectable families in the city, noted on their part for gracefulness of movement, gravity of manners, extreme politeness, and genuine hospitality.

On one occasion, after dinner, a handsome Mexican saddle elicited the attention of the guests, and to my surprise the next day a servant came to my tent with a note, and the saddle, "begging me to accept it with consideration," etc. A few days afterwards I returned the saddle, with a small present, upon the grounds that it was too handsome for daily exposure in service, etc.

Lieut. Randolph Ridgely brought with him a fine old setter dog, and, as partridges were abundant, I found exercise and amusement in hunting. Lieut. J. F. Reynolds was generally with me, and we would return with all the game we could carry, as the birds were tame and numerous. We also enjoyed the waters of the hot springs near by, now quite a resort for invalids.

On the 27th of October, Capt. R. Ridgely was killed by his horse slipping and falling in the main street of the city, where the smooth natural rock was the pavement. He was, in my estimation, "the fearless and irreproachable knight," the Bayard of the army. What a ball is to a young lady, a fight was to him; it made his step light and his eye radiant with delight, while joyous smiles beamed from his face. It seemed the very irony of fate that he, who had raced his steed on the sea wall of Charleston, and leaped over into the ocean unharmed, should meet an untimely end from a horse falling in an open street. His father lived on Elk Ridge, near Baltimore, a gentleman of the olden school, of an age of the courtly past, and as John Randolph, of Roanoke, was a frequent visitor there, Randolph Ridgely was named for him.

The death of Capt. Ridgely promoted Bragg to his company, and Capt. T. W. Sherman to Bragg's company. Thus Bragg now became the commander of the late Maj. Ringgold's battery of artillery.

It would appear as if some State governor, or some idle general would issue a "Pronunciamento" every new moon in Mexico, in hopes of becoming President of that republic; and thus it was that half the people of Mexico could not tell who was President. And now Paredes was deposed, and Santa Anna, who was permitted to enter Mexico by the United States authorities as a man of peace,* reigned in his place. About the middle of September he arrived in the city of Mexico, and hastened soon after to San Luis Potosi to assume the command of the army thrice defeated by Gen. Taylor.

To carry out the wishes of the War Department, to have Tamico captured, Gen. Taylor started for Victoria, a small town, the capital of the State of Tamaulipas, on or about the middle of December, with the troops commanded by Gens. Twiggs and Quitman, leaving Gen. Worth in Saltillo with his division.

On reaching Montemorelos he received information from Gen. Worth that Santa Anna was marching on Saltillo, and turned back with all the troops except those under Gen. Quitman and our battery. Gen. Quitman was to continue on to Victoria. The march was uninterrupted down this beautiful and fertile valley. On our right towered the lofty range of the Sierra Madre Mountains in one unbroken chain and sharp serrated edge, that looked thin enough for a man to sit astride of. In fact, at Santa Catarina, there is a vast hole through this ridge near a thousand feet below the crest, through which clouds, as if in another world, could be seen moving by day, and stars by night.

The town of Linares is in a rich, wide, and beautiful valley or plain divided into large sugar estates cultivated by peon labor. The orange trees were very large, and all the citrus fruits abundant. As we journeyed on, one day Christmas came, and as usual it came on time, and, although we were in the land of the saints, we had not faith enough to believe that Santa Claus would make us a visit. So I went into the mountains in quest of a wild turkey for dinner, and failed to kill one. What were we to do? Reynolds or our servants had succeeded in procuring some eggs. With them visions of pudding and "egg-nog" arose. We could get "pulque," get "aguardiente," from the maguey plant, but it was villianous fire water. In this dilemma I sent my servant in quest of our doctor—Dr. C. C. Keeney, I think it was—to tell him to call immediately. The eggs were all beaten up ready. The doctor arrived. We made him a prisoner, and told him that he could not be released until

---

* It was understood that Santa Anna was to end the war by making a treaty of peace, but he deceived President Polk.

he wrote a note to his steward to send him a bottle of brandy and a bottle of rum. He did it on the ground that we all were in want of a stimulant, and on this occasion the doctor took his own prescription. When Plymouth Rock smiles, wonder not that we, far away from home, tried to make the service suit the day, and the day to be one of rejoicing that immortality was brought to light.

We encamped one night at a hacienda not far from Victoria. The owner was very civil and kind; invited us to his drawing-room, walked with us in his large orange grove laden with golden fruit, which was protected by a high stone wall. He possessed a vast sugar estate, and said that he had over five hundred peon laborers on it. As far as we could see there was only sugar cane.

On the 29th of December we marched into the great square, or plaza, of Victoria without meeting with any resistance. The troops were drawn up in line, the officers to the front and facing the alcazar.

The alcalde left his office, crossed the plaza, and after a short address presented the keys of the city to Gen. Quitman. The Mexican standard was hauled down, and as the United States flag was thrown to the breeze the band began to play, when all at once, in emulation, three or four jackasses began to bray, and bray, and drowned all proceedings, amidst roars of laughter that could not be restrained, especially among the volunteers.

We had been in camp but a few days when Gen. Taylor arrived with Gen. Twigg's division, and almost at the same hour Gen. Patterson came in from Matamoras with a large force.

Before I tell you any more I must inform you of certain proceedings and events that happened or took place in the past. One was that the President had ordered the commander in chief, Gen. Winfield Scott, to take the field as he desired, and to proceed to Vera Cruz, and advance on the City of Mexico from that place. Of course all the troops in Mexico were subject to his orders. Accordingly, when Gen. Scott came to the mouth of the Rio Grande, he made known to Gen. Taylor the particular troops that he wished him to order to Vera Cruz by duplicate dispatches. The letter sent to Monterey reached there after Gen. Taylor had started for Victoria. It was reported, and I presume it is true, that the letter was opened and read by Gen.

Marshall. If so, then he knew its importance. He committed two grave errors: First, he should have known that it was all important that the dispatches should be so sent as not to fall into the hands of the enemy; and secondly, he should not have required an officer to go to almost certain death when it was not necessary. What did he do? He placed these dispatches in the hands of Lieut. John A. Richey, and sent or permitted him to carry the dispatches *alone* through the enemy's country one hundred and fifty miles to Gen. Taylor at Victoria. The consequence was that as Lieut. Richey was leaving the town of Villa Gran he was "lassoed" by a Mexican, pulled from his horse, murdered, and the dispatches forwarded in all haste to Santa Anna, who learned how Gen. Taylor would be stripped of all the United States troops and most of his volunteer force, how Gen. Scott was on his way to Vera Cruz to capture that city, and then to march on his capital.

Santa Anna's decision was prompt and decided. It was what a great commander would have done. He decided to attack Gen. Taylor without delay, defeat him, if possible, recover all the territory lost, even to the Nueces river; then fly to the defense of his capital in time to meet Gen. Scott before he passed the strong defenses of Cerro Gordo.

He did not succeed in defeating Gen. Taylor, but he met Scott as he had planned to do. This was told by Col. Iturbide, a son of the last emperor of Mexico, whom I met after the war.

When Gen. Taylor received the duplicate of the orders from Gen. Scott at Victoria, and learned how he was to be stripped of nearly all the gallant men who had won for him the three battles, he gave the necessary orders for the departure of the troops called for, and this embraced the divisions of Gens. Worth and Twiggs, and most of Gen. Patterson's forces. In short, all the *regular* troops were sent to Vera Cruz, except four field batteries of artillery and two squadrons of dragoons, in all about six hundred men. I will not write here my opinion, as formed from observation or otherwise, of Gen. Taylor's equanimity of mind on that occasion. However, it was reported that by mistake he once put mustard in his coffee instead of sugar. Wonder not at his perplexity. He had enough to irritate him. He had some apprehension, no doubt, that the enemy might make an advance from San Luis Potosi on his now small force; but what wounded his pride,was—Apollyon behind him—the party opposed to the annexation of any territory south had expressed a wish that our troops might be welcomed by the Mexicans with "bloody hands and hospitable graves;" and the administration, alarmed at his growing popularity with the Whig party, hoping to divide or parallel his fame with another, sent Gen. Scott with such an inadequate force that *he* was obliged to deprive Gen. Taylor of such troops as I have stated. So Gen. Taylor had Santa Anna in *front*, the jealous administration and the anti-annexation party in Congress to fight *behind* him. The sequel will disclose his intrepid character, and his triumph in the end over all.

In the latter part of January Gen. Taylor took his departure from Victoria for Monterey. His escort consisted of Col. Jefferson Davis's regiment of Mississippi Rifles, two squadrons of dragoons, and our battery. My heart was not so light nor my feelings so buoyant as when we went journeying southward. I have mentioned how Lieut. Richey was murdered at Villa Gran and his dispatches taken. When Gen. Taylor reached that town he directed our battery and the dragoons to be halted in the plaza, and, sending for the alcalde, held a court to investigate the murder of Richey. The murderer was demanded. The alcalde said that he did not know who was the guilty man, and could not produce him. The general did not credit his story; said he would hang him if he did not give information as to who was the criminal. The alcalde was very much frightened, and turned pale and trembled. The examination of such persons as were called was fruitless, and ended in Gen. Taylor notifying the alcalde that he would levy a contribution on the town of (I believe) some $50,000 as indemnity, which would have to be paid in three weeks unless the murderer was caught and delivered to him. In all this the priests assisted the alcalde, and endeavored to pacify the General.

When the court left the hall the General discovered that his baggage wagons had been halted, and that vexed him, and to further irritate him, a piece of artillery blocked the road by not being able to get up a steep hill. The General pulled the driver's ear, got the piece up, and ordered it to remain outside the road until everything had passed. When he rode away, I ordered the gun into the road, and it was driven on. I never learned whether the murderer of Richey was apprehended or not.

When we arrived at Monterey we went into our old camp at Walnut Springs. We had some idle time to ride out in the country. The scenery around Monterey is very beautiful. There are near the city two isolated mountains—Saddle Mountain and Mitra Mountain—behind which the chain of the Sierra Madre rises in towering grandeur from the plain to the height of near five thousand feet, stretching beyond vision as one vast wall of rock, with a serrated edge seemingly as sharp as a saw, and inaccessible to man. Nearly every morning a canopy of clouds would form around the breast of Saddle Mountain, extending overhead to the distance of five or six miles. Gradually, as the day advanced, the clouds from the outer edge would sail gently away one after the other, disrobing the mountain and exposing the beauty of its form to view.

Once I was on the mountain above the clouds, in the bright sunshine looking down upon this billowy sea. Beyond was the lofty ridge glowing in the sun; around, hiding the plain for miles distant, was an ocean of clouds white as snow, softer than carded wool, lighter than down, rolling and swelling as silent as the heavens above them. Then they floated slowly away, melting into air, and left me to look down on the gross earth to which I must return.

When Gen. Worth believed that Santa Anna was on the march to Saltillo, Gen. Wool left Parras and hastened to Agua Nueva, and held that place, which is seventeen or more miles in advance of Saltillo.

Sometime in the early part of February our company left Monterey, and we began our march to Saltillo. Moving west, we passed the bishop's palace. Thence the road runs along the base of the Cerro de la Mitra Mountains for miles, with the Sierra Madre on the left; and, although this immense ridge was about eight miles distant, it was so abruptly high and the atmosphere so clear that it appeared not more distant than one could cast a stone.

Marching on, we passed some mills; then through a valley in the mountains, highly cultivated, trees bordering the road, and then down an incline to the hacienda of Rinconada, closed in by mountains. The road then ascends by a high grade to Los Muertos, thence on to Saltillo. The ascent to Los Muertos reminded me of Thiers's description of the road rising up the Incanale to the plateau of Rivoli, in his account of that battle in Napoleon's Italian campaigns. I am sure no troops could advance up that incline, straight and narrow, against well-served artillery. It was not fortified by the Mexicans to any extent, because it could be turned by two distant passes. This march of sixty odd miles was interesting in a high degree. Lofty mountains, deep valleys, wild, narrow passes, beautiful green fields in cultivation, babbling brooks surprising me at every turn. During this march from Monterey to Saltillo we made or gained an elevation of over four thousand four hundred feet, and we were now over six thousand feet above the ocean. The city is built on a slope that rises across the valley from mountains to mountains. You must understand that when we rose from out that steep ascent at Los Muertos there was apparently a plain before us, but really it was a valley, with continuous mountains on either side, all the way to Agua Nueva; thence, on south toward the City of Mexico as far as the eye could see were blue peaks towering in the sky.

As you will soon have a battle on hand " and a famous victory," I will here give you some idea of the ground. Leaving the city of Saltillo and going south, the first place of note is the hacienda of Buena Vista,* five miles distant, with its thick adobe (sun-dried brick) walls and flat roofs; next, a point eight miles from the city called La Angustura (the Narrows), which became the center of the battlefield. Farther on is Encantada, the enchanted place, and then Agua Nueva, nearly twenty miles from Saltillo. The ravines on the left of the road at Angustura ran back to the base of the mountain, and to the right of the road were deep gullies (barrancas), some extending to the mountains on the west. At one place the ravines on the left and the gullies on the right approach so near that there is room only for the road, forming the Narrows.

It was about the 8th of February when we reached Saltillo, and soon after we were sent to the front at Agua Nueva. From many sources came corroborative testimony that the enemy was advancing on Saltillo by detachments. Seventy

---

* "Beautiful View."

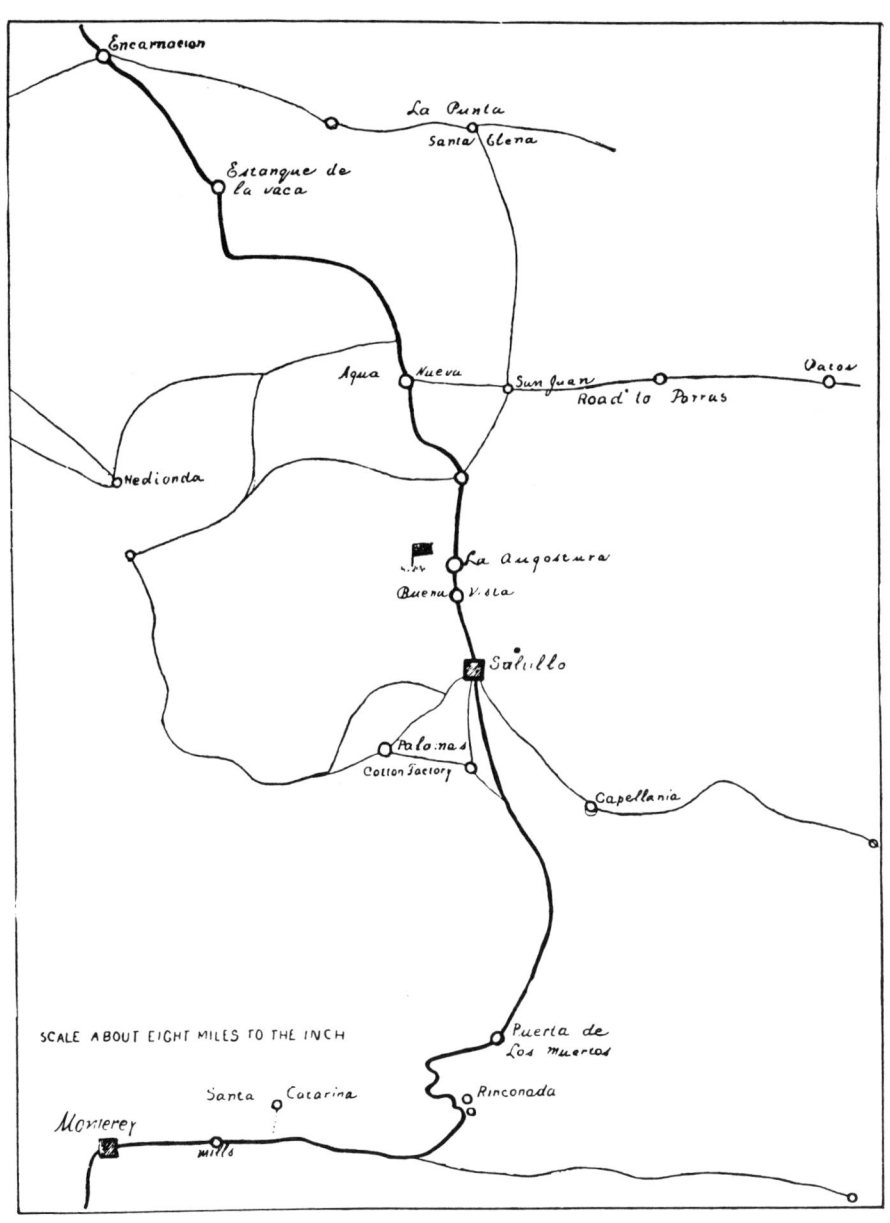

MAP OF THE COUNTRY NEAR BUENA VISTA.

volunteers, under Majs. Borland and Gaines, were captured at Encarnacion, within twenty miles of where we were encamped. On the 20th Col. May was sent to Hediondo on a reconnoissance, and some of his troops were captured, but he returned with the information given him by a deserter from the Mexican army that Santa Anna, with an army of twenty thousand men, was at La Encarnacion, only twenty miles distant from Agua Nueva. May got back early on the morning of the 21st, and a few hours after Maj. McCulloch arrived with like information, with this difference: He went to Encarnacion, climbed a lofty peak that overlooked the encampment of the Mexicans, and computed their number *for himself*. This was confirmation strong.

On the 20th I went hunting with Lieut. R. L. Moore, of the Mississippi regiment. The day was warm; the winds were in their caves; an ominous silence pervaded all nature; the sun did not dazzle the eye, and was distinct in outline, like the full moon; the game was tame and stupid; Moore was heavy of heart and dreamy. There was something peculiar in this silence—like the desert—like the stillness that oft precedes the tempest and the earthquake. Did Moore have a premonition of his death? He fell in the coming battle. The day left a lasting impression on my mind, it was so weirdlike and mystical.

> "By a divine instinct men's minds mistrust
> Ensuing danger; as by proof, we see
> The water swell before a boisterous storm."

On the 21st, as I have mentioned, both May and McCulloch returned to camp. Bragg, in his usual sarcastic manner commenting on May's expedition, remarked: "I perceive that it is harder to *lose* one's reputation than to make it."

It being an open country for some distance around Agua Nueva, Gen. Taylor, considering the great superiority of the enemy in numbers, resolved to fall back to Angustura, the narrow pass, near Buena Vista. Our company went into camp on the plain above and near the city. On the morning of the 22d, we moved down to the site selected for the field of battle. If the Hudson river, where it passes through the Catskill Mountains, were dry and wider, and its surface furrowed by deep ravines and water gullies crossing it, it would resemble the field of Buena Vista.

Capt. Washington's battery of eight guns was placed in the

road at the Narrows. Thence a ravine ran in a southeasterly direction. At the mouth of this ravine, on the plain, the line of infantry commenced and extended on the left toward the mountains. The howitzer which I commanded was put in position on the left of Col. Bissell's Second Regiment of Illinois. Lieut. G. H. Thomas had his gun on the right of this regiment. It was not long before away in the distance clouds of dust were seen growing larger and nearer as the cavalry came in sight; then came artillery and infantry moving to their right and confronting our line, with bands playing and banners waving. Hours were consumed in this movement. In the meantime Gen. Santa Anna under a flag of truce sent to Gen. Taylor a long communication, particularly informing him that he was surrounded by twenty thousand men, and to avoid being cut to pieces, called on him to surrender at discretion, that he would be treated with the consideration belonging to the Mexican character, etc., and inscribed it: "God and liberty! Camp at Encantada, February 22, 1847. Anto. Lopez de Santa Anna."

It was in the Spanish language, and had to be translated to the General. Turning to Maj. Bliss, his adjutant general, he announced a very forcible reply that was toned down by Maj. Bliss to the following:

HEADQUARTERS ARMY OF OCCUPATION, }
NEAR BUENA VISTA, February 22, 1847. }

Sir: In reply to your note of this date summoning me to surrender my forces at discretion, I beg leave to say that I decline acceding to your request. Z. TAYLOR,
Major General U. S. A., Commanding.
Senor Gen. D. Anto. Lopez de Santa Anna, Commanding in Chief, Encantada.

As no signs of an advance had been made, and as none could be attempted until after the return of the flag of truce, I rode down to where Gen. Taylor was to learn the purport of the dispatch. I regret now that I did not write down the exact words made by the General in his verbal reply.

I am sorry that I have no time to write you a description of this battle, but you will find it in some of the histories of this war. I can only tell you what relates to me and what I saw and heard.

At 3 P.M. the firing of a solitary gun by the enemy was the signal for battle; and immediately the enemy began ascending a ridge of the mountain on our left. At the same time our troops began climbing up another. These two ridges, like the sides of a triangle, met at a point halfway up the mountain side; so the higher they went the nearer they approached each other. This skirmishing on the mountain continued long after dark, and the bright flashes of the muskets imparted an interest to the surroundings.

When this prelude terminated, under the watchful sentinels, the two armies rested as best they could during the night. If you will bear in mind that the height of Mount Washington is 6,234 feet, and that the plain or valley of La Encantada is 6,140 feet above tide water, you will not be impressed with the idea that we were slumbering in an atmosphere as balmy as Egypt. On the contrary, the wind swept along the valley like a young Dakota blizzard.

Maj. John Munroe, one of the kindest men to be found in the army, may have derived his knowledge of Connecticut "bundling" from the veritable historian Diedrick Knickerbocker or otherwise; but be that as it may, he suggested to Lieut. J. F. Reynolds and me that we should "bundle" to keep warm during the night. So a blanket was spread on the ground and the others used for covering. The Major slept to windward, and Reynolds to leeward. In all my varied experience in life I cannot recall a night when I came so near perishing from cold. Yet there was nothing severely frozen, only the wind carried off all the heat from our bodies. When we got up I could not keep my teeth quiet. Some of the men of the company had a little fire, and we warmed our hands. Everybody was shivering. My servant was in camp at Saltillo, and I do not remember getting any breakfast; I know I had no dinner or supper.

Santa Anna was very considerate in not having reveille till a late hour, and then it was sounded in one command after another, perhaps to impress us with the number he had. Everything was done with Spanish gravity suitable to the occasion. There was no running to and fro, but decorum marked their proceedings, for I had an opportunity to judge. There had been some skirmishing since daylight up in the mountain, which was merely a side show. I was ordered by Col. Churchill to go to the base of the mountain and ride down the side of the ravine in front of the enemy to ascertain if it could be crossed by artillery. I did as directed, and was not fired at. This was before

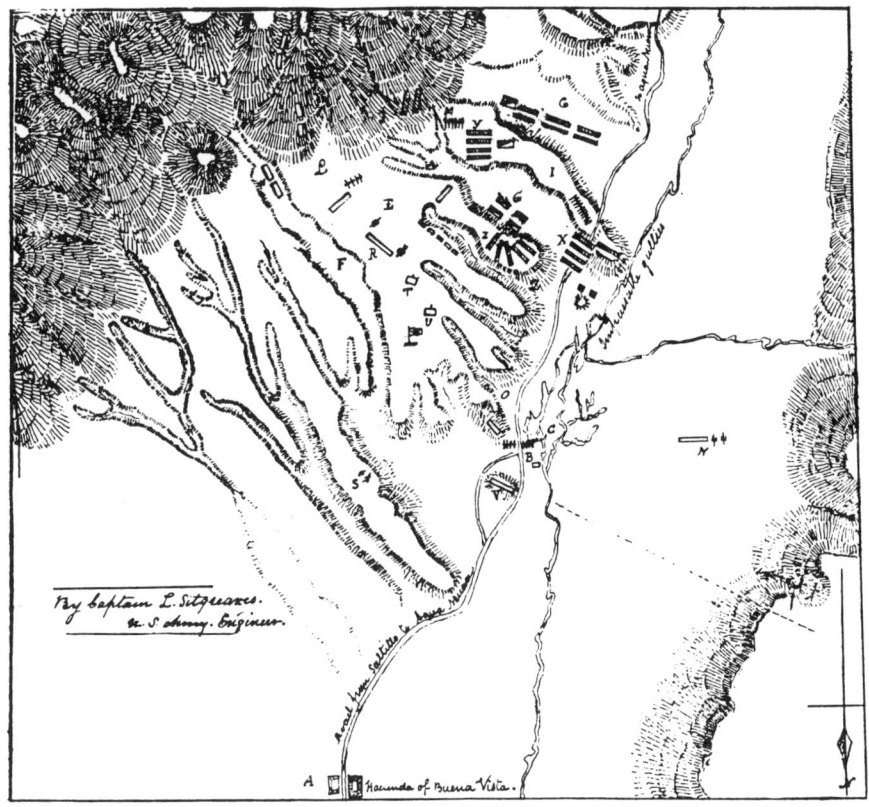

PLAN OF BATTLE OF BUENA VISTA.

Fought February 22, 23, 1847.

Headquarters of Taylor.
A—Hacienda of Buena Vista.
B—La Augustura.
C—Deep gullies.
D—High land.
E—Plateau.
F—Ravines.
G—Broad ravine.
H—Encampment.
I—Elevated ridge.
J—Occupied by enemy on the 22d.
K—Slope of the mountain occupied by our forces on the 22d.
L—Position of O'Brien's and Indiana Regiment.

M—Enemy's battery.
N—Bragg's Battery and Kentucky Volunteers.
O P Q—Gorges.
R—Second Illinois and Lieuts. Thomas's and French's guns.
S—Two of Sherman's guns.
T—United States dragoons.
U—Texas Rangers.
V—Lane's Indiana Volunteers.
W—Arkansas and Kentucky cavalry.
X—Column of first attack.
Y—Lombardeni's Division.
Z—Pacheco's Division.

the heavy masses of infantry were put in motion. I reported the ravine impassable for artillery.

The enemy's infantry was formed into three columns of attack. One moved down the road toward Washington's battery. The central one was composed of two divisions commanded by Gens. Lombardini and Pacheco. Their third column had been deployed already, and a part of it had been skirmishing all the morning on the mountain side. I took the greatest interest in the central column. Pacheco managed to get his division in a ravine by entering it at the gorge, and moved up concealed, directly in front of us. I tried to burst shells over them by shortening the fuses, as they were only about one hundred and fifty yards distant. Their firing increased rapidly. As Lombardini was advancing across the plateau to Pacheco's right, Pacheco's division rose from the ravine (to form line with him) directly opposite the Second Illinois troops. Instantly Bissell's and Lane's infantry opened fire on them, and Thomas and I used canister as rapidly as men (so well trained as ours were) could serve the guns.

Unfortunately some of Lane's troops gave way and fled, and this enabled the enemy to gain our left flank and rear. At this time I was struck with an ounce musket ball in the upper part of the right thigh while my left foot was in the stirrup in the act of mounting my horse. The shot was not painful at all, and the sensation was that of being struck with a club. I was put on my horse, as I could not walk. Soon after, to prevent being entirely surrounded, we were ordered to fall back toward the road, and came into line facing toward the mountain, and opened fire, now taking the enemy in flank and rear as they were crossing the plain. I refused to be taken from my horse and put in a wagon, knowing I would be "lanced" by the Mexicans in case of disaster, so I sat on my horse all the rest of the day walking him sometimes to the battery when it remained in one place any length of time. In the attack made in our rear Reynolds came by with his guns, and we drove back a large body of cavalry alone. Reynolds at the caissons prepared the shells, cut the fuses himself, and I directed the firing until the Mexican troops were driven beyond the range of the shells. He then moved in pursuit at full gallop and left me alone. The enemy was now in our front, left flank, and rear. When Reynolds left me I concluded to go to the hacienda of Buena Vista, now close by; but before I reached there I noticed the Arkansas and Kentucky cavalry forming in line a little way to the east of the hacienda, and at the same time I saw a brigade of the enemy's lancers coming from the base of the mountain to attack them. As I had never seen a cavalry fight, I watched it with a great deal of interest, being close by. The enemy were over two to one of ours. They came on in solid column, received the fire of our men without being checked at all, rode directly through our men, using their lances freely on every side. After passing over our troops they went near the hacienda, and were fired on by our men on the top of the building as they passed by. This brigade of lancers crossed the road to the west, then went south and joined the army where Santa Anna was, thereby having made the complete *circuit of our army* during the battle.

When this affair was ended I saw another body of the enemy's cavalry coming down from near the mountains heading for the hacienda, and our infantry moving to intercept them. Observing large crowds around and in the buildings, I went to them. I asked them, I begged them, implored them to fall into line, not to fight, but to show themselves to the enemy. I got about twenty into a company, and while waiting for others to join one by one those that I had asked went into the building for their companions until finally I was left alone, none of them returning. By this time the cavalry referred to came on down in splendid style, and, instead of making a headlong charge, halted in front of the Mississippians and Indianians under Col. Jefferson Davis, and were repulsed with heavy loss. One of the guns of our battery was also engaged in this isolated fight. Why this cavalry rode down into the very jaws of death and came to a halt I never heard explained.

Weary, tired, and weakened by loss of blood, with my leg stiff and useless, I rode into the court of the hacienda, and was taken from my horse and carried into a very large room and laid on the floor. The whole floor was covered with wounded. I was placed between two soldiers. One had both legs broken below the knee. The scene almost beggars description. The screams of agony from pain, the moans of the dying, the messages sent home by the despairing, the parting farewells of friends, the incoherent speech, the peculiar movements of the hands and fin-

6

gers, silence, the spirit's flight—to where? And amidst all this
some of the mean passions of humanity were displayed. Near
me was a poor soldier hopelessly wounded. He was cold, and yet
a wretch came and, against remonstrances, took the blanket off
him, claiming that it was his.

On the field I was twice taken from my horse by the surgeons
and had the wound probed, but no probe could reach the ball.
No surgeon was at the hacienda, so there I remained until after
dark. I think there must have been seven or eight hundred able-
bodied men at the buildings who had left ranks. When the firing ended Gen. Taylor came. A tailboard of a wagon was
brought in, I was placed on it and carried out and put in a common wagon (by the General, Dr. Hitchcock, Col. May, and some
others) between two wounded men. One of them was Col. Jefferson Davis, the other a lieutenant of volunteers. I said to the
General I hoped he would gain a complete victory on the morrow, and his reply was: "Yes, yes, if too many of my men do
not give me the slip to-night." I think he made this reply because he was mortified and pained to find so many men at the
hacienda who had deserted the field, many of them by carrying
off the wounded and not returning to their companies.

I was taken to our camp at Saltillo, put on the ground in my
tent with but little covering, and left alone. Where my servant was I know not. The camp was silent, every one being away
on or near the field of battle. It was to me a night of bodily
suffering. About daylight I heard footsteps and called aloud,
and was answered by a passing soldier coming to my relief.
That morning I was moved to a hospital and received medical
attention, and soon after I was sent to a private house occupied
by the wife of one of our soldiers, where I received every care
and was made comfortable.

When I left my gun I went in search of an army surgeon, as
I was urged to do by Lieut. Thomas, because I became dizzy and
had to be taken from my horse for a while. I found Dr. Hitchcock somewhere in the field and exposed to some fire from the
enemy in front. He advised me to take a wagon and go to the
hospital. He was extracting a ball from Capt. Enoch Steen, of
the dragoons, who was wounded, and who, perhaps to divert his
mind from what the doctor was doing, or for relief from pain,
was cursing two men who had stopped on their way back to

their company to see the operation performed. He ordered them away, called them cowards, and other vile names; but still they moved not until a musket ball came passing by more closely than others, knocked the hat off the head of one of them, and left his head white where it cut the hair from his scalp. He dropped his musket and jumped and danced around like mad, crying out, "I am killed, I am killed," to Steen's amusement and relief from the knife, by diverting his attention.

After the right wing of the Mexican army, which had gotten away behind us, had been checked, it began to fall back along the base of the mountains, and succeeded finally in reaching the position it started from by a *trick* of Santa Anna's. Under a flag of truce, which our troops respected, he sent a message to Gen. Taylor "*to know what he wanted,*" and when our troops stopped firing he withdrew his right wing.*

After this came the last great effort of the enemy. He massed his troops and made the second grand attack very much as he did in the morning, and over the same ground. How near he came being successful by this sudden attack on the force centered about Angostura while so many of our men were away near the base of the mountains in our rear, you will find in the published accounts of the battle; and it was caused by the enemy making the attack before our troops could get on the plateau by reason of the circuitous route around the ravines that could not be crossed. I did not see this last struggle. Lieut. O'Brien lost his guns. Bragg would have lost his in a few minutes had not our battery and Davis's and Lane's regiments arrived the moment they did to meet the advancing mass of the enemy. It was a death struggle. Our concentrated fire swept away the advancing line, the second faltered, halted, fell back, and the field was won.

Santa Anna, when referring to this battle, frequently declared that he "won the victory, only Gen. Taylor did not know when

---

*The Mexican story is: That a Mexican lieutenant in the first line got mixed up with our troops and feigned a *parley* and was carried to Gen. Taylor. This was followed by his returning to the Mexican line accompanied by two American officers to have an interview with Santa Anna. Then our line stopped firing and theirs did not. If this Mexican officer bore a flag of truce, it would explain why we stopped firing, and I am quite sure he did.

he was whipped," and just stayed there, while *he* was obliged to go back for water, provisions, and forage, and left the field to Taylor. I take this occasion to express my gratification to Santa Anna, even at this late date, for not staying on the field he had won, and I acknowledge his distinguished consideration in permitting me to remain at Saltillo. How vexatious it must have been to Santa Anna in his old age to recall to mind that the ignorance of Gen. Taylor in not knowing he was whipped so changed his destiny, and no doubt he thought how truthful is the line:

"Where ignorance is bliss 'tis folly to be wise."

We had present 4,691 officers and men, and our loss was: killed, 272; wounded, 388; missing, 6; total, 666. The relative number of wounded to the killed is very remarkable. Usually there are five or more wounded to one killed. The enemy numbered over 20,000 men. Although their reports place their loss at over 4,000, it falls short of the real number.

At dawn on the following morning it was discovered that Santa Anna had retreated to Agua Nueva. Gen. Taylor, with a proper escort, rode to Encantada and sent Col. Bliss to Santa Anna for an exchange of prisoners captured before the battle. This was effected. The wounded Mexicans even from Encarnacion were removed to Saltillo for medical care.

Here we have the achievements of one plain, unpretending practical, common sense man, who was ever observant of duty, and whose declaration was, "I will fight the enemy wherever I find him," summed up in four victories—Palo Alto, Resaca, Monterey, and Buena Vista. Success, ordinarily, is the measure of the greatness of a soldier.

CHAPTER VII.

I NOW come back to personal matters. The weather was springlike. The door of my room in Saltillo opened on the street on a level with the pavements, and through it and the windows I could see all the passersby, and it imparted a cheerfulness to the surroundings.

My physician was Thomas C. Madison, United States army, a most estimable gentleman and skillful surgeon. Several consultations were held in my case. They would not cut for the ball because they could not discover where it was. I was becoming emaciated, and felt conscious that I could not live unless the ball was removed. I had now been on the cot over forty days, and I demanded that they should extract the ball, for I could tell them *where* it was. So next day Dr. Madison came, and with him Dr. Grayson M. Prevost. They declined to use the knife, but promised to come on the morrow, and Dr. Madison came alone next morning. No one was present but my servant. I placed my finger over where I was sure the ball was then located, and told him to perform his duty, that I was responsible for the result. In those days there was no anæsthetic known, and surgical instruments were not often made for special purposes. As I predicted, the doctor found the ball. I was watching his face intently, and the moment he touched the ball I saw an expression of delight come over his countenance. Suffice to say, for the want of modern instruments, he cut a gash, or hole, large enough to insert his finger and a large steel hook to get the ball out. I think the doctor was in a better humor than I was, for I had said bad words to my servant for not holding my foot. I found afterwards it was the tetanus that cramped or contracted the muscles of the leg. In three days I managed to sit on the side of my cot; and some days after, with crutches, I went to the door and looked into the street.

And now I must tell you a little incident. From my cot I could see a Mexican woman who almost every afternoon would sit on her doorstep. She must have been very old, for her hair was as white as snow, her cheeks were bony, and her hands without flesh. She must have sympathized with me, though her enemy in war, for on seeing me at my door she rose from her seat, made a slight courtesy, and soon after sent me a bunch of fresh flowers by a little girl.

"One touch of nature makes the whole world akin."

Sometime early in April I was informed that I could have an ambulance, with leave to return to the United States and report to the Adjutant General in Washington.

I was furnished with an escort of *two men* on horses and my servant, five in all, to pass through the enemy's country to Monterey, a protection really inadequate. We reached Rinconada late in the day, and my bed was the counter of an abandoned store. The next day we arrived at Monterey safely, and I was made very comfortable by the quartermaster. I remained in the city until a train of wagons left for Camargo for army supplies, and when we started I took one "last, long, lingering" look at the surroundings of the city which had but a few months before been to me so pregnant with exciting events.

The journey to Camargo was devoid of particular interest. I found a government steamer there, and took passage for Point Isabel, or Barzos Santiago. On the trip down the river we saw a great many cattle that, in attempting to get water, had sunk in the mud to perish. Some had only their heads visible; others, a part of their bodies. It was a piteous sight to see the poor beasts, while yet alive, being devoured by buzzards.

When I arrived at Matamoras Capt. W. W. H. Davis came down to the steamer to see me. He was a student with us at Burlington, N. J., and was a general in the United States army during the late war, and is now a resident of Doylestown, Pa.

When in Matamoras he was a member of the staff of Gen. Caleb Cushing. He had retained my mail, and brought it to me on the steamer. Among the letters was one from Hon. Garret D. Wall informing me that the citizens of New Jersey had caused a sword to be made for me, and had placed it in his hands for presentation, at such place and time as would suit my convenience. This was a surprise to me, for no one had informed me of these matters.

On arrival at Point Isabel there were a brig and a steamer ready to sail for New Orleans. I was put on board the brig, but it was so dirty that I could not remain, preferring to risk my life on the old sidewheel steamer James L. Day. As I was taken ashore I met Col. McClung, of Mississippi, also wounded, going on the brig, where he remained. On the steamer were some officers on their way to New Orleans from Gen. Scott's army, and among them was Gen. Gideon J. Pillow, who was wounded slightly at Cerro Gordo. The steamer was unfit for a voyage on the ocean, although the weather was calm and the sea smooth. I amused myself watching from my cot the partition boards slide up and down, caused by the gentle rolling of the vessel. On reaching New Orleans we landed aside of some ship, on which I was placed, put in a chair, hoisted up and run out the yard-arm, and lowered on to the wharf.

I think we arrived in New Orleans about the 18th of May. At the St. Charles I met a number of old friends, army officers and civilians, and among the latter were Col. Bailey Peyton and S. S. Prentiss. In a few days I learned to locomote very well on one leg and my crutches.

Some few days after we arrived in the city a grand illumination and street procession was gotten up to celebrate some victory of our army in Mexico, and late in the afternoon a committee called on me to participate. About 8 P.M. Col. MacIntosh and myself were escorted to a barouche drawn by four white horses, to take our place in the line of procession. The streets were crowded with people. The horses did not like the crowd, the shouts, the music, nor the transparencies, and manifested it by frequently standing upon their hind legs; and had it become necessary to get out of the carriage, I was not able to do so. The Colonel and I were put on exhibition as two " heroes " from the war. The Colonel, as you remember, deserved it, for he was once pinned to the earth with bayonets and lances. One bayonet went in his mouth and passed through his neck into the earth. I rejoice to say we were returned to our landlord, from whom we had been borrowed, safely. I write this to show you how evanescent these things are. To-day we are the idols of the crowd; to-morrow we pass along the same street unobserved, unheeded, unknown save to friends. So passes away much of the glory of this world.

One evening after tea Col. Peyton and Mr. Prentiss asked me if I was able to join them in a short walk down the street. We had gone but a little way when, passing a door, we heard some one speaking, and loud applause in a hall, the floor of which was on a level with the pavement. Mr. Peyton said: "Let us go in." It proved to be a political meeting called for the purpose of expressing a preference for some one of the prominent men in the Whig party for the presidency. Mr. Hunt, who was speaking, closed his address in a few minutes after we entered. We were close to the door by which we had entered. Some one saw Mr. Prentiss, and called out: "Prentiss!" He turned to gain the street, but the crowd would not let him pass, while "Prentiss! Prentiss!" came from a hundred mouths. He exclaimed to his friend: "Why did we come here?" There was no alternative but to face the standing crowd. He uncovered his head and in a few words excused himself. It was in vain! The cry was everywhere: "Go to the platform!" Getting into a chair that chanced to be near the door, he spoke somewhat as follows, as I recall it after a lapse of near fifty years:

Mr. Chairman and Friends: As I was passing along this street with some friends I saw lights in this room and heard loud applause, and we entered to ascertain what was the object of the meeting, and from the closing remarks made by the distinguished gentleman who has just taken his seat I can infer the object of this assemblage.

When a young lady has been robed for a grand ball her maid opens and places on the toilet table before her her jewelry case, that she may select such as will be the most appropriate for the occasion. She takes out the sapphires and arrays them on her person to embellish her charms, but she places them on the table before her. The attendant encircles her swanlike neck with pearls, emblems of her purity, but she has them placed beside the sapphires. They put diamonds in her ears, and the sparkling cross rests on her bosom, flashing incessant lights as it rises and falls with every breath. She surveys them carefully; then has them removed and put aside also. And now rubies, the most costly of stones, are contrasted with her fair complexion; and at last they too are removed and laid with the others. She surveys them all, contrasts their qualities, and as each would be alike appropriate for the occasion, she stands undecided which is preferable. Now, Mr. Chairman, when I open the *casket of Whig jewels*, and gaze on their varied brilliancy, I am as undecided as the young lady was. They differ in some respects, but each is qualified for the opportunity, and I hesitate which I would commend as most worthy to occupy the presidential chair.

How nicely he evades an expression of preference for any one for the office, and this without offense to any of the aspirants!

While speaking of Mr. Prentiss I will relate to you as best I can a story of his reply to Mr. P., who accused him of intoxication while they were each making the joint canvass for Congress from Mississippi. And I will premise it by stating that P. had the reputation of being a lover of whisky. It was before a large and appreciative audience of Prentiss's friends, and in joint debate that the charge was made. In replying to that Mr. Prentiss said in his rejoinder, as I heard it related:

Ladies and Gentlemen: Many of you know me well, you have been present with me at numerous social entertainments, and I acknowledge it is true that I have a taste for the light wines of Italy and the pleasant wines of France. Wines have been the common beverage of mankind on festive occasions from the remotest ages. They impart a genial warmth to my feelings, a glow of tenderness to my heart, awaken my imagination, enlarge my sympathy, and give to music enrapturing charms, until in the fullness of joy I forget the ills of life and love my fellow-men.

I assure you, my friends, I have never been drunk from drinking whisky: but my opponent here is never so happy as when he retires to his room and draws from the closet his demijohn of whisky, throws it over his back, tips it over his shoulder: and no music is so sweet to his ear as the sound of the whisky singing "gurgle, gurgle, gurgle," as it leaps into the cup, save only that other sound of "gargle, gargle, gargle," as he pours it down his capacious throat.

I have told you that I have never been drunk from *drinking* whisky. But by whisky, ah! I remember me now; I was once made drunk, and it happened in this way. Sometime ago I had occasion to attend court in a remote county, sparsely settled, and where there was but little accommodation for the court. I arrived after night and repaired to the house pointed out to me where I could get lodging. The proprietor said his rooms were all full, but there was one room occupied by a lawyer that had a double bed in it, and perhaps he would share it with me. When I was ready to retire the landlord took a tallow candle and conducted me to the room. By the dim light I saw my present opponent in bed asleep, oblivious to sounds. I retired and slept by his side. When morning came

I found myself possessed of a strange feeling; I was dizzy, sick, drunk. Yes, *drunk by absorption!*

When Mr. Prentiss began the great speech he made in New York City a clergyman took his watch from his pocket to note the time; and two hours after, when Mr. Prentiss fell exhausted, this clergyman felt his pocket for his watch. It was gone, and he thought he was robbed, until he discovered his watch open in his left hand. He was so captivated and *en rapport* with the wonderful orator that he was oblivious to time, and stood there in the vast crowd listening to the words as they fell from his lips. Turning to a friend, he exclaimed: "Never tell me that man is not inspired."

I could tell you many things about this remarkable man, but time and other matters forbid. I will say, however, that I believe that *Alexander Hamilton* and *S. S. Prentiss* head the list of all men in the United States who have achieved greatness in early life. Prentiss's oratory burst on the people like a meteor athwart the sky, and ended as suddenly with his early death.

When I left New Orleans the surgeons advised me that I should go by water as far as I could on my journey north, and avoid the shaking of the railroad cars. I took passage on the steamer Chancellor for Louisville, and when we backed out from the levee and headed up the river we saw a steamer—the Belle of the West, I think it was—close behind us, and then the race began. For fifteen hundred miles it was a bitter struggle; first one ahead and then the other, according to the landings made. Now the Belle would be ahead and then our pilot would quit the main channel and by taking the "chutes" come out ahead. Then we would be overtaken and run side by side. Often the two boats ran with their guards touching, allowing the passengers of the two steamers to converse with each other and have a jolly time. On the Belle was a lady with her three daughters, of whom you will hear more hereafter. At Paducah, finding a number of barrels of resin, our captain bought them to use with the wood to increase the steam. So on and on we went, with boilers hissing and volumes of black smoke rolling from the smokestacks or chimneys, forming great clouds that were wafted away by the winds. After five or six days and nights of clanking of the fire doors, ringing of the bells above and below, and the blowing of whistles, we arrived at Louisville just fifteen minutes behind the Belle.

When I look back on the danger incurred from the explosion of a boiler, I cannot recall to mind one word of protest from any passenger against carrying such a high pressure of steam, or of asking the officers to desist. On the contrary, every one would shout for joy and wave their handkerchiefs on the passing boat.

However reprehensible, those races were common in the palmy days of steamboats on the "Father of Waters."

From Louisville I went to Cincinnati, thence on a small steamer to Pittsburg. Here I took passage on a canal boat for the east. As time was no object to me, I was not impatient of delay, and enjoyed the wild mountain scenery of the Alleghanies, and the pretty views along the blue Juniata; and as chance would have it, among the passengers were the lady (Mrs. J. L. Roberts) and her daughters that were on the Belle of the West, to whom I was presented by the gentleman who came to Pittsburg to meet them. They went by canal because one of them had been injured by having been thrown from their carriage. From this time on they were kind friends of mine, and I recall with delight the many happy days that I subsequently passed at their home on their plantation back of Natchez, Miss.

I reached home in June, and my father and mother welcomed me—whom the newspapers had reported killed in battle—with a joy not unlike that given to him for whom the fattened calf was killed.

I soon reported at the Adjutant General's office, and was given indefinite leave. Returning home, I received a note from a friend in the office of the Quartermaster General soon after, telling me that there were some vacancies in the quartermaster's department, and that if I would return to Washington and report to the department for duty I might be made captain and assistant quartermaster in the regular staff; but I did not go until sometime in July.

I received a letter from Senator G. D. Wall stating that it was the wish of the committee that I should be in Trenton on the fourth of July to receive the sword that was to be presented to me. So I repaired to Burlington, and in company with him and the Rt. Rev. G. W. Doane, bishop of New Jersey, went to Trenton. When the people were leaving the hotel for the public hall where the presentation was to take place, the Senator sent me the manuscript of his intended remarks. It was too late to write anything in reply, as the carriages were waiting; so we got in and went to the hall. I was very much frightened. There were many on the stage or platform, and among them an officer of the navy in uniform. I had on a citizen's dress.

Mr. Wall made a very appropriate address, and delivered the sword to me. I am sure that I made a very poor reply, and the only good thing was its brevity. But think of it! Wall did not say anything that he had written, but made an extempore speech, much to my surprise. When it was ended Senator W. L. Dayton said to the General: "You made an excellent address." "Well, I have a much better one in my pocket," was his reply. As I was comparatively a stranger to most of the large audience, I think the officer in uniform was taken for me, for when I rose to receive the sword there was a hum of surprise all over the house. I was glad when the presentation was ended. The next thing in order was to dine with the "Society of the Cincinnati," of New Jersey. I was invited to dine with the "Society of the Cincinnati" of Pennsylvania also, but declined. One dinner was ample, and I was not strong.

In a day or two I returned to Washington. I was ordered by Dr. A. S. Wotherspoon to quit all labor, and after he had bandaged my leg he kept me on my back three weeks. It did no good; no adhesion of the parts was made. I was vexed; so I took from my trunk a bottle of I know not what, obtained in New Orleans, only it smelled of turpentine, and injected it into the wound. I got up in the morning to go home, but lo and behold, the bandages were all saturated with blood and the wound inflamed. So, instead of going home, I was put on my back again. However that injection inflamed the sinus in my leg, and when bandaged again all the interior grew together, and in three weeks I was on my crutches, and my toes, or foot, touched the ground for the first time for about six months. So I was permanently cured by accident.

I had made application to the President for the appointment of assistant quartermaster some time in June. Now one day in July, when I was kept in bed by the doctor, a friend of mine, Mr. Nugent, came to my room to impart to me the information that I would not get the appointment because I could not "take the field," and that it would be given to Lieut. A. W. Reynolds, who was in Philadelphia on recruiting service. Nugent was connected with a newspaper, and was at times an assistant in the office of James Buchanan, Secretary of State, if I remember aright. On that day J. W. Forney, editor of *The Pennsylvanian*, a Democratic paper in Philadelphia, was in the office of Mr. Buchanan, and agreed to throw George M. Dallas, Vice President, overboard and support Mr. Buchanan for the presidency provided certain things were done by him for Mr. Forney. One of these items was that A. W. Reynolds should be appointed assistant quartermaster. I asked Nugent what special service Reynolds had rendered, as he had not been in Mexico at all, to entitle him to promotion. "Why he has always carried his *recruits* to the polls to vote for Forney's Democratic friends." And thus it was; and on the 5th of August Reynolds was appointed "to take the field." Reynolds was a genial fellow, and "took the field" by remaining in Philadelphia until the spring of 1848, when he went to Matamoras to bring some mules to the States.

Lieut. Derby, alias John Plœnix, alias John P. Squibob, that prince of humorists, and I had now located ourselves on Fourteenth Street, near Willard's, expecting to have a pleasant time during the coming winter, when one day about the 8th of September a messenger from the War Department brought me a note asking me if I was able to go to the arsenal at Troy, N. Y., to select a six-gun field battery, caissons, harness, etc., all complete, and take it with me, by way of the lakes and canal, to Cincinnati, Ohio.

I replied that I would leave immediately. While at Troy I met Gen. Wool. He had come home from Buena Vista. He had some friends to meet me at a dining, and I remember his pun on a young lady to whom I was presented, "Miss Hart, one of *deer* family." The battery was shipped on a canal boat to Buffalo. I went by train. Stopped in Rochester all night. The next morning, October 16, the ground was covered with snow, which made me apprehensive that the navigation by canal would close in Ohio before I could reach there. When the steamer arrived at Cleveland the water had been let out of the canal, so we went on to Toledo. From there I went on to Cincinnati by passenger boat. I was the only passenger, except local ones getting on and off along the route. Toledo was no town at all, and the sidewalks were "paved" with gunwales of barge boats, and here and there a plank, and the mud!

I remained in Cincinnati during the months of November and December idle, awaiting orders. There were many parties given, and the society people were pleasant and accomplished. During the day, however, nearly all the men were busy, and I used to say there were but three young men idle in the city—Grosbeck, Febiger, of the navy, and myself.

Early in January, 1848, Senator J. D. Westcott informed me that the President had appointed me captain and assistant quartermaster, and sent my name, among others, to the Senate for confirmation.

The commission is dated January 12, 1848. I had been in the service only four and a half years and had received six commissions — viz., brevet second lieutenant, United States army; second lieutenant, Third Artillery; brevet first lieutenant, United States army; first lieutenant, Third Artillery; brevet captain, United States army; and captain and assistant quartermaster in the general staff of the army, outranking some officers that had been from twelve to eighteen years in service. The brevets were bestowed for "gallant and meritorious services at the battles of Monterey and Buena Vista, Mexico."

When I was informed of the appointment I went up the river to Brownsville, Pa., thence to Cumberland, Md., by stage. The weather was intensely cold. Snow covered the plains and the mountains, and travel had made the roads very smooth and slippery. In going down Laurel Mountain we barely escaped an accident. The stagecoach, when held back, would swing around on the icy incline and go down sideways, and to prevent this the driver gave reins to the horses and we were descending at a gallop, when turning a point we met an eight-mule team that had the inside track, leaving our driver just a possible space to pass. He measured the space and saw the danger instantly, barely missed the hubs of the enormous wagon, and, as he sheered in behind the wagon, our hind wheel on the right threw down the mountain side a quantity of earth, snow, and rocks. There were nine of us in the coach, which gave us the privilege of stopping at night. A member of the Senate from Missouri was opposed to the delay; he must be in Washington, and so the party was divided. The narrow escape from death settled the matter, for when we got out for supper no one said to the driver: "We will go on to-night."

On arriving in Washington I was ordered to report to Gen. Thomas S. Jesup, Quartermaster General of the army. He received me courteously, but observed in a pleasant manner: "Capt. French, neither you nor Capt. Rufus Ingalls were recommended by me for appointment in my department; you were commissioned over officers that I recommended. Besides, the regulations of the army forbids any officer from becoming a captain and assistant quartermaster until he has been *five years* in service, and neither of you have been in the army five years."

It was suggested to him that experience was a slow but very good teacher; that one of his last appointees had not been in the field, while Capt. Ingalls and I had served nearly two years in Mexico, and from experience had derived some knowledge of the duties of officers of the department which should overbalance length of years of service in garrison at home, and that we should not be condemned before trial.

It is a remarkable fact that Gen. Ingalls was retained, from the beginning to the end of the war, as the chief quartermaster of the Army of the Potomac under its many commanders. It is proof of his great administrative ability.

CHAPTER VIII.

I WAS ordered to report for duty to Col. D. D. Tompkins in New Orleans, and remained there some three months. From that city I was put on duty at Baton Rouge, La., where Gen. Taylor and his family were living at the barracks. Of his staff, Col. Bliss, Maj. Eaton, and Capt. R. S. Garnett were with him. One day I was walking down town with Mrs. Taylor and her daughter Bettie, when a steamer landed, and brought the news of the General's nomination for President. Mrs. Taylor expressed regret that he was nominated; said "he had honors enough;" but added, however, "Since he has become a candidate, I hope he will be elected, and if he be, I will not preside at the White House."

From Baton Rouge I went to New Orleans; thence to Vicksburg, Miss., July 4, 1848, to muster out of service the regiment of Mississippi riflemen commanded by Col. Reuben M. Davis. We lived at the Prentiss House, kept by that prince of landlords, Gen. McMacken, who always "cried" his bill of fare. He said that when he kept a hotel in Jackson, Miss., he was obliged to do so, because so many of the members of the Legislature at that time could not read the printed ones, and he continued it to the day of his death. He was exceedingly pleasing in manners. On one occasion, seeing a gentleman of a commanding presence enter the dining room and seat himself at the table, he welcomed him with: "Good morning, general." "That is not my title, sir." "Ah, excuse me, judge." "Mis-

taken again, sir." "Well, bishop, what will you be helped to?"
"Why do you call me bishop?" "Because I am sure that you
stand at the head of your profession, whatever it may be." That
gentleman was Bishop Leonidas Polk, afterwards a Confederate
general.

During the summer and fall there was yellow fever in Mobile
and New Orleans; but no one regarded it, except to leave the
cities at night if possible; during the day business went on as
usual.

On my return to New Orleans I was ordered to Mobile, Ala.,
to take charge of government property, and to muster out a
company of Alabama cavalry. This finished, I was kept there
awaiting orders. In the meantime the army from Mexico had
returned, and was encamped at East Pascagoula, and in September I was ordered there.

The evening I arrived there was a ball given at the hotel. I
met there a young, tall, and pretty lady from Mobile, with whom
I was acquainted. She personated the morning star. Leaving
the "floor," she took a seat on a sofa beside Gen. Twiggs, and
I seated myself on the other side of her. She declined several
sets, and I remained talking with her. All the while the General said but a few words. The windows were open, and I felt
some one on the gallery pull my hair. I went out to ascertain
the meaning of it. Two or three officers came up, and said:
"French, don't unpack your trunk; you will be ordered away
in the morning. Don't you know that young lady is Gen.
Twiggs's fiancée? He is as jealous as a Barbary cock." I mention this because of something hereafter.

I remained in Pascagoula until the army had been sent hither
and thither, according to the wants of the service. The last
shipment of troops was some cavalry to Galveston, and I followed on after them, last of all, in an old propeller. It so happened, as I was leaving the wharf, that a captain of a vessel had
just made an observation of the sun to get the time, and I set my
watch by it. When we got out on the gulf a cyclone came on.
The ship had no chronometer, and only anthracite coal, which
made but little steam. The propeller was now spinning in the
air; then motionless when under water. Finally the captain had
to run before the wind to the south.

Some days after, when running north, we saw land, and made

7

observations. I got the longitude from my watch. It said thirty miles from Galveston. The captain said that the land was the mouth of the Sabine river. Two hours after, we saw the shipping in Galveston, proving my observation correct. The wind was still blowing hard. No pilot boat could come out for us. It was a government ship, and I ordered the captain to make the harbor. The trouble was to find the outer buoy. Finally it was discovered, and we got in safely.

Gen. Twiggs had been assigned to the Department of Texas, and I found him in Houston. We remained there a few days; and, when the dragoons started for Austin, Twiggs, his aid, Capt. W. T. H. Brooks, and I took the stage for Austin also. It had been raining all day and all night when we started. From Houston to a small mound on the prairie twenty-five miles on the road the land was all under water, and still it rained. We crossed the Brazos river about noon, and went on in the rain, which continued all night. At 2 A.M. the driver turned out of the road, and down went the coach till the body was on the ground. The driver said that there was a farmhouse about four miles farther on. A horse was unhitched, and Gen. Twiggs was put on it bareback to ride to the house. Two passengers went on foot. I had in a satchel $5,000 in gold (government funds), which was in the box under the hind seat. Brooks said that he would stay there and guard it, if I would go on and get help. I also mounted a horse and overtook the General. When we reached the house, the farmer got up, had a fire made to dry our clothing, and agreed to send some mules to bring in the coach. The General made so many abusive remarks about Texas and the people that the farmer got mad, and said that the stage might "stay where it was;" but when he was satisfied that the remarks made by Twigg were not personal, he started the servants for the coach. The General and I had to rest in the one bed the best we could.

The coach came up about eight in the morning. The General declared that he would go no farther, but return to New Orleans. Now, the truth was, he wished to go back to meet that young lady. I was told that when she returned to Mobile some of her old and experienced friends persuaded her to marry a younger man, who had long solicited her hand. When the General reached New Orleans he was sadly disappointed; but he found consolation soon after in marrying the widow of Col. Hunt, late of the United States army.

We left Taylor's (the farmer) the same day, and went on to Plum Creek; and, as it was not fordable, we had to stop with a widow and her two daughters. Her house had only one room, and a cock loft gained by a ladder. The following persons found shelter with the family that night—viz., Maj. Ben McCulloch, Durand and his two sisters, our two passengers, the postmaster, Brooks, myself, and the stage driver—thirteen in number.

After supper was over our hostess lit her cob pipe, and enjoyed her evening smoke, after which she politely offered it to those inclined to indulge. When the time arrived to retire, the old woman had no trouble in disposing of her ten guests. She merely said, "You men can go aloft," and there on the floor we passed the night. It was well that the General remained at Taylor's. The morning dawned clear, but the creek was not fordable until noon. In the course of time the stagecoach reached Austin, where I remained during the winter, furnishing transportation for troops to the frontier; and where they were located are now to be found the cities of Waco, Dallas, Fredericksburg, etc. The sword plants the banner, and a city is built around it.

In the month of February, 1849, I received an order from the Quartermaster General to go to San Antonio and fit out a train to go to El Paso with the troops to be stationed there. For that purpose I bought one thousand one hundred and eighty oxen, and collected about two thousand head of mules, six hundred of which were wild mules from Mexico, and I have never had any admiration for that animal in his native state since, for, like his sire as told in the book of Job, "neither regardeth he the crying of the driver."

To-day (November 22, 1894) is my birthday, and I am now six years past the time alloted to man by the psalmist. For this I am truly grateful to Him from whom all blessings flow, and I will henceforth endeavor to walk humbly before him.

I had established my camp on the prairie about nine miles from the city, where there were almost four hundred hired men. In March the cholera made its appearance, and in a malignant form. Some cases occurred in camp, and, as I could not get a physician to go out there, I wrote for Dr. Baker, of Austin, an elderly man, to come over and take charge of it. On his arrival I furnished him with a mule, and gave him directions to find the camp. Night came on, and no doctor returned. The next morning about nine o'clock he rode up to my office with his umbrella under his arm, his mouth drawn up, the picture of despair. I asked him: "Are many sick in camp?" He shook his head in the negative. He was invited to dismount and come into the office, which he did, and told his grievance. It appears that he found camp, attended to the few sick, and started to return to the city. When he reached the Salado, a small stream a few miles from town that was about ten feet wide, his mule declined to cross the creek; neither would she wet her feet, as the doctor did, and be led over. All attempts were futile. So, worn out, the doctor sought the shelter of a tree, and sat there all night holding in his hands the bride reins. In the morning the animal was still stubborn, and the doctor in despair. No lone sailor on a raft in midocean hailed an approaching sail with more delight than did the doctor a Mexican coming down the road. He made known his trouble to the Mexican, who said: "Si, Señor, me fix him." The man got off his own mule, mounted the doctor's, rode off about fifty yards; then applying whip and spur at every leap, the mule could not stop, but was plunged into the water. He rode quietly across three or four times, and then the doctor had no more trouble. The next trip the doctor was furnished with a pony. He was a kind old gentleman, and went on with us to El Paso as physician.

In May Gen. Worth arrived to take command of the department. A few days after, he died of cholera, and the command devolved on Gen. W. S. Harney.

The expedition to Paso del Norte was under the command of Maj. Jefferson Van Horne, Engineer Officer Col. J. E. Johnston, and the Quartermaster (myself). The object of the expedition was to march a part of the third regiment of infantry to Paso del Norte to garrison that place, and my train was to convey public stores there for their future use and to open a public road to that point now called El Paso. There was no road, not a path, from San Antonio to Paso del Norte. All was an unknown, untrodden extent of plains, hills, and mountains over which perhaps no white man had ever traveled, except two

United States engineers who had ridden over it in returning from New Mexico.

We left San Antonio June 1, 1849, and arrived at El Paso early in September. We remained there nearly a month. At that time El Paso was a town on the Mexican side of the Rio Grande river. There was but *one* building on the Texas side, and that was the Maggoffin's hacienda. Vegetation at El Paso grows very rank, and fruit exceedingly fine. The grape attains a large size, and bunches weighing four pounds were common. I brought with me cacti, in form like an acorn, and so large that the hoops had to be removed from a clothing tierce (a small hogshead) to put a single one inside for transportation.

I pass over all description of the country and incidents of the journey home, because I leave you the original diary, and my report was published by the United States government.* The oxen and wagons drawn by them were all turned over to the post quartermaster, and I returned with the mule teams only.

Our return to San Antonio was over the Guadalupe mountains, down Delaware Creek to the Horse-head crossing of the Pecos river, thence down that stream to where we crossed it on our way out. There is now a railroad from San Antonio to El Paso, following generally our route, which runs on to the City of Mexico.† Remaining in San Antonio long enough to make out my accounts, I proceeded to New Orleans. I there found Gen. Twiggs in command, and called from courtesy to see him at his headquarters. His aid, Capt. W. T. H. Brooks, who, as I have related, remained in the stage when it sank in the mud, informed me that the general commanding said I must shave off my beard, as a general order to the effect had been issued by the adjutant general. I did not obey, as I was under orders from the quartermaster general to return to Washington, and did not consider myself in his command at all. The next day I was at the general's office unshaved. He made no remarks to me about it then, but some time that day Brooks came to the hotel and ordered me to have my beard cut off. I did not go to the barber. The next day I left New Orleans resolved to beard the adjutant general in his den in Washington. On ar-

---

*Senate Document.
†Also to San Francisco, Cal., as was then predicted.

rival there I found the shaving order not enforced, and thus I saved my beard.

As I never met Gen. Twiggs again while I remained in the United States army, I will take my leave of him. He was not a man well beloved by officers or soldiers; he possessed no magnetic power; he was not genial in temper or disposition, and yet he enjoyed a joke, and at times made a pun. He entered the army in 1812. When that war terminated he was a captain. On the reorganization of the army he was retained in service and made a major. Being asked in what battle he gained his promotion, he replied "in the *affair* at *Ghent*," meaning the treaty of peace with Great Britain. There was in the second regiment of dragoons an officer named A. D. Tree, who possessed a frailty from which the General was not exempt. On account of this, complaint was made to the General about Tree. The General sent for Tree and asked him about the matter. His reply was: "You cannot blame me; just as the Twigg is bent, the Tree is inclined." The common influence of example was tacitly acknowledged, his wit appreciated, and he withdrew under words of advice from lips that smiled. When Twigg's native State seceded from the Union, he resigned from the army and entered the service of the Confederate States. His advanced age kept him from active operations in the field. He had left in New Orleans the sword presented to him by the State, together with his silver plate, and it was all seized by Gen. Benjamin F. Butler, United States army, when in command in that city.

While I was absent in Texas, on the 8th of February, 1849, the Governor of the State of New Jersey, in pursuance of a resolution passed February 10, 1847 by the Legislature of that State, directing him to procure swords to be presented to Capt. W. R. Montgomery, Lieut. N. B. Rossell, Fowler Hamilton, and Samuel G. French, of the United States army, for brave and gallant conduct displayed by them in the battles of Palo Alto, Resaca de la Palma, and Monterey, made the presentation. Richard P. Thompson, of Salem, N. J., acting in my behalf, received the sword for me, and I am sure I will be pardoned for relating some of the proceedings.

Gov. Haines, in his address, was pleased to say in reference to me at Palo Alto:

While the battle was fiercely raging, a body of Mexican lancers made a movement to the right, apparently with a design upon the trains. The Fifth Regiment of Infantry, with two pieces of artillery, were ordered to advance and check them. To form in square to receive the impetuous charge of the horsemen and to repel them, was the well-performed duty of the Fifth Infantry; to scatter them in all directions was the quick work of the battery under First Lieut. Ridgely, assisted by Second Lieut. French.

At Palo Alto, and Resaca:

The bearing of Lieuts. French and Hamilton in both these sanguinary engagements was marked for its gallantry and courage, and merits our highest praise. Of the former it is sufficient to say that he served a battery in conjunction with Lieut. Ridgely, and in that duty contributed largely to the success of our arms.

At Monterey:

Lieut. French performed deeds of daring worthy of commendation. He was exposed during the attack to imminent perils. Among others, the battery under his command advanced through the blood-stained streets of the well-fortified town in the face of the enemy's artillery and amidst showers of balls from the musketry upon house tops. Of the five who served his gun, four were shot down by his side. These are the battles, and this but a small part of the brave and gallant conduct referred to by the Legislature in their resolution, and for which, in the name of the people of the State, they desire to thank and to honor you. That they have not misjudged is manifested by your subsequent conduct.

In the bloody and desperate conflict of Buena Vista, Lieut. French bore himself with great intrepidity, and was severely wounded. For his gallantry he has been promoted to the rank of captain, and we have to regret that his services in a distant part of the country deprives us of the pleasure of his company here to-day, and requires him to be represented by his friend.

Richard P. Thompson, Esq., on my behalf spoke as follows:

Sir: In behalf of Capt. French, to whose patriotic services you have alluded in terms so eloquent and just, I accept with profound gratitude this beautiful sword—the proudest testimontal a brave man could desire from his native State.

It is a soldier's duty to obey with cheerfulness and alacrity the call of his country—his post of honor is on the battle field, amidst the "pride and pomp, and circumstances of war,"—his loftiest ambition to bear that flag to victory that never knew defeat, and to win for himself the approval of his countrymen. When on the bloody fields of Buena Vista, Palo Alto, Resaca de la Palma, and Monterey, Lieut. French periled his life for his country, one bright and sunny hope animated his young and gallant spirit, and this day, sir, finds that glorious hope fulfilled. Here, in sight of the battle ground of Trenton, the descendants of heroes are proving to the world how Jerseymen appreciate and reward the heroism of her sons.

To Capt. French, now absent on military duty, the events of this day, sir, shall be faithfully transmitted, and I can well imagine how his manly heart will overflow with gratitude. The perils and privations he endured, the pain and anguish of his wound, will be forgotten in the joy of this event—in the knowledge that the Legislature of his beloved State, with a magnanimity alike honorable to themselves as to him, have placed in his hands this mute but eloquent certificate of brave deeds in his country's service.

In accepting for him this evidence of the regard in which New Jersey holds his bravery, in the presence of her assembled representatives, and of this bright and beautiful array of her mothers, wives, and daughters, I pledge myself to you, sir, her chief Executive Magistrate, that my brave young friend will treasure it as the proudest gift of his life—that its keen and polished blade shall suffer no stain from his dishonor—that in peace he will guard it with a soldier's fidelity, in war defend with it the honor of his country—unsheath it never in an unholy cause—and part with it only when he shall be laid at rest " beneath a soldier's sepulcher."

The inscription on the scabbard reads:

Presented by the State of New Jersey to Lieut. Samuel G. French, of the third Regiment, United States Artillery, for brave and gallant conduct displayed in the battles of Palo Alto, Reseca de la Palma, and Monterey. Subsequently distinguished at Buena Vista, and promoted to the rank of captain.

AEQUM EST MILITEM
INTREPIDUM
HONORE
AFFICERE.

And so my good friend Mr. Thompson relieved me from the embarrassment of returning thanks, publicly, for the sword delivered by the Governor.

While on this subject I will here remark that this sword and the former one were taken from my summer home in Woodbury, N. J., in the absence of the family, and with all personal property and realty sold by the United States marshal at public outcry under the confiscation act of 1862.*   Were the proceeds covered into the treasury?

I arrived in Washington during the winter of 1849–50, and made a report of the expedition that was published by the government as I have stated.   The Quartermaster General, or the War Department, kept me all the year 1850 in Washington, or within call, for any special duty required.

* Until charged, tried, and convicted of treason is confiscation legal?

Soon after my arrival in Washington I was honored with an invitation to dine with the President. I had the pleasure of taking in to dinner Miss Taylor, a young lady from Louisiana. The guests were too many for any general conversation, and nothing of moment occurred.

I was in Philadelphia when the news of the death of the President was received, July 9, 1850. Having been with him in all his battles in Mexico, I was pained to hear of his death, and that I had lost a kind friend. He had lived a soldier's life until elected President, and had never heard the voice of detraction, or his name mentioned except for praise, until he was forced into the political arena.

A lady friend of mine told me that she had a room at the hotel adjoining the General's reception room, and thus involuntarily heard much wrangling about the formation of his cabinet. Delegations of politicians from different States would go so far as to demand that certain men should be members of his cabinet as the price of loyalty to the party and support of his administration. The enemy on the battlefield never perplexed him as did his political *friends* and the pressure for appointment to office. He whose order and every word was obeyed now found himself confronted by the bitterest opposition, which perplexed him in the extreme, and, no doubt, it shortened his days. Brave, honest, pure, sincere, as a soldier he never deviated from the path of duty; and if we consider that the world has limited the fame of a soldier to one single measure, *deeds performed*, by this test his fame is imperishable. His every success was achieved by his daring, steadfast determination to do his duty, and fight the enemy wherever he found him, regardless of all odds. In this respect he might be paralleled with Nelson.

Mr. Fillmore now became President. Soon after this the Gardiner claim was being investigated, and I believe there were six commissioners to be sent to Mexico to examine the *mine*. The President was to name two of these commissioners; the Senate, two; etc. I was informed by the Adjutant General that the President instructed him not to send me on any duty out of the city, as he purposed to name me as one of his commissioners. However, about a month after this, Senator Soule, of Louisiana, came to the department to see me, and I believe my knowledge of the Spanish language did not come up to his expectations;

and, if I remember aright, Lieut. Doubleday was named at his suggestion.

It was about this time that Capt. Ringgold, of the United States navy, asked me urgently to go with him as the artist on an expedition to make a coast survey of Kamchatka, and thence on south. He consulted the Secretary of War, and obtained permission for me to go if he made the application. He spoke of the climate in summer, and said in the fall we would sail for the Sandwich Islands and pass the winter there. The expedition was a tempting one, but other considerations induced me to decline going. Capt. Ringgold was a brother of Maj. Ringgold, who was killed at the battle of Palo Alto.

I think it was during this autumn that I was sent to Louisville, Ky., to purchase horses for the cavalry.

About the middle of December Col. Joseph Taylor, Maj. Gaines, his two daughters, and I took passage on a steamer for Cincinnati. There was much floating ice in the river, and snow began to fall, and it turned very cold. The captain ran into the mouth of the Kentucky river to avoid the heavy drift ice. In the morning we found the steamer fast in frozen ice, and wagons and sleighs came alongside. Gen. W. O. Butler came on board to see Col. Taylor, and, as there was no prospect of the steamer leaving for weeks, arrangements were made for Gen. Butler to send us on to Florence in his common two-horse farm wagon. The next morning the trunks were put in for seats and we started on our journey, The country was covered deep with snow, and the thermometer was fourteen degrees below zero. I walked behind the wagon nearly all the way to keep warm. The driver's hands were nearly frozen, and in crossing an awful ravine the horses were not checked and the wheels on one side would have missed the bridge and all in the wagon been killed had not my trunk fallen out in front and stopped the wagon. Fortunately no damage was done, The driver was to blame for not telling us his hands were half frozen.

It was dark when we reached Florence, and for once fire could not warm me for hours. Next day Col. Taylor bargained for a jumper (sled) to take him and me to Cincinnati. We crossed the river on the ice, and were driven up to the door of the hotel in the jumper. Next day Hon. Salmon P. Chase joined Col. Taylor, and we went on to Washington together.

CHAPTER IX.

IN the early part of January, 1851, Gen. Jesup told me that
he would have to send me to El Paso again. I suggested
that some other officer be ordered on that duty, as I had made
the trip once. He said that there had been no rain in Western
Texas for over a year; that the report was the troops were out
of provisions, and as I had been over the road and knew the
country, I must go again; that he would not under such circumstances intrust the expedition to any one else. This was complimentary, to be sure, and I pointed out the difficulties that
would be encountered on such a long journey over a now barren
country, destitute of water and grass; but told him I would do
the best I could to make the expedition a success.

Capt. Lorenzo Sitgreaves, topographical engineer, United
States army, was in the city under orders to make a survey
of the Gila river, and, as he had to go to El Paso, would accompany the expedition. With him was Dr. S. W. Woodhouse,
of Philadelphia, Pa. In due time we went to New York, and
sailed for Havana, Cuba.

In Havana at the hotel were P. T. Barnum with Miss Jennie
Lind, James G. Bennett and wife. We remained in the city
about a week, and then took steamer for New Orleans. Capt.
Hartstine, of the United States navy, commanded the steamer.
He gave Miss Jennie his stateroom on deck. I was sitting with
Miss Jennie in her room when we entered the Mississippi river.

Soon a sweet little girl came in, and, dropping on her knees before the songstress, said: "Miss Jennie, you promised that you would sing for me when we got in smooth water. Please do, for the winds and waves are still." And she sung "I Dreamt I Dwelt in Marble Halls" and "Home, Sweet Home." O how melodious her voice sounded to us alone there far away, where the waters of half a continent mingled with the ocean, and awakened new emotions that moistened the eye with a tear! I heard her sing on the stage, but I remember better her songs to the little girl. She asked me about the length of the Mississippi river, and her astonishment was great when I informed her that she could go all the way from where we were, if the river were straightened out, to her home in Stockholm.

When we arrived at the landing in New Orleans there were perhaps a thousand persons present. The police appeared helpless. To land the ladies looked like an impossibility. How could they get through that crowd to the carriages? Miss Jennie would not attempt it. After a long time Barnum's tact accomplished it. The crowd had seen both Miss Jennie and Barnum's daughter on the deck when the steamer arrived. They were now below deck in despair. Barnum arrayed his daughter like Miss Jennie, covering her face with a thick veil, gave her his arm, and met the crowd, worked his way through to a carriage that was covered with people, and finally got his daughter inside, and jumped in. The carriage moved slowly on, the mob after it to see her get out. Then Miss Jennie was landed, and put in another carriage that followed. But the crowd discovered the deception, met Miss Jennie, and escorted her to her hotel. All this was merely a desire to see a distinguished vocalist. An hour or two after, we also got on shore. I have failed to tell you that Dr. Fisher, of Philadelphia, was one of our party. He was employed by me as physician to render medical services to the civil employees on the expedition. From New Orleans we took steamer to Galveston, where we were detained some days.

How often do extremes meet! In New Orleans we had just listened to the sweet voice of Jennie Lind; here we were entertained by an old negro slave with music drawn out of a cheese box made into a banjo. He knew but one song, and as he played it over and over we paid him to quit instead of encouraging him to continue. It made me feel very sad to see the poor fellow trying to please the people at the hotel with his rude banjo and song. What a fall from a Cremona or Stradivarius to a cheese box!

From Galveston we sailed to Indianola, and thence to San Antonio by stage, where we arrived February 24.

As it will be too much trouble for me to abbreviate my report of this expedition, I will, mainly for preservation, give it in full:

REPORT.

WASHINGTON CITY, November 2, 1851.

General : I have the honor to inclose to you the accompanying report in relation to the late expedition to El Paso, made in compliance with the following order:

QUARTERMASTER GENERAL'S OFFICE, }
WASHINGTON CITY, January 14, 1851. }

Sir: A large supply of stores for El Paso is on the way from Baltimore to Indianola, Tex., as you are aware, to meet an apprehended deficiency of subsistence for the troops at that post and its dependencies in New Mexico. This supply is to be taken to its destination in a public train. You are selected to take charge of and conduct it. You will proceed to San Antonio, and report to Maj. Babbitt for that service. On your way thither you will stop at New Orleans, and ascertain from Col. Hunt the state of the wagons which he has shipped to Indianola by orders from this office; and if they are not in every respect in a condition for the service in which they are to be employed, you will call for whatsoever you may think necessary to the efficiency of the service. Should you obtain information on the route of the loss of any of the wagons shipped recently from Philadelphia, you will take measures to replace as many of them as you may think necessary.

The expenses of the department are enormous, and they must, if practicable, be reduced. You must therefore carefully avoid any expense not absolutely required; but at the same time, economy is not to be carried so far as to impair efficiency.

Maj. Babbitt has been written to and informed that you are to organize a train under his instructions, or to aid him in organizing it, and that you are to have charge of it. Let that service be performed in your usual manner, and with your accustomed energy, and I am sure all will go right.

All the operatives employed must go armed, and if a small escort be necessary in addition, the commanding general I have no doubt will direct it. Let it however be as small as possible, so as not to use so large a portion of the supplies as are usually required for escorts.

Collect all the information you can in regard to the country, its resources, the condition of the Indians who roam over it, what are their numbers, and how they can best be controlled; also whether settlements might not be formed on the route sufficiently strong to protect themselves from the Indians. and furnish supplies for emigrants and troops.

With entire reliance on your energy, talents, and zeal, I am respectfully your obedient servant, TH. S. JESUP, *Quartermaster General.*

Capt. S. G. French, Assistant Quartermaster, Washington City.

In pursuance of the above orders I proceeded to San Antonio, and reported for duty on the 24th of February, and commenced making preparations f)r the organization of the train. Many of the wagons required for the service, and all the stores, were still on the coast, and all the available means that Maj. Babbitt had were immediately employed in bringing them to the depot at San Antonio. An estimate of the number of animals that would be required was made, and, as there were not enough in his possession, some three hundred were received by purchase, and formed into teams for the road, and a small train thus organized was dispatched to Indianola to hasten up with the subsistence. But little hired transportation could be procured, for the severity of the winter had destroyed all vegetation, and the cattle could barely subsist. Some of the stores thus sent by the citizens from the coast were nearly or quite a month on the road up to the depot at San Antonio. By the last of April most of the stores had arrived, the requisite number of employees had been engaged, and the loading of the wagons was commenced. As they received the loads, they were sent in small detachments to Leona, the point I had designated as the general rendezvous. By the 7th of May the last train left the depot, and I started with it for Leona. The supplies for El Paso were kept separate from those drawn for the escort and employees, and, in order to avoid the expense of transporting salt provisions for the command, I received from the commissary of subsistence eighty days' fresh meat, the beeves being driven along by men in the employ of the contractors, and furnished when required. As the Indians on the borders had manifested considerable hostility during the spring, I deemed it necessary to ask of Maj. Gen. Harney, commanding the department, the protection of an escort. For this service a detachment of eighty men from the first regiment of infantry was ordered; but, as the transportation of their subsistence would incur considerable expense, I thought it consistent with proper economy and perfect safety to suggest its reduction to fifty men. The number was accordingly diminished, and on my reaching Fort Inge I found the escort there under the command of Capt. B. H. Arthur awaiting my arrival, and I will here express my obligations to him for the cheerful aid he always afforded me.

I encamped at the rendezvous on the 11th. On the 12th the last of the wagons arrived, and the day following was passed in making final preparations for our departure. The entire expedition, comprising one hundred and fifty wagons (including three belonging to Maj. Backus,* Capt. Sitgreaves, and Lieut. Williamson, *en route* to New Mexico) and over one thousand animals, moved on the 14th, and encamped on the banks of the Nueces. These numbers were further increased by those of citizens availing themselves of our protection to pass through the Indian country.

The march was now continued without any accidents or unnecessary delay, until the night of the 23d, when we were visited by a thunderstorm, accompanied by such violent gusts of wind as to prostrate all our tents and expose us to the rain till morning. We were encamped in the valley

---

* Maj. Electus Backus went to Fort Defiance, among the Navajoes, and destroyed the influence of their god—the dancing man—by a piece of jugglery in making a stuffed figure to represent their god, and by means of wires making it dance. Peace followed this exhibition by a treaty.

of the San Pedro river, and, knowing that it was subject to sudden over-flows from heavy falls of rain, I examined the ford the next day about noon, and could perceive only a slight rise in the water, and therefore commenced crossing the baggage wagons, giving directions for the main train to follow soon after; but no sooner were the former completely over than in the space of a few minutes the waters rose several feet, thereby completely cutting off all communication with the main train for nearly two days. The waters having subsided enough so as not to enter the wagon bodies, the stream was passed, and we continued the march again without interruption to the Pecos river. We found the water of this stream low: but an examination of the ford led me to believe that it was still too deep to pass over in safety, and I was obliged to cause three cylindrical iron rods, or wires, that had been left across the river by the contractors for the year previous, to be raised and secured to the shores by means of strong cables, which being planked over formed a suspension bridge forty feet in length, over which the wagons with the stores were run by hand. About seventy wagons had been thus passed across, when the end of one of the rods that was bent at a right angle broke, and the bridge became impassable. A second examination of the river led to the discovery of a ledge of rocks affording a good bottom, where the rest of the wagons were driven across with but little difficulty. The west bank of the river having been gained, we resumed our journey. At the Comanche Springs we were overtaken by Col. J. D. Graham, U. S. army, topographical engineer, on his way to the Mexican Boundary Commission, who continued with us to El Paso.

The disappointment arising from not having water where on former occasions it had been characterized as permanent or living, together with the parched-up condition of the country, caused me to move with more circumspection. The Lempia was found dry its entire length, excepting one place, that was a mile distant from the road and almost inaccessible to animals, and another at its source at the Painted Camp. I therefore remained at the last-mentioned place, and sent expresses ahead to look for water, which resulted in the discovery of a pool in a ravine twenty miles in advance, to which point we moved. The condensation of vapor on the mountain sides caused some rain to fall about ten miles farther on the road, where the men in advance, by digging trenches on the plain, drained it from the surface where it had not been absorbed, in sufficient abundance for all the animals. Preparations had been made in anticipation of a long journey without water, by filling all the water barrels and kegs at the Lempia. There was now but little hope of finding water short of Eagle Springs, sixty-five miles distant, and the weather being extremely warm, and the roads excessively dusty, I started at two o'clock A.M.; but, much to the joy of every one, a small hole containing water enough for a part of the advance train was found about sunrise, and two others containing sufficient to allow each animal a few quarts were discovered where we halted at noon; again about sunset some was found in a small water gulley in Providence Creek, and each animal was given a few gallons as they passed by and moved in advance in quest of an encamping place where there was some grazing for the animals. But the dryness of the herbage seemed only to increase the thirst of the poor mules, and all night they kept up a continued braying. At one A.M. I again started for the springs, still twenty-nine miles distant, halting at eleven o'clock to give the animals all the water in the kegs and to permit them to graze. Our baggage wagons and the advance of the escort continued on to the springs, which, to the astonishment of all, were so nearly dry that the few animals with us scarcely got enough to slake their thirst. I immediately set some men to the task of digging out the springs, and dispatched a party several miles up the mountains to where on a former occasion a large stream was found running, but they returned and reported it perfectly dry. As to procuring water from the springs where the men were digging, it was an impossibility. While thus perplexed, a thunder shower that hovered around a distant peak of the mountains, and then rolled up the valley, for a time inspired hope, but like the cloud it soon passed away. About four P.M. the trains arrived, and I directed them to continue the march all night to the Rio Grande, thirty-two miles distant. All day difficulties had been accumulating. In the morning an express had overtaken us, giving the information that some of the mules belonging to the Boundary Commission had strayed for water during the night, and they were unable to move from Providence Creek. They could not be left there without water; and, lest the missing animals should not be recovered, I caused four teams to remain at Eagle Springs; so that, should their animals be irrecoverably lost, I might give assistance to get their wagons up to the springs the next day, and resolved to remain in camp till two o'clock the next morning, believing that ere then they would reach our camp, which fortunately was the case. At two o'clock in the morning I left the springs, and arrived at the mouth of the cañon * through which the valley of the Rio Grande is gained, about nine A.M., and found in it near twenty wagons blocking up the passage, the animals exhausted for want of water and from fatigue. They were immediately loosed and driven to the river, eight miles distant, where the main body was encamped, and in the evening these wagons were brought into camp from out the cañon where they had been left. Thus, from not finding water at Eagle Springs, and being obliged to continue on to the Rio Grande, the trains were forced to make a march of *ninety-six* miles *in fifty-two consecutive hours,* the last *sixty miles* having been made in *thirty hours.* These marches were as disagreeable as can well be imagined, and continued to be so to the place of destination, owing to the intolerable heat, the thermometer during the day in the shade standing at 110 degrees, and to the immense volumes of dust that rested on either side the road like a cloud, obscuring everything from the view, except when wafted away by the wind.

We reached El Paso on the 24th of June, forty-nine days after leaving San Antonio, during which time thirty-nine only were passed in traveling. The stores were all delivered in good condition; and an estimate being made of what would be required on the return trip, I found more salt pro-

---

* Pronounced canyon.

visions on hand than were necessary, and therefore caused a part of them to be left at San Elizario, whereby the supplies were increased by about eighteen hundred rations. As soon as the stores were delivered and I could complete my duties, the journey homeward was commenced. We left El Paso on the 7th of July, and reached San Antonio on the 9th of August. The same difficulty in regard to water was not experienced when returning; for at Eagle Springs Mr. Smith, a gentleman who had charge of a small train of wagons, arriving there about a week after us, finding no water, remained there in camp while his animals were being driven to the Rio Grande, thirty-two miles distant, and dug out the springs to a capacity four times greater than I had left them. I also divided the train in sections, marching on consecutive days, so as to let the springs fill during the intervals between the departure and the arrival. The marches were always made with a view to favor the animals, and the time of starting, etc., was determined by the circumstances of distance, the weather, grazing, and water. On the journey out, I generally had the animals corralled at night for safety when there was no moon; but after the stores were delivered, and the main object of the expedition had been accomplished, more risk could be afforded; and accordingly, from the time we left the Rio Grande until the arrival at San Antonio, the animals were herded all the time excepting when in harness. By thus giving them every opportunity to graze, and always traveling with a view to favoring them, I am pleased to state that they returned to the depot in about as good condition as when they started, after marching a continuous journey of more than two thousand miles, if the trips to the coast from the depot be included. The loss of animals from deaths, straying, thefts, and otherwise, from the rendezvous to El Paso and back, was two and a fraction to each hundred. No Indians were ever met on the route, though the guard at night on two occasions fired on what were supposed to be Indians. Often they hovered near our camp, making signal fires on the mountains.

In regard to the country through which the route lies, you were furnished with a description in a former communication. Of course all the peculiar characteristics that it has obtained from the formations remain the same; but every feature of productiveness and beauty, derived from the seasons in their annual course, is sensibly changed, and to the eye it presents but little that is attractive, owing to the drought. From the Nueces to the mountains, which divide the waters that flow into the Pacific from those that flow into the Atlantic, the whole country appears altered. But little rain has fallen for near two years, and hills that before were clothed in verdure now are bare. Valleys that seemed to vie in fertility with the most favored appear sterile; and plains where two years ago the tall grass waved like fields of wheat now are rocky and barren. Parasitical plants hang leafless to the trees, and the mistletoe has ceased to put forth its buds. Where the prairie had been swept over by the fires of the previous summer the surface of the earth was still black and covered with ashes, and nothing green showed that the spring season had passed. The vegetation of the previous years had become so dried and withered by the scorching rays of the sun that it appeared cineritious, crumbling into ashes

8

or dust when pressed in the hand or trodden on by animals. The little lakes that once bordered the streams were dried up, and the streams themselves had often ceased to flow. Even the prairie dogs had forsaken the central part of their town, from starvation, and inhabited the suburbs bordering on the vegetation that widely encircles them, remote from their former homes. It seemed as if Providence had withdrawn his protecting care and left the country to itself. I never before had such a negative proof of the fertilizing properties of rain and dews. The general aspect of that vast extent of country west of the Nueces is thus changed from what it was two years since, when it was an untrodden wilderness unknown to the white man. A general drought has prevailed, and it was only occasionally that green grass was found where a shower had passed in the spring. Notwithstanding the tide of immigration settling into the country, the acknowledged enterprise of our people, the rapid subjugation of the wild lands to useful purposes by the settlers, and the utmost protection that may be given to the advance of all our settlements—yet such are the few attractions that most of that region of country, on the route west of the intersection of the table-lands with the Rio Grande, Northern Mexico, or perchance to the Pacific Coast, it will be a long time before it can attract the attention of agriculturists, or even become a pastoral country to any great extent. The establishment of a mail route from San Antonio to El Paso may cause a small post to be established at Live Oak Creek or Howard's Springs, but, generally speaking, the San Felipe limits the fertile portions of Texas (south of the great plain) in a westerly direction.

I have endeavored to collect some information in regard to the Indians, as required by your orders, and from having been on duty in Texas principally, since 1848, during which time I have traveled over a considerable portion of the country they frequent (in the south and west as far as New Mexico), some conclusions I have arrived at may differ from the generally received opinions in regard to them.

Their numbers appear to have been considerably overestimated, if the report of men who have been among them can be relied on, and the information gained by Lieut. Col. Hardee in his late expedition to their country be correct. It is believed that the entire number, including all ages and the different sexes, of all the tribes that frequent the border settlements of Texas, in the Eighth Military Department, does not exceed four thousand.

The respective numbers of the different bands may be set down (by their own computation principally) about as follows: Delawares, 63; Shawnees, 70; Tonkaways, 300; Quapas, 200; Caddoes, 160; Anadoces, 200; Iones, 113; Keechies, 48; Tawacanoes, 140; Wacoes, 114; Lepans, 350; Lower Comanches, 700; and the Northern Comanches at 1,500. These tribes roam over the country watered by the Red, Trinity, Brazos, Colorado, Nueces, and San Pedro rivers and their tributaries near their sources. The Northern Comanches have the most extensive range for the pursuit of the buffalo to the north of the Canadian. They traverse the entire country to the south, and by their ancient warpaths cross the Pecos, continue to the Rio Grande, enter Mexico, and carry their depredations far into the interior of that distracted country. The southern band of Comanches, and all the other tribes enumerated, are found frequently associated together, and on seeing the northern portions of the line near their home visit those posts in seeming friendship.

That barren, dreary, and desolate region immediately west of the Pecos has not sufficient claims to be in possession of any Indians. The Northern Comanches pass over a portion of it as they wander alternately from the north to the south, and the different bands into which the Apaches are divided approach its borders from the north and west.

The Apaches are divided into numerous bands, and, united with other tribes in New Mexico, have been variously estimated at from fifteen to thirty thousand, the former being perhaps nearer the truth.

The condition of all these Indians, except some few of the Delawares, is truly lamentable. Denied the possession of lands and a home, despising industry, and regarding labor as degrading, no provision is made for subsistence by the cultivation of the soil; but, depending entirely upon the flesh of the horse, the mule, the uncertainty of the chase, and the few wild products of the country, they wander about exposed to all the vicissitudes and every ill of life that can arise from disease, extreme exposure to cold, nakedness, and hunger bordering on starvation, leading an existence more filthy than swine, and as precarious and uncertain as the wolf; and this life is rendered, if it be possible, even yet more intolerable by the almost entire absence of laws respecting property and the rights of the individual. Their views of property tend toward socialism, without that restraint by which the strong are prevented from plundering the weak, and but few injuries have legal redress. However strongly their condition would seem to appeal to philanthropy for relief, much sympathy is lost in the remembrance that their code of morals inculcates many of our vices as their cardinal virtues, and regards our virtues as so many vices or traits of weakness, while their atrocious barbarities shock every sensibility of nature and humanity. The experience of the Jesuit fathers, other Christian missionaries, and learned professors would almost incline us to believe that the Indian is endowed with certain instincts, as they might be called, that are inherent in his nature, and not always directing him to good, which neither separation from his people, education from infancy, the attainments of academies, attractions of wealth, the refinements of society, nor the doctrines and precepts of Christianity can destroy; and, after all, he stands in nature an Indian still. Be this as it may, of one thing we are certain, they are thrown on our borders and violate our laws, and it becomes a question how best to control them, and what policy to pursue in our relations with them. They are now being encroached upon by settlements on the frontier that will soon encompass them on many sides. We are circumscribing their bounds, limiting their hunting expeditions, and destroying their game. And there is no checking these encroachments, for the State of Texas claims possession of all the domain within her boundaries, and no act of the agents of the Federal government can at present cede them a portion of her territory, or military force restrain the lawless traders established in the Indian country. Treaties may be effected with them, but they cannot stipulate to restrain citizens from settling on their hunting grounds, nor grant them many immunities. It is, under the present condition of affairs, vain to suppose that the most skillful combinations for military operations can check a famished, wild, and degraded people from committing depredations on the lonely roads and extended prairies, for the purpose of clothing their naked women and children and to satisfy the calls of hunger; and more especially so when these very acts are not regarded as wrong, and are the only steps by which the untutored brave gains distinction or renown among his people and receives the awards due to valor. Theft with them is no crime, but only a legitimate profession. In all civilized communities ambition is satisfied in pursuing innumerable channels of a civil nature. The Indian has but two, war and the chase, and they are now no longer pleasures, but made a burden by the stern necessities of providing subsistence.

How to control these nomadic tribes various plans have been suggested, but all calling for legislative action, and I feel a reluctance in alluding to them. But I know of none more humane in the end than *to teach them the power of our government*, then grant them a territory, dismount them as far as necessary, feed and clothe them to a sufficient extent to make them dependent on our agents, elevate the character of their war and council chiefs in the estimation of their respective tribes by treating them with some distinction and consideration, whereby their influence over the bands will become greater, and they will become instrumental in carrying out our wishes. Encourage the cultivation of the soil, and establish a few plain, salutary laws for their government and for regulating the intercourse of the whites with them, and have them enforced by the aid of the military; and then, perhaps ere long, tranquillity may be known on the frontier where for so many years partial war has been waged. A similar policy might be urged from other considerations, especially to prevent the immense amount of claims constantly growing out of what are alleged to be Indian depredations, and the expense of maintaining so large a force remote from points where the supplies are drawn.

Were the State of Texas to grant the Indians within her borders a definite territory, ceding the jurisdiction thereof to the United States, so that the proper laws regulating the intercourse of the whites with them could be established and enforced, and were they but partially clothed and fed, the State would have peace on the frontier, immigration to her shores would increase, the immense resources of the country would be developed, and prosperity, spreading happiness among her people, would spring up over her entire dominions.

The service upon which I have been engaged has induced me to urge upon your consideration the propriety of recommending to the honorable Secretary of War the necessity for, and the advantages that would be derived from, a legislative enactment whereby a limited number of employees could be enlisted in the service of the department for a term of years, subject to such rules and regulations as in such cases may be established by proper authority.

When passing through Galveston I had the pleasure to examine the establishment of Mr. G. Borden for the manufacture of meat biscuit. Two cans, in a crushed state, containing five pounds each, were purchased, and on our journey to El Paso and back it was almost constantly used; and, in connection with vegetables, was found an excellent article. We had no such object in view as to test the usefulness to any extent, but from its convenience and palatable qualities it naturally came into daily use. I gave away one can of it, which served a party of four persons, who came from New Mexico to San Antonio without pack animals, as a reliable dependence for food on a journey of about six hundred miles to the nearest settlements. They made it a substitute for animal food excepting when they chanced to meet game, and spoke of it in commendable terms. In forming a *part* of the ration it would commend itself, economically, in a degree somewhat proportionate to the diminution it would make in the weight of the ration; but the military advantages it would afford, where land transportation is difficult, and certain results are to be obtained, cannot be so well calculated. In many points of view it commends itself so favorably, as a component part of the ration for particular service, that it is worthy of more than a single trial.

During the months of March and April the teams were employed in bringing up the supplies for the troops in the Eighth Military Department, and were sent on any other duty that the service required, and were not confined exclusively to transporting the stores destined for the troops in New Mexico. The provisions for the escort were conveyed from San Antonio; and from the forage that I received were fed the animals belonging to the officers' teams, and some was issued to the train of the Boundary Commission in the service of Col. Graham. These and other circumstances connected with the general duties of the service have rendered it impossible for me to present you with more than an approximate estimate of the cost per pound for transportation to El Paso. I have embraced in the calculation the cost of freight of the provisions for the escort; the transportation of the rations for the employees of the department, and the value thereof; the compensation for service of all persons connected with the train; the loss of animals; incidental expenses, etc.; and find the cost per pound, from the Gulf to El Paso, to be about nineteen cents. This will not exceed the expenses per pound under the contract for the previous year, but it exceeds that now paid citizens who own small trains and are carrying, to a limited amount, by four cents per pound. To the government the forage for the animals has been a heavy item of expenditure, and although I allowed only a third of the rations of corn, without long forage, yet it has, owing to the exorbitant price it commands, amounted to over two-fifths of the entire expense of the expedition.

When the grazing is good small trains of twenty or thirty wagons may avoid the use of grain almost entirely by traveling more slowly and stopping oftener to graze; and if the department will thus risk supplies without escorts of any kind, it may, to some extent, diminish expense, but it will be attended with more uncertainty.

It may be gratifying to you to learn that during the time we were absent on the journey, with the exceptions I have mentioned, nothing of note occurred. The trains were always ready to move at the hours designated, and would come into camp without any of those vexatious delays caused by animals "giving out" from fatigue, or the breaking of wagons, or other accidents generally attendant on such expeditions.

Respectfully your obedient servant, S. G. French,

Captain and Assistant Quartermaster.

Maj. Gen. Thomas A. Jesup, Quartermaster General, U. S. A., Washington, D. C.

The officers who accompanied me were Capt. B. H. Arthur, in command of the escort, and Col. J. D. Graham, Maj. Backus, Capt. Sitgreaves, Lieut. Williamson, who availed themselves of the protection of the expedition to go to El Paso; also my brother, John C. French, Bishop Lama, and Mr. Wright, collecting plants for Prof. Gray. His herbarium and large plants filled three wagons. I brought several loads of cacti, embracing about sixty varieties. Unfortunately they were all frozen in transit from New York to Philadelphia, an almost irreparable loss.

During the winter of 1851–52 I occupied a desk in Gen. Jesup's private office. The morning hours, from nine to twelve, were generally given to visitors calling on business or socially. Often were the battles of Niagara, Lundy's Lane, and Chippewa fought over again, until the hour to dine was at hand, and, when visitors ceased to call, the General would look over the morning's mail, then hand the letters to me to answer, telling me what reply to make to every letter. I found it very difficult at first to answer so many letters handed to me one after another, the answers to each verbally given me. Besides I seldom reached the hotel until dinner was over.

The General used to tell me all about the war of 1812. How he was ordered to Hartford on some ostensible service, but really to watch the proceedings of the Secession Convention held at Hartford. Daily he reported to President Madison, as far as possible, what the proceedings were. They had the desire to *secede,* but were apprehensive of the consequences.

As I have before me the proceedings of the Hartford Convention, and an attested copy of the secret journal of that body published in Boston by O. Everett, 13 Cornhill, 1823, I will give a few extracts from the journal.

MEMBERS OF THE CONVENTION.

From Massachusetts: George Cabot, William Prescott, Harrison Gray Otis, Timothy Biglow, Nathaniel Dane, George Bliss, Joshua Thomas,

JOHN C. FRENCH

Hodijah Bayliss, Daniel Waldo, Joseph Lyman, Samuel W. Wilde, and Stephen Longfellow.

From Connecticut: Chauncey Goodrich, James Hillhouse, John Treadwell, Zepheniah Swift, Nathaniel Smith, Calvin Goddard, and Roger M. Sherman.

From New Hampshire: Benjamin West and Miles Olcott.

From Rhode Island: Daniel Lyman, Benjamin Hazard, and Edward Manton.

George Cabot was chosen President of the Convention.

Convention assembled December 15, 1814, and prepared rules and orders.   1. Meetings to be opened each morning with prayer.   .   .   .   2. The most *inviolable secrecy* shall be observed by each member of the Convention, including doorkeeper, etc.   .   .   .

December 16, 1814, committee met,   .   .   .   opened with prayer.   .   .   . Committee reported the following to be proper *subjects* for the consideration of the Convention:

The powers claimed by the Executive of the United States to determine conclusively in respect to calling out the militia of the States into the service of the United States, and dividing the United States into military districts with an officer of the army in each thereof, with discretionary authority from the Executive of the United States to call for the militia to be under the command of such officer.   .   .   .   The refusal of the Executive of the United States to supply or pay the militia of certain States when called out in their defense.   .   .   .   The failure of the Government of the United States to provide for the common defense,   .   .   .   leaving the separate States to defend themselves, etc.

December 17, 1814, met and opened with prayer,   .   .   .   and adjourned.

Monday, 19th, met as usual.   (Proceedings of no importance.)

Tuesday, December 20, and 21st, 22d, and 23d as well, opened with usual prayers and adjournments.

Saturday, December 24, 1814, opened with prayer by Rev. Dr. Jenkins. .   .   .   The committee appointed to prepare and report the measures as it may be proper for this Convention to adopt respectfully report:

Article 1. Complains about the unconstitutional attempts of the Executive Government of the United States to infringe upon the rights of the individual States in regard to the militia.   .   .   .   Recommends the adoption of decisive measures to protect the States from usurpations, etc.

Article 2. Recommends the States to make provision for mutual defense by retaining a portion of the taxes.   .   .   .

Article 3. Recommends certain amendments to the Constitution of the United States as follows:

(1) That the power to declare and make war by the Congress of the United States be restricted.

(2) That it is expedient to attempt to make provision for restraining Congress in the exercise of an unlimited power to make new States, and to admit them into the Union.

(3) That the powers of Congress be restrained in laying embargoes and restrictions on commerce.

(4) That a President shall not be elected from the same State two terms successively.

(5) That the same person shall not be elected President a second time.

(6) That an amendment be proposed respecting *slave* representation and slave taxation.

On motion it was voted that this Convention be adjourned to Monday afternoon at three o'clock, then to meet at this place.

Monday, December 26, 1814, the Convention met pursuant to adjournment, etc.

On the 26th, 27th, and 28th nothing of importance was done.

On the 29th, after prayers, a proposition was referred to the committee appointed on the 21st inst.:

That the capacity of naturalized citizens to hold offices of trust, honor, or profit ought to be restrained; and that it is expedient to propose an amendment to the Constitution of the United States in relation to that subject.

But this is enough to show the drift and patriotism as they saw and *felt* it.

One day, being late to dinner as usual, the table at Willard's was nearly deserted; but seeing Gen. Harney, I took a seat beside him. Soon after, Gov. W. P. Duval, of Florida, came, and, seeing Gen. Harney, he came over and was seated between us. I knew he was a good raconteur, and hoped to have him relate some Florida stories. After he and the General had talked over their experiences with the Seminoles and the Florida war, I asked him to relate some of his adventures in early life. He began the story of Ralph Ringwood, with his schoolboy days, the imported "jack," putting him in the smokehouse, the fright of the old negro housekeeper, Barbara, when she opened the door and the jack brayed, his leaving home, and so on all the way through as related by Washington Irving, with this difference, that he embellished it with many more incidents. He gave us an amusing account of his first visit to New York City. When he reached Washington City President Jackson invited him to dine with him privately. He was not familiar with regular courses at dinner, and came near getting nothing to eat, for while he would be telling a story to Jackson the servant would take his plate away, provisions and all, and put an empty one there. This occurred so often that when he was "helped" again, while talking to the President, he held on to his plate by holding his fork in it perpendicularly, pressing it down hard. The Governor was a very amusing story-teller, and I think he said the way "The Experiences of Ralph Ringwood" came to be published was: Being at West Point Academy, a member of the Board of Visitors, he was invited by Mr. Kemble, who lived on the shore of the Hudson opposite West Point, to dine with him, and there he met Irving and Spaulding and related to them his experiences in early life.

From the time I returned from Mexico, in 1847, until 1854 I was retained on duty in Washington City, to be sent on such incidental service as occasion required, and I am happy to tell you that during all these years I enjoyed the confidence and respect of all the officers in the War Department.

There were long periods of leisure, and I passed much of my time at the Capitol interested in the Congressional debates, especially in the Senate, where, through a friend of mine, I generally enjoyed the privilege of the seats under the gallery or on the floor. I have listened to Everett, the scholar; Sumner, the rhetorician; Choate, the lawyer; Calhoun, the metaphysician; Clay, the orator; Webster, the expounder, and all the other Senators in their best efforts day by day, and I must declare Henry Clay the most eloquent and persuasive speaker of all. The glowing words fell from his lips as though they had been touched by a burning coal from the altar of Elijah on Mt. Carmel. The great natural gift of Savonarola was his. I could illustrate his wonderful magnetic power over men by many occurrences.

In the Metropolitan Hotel the hall leading from the entrance of the office was long and wide. Seats were arranged to the wall on either side, and in this hall, at night, prominent persons were wont to assemble. An Englishman of high official position, on a visit to this country, had arrived in Washington and was a guest at the hotel. In the evening a number of Senators and government officials called to pay their respects to him. Now, without regard to the order of arrival, I will merely observe: When Mr. Cass entered the hall a few persons spoke to him on his way to the office. His card was sent up and he was shown to the reception room. Mr. Clayton came in and was shown up. Mr. Webster arrived, in buff vest and blue coat, and a cloud on his brow, and on his way to the office exchanged a few words with some of his friends. After a while Mr. Clay came. Instantly all rose from their seats. Though the hall was filled, the crowd pressed around him. He had a pleasant word for every one, and the gracious reception he gave them was so magnetic that with difficulty he reached the office and parted from his friends, leaving them *en rapport* with him from sympathetic cheerfulness. When

I was first introduced to Mr. Clay he said, "Ah, an élève of the Military Academy, I suppose?" and then spoke in commendation of the school. I felt sure the shade of his son rose up before him, for he was educated there, and was killed on the battlefield of Buena Vista. I once related to Mr. Clay a story I had heard about James K. Polk. His reply was emphatic: "It cannot be true. No man with such a heart could ever have been President of the United States." Contrast with this Mr. Benton's remark about Stephen A. Douglas: "He can never be elected President of the United States. His coat tail hangs too near the ground." I never heard Mr. Benton make a speech in favor of a measure; he was generally in opposition. If asked who I regarded the finest speaker in the Senate at that time, I would reply: "Henry Clay." I think his reply to Mr. Soule, of Louisiana, on the boundary of New Mexico the best speech I have ever heard. He was the most self-reliant man I ever knew. Gen. Jesup, who knew him well, told me that Mr. Clay's self-reliance prevented him being elected President. He would frame a bill on an important measure, introduce it, and whip the whole Whig party into supporting it. Mr. Webster and other great men in the party disliked coercion, and their support would be lukewarm, when he might have had their hearty coöperation if he had, before presenting a bill, called them to his room, shown it to them to make suggestions, and asked their support in advance, and made them feel that it was their bill as well as his. But no; he was a great leader of men, and commanded them to follow. That is well in military affairs, but in politics it creates jealousy where the leader is not established by law. In the Senate, where acts are recorded, he did command; in politics the vote is secret, his rivals were envious and, at heart, indifferent to his success, and he fell from his own greatness in the struggle for the presidency.

I recall what Gen. Jesup told me of Clay's duel with John Randolph, of Roanoke. When Randolph called Clay "a being so brilliant and so corrupt, only to be compared, indeed, to one thing under the skies—a heap of rotten mackerel by moonlight, that shines and stinks," Clay challenged him. Gen. Jesup and Dr. Hunt were Clay's seconds, and Gen. James Hamilton and Col. Tatnell were Randolph's. Gen. Jesup carried the cartel to Randolph, who referred him to Hamilton. The preliminaries were arranged and the parties met on the Virginia side of the Potomac above the bridge over the Little Falls at 4 P.M. April 8, 1826. Randolph drove out there in his morning wrapper. Randolph declared that he would fire in the air, against which Hamilton remonstrated in vain. Without relating the particulars of Randolph's wearing gloves, and how, therefrom, his pistol was prematurely discharged, I will only observe that at the word Clay fired, the ball passing through Randolph's wrapper without touching his person; then Randolph fired in the air. Seeing this, Clay advanced, seized Randolph in his arms, and exclaimed, "I hope, my dear sir, you are not hurt. What do I not owe you?" Randolph exclaimed, "Mr. Clay, you owe me a new wrapper," pointing to the rent made in it by the pistol ball.

But what I wish more particularly to relate is that many years after this, when Randolph was passing through Washington on his way to Philadelphia, he was driven to the capitol, a sick man, and carried into the Senate chamber and placed on a sofa. It so chanced that Clay was then speaking, and Randolph exclaimed: "Raise me up! be quick, that I may hear that matchless voice once more." What testimony to Clay's eloquence!*

Randolph was Minister to the court of St. Petersburg. He died on reaching Philadelphia, and his last words were: "Remorse! remorse!"

---

* When I was stationed in Louisville, Ky., in 1850, on one occasion Thomas F. Marshall, Dr. Matthews (who was with us in Mexico), and I were at the Galt House. Marshall and the Doctor became engaged in repartee. The Doctor was a master of wit. Marshall acknowledged defeat, and invited us to dine with him next day at the Louisville Hotel, and we accepted his invitation. When the morrow came the Doctor was a little reluctant to go, fearing another encounter. However, at the hour Marshall was on hand. He was an entertaining host, and among his many anecdotes he related the treatment he once received from Henry Clay.

Marshall was opposed to Clay in some local political issue, and the day after the election many people assembled at the courthouse in Lexington to get the news. Clay was in the rotunda surrounded by friends when Marshall entered and approached the crowd. Clay saluted him with: "Good morning, Mr. Marshall. What is the news from Woodford County?" Marshall answered, "We traitors have been defeated;" and instead of extending his hand to "Tom" and saying, "O come back to the Whig fold!" he waved his long arm and exclaimed, "May that ever be the fate of all traitors!" Marshall said the repulse of his proffered friendship astonished him, but it was Clay's *imperious* way.

Washington was the home of many eminent men, remarkable for their integrity in the administration of their duties, purity of character, and modest manner of living. In the army there was Gen. Scott, the brave and successful soldier. He had a few eccentricities in regard to language. He called a lieutenant a "leftenant;" a clerk, a "clark." If any one failed among us youngsters to not give "guard" the letter "u" long, he would be corrected; and as president of military boards he would assume to be recorder, and generally wrote the proceedings himself. The press ridiculed him for writing "sparcely settled" and "conquering a peace," and the Democratic party harped on his "hasty plate of soup" when he was nominated for the presidency; to such mean tricks will a party descend.

There was Gen. Nathan Towson, who so gallantly captured the British brig Caledonia under the guns of Fort Erie, in October, 1812, ever a polite gentleman; and Gen. George Gibson, J. G. Totten, and T. S. Jesup, the last twice breveted for gallant service in the battles of Chippewa and Niagara. And I often met Col. George Croghan, noted for gallantry in defense of Fort Sandusky, and of whom President Jackson said, when charges of intoxication were presented to him against Croghan, "Tear them up; Col. Croghan may *drink* whenever he pleases;" and Col. J. B. Walbach, who was, if my memory serves me aright, one of the defenders of the Tuilleries when it was destroyed.

There were, of course, many naval officers at the capital, and a jovial, good set of men they were. Commodore R. F. Stockton resigned after the explosion of the "big" gun (the Peacemaker) on the propeller Princeton, and soon afterwards represented the State of New Jersey in the Senate. Lieut. Stockton was, as I was told the story, on the U. S. ship Delaware (in the harbor of Gibraltar), commanded by Commodore Pattison. Dining one day at a hotel on the neutral ground, among others present were three young English officers of the garrison and a young man, captain of a fine American ship. The three officers had indulged freely of wine, and made some offensive remarks to the young captain, who resented them, and I think threw his plate at their heads. When challenged, they refused to fight him, on the ground that socially he was not their equal. Stockton handed them his card, and exclaimed, "I will take that gentleman's place; you cannot refuse to fight me." He fought all three and wounded them, and then challenged all the officers of the garrison. When the commandant of the fortress heard of it, he called at once on Commodore Pattison and in a good-natured way suggested to him to get his madcap officer on board ship as soon as possible and make a few days' cruise, or he would have no officers of the garrison left to command the guns. Pattison acknowledged the necessity, weighed anchor, and went seaward.*

When John Howard Payne was Consul at Tunis, in 1841, he incurred a debt for the repairs of a building for the consulate. The bey refused to pay the bill, as he had formerly done to the foreign Consuls. This claim had been pending since Payne's death, in 1842; so, in hopes of settling the matter, Capt. Van Rensselaer Morgan was given a good vessel and ordered by the Secretary of the Navy to proceed to Tunis and adjust the claim if possible. Selecting his officers, he sailed for the Mediterranean. One of his officers selected was skilled in international law, and from the state papers made out a strong case in favor of the United States. Capt. Morgan was a plain, unpretending man, possessed of much common sense. On arriving at Tunis, he was informed that the bey was at his country palace, a few miles distant. The captain procured a carriage, and took two of his officers with him and drove out to see his mightiness, the bey— a prince in rank.

When admitted to the audience chamber, instead of making salaams he walked directly up to the bey and in a frank and friendly manner took his hand and, shaking it heartily, said: "How do you do, Mr. Bey, how do you do? Don't get up, Mr. Bey, don't get up; I will take a seat alongside of you. I hope you are well. How are Mrs. Bey and the children? I hope they are *all* well. I have been a long time coming, and I am glad to see you, Mr. Bey. We have a fine ship; you must come and see us, Mr. Bey, do come." The Captain, after a short interview about current events, rose to leave, and with some expression of solicitude for the bey's health, he retired a few steps, when, suddenly stopping, he turned to the bey, drew from his pocket a large envelope, and remarked, "O, Mr. Bey, I forgot to hand you these papers. Here they are. Don't read them now; you will have plenty of time to do that before we leave."

*I give this story as related to me by a naval officer.

When the Captain was on his way back to his ship, an officer of the court, riding furiously, overtook him, rode past, and, planting his horse in front of the carriage, stopped it, and, bowing, exclaimed: "O howadji, the bey says that claim will be paid." *

A few years ago I was the guest of Commodore Morgan at the life-saving station on Indian River, or rather on the broad Atlantic near Indian River inlet, and I regret that I did not think to ask him to tell me the story himself.

Society in Washington in the forties was largely Southern, and had not lost the courtly dignity and grace of colonial days. It was quiet, gentle, and refined, where it is now loud, boisterous, and rough in a measure, from the power of suddenly accumulated wealth that dominates over all the conditions of life, social and industrial. On New Year's and other occasions we used to call on Mrs. Madison. Her face retained marks of that beauty that has been transmitted to canvas and adorns the East Room of the presidential mansion. I have seen her wearing a turban.

On the 1st of April, 1853, I received a letter informing me of the death of Joseph L. Roberts, who died on the 28th of March previous at his residence on his plantation near Natchez, Miss., and requesting me to come there immediately, if possible. Gen. Jesup, ever considerate as he was, gave me leave to visit the family. Mr. Roberts had been the cashier of the branch Bank of the United States at Norfolk, Va., then president of the branch Bank of the United States Bank of Pennsylvania, and at his death was the agent of the latter institution. His wife was Miss Mary Symington, one of the beautiful women of Philadelphia.

As I had been engaged to Miss E. Matilda, their second daughter, we were married on the 26th of April, 1853, and soon after we went to Washington.

I remained on duty in the War Department until the spring of 1854. As I had become tired of hotel life, and wished the quietness of a home, I requested Gen. Jesup to assign me to some Western post, and he sent me to Fort Smith, Ark.

The military reservation of Fort Smith is separated from the town by a street, and the dividing line between Arkansas and the Choctaw Nation runs through the garrison grounds. When

---

* Told as related to me.

Mrs. French crossed the street and went into the town, I became both the commander and the garrison, and "my right there was none to dispute."

My duties were light and were mainly receiving and forwarding supplies to the troops stationed at Forts Washita and Gibson. Several times I went in a light carriage to Fort Washita, through the Choctaw people, a distance of one hundred and eighty miles, accompanied by only my servant boy. The accommodations on the road were always clean and good and the people kind. On one occasion my duties required me to go from Washita to Fort Towson (eighty miles), on the Red river, to examine the public buildings and sell them. Col. Braxton Bragg fitted me out on a mule with a hard saddle, and I started off alone. That day I rode forty miles to "the boggy" without seeing any person; rested at night with an Indian family, and rode the next day to Fort Towson. I was met there by a committee of Choctaws, wealthy men and well educated. One of them owned slaves in number sufficient to raise three hundred bales of cotton yearly, and "lived sumptuously every day." They went with me to examine the buildings. It would have been folly to sell and destroy such property, for it would bring nothing. So I recommended that it be deeded to the Choctaws for an academy, and it was given to them.

I made a journey to Fort Gibson through the Cherokee Nation. I had been advised to stop and take breakfast with an Indian family, for I would there, no doubt, see two beautiful and accomplished girls, members of the family. Report had not done them justice. There was only a delicate shade of Indian color in the white skin. They were lithe, tall, and graceful; and nature gave them hands as beautiful as ever Praxiteles shaped in marble. They had lately returned from Troy, N. Y., where they had been educated by Miss Willard. Pope's

Lo the poor Indian, whose untutored mind
Sees God in clouds, or hears him in the wind,

does not apply to the Choctaw and Cherokee Indians; many of them are well educated. I became acquainted with John Ross, chief of the Cherokees, in Washington, and lately sent to Mr. Clyde, of New York, a letter from John Ross to frame and place in the saloon of his steamship Cherokee.

9

Indian blood is being rapidly diffused with the blood of the white man—a half-breed, quarter, and eighth.　Fred Douglass is dead—a mulatto.　Shall we credit his intelligence to the white blood or the negro?　Suppose he had been an octoroon? What then!

Sometime during the year 1855 Col. Henry Wilson made Fort Smith his headquarters, and with him came Lieut. J. H. Potter, adjutant of the Seventh Infantry, who was a classmate of mine.　He was a jovial, good fellow, and a wound in his leg made it an excellent indicator of rain, and was used to guide us on hunting expeditions.　Partridges were numerous, and during the hunting season nearly every afternoon Mrs. French and I in a carriage, and Lieut. Potter on his pony, would ride over the prairie and have rare sport.　We had well-trained dogs and open shooting, and time passed pleasantly on.　From this dream life I was awakened to make a visit to Natchez, Miss., on business connected with the estate of Mr. J. L. Roberts.　In company with a French planter on the Teche, in Louisiana, whom I invited to go with me, I started in an ambulance for Little Rock.　The weather was bitterly cold, the thermometer being ten degrees below zero.　The close of the second day brought us to the usual "stopping place," but all accommodations were occupied by the sheriff, guards, and prisoners.　The owner of the house told me I would have to go on to Little Rock, unless Capt. ——, who lived seven miles farther on, could be induced to let us stay overnight with him; but that he was a misanthrope, and would see no one.　The gray, leaden sky, the biting wind, the snow that was falling in dry pellets, and the bitter cold made our situation desperate, and induced me to try the Captain with a little adulation.

How lonely and dreary everything was!　I knocked at the door, I heard the bolts slide, and the door was slowly opened by the Captain.　I introduced myself to him, and told him that I was informed he lived here; that, regarding him as a Mexican veteran, I had called to pay my respects to him; that I was present and witnessed the gallant fight his command made with the Mexican lancers at the hacienda of Buena Vista; that I never was so cold before in my life, except the night of the battle of Buena Vista.　He was silent till I finished.　He took my hand, and said: "Come in."　He ordered the horses taken out, intro-

duced me to his wife, and we passed a pleasant evening before
a great blazing fire. Doubt not my word, but no one in Arkansas then believed that we entered the portals of that door.

Learning that no steamers could reach Little Rock, we went
to Duval's Bluff, on the White river, for a boat; got on the first
one that arrived. The Captain said he was bound for Memphis,
but would land us at the mouth of the White river to get a
down boat.

When near the mouth of the White river, the captain of the
boat informed me that the wharfboat at the mouth of the river
had been removed, and that he would carry us up the Mississippi
until we met a down boat, and put us on that. The wind was
blowing violently, and the river full of floating cakes of ice;
and when we met a boat, so violent was the wind, it would not
answer our hail to stop, and we went on up. In the midst of
all this snow, ice, and gale the boat caught fire in the hold, and
the flames burst up the hatchways very high. The hatches
were soon covered with wet mattresses, steam driven into
the hold, cotton on deck thrown overboard, and the boat landed where the bank was high and the water deep. Baggage and
furniture were put on shore, and fires built. Holes were bored
in the hull of the boat, but the cotton on fire could not be extinguished. About dusk the captain announced that he would put
the baggage on the boat again and run up the river three miles
to a place where he could scuttle her in shoal water and put out
the fire. All the passengers walked through the deep snow to
the landing above, except one man and his wife, the Frenchman, and myself. It was not pleasant to be on the river in such
a gale, and with the boat deck hot from the fires beneath; and
when we did land and made fast to a wood barge, the owner, seeing we were on fire, ran out and cut our line with his ax to send
us adrift. What a punishment the crew of the steamer gave
him for cutting our line!

In time a steamer going up took us on board and carried
us to Helena. After trials innumerable, and too long to write,
I reached Natchez safely. Nothing during the late war equaled
this journey in the suffering I leave untold. I rode out to the
residence of Gen. John A. Quitman, and asked him to go on my
bond. He said: "Certainly I will. Take dinner with us, and I
will then go down with you." When we reached the clerk's office,

he asked Mr. Inge, the clerk, what the amount would be, and I think he replied about one hundred and eighty thousand dollars. Asking for a *blank* bond, he signed it, and said: "Fill this out when necessary with any sum required." It was a kind act, and all he said was: "If you should have any trouble, let me know it, and I will aid you."

Mrs. Mary S. Roberts died April 5, 1854, and it devolved on me to take out letters of administration on the estate. I then returned to Fort Smith and continued on duty there until March 29, when I tendered my resignation. A reply to this letter was as follows:

ADJUTANT GENERAL'S OFFICE,
WASHINGTON, D. C., April 24, 1856.

Sir: Your letter of the 29th ult., tendering the resignation of your commissions of first lieutenant, Third Artillery, and captain and assistant quartermaster has been received and laid before the Secretary of War, by whom I am instructed to say that, as your communication appears to have been written under an impression that your leave would not be extended, he desires that you will state, with as little delay as practicable, if this supposition be correct, or whether it is your intention to leave the service in any event. A decision upon your letter of resignation will be deferred until you are heard from upon the subject.

I am, sir, very respectfully, your obedient servant,

S. COOPER, *Adjutant General.*

Capt. S. G. French, Assistant Quartermaster, United States Army, Greenville, Miss.

As I had now, among other property, a plantation on Deer Creek, near Greenville, and over a hundred servants on it, I asked in reply that my resignation be accepted. To this letter I received an answer: "Your resignation has been accepted by the President of the United States to take effect the 31st inst. [May]."

While living at Fort Smith, Ark., was born Matilda Roberts French, on the 16th of August, 1855.

The summer of 1856 was passed mainly in Canada, and in the autumn we returned to the plantation. In the spring of 1857 Mrs. French and her little girl went on a visit to her sister, Mrs. John C. French, in San Antonio, Tex., and in May following I joined her there. And here a great sorrow crossed my path.

On the morning of June 13 Mrs. French greeted me with joy and hope, but ere the day was passed her life ended in that sleep "that knows no breaking." She went to the grave for her baby boy, and took him with her. O, the irony of fate! She, the peer of the noblest, crowned by every grace, the idol of the house, the gentle mother, the handmaiden of charity, the priestess of religion, a believer in its promises, bowed to His will, and left all that makes life attractive before age or disease or disappointment or grief or sorrow had chilled her heart, and left a smile on her face for weeping friends, when her pure spirit rose to meet her God. Her remains rest with her babe on her breast, beside her parents, in a vault at Laurel Hill Cemetery, Philadelphia, Pa., where the waters of the beautiful Schuylkill gently flow by the portals of her tomb.

I remained in San Antonio until autumn, when I returned home. In March, 1858, I embarked on the steamer Europa for Liverpool. As I leave you my journal of travels in Europe, I shall mention only some of the principal places visited.

Most of the traveling in Italy was in private carriage, and only in daylight. In Naples, Rome, and Florence I remained a month each. From London I went to Paris, Lyons, Marseilles, Toulon, Naples, Rome, Florence, Pisa, Modena, Bologna, Mantua, Verona, Venice, Milan, Como, Isola Madre, Isola Bella, Simplon Pass, Domo-dosola, Martigny, Chamoni, Geneva, Bienne, Berne, Interlaken, Wingen Alps, Grindenwald, Basle, Baden-Baden, Ulm, Munich, Salzburg, Ischl, Lintz, Danube River to Vienna, Prague, Dresden, Berlin, Potsdam, Frankfort, Wiesbaden down the Rhine, Cologne, Liege, Brussels, Waterloo, Paris, London, Windsor Castle, Birmingham, Sheffield, Doncaster, Carlisle, Edinburgh, Sterling, Callander, The Trosacks, Lake Katrine, Dunbarton, Glasgow, Belfast, Irish Causeway, Dublin, Chester, Liverpool, home.

Soon after my return from Europe I was kindly invited by Benjamin Gould to make him a visit in Boston. His son, N. Goddard Gould, had, as I have stated, been my traveling companion for many months. Their home was in Penberton Square. The family was composed of charming, refined, cultured people, and I retain only pleasant recollections of their kindness.

I passed the winter in San Antonio, Tex., and the summer at Rye Beach, N. H. This year (1859) some notable events occurred that had important bearings in shaping the history, if not the destiny, of the country.

Harriet Beecher Stowe's publication of an imaginative work, "Uncle Tom's Cabin," Hinton Helper's pamphlet called a manifesto, and John Brown's raid in Virginia, to raise an insurrection among the slaves and to kill the whites, like distant thunder, presaged the coming storm.   His purposes of *murder* were well known to many prominent abolitionists of the North, who assisted him by contributions to obtain arms to carry out his murderous designs.   The party consisted of the old murderer, his three sons, thirteen white men, and five negroes from the North.   They obtained possession of the armory at Harper's Ferry October 16, killing a negro, the mayor of the town, and other citizens.   On arrival of the United States troops under Col. R. E. Lee, the armory was captured.   Some were killed in the assault, and the remainder taken prisoners. These were tried and hung.

This infamous outrage on the State of Virginia, instead of being condemned by the people of the North, won their admiration, sympathy, and love for John Brown, and by some he is compared to our Saviour, and "his soul is still marching on," without peace or rest, like the wandering Jew—on, on—a punishment for his crimes.   These events induced an uncalled for and unjust feeling of hatred toward the South, and the intensity of this hatred is most significantly displayed in the *apotheosis* of this murderer, and the *consecration* of his crimes.   Could this be otherwise than a warning to the Southern people?   The statutes made by the Northern States for the *abolition* of *slavery* never *set free* a *living slave*.   They emancipated only the *unborn*.   Now you can comprehend the difference between *abolition* and *emancipation*.

After the war began many unusual expedients were resorted to designed to increase the wild frenzy of the people North. Among them was the spectacle of Henry Ward Beecher selling slaves from the pulpit stage of his Plymouth Church, Brooklyn. So noted was this exhibition that it is related as one of the eight notable events of the nineteenth century.   I attribute this act of his to *heredity*.

CHAPTER X.

I SPENT the summer of 1860 at Rye Beach, Boston, and in Canada. When I returned I found the animosity between the two great political parties very bitter. Slavery, for the first time in the history of the United States, had consolidated all the "isms" and all parties against the South, and nominated Abraham Lincoln for the presidency, save only the Democratic party, and that was divided. On my journey home I found intense excitement all the way on account of a sectional nomination for President, and the election of Lincoln was deemed an open declaration of hostility to the people of the South, and drove them to the act of secession. And the people of Mississippi, in convention assembled, repealed all the laws and ordinances by which she became a member of the Federal Union, and on January 9, 1861, she was a sovereign and independent State.

About the middle of February I received a verbal message from the Governor, J. J. Pettus, that he wished to see me, and soon after I went to Jackson. The Governor informed me that I had been appointed a lieutenant colonel and chief of ordnance in the army of the State of Mississippi on February 12, 1861.

On assuming the duties of the office I found the State destitute of all military supplies and without arms. Investigation showed that a mercantile firm in New Orleans had offered, immediately after the act of secession, to furnish arms from England or Belgium, but it was declined.

Weeks after, the Governor sent an agent to Europe to purchase arms, but it was too late to get any in England; but in

Belgium he obtained some muskets, and shipped them on a vessel that reached the mouth of the Mississippi river just as the blockading ships arrived there. Discovering the blockade, the vessel bore away for Havana, and stored the arms there. From Havana they were afterwards brought over and landed in small quantities. I built a powder house, and asked permission to go to St. Louis and purchase powder, and it was refused on the ground or belief that I would be arrested there, and that he, the Governor, would have to arrest a person as a hostage in my place. Afterwards I wrote to a friend in St. Louis, and obtained two hundred kegs (I think that was the number) of powder and fifty-four sets of artillery harness, and this was done after the town of Cairo, Ill., was garrisoned by Gen. Grant.

I purchased *every* yard of flannel that could be obtained in New Orleans, Natchez, Vicksburg, and other towns for artillery cartridges, and all the paper suitable for making cartridges for small arms, even including wall paper, and could not get enough. I was offered by a person whom I knew in Philadelphia a machine for molding lead balls with die for all caliber of small arms (made for the Governor General of Cuba) for a moderate sum, but the Governor disapproved of getting it. Then I made arrangements to have one thousand large Colt's pistols with holsters, etc., sent me from Philadelphia. Twenty thousand dollars in the treasury was placed to the order of the express agent in Jackson, payable to him on delivery of the goods. He succeeded in getting them as far as Baltimore, and there they were seized or stopped. This was in April.

When all arrangements were made for putting up ammunition, the Confederate government could not send me a person that had ever seen a cartridge made, and I had to teach the women how they were put up. The same was true of artillery ammunition. The guns were cast in Richmond, Va., but the carriages were made in Jackson. In making artillery harness difficulty was experienced in procuring leather, and not one person could be found in the State that had ever made a leather horse collar, so dependent were the people of the South for most of the manufactured articles in common use.

As for arms for the infantry and cavalry, we literally had none fit for use. The flintlock muskets found in the arsenal at Baton Rouge, I shipped from time to time to my merchant, Walter Cox, in New Orleans, who employed a gunsmith to alter them to percussion lock; and caps for the guns came in small quantities smuggled over the line from Tennessee. However, as fast as possible the organized companies were supplied with arms such as we had and very good ammunition, and went to their homes to await orders.

When the supply of arms was exhausted I was directed by the Army Board to issue an order for the purchase of shotguns, with which the Governor was bent on arming the troops. He would "o' nights" come to my room and tell me long yarns about how his father, or grandfather, once with a party armed with shotguns loaded with buckshot waylaid a band of Indians, and killed them all. Elated with this legendary story, he wanted *his* army to be supplied with shotguns, so that he might annihilate the pestiferous Yankees, should they invade *his* domain. Gens. Alcorn, Dahlgreen, and O'Farrel were to superintend the collection of these deadly shotguns in their respective departments, and I was ordered to write out instructions for their guidance. Now, lest we should be burdened with a lot of worthless arms, they were informed that it was not expected they would purchase the costly shotguns at high figures, nor were they to buy guns made of "two-penny skip iron," nor "sham-dam barrels," cast-iron barrels, etc.

Alas! when these guns began to arrive the god of war never beheld such a wonderful collection of antique weapons as came in for the Governor. There were guns with only a vent, to be fired with a live coal, guns without ramrods, barrels without stocks, stocks without barrels, guns without cocks, cocks without pans. One gun, I remember, consisted of a barrel that flared out at the muzzle like a bell nailed on a crooked cypress rail, without cock, having only a pan and vent, requiring one man to hold it and another to "touch it off." It was a valuable collection for an antiquarian, but useless in war. I am particular in describing this remarkable collection of arms, because I never saw any of the arms sent South by Secretary J. B. Floyd, and I don't want any Northern writer to accuse him of having sent these shotguns privately to aid "rebellion." A *private* and *confidential report* of all the arms found in the various arsenals, and all arms in the possession of the Confederate States, was sent me by the Chief of Ordnance of the Confederate government.

It showed a beggarly array of trash not unlike Pettus's collec--
tion turned over for me to issue to his troops, to ambush the
Yankees should they invade his territory.

I must here, as a contribution to war history, say a few words
about the Governor's *grand strategy.* Several companies of
Mississippi troops crossed out of his State, and went to the
front in Tennessee, and were received by the Confederate army
then with Gen. G. J. Pillow to hold the enemy in check. For
some offense a few of them were put in the guardhouse. They
made their escape, and came to Jackson. The Governor, Wiley
P. Harris, and myself were in his office, when two long-haired
men came in, and asked for his excellency. "I am the Governor," was the reply. They told him how they had been put
in the guardhouse, etc., and his reply was: "Go back to your
company, and tell Gen. Pillow that, notwithstanding you have
been mustered into the Confederate service, you are by fiction
of law supposed to be in the State of Mississippi, and still in my
command, and not subject to his orders," etc.

On another occasion Capt. Manlove had organized a company,
and by purchase or otherwise had armed it with the Mississippi
rifles. When the Governor learned that they contemplated going to Richmond, he told me to issue an order requiring them
to turn in their arms. Capt. Manlove came over to see me about
it. He was informed that it was an order of the Governor, and
would have to be obeyed. After dinner he asked me privately
what I would do if I were in his place. I told him I could not
advise him, yet he could go home at once, muster his company,
get on the night train, and in the morning be beyond his jurisdiction. He did this; but when the Governor learned that they
had passed through the city during the night, he telegraphed
Gen. Charles Clark, at Iuka, to stop the company and disarm
them, which he refused to do. Capt. Sweet had an artillery
company in Vicksburg with four guns, horses, and ammunition,
complete for the field. He came over to see me lest his guns be
taken, and in a few days after he was reported to be in Tennessee in front of the enemy. And so very properly the army of
Mississippi became less and less, by the troops themselves going
quietly to the front or by his sending or loaning troops for Pen--
sacola and Tennessee, etc. I have no desire to make any reflec--
tions on the Governor, except to point out how his war policy

would have been ruinous to the Confederate cause, had he been permitted to invite the enemy to invade the "sacred soil of Mississippi" to gratify his desire to ambush them and kill them with shotguns. This opportunity was afforded him in 1863.

By the latter part of August most of the Mississippi troops were in the Confederate army, and I had worked up and issued all the war material that could be obtained, and was comparatively idle.

In October I made a visit home in Greenville, and one night the servant came in with the mail. I opened the letters and read them, but among them was a yellow envelope from Greenville that I did not open, supposing it to be a bill, and turned my attention to the papers. When mother and sister rose to retire, I opened this envelope, and behold! it was a dispatch from the President, saying: "Will you accept an appointment of brigadier general? Answer." And the question then was, what should I do? Should I raise a company of cavalry or accept this appointment? They advised me to accept. Ten days after, I telegraphed the President accepting the appointment. During that time I was in Jackson closing my ordnance accounts. Why I did not accept the appointment at once I cannot understand now, unless it was so unexpected that I took time to reflect the matter over. The date of the appointment was October 23, 1861. I had been appointed a major of artillery in the *regular* army of the Confederacy April 2, 1861.

CHAPTER XI.

IN obedience to orders received, I went to Richmond in November. I called on the President, and then reported to the War Department for duty. Secretary Benjamin told me that he would put me on duty at Norfolk; but for some reason, when the order came, I was directed to relieve Gen. Trimble and take command of the troops at Evansport and the batteries there, and blockade the Potomac river to prevent communications with Washington City by water.

An earthwork at the mouth of the Quantico had been constructed, and contained nine or ten nine-inch Dahlgren guns. To these I added five or six heavy guns. These latter guns were far apart, and mounted in circular pits sunk in the earth. Thus isolated, they commanded the river afar, both up and down, and no concentrated fire could be made on them all at the same time. One was a large English Armstrong rifled gun. The infantry force was composed of the regiments of Cols. Brockinbrough, Virginia; J. J. Pettigrew, North Carolina; W. B. Bate, Tennessee; Col. J. J. Judge, Alabama; Col. Thomas, Georgia; Walker, Arkansas; Fagan, Arkansas; Bronough's battalion, Arkansas; Col. Snowden Andrews's battery of field artillery, Maryland; and Capt. Swann's company of cavalry. Capt. Chatard, Capt. McCorkle, Lieuts. Simms and Wood, C. S. navy, were given command of some of the land batteries and the

JEFFERSON DAVIS

steamer Page. On the Maryland shore opposite us were the brigades of Gens. Hooker and Sickles, and some water batteries of Parrott guns: and above several ships of war were blockaded, and below such ships of war as came up from time to time. With this force the river was closed to navigation; and as Lord Lyons, the British minister, remarked in one of his dispatches, "Washington is the only city in the United States that is really blockaded."

The ammunition found in the magazine for the large guns was very indifferent. The powder was a mixture of blasting with rifle powder. Sometimes the Armstrong gun, at the same elevation, would not throw a shell more than halfway across the river; then again far over the river.

During the whole winter, notwithstanding a great deal of shelling from the steamers below us and the opposite batteries, nothing of importance occurred. It was only the thunder of big guns.

I think it was on the 5th of March that I received, confidentially, verbal orders to remove all stores to Fredericksburg, and to be prepared to fall back on the 8th inst. All property was removed except the heavy guns. Some of them were thrown into the Potomac, and the remainder spiked and the carriages destroyed. On the 8th the troops in my command were on the road to Fredericksburg. On the night of the 13th a telegram was handed me, saying: "Come to Richmond immediately." I reached that city early next day. Calling on the President, he told me that I must go at once to New Berne, N. C., and relieve Gen. L. O. B. Branch, take command of the forces there, and call at Gen. R. E. Lee's office for instructions. I found Gen. Lee at his home, and he said: "I want you to go to New Berne, and drive Burnside away from there when he attacks the place. When can you go?" I said by the first train, requesting him to have my staff and horses sent me as soon as possible. The train was to leave in the afternoon. Next came a message from the President, telling me that he wished me to call at once. I did so, and he then informed me that he had just received a dispatch that New Berne had fallen, but that I must go down and assume command.

I found Gen. Branch at Kinston. He received me very cordially, and offered to aid me. I disliked to hand him the orders, because they were written before they knew the battle had been fought. I made an inspection of the troops, and found them cheerful and seemingly not at all discouraged by their defeat. This was on the 17th. On the 20th I received a dispatch ordering me to Wilmington, as there was some apprehension of that place being attacked, and I went there without delay. Gen. Joseph R. Anderson succeeded to the command at Kinston.

On arriving at Wilmington, the first duty was the immediate examination of the defenses at the mouth of the Cape Fear river. Fort Caswell was in fair condition for defense, and any vessels passing it would meet river obstructions while under short range of the guns. Fort Fisher was a small unfinished work, consisting of a casemate battery *fronting the ocean*, and a line of works, nearly at right angles with this, that ran back inland. This latter line constituted the land seaside defense, while the guns also commanded the channel and the entrance thereto. This face I continued inland to the edge of the marsh, making it perhaps a third of a mile in length. From my assuming command in March until I was ordered to Petersburg in July I gave this fort much care, and kept a large force at work. Commencing at the right of the casemate battery, I caused a line of revetment to be put up, extending parallel with the ocean, a distance of perhaps half a mile; knowing the winds would blow the sands up and make a glacis in front; and so the windstorms blew thousands of tons of sand, forming a smooth slope to the seashore. From this front we constructed a line back to the marsh, and thence up to the line running back from the casemate. It was an enormous work, and its garrison should not have been less than three thousand men. Outside the sea front, near the ocean, I sunk a pit, as deep as admissible, and mounted the largest of the Tredegar guns, that swept the horizon in every direction.

Maj. Kendrick was in command of Fort Fisher for some time. I believe it was at his own request that he was relieved, and I put Col. William Lamb in command in his place, and he remained there until it was captured, January 15, 1865. I mention this because it is a part of the history of the fort.

There were many incidents connected with Fort Fisher whilst in my command at Wilmington. I had constructed a telegraph from Wilmington to Fort Fisher. One morning early I received a telegram stating that a " blockade steamer " had been run ashore near the fort, designedly, because she was fired on by the blockading ships and had much powder on board, and that a messenger had reached the fort, asking the commander to sink his steamer to *save the powder*, and asking me for orders. However, before he got my reply to "not fire a shot at the steamer," a shot was fired at her from Fort Fisher, and, striking below the water line, she gradually filled. All the shells of the enemy fell short. We took charge of the abandoned steamer, and sent two lines from her to the shore, and with the labor of two hundred men removed all the cargo to the depth of six feet in the water. The brandy, whisky, ale, powder, medicines, and above all six Whitworth field guns, were landed. Two of these guns were kept at Fort Fisher. As their range was about six miles, I instructed Col. Lamb to select good men for them, and practice with them inland, so as not to let the enemy know the range. When this was done, one bright day when all was quiet, and the lazy blockaders were lying at anchor about three miles off the fort, these two guns opened on them, creating a lively scene. Black smoke began to stream up from the smokestacks of the steamers; sails were thrown to the wind from the ships in all haste, and the squadron went seaward. When they returned, they anchored out of range, and from this time on I requested all blockade runners (steamers) on arriving to make the mouth of the channel at dawn and run in by daylight out of reach of the enemy's guns.

Soon after this another steamer came in from Nassau, and Capt. McCorkle, of the navy, and I got into a yawl with two sailors and went out to meet her. We found a young "my lord" from England, who had run the blockade to carry a "free lance" and have some "fun" with the Yankees. He had been pent up on shipboard and was full of life, and asked us to take him ashore in our boat. When we shoved off, he insisted on taking one of the oars for mere relief to the exuberance of life. We had almost three miles to row, and McCorkle, as boatswain, managed the rudder so as to give him an opportunity to display his strength. When he began to weaken, McCorkle would cry out, "Give way, my lord," to encourage him. When we reached camp, he was not so restless; but he was a jolly good fellow, and I hope he had an opportunity given him to gratify his inclination to fight.

10

My volunteer aid, Baker, was given a month's leave. He obtained a small boat and loaded her with nine bales of cotton, and, with only a small boy to tend the jib sail, put out for Nassau, reached port safely, and sold the boat and cargo. He returned on a vessel that ran the blockade at Charleston, and brought me a "pith" India hat, gloves, kid gaiter shoes, and other acceptable articles. With him on the steamer came a distinguished officer, carrying a saber as large as the sword of Wallace, who was "spoiling" for a fight, as he expressed it at a dinner given him by some of the officers in Charleston. He was a genuine, good soldier, entered our service, and often distinguished himself while chief of staff for Gen. J. E. B. Stuart.

I was kept very busy during my stay in Wilmington in constructing defensive works. I *fortified the city of Wilmington;* put up, or mounted, isolated guns on the bluff banks of the river, and otherwise defended the city from the approach from seaward.

And now were "fought the fights" around Richmond, and I was down here digging dirt without much honor or renown, and when they terminated an order came, July 17, placing me in command of the Department of North Carolina and Southern Virginia. Gen. W. H. C. Whiting was given the command of the defenses of Wilmington, and I was requested to name certain counties around the city to give him a separate command. He continued there until Fort Fisher was captured, as stated, on January 15, 1865. Although it was subjected to a terrific bombardment, the report shows that out of forty-seven heavy mounted guns twenty-five of them and their carriages were serviceable when captured. How difficult it is to destroy sand forts!

Fort Sumter, with its walls crumbled into dust by four years of bombardment, never was captured, and its defense stands *alone*, unparalleled in the history of the world, and before which all others pale. See Jollification Order, Vol. L., No. 106, page 1143, "War Records," when information was sent to the United States troops that the Confederates had left the fort.

Occasionally some war steamers would come near enough to throw shells into Fort Fisher, but they did very little damage.

The main annoyance was the reports given out that every large naval expedition was designed for Wilmington. On one of these occasions a company of volunteers, mainly *lawyers and the like*, most elegant men, arrived in Wilmington from Fayetteville and tendered their services to defend Fort Fisher. Although I had learned the destination of the fleet was not the Cape Fear river, I accepted their services, sent them to Fort Fisher, and put them to work with wheelbarrows and shovels to build ramparts. It went hard with them at first, but after a while they considered it as being a rather good offer too prolonged. Their complexions were soon tanned, their hands blistered. They, however, made the time pass away merrily, worked hard, slept well, improved in health, and when their time expired Capt. Devereux and his companions thanked me for the opportunity given them to fight for the cause, and making the fort impregnable, as they expressed it. They enjoyed working because they were men of character.

The battles around Richmond had been fought, and Gen. McClellan driven to seek shelter at Harrison's Landing, on the James river, under cover of the heavy guns of the navy. Gen. R. E. Lee's army rested around Richmond. My line of defense commenced on the James near Drewry's Bluff, thence down the James, down the Blackwater, thence on to the mouth of the Cape Fear river, over three hundred miles in length, with the enemy at intervals along the front at Norfolk, Suffolk, Washington, Plymouth, New Berne, and other places, constantly threatening and making raids. It was imposing on me unceasing labor and a grave responsibility; and I will here remark, once for all, that during my command of this department, although Smith, Hill, and Longstreet were temporarily in command, at intervals, they did not remain in the department any length of time, or interfere with the defense.

Sometime toward the last of July Gen. D. H. Hill, who had no command, came over from Richmond, and as no defensive works had been constructed for Petersburg, the matter was mentioned, and it resulted in our riding out and selecting a point on the Appomattox river to start from; and we determined on the line to the City Point railroad, thence on by the farms of Hare, Friends, and Dunns. And as I may not refer to it again, I will state I went to work with my troops, and, staking out the line, *constructed the entire works around the city,* crossing the Jerusalem pike and on to the lead works on the P. and W. railroad. It took one year to build this line, and it served a good purpose in the end, and gave one year of life to the Confederacy.

On the evening of July 28 Gen. Hill handed me a letter from
Gen. Lee stating that he would send over to Petersburg the next
day Gen. W. D. Pendleton, his chief of artillery, with six batteries.   To these other batteries could be added as desired, the
whole to go down to Coggins's Point, on the James, and attack,
at night, the shipping and camp of the Federal army at Harrison's Landing, on the opposite shore; and that I should command
the expedition, etc.   Accordingly I increased the number of
guns to seventy-five, and designated Gen. Daniel's brigade as the
escort.   We started on the morning of the 30th, intending to
make the attack that night.   The forces were halted in the woods.
I then rode down with Gen. Pendleton to the dwelling of Mr.
Ruffin, on the river, to reconnoiter the grounds and select positions for the guns.   At Ruffin's I took off my coat, put on a
straw hat, hoisted an umbrella, and in the seeming garb of a
farmer examined the shore, rode down to the river and watered
my horse near a war steamer.   After going down a half mile I
returned.   It was then growing late, and we started back.   To
my astonishment, in the darkness, I met the artillery moving
toward the river.   As not one captain had any idea of the ground,
every gun was ordered back, and such trouble to encamp, by
reason of the intense darkness, seldom occurs.   Gen. Hill, who
was in camp, said we would "be *discovered next day*," and he
returned to Petersburg.   The next morning the captains of the
batteries were instructed to go through the clover fields to the
river bank and select positions for their guns.   This was done
without attracting the notice of the enemy, or the hundreds of
vessels in the stream.

As the day closed a drizzling mist made the darkness *thick*.
Like the interior of the Mammoth Cave, it could be felt, but not
seen.   However forty-five guns were put in position, exclusive
of the two long Parrott guns captured at Manassas.   Amidst
such darkness what a beautiful sight was before us! Ten thousand
lights from the shipping and the camp shone the brighter from
some reflection of the darkness that should have obscured them.
At midnight the battery on the right was to open fire, to be followed in quick succession along the line, and in a minute it was
a continuous fire.   Soon the lights were all extinguished, save
one or two on some lone craft in the river.   When the firing
commenced all the monitors and other war vessels moved up the

river to meet the *ironclad* built in Richmond that was reported to be ready to come down the river, and so we were not subjected to any fire except from one gunboat, and from some Whitworth guns that sent bolts, whistling like birds, high over our heads. As the day dawned the guns were withdrawn and we returned to Petersburg. The report of Gen. Pendleton and my own can be found in the war records. There were no casualties on our side. It was real amusement.

Officers of the Union army, years after, gave me accounts of the wild confusion in their camps. Unexpected as a midnight earthquake it burst upon the slumbering army. Horses and mules broke loose and ran affrighted over the grounds, stumbling over tent cords. Captains shouted everywhere for men to fall in line. The blue was here and there mingled with midnight summer's sleeping uniforms of white indescribables, airy and cool, that were seen only by the light of bursting shells. Gen. Alfred Pleasanton told me he could find nothing in his tent to put on, except now and then by the light of the shells, and my good friend, Gen. Rufus Ingalls, in the first letter he wrote me after the surrender, said: "You don't know, dear Sam, how near you came killing me that night, which, had it happened, would have been a great sorrow to you." I was informed that a war correspondent wrote a letter severely criticising Gen. McClellan's inability with eighty thousand men to offer any resistance to this attack, that was successfully used, with other charges, by his enemies to have him relieved from command of the Army of the Potomac. McClellan, perhaps mortified that his position was shelled without being able to make any defense, treated the matter very lightly in his reports. He had not taken the precaution to place any guns on the river bank, and the intense darkness prevented moving artillery through his camp. Besides, he could not use guns, as the ships and vessels of every kind lined the river shore and were in the way.

Gen. Lee directed me to have my scouts watch McClellan's movements closely, especially movements of the shipping down the James. In time I reported the departure of the transports, and the crossing of the Chickahominy with the infantry. Soon after followed the battles of Cedar Run, August 9; the second Manassas, September 2, where Pope met his reward; then Fredericksburg, December 13, where the vain Burnside was defeated.

There is an incident connected with this last battle that I will here relate, although it has been published in a magazine called the *Confederate Veteran.*   The Federal army had crossed the Rappahannock river and formed in line of battle to attack the Confederate army on the heights beyond.   Maj. Pelham commanded a battery belonging to Stuart's cavalry, away on our right flank, in age a youth, in character a hero.   When the Federal line commenced to advance, in full view of friends and foe, in the silence that often precedes a great battle, Pelham, with a piece of artillery, dashed forward between the two armies, halted, a puff of smoke, a shell burst over the Federal line, and in a moment the fire of twenty batteries centered on that lone gun; and there, amidst shrieking shot and bursting shell, flame and smoke, that detachment of Frenchmen worked their gun and stayed the battle near an hour, all the while singing the "Marseillais," which was now and then heard for a moment, borne by the fitful breeze, in the break of an almost continuous roar of artillery.   France and glory evermore abides in the hearts of Frenchmen.   Macaulay, in his lays of ancient Rome, tells in song the story of Horatius and his two friends defending the bridge over old Tiber against the hosts of Lars Porsena, and here is a deed of modern date that rivals that of old, and some day it will be a theme of inspiration for a poet.   A boy, one gun, eight Frenchmen holding in check so long eighty thousand men!

Sometime in November, I think it was, I received a dispatch from the President to come over to Richmond.   On calling at the President's house I found Gen. Lee there.   The General asked me what was the least number of troops I would require, for a short time, to hold my line.   Reflecting awhile, I said about six thousand.   His reply was: "That is reasonable.   When you return order all above that number to report to me."   Now I write this as an illustration of the delicate consideration Gen. Lee had for the officers under him.   He could have ordered from the department such troops as he desired, without seeing me, but he was ever a gentleman, and considerate to every one.

I have not the date, my papers having been turned over to my successor, but it was during the winter of 1862–63 that Gen. Foster made a raid from New Berne up to near Tarboro, N. C., and as soon as I could ascertain his designs and objective point

I began to concentrate troops to meet him. I assembled about eight thousand troops at Tarboro. Foster was at a village about twelve miles distant. During the afternoon he marched on one road toward Tarboro, and I moved on another to meet him, and on the road that he was reported to be on. When night came we were near each other on different roads, and preparations were made for battle. In the morning Foster was far away on his road to New Berne. It was cold, and snow covered the ground, and pursuit was useless except by cavalry. There was brought to me an old negro slave who was with Foster during that night, and the following was his story:

Well, master, I will tell you how it was. You see I was going from Tarboro out on that road unbeknownst that the Yankees was there. Well, for sure, some of dem Yankees on horseback cried, "Stop dar," and asked me, "Where you live, and where you goin'?" I told how it was, and they said, "Come along, old man," and they took me to the ginneral. He was in a house sitting on a sofa, and he says to me, "Are you from Tarboro?" and I said, "Yes, master;" and then he says, "Take a seat here." So I sot down just this way. He was on this side of me, and I was, as it might be, on tother side of him. He looked kind to me, and says to me: "You know we are friends of the colored people, and so you must tell me de truth." Then he says: "Mose [for I had done told him my name], Mose, are there many soldiers in Tarboro?" I told him there was in de morning more men than I had ever seen in my life, and I tells him where they went to. Then he asks me: "Mose, have they much cabalry?" "Cabalry? what you mean by dat?" "Have they many men on horses?" And I says: "Bless your soul, master, I neber have seen as many blackbirds in de cornfields as dey have horses thar; everywhere you go you see dem men on horses." "Have they many guns?" "Sure, ebery man hab a gun." "You don't understand me, Mose," says he; "have they many cannon on wheels?" Then I ups and tells how when dem cannon went out of town I sot on de ground on my knees in a joint of fence in a cornfield on tother side de road and looks through de rails and counts them, and dar war, for sure, just sixty-four of dem. Next he asked me what ginnerals were there, and I told him I ain't particlarly 'quainted with dem, but that I had heard tell of Ginneral Martin there, who had but one arm. Then, after thinking for some time, he called a man and told him to take care of me and not let me get away. Soon they beat de drums and blowed de horns, and they all got ready and was going back, and in the big crowd I slips out, and, bless the Lord, I am home here with de ole woman and children.

Whether Foster was influenced by the information he got from old Mose, I know not, but such was the old negro's story as he related it to me the next day, as I remember it.

I am quite sure vandalism (especially stealing) commenced in New Berne, for the pianos and furniture shipped from there decorate to-day many a Northern home. At Hamilton most of the dwellings had been entered, mirrors broken, furniture smashed, doors torn from their hinges, and especially were the feather beds emptied in the streets, spokes of carriage wheels broken, and cows shot in the fields by the roadside, etc. It was a pitiful sight to see the women and children in their destitute condition. Alas! toward the end it was an everyday occurrence, and the main object of small expeditions was to steal private property.

Pretty early in December a lady correspondent, outside of New Berne, informed me that it was reported that the troops in the town were to move out and attack Wilmington, or destroy the railroad to that place. I kept Gen. G. W. Smith, in Richmond, whose command embraced the State of North Carolina, advised of the information received, and he went through Petersburg, stopping to see me, and then went on to Goldsboro, N. C., to await developments.

My diary says:

Left Petersburg December 15, in the evening train for Weldon. From there ordered the horses and equipments by land road to Goldsboro. Also, by command of Gen. G. W. Smith, I ordered Col. Martin's regiment to Goldsboro. I left in Petersburg, awaiting transportation, the Mississippi regiments and some of Daniel's Brigade and Bradford's Artillery. Leaving Weldon, I proceeded to Goldsboro, and arrived there at 7:30 A.M. on the 16th, and took the train to Kinston. Reached Mosely Hall about 10 A.M. Found Gen. Evans there. At this time there was heard heavy firing at the Whitehall bridge over the Neuse river. The firing increasing rapidly, I sent to Gen. Robertson Col. Burguin's regiment, and Gen. Pettigrew to take command if it should prove to be a determined attempt to cross the river, which I doubted. This regiment did not reach there in time to render any material assistance. The troops engaged were Leventhorpe's Eleventh North Carolina, a part of Feribee's and Evans's Brigades, Jordan's Thirty-First North Carolina, and two pieces of artillery. A battery I sent did not reach there until the fight was over. In this affair we lost about thirty killed and wounded. We had about five hundred men engaged, and the enemy four regiments and fifteen pieces of artillery, and their loss, from inferior position, must have been about one hundred.

Being satisfied that the attempt to cross or to put down a pontoon bridge was frustrated, if seriously contemplated, and that the objective point was Goldsboro and the railroad bridge there, I ordered Col. Rodgers up from Kinston, who had been there all day in possession of the town, and sent him and Evans's Brigade forward to Goldsboro in haste, and informed Gen. Smith that the enemy was moving up the river; and made every effort to get our force to Goldsboro. Gen. Pettigrew moved with Burguin's and Leventhorpe's regiments for that point, leaving a strong force and two guns at Whitehall. The train that took Rodgers did not return until about 4 A.M., and left soon after with troops. Seeing them off, I started on horseback with staff and rode to Goldsboro, and reached there at 9 A.M. and reported to Gen. Smith.

The guard that was left at Mosely Hall was directed to take an account of the cotton burned there, and to save the rope and bagging.

When I reached the depot near Bear Creek I there found Burguin's regiment and a down train. It brought me an order from Gen. Smith to leave Gen. Robertson in command of the troops at Whitehall and Spring Bank bridges to hold them. Gen. Martin was left in command at Mosely Hall. I have since learned that the enemy left eighty men unburied at Whitehall. They removed the wounded. Seventy stand of arms were collected. During this time Gen. Clingman, with his brigade, was on the right bank of the river.

When Col. Rodgers was ordered from Kinston I directed that the command of Wallace should proceed direct to Goldsboro from Greenville, and not stop at Kinston to support Col. Rodgers, as he had been ordered away.

In consequence of the movements made, as has been stated, the condition of matters on the morning of the 17th, was as follows: Clingman was over the river on the right bank with his brigade (Cantrell's, Shaw's, and Marshall's regiments) and some artillery; Evans, with his brigade and the Mississippi troops, in the town; Rodgers, near by; and Burguin, *en route*, near at hand. When I reached the town and reported to Gen. Smith he told me he had ordered, early in the morning, Gens. Evans and Clingman to make an armed reconnoissance on the other side of the river. For some reason, not known to me, it never moved or got off until the enemy attacked the bridge.

About 2:30 P.M. I was informed that the enemy was advancing on the Goldsboro bridge (the railroad bridge over the Neuse), and the cannon were heard in the distance. Pettigrew started to join Clingman on the other side of the river. Smith sent for me to come to his office. I remained with him about an hour, urging forward troops. Gen. Smith then went to the hotel for his sword, coat, etc. When he returned I picked up my saber and said: "If you have no particular use for me here, I shall go down to the field." To this he replied: "Very well."

Riding down I overtook the Hon. W. Dortch, Confederate States Senator, and Gov. Z. Vance. They wished to show me some fords in the river. I found Pettigrew examining them also. I then galloped on for the field, and found Gen. Smith there. He had passed by while we were locating the fords. On arriving on the field I found most of our troops in the edge of the woods. I moved them across the field to the railroad, which afforded some protection. The enemy were drawn up in line on some rising ground somewhat obliquely to the railroad. Their right was about seven hundred yards distant, and the left four hundred. There was really but little firing except artillery, and that was at the one gun we brought on the field. Evans, on our left, ordered a charge over the open field toward a battery. The regiment making the charge suffered considerably from canister shot, and as soon as possible I recalled it. It soon became dark, both lines maintaining their positions. Smith now came over to the left, and called Evans, Pettigrew, and me, with Stevens, engineer, to consult or counsel with him on the question of remaining or withdrawing. All but Evans favored crossing back to camp.

The diary is too full of detail to quote. We recrossed because the weather was intensely cold, and the troops had no blankets or provisions, and would be unfit for service if they remained there. Next morning Foster was on his return to New Berne. Had Smith seen to it that Evans had crossed over, and with Clingman's Brigade and his own moved as directed, the bridge could not have been burned, as it was, by a party of six men. Reports said Foster had eighteen thousand men and eighteen pieces of artillery; we had nine thousand, with nearly twenty pieces of artillery. The whole matter was probably a demonstration in favor of Burnside at Fredericksburg. Our troops were not properly handled at Goldsboro.

From Goldsboro I returned to Petersburg on the 24th. On January 5, 1863, I left Petersburg for Weldon on account of information of an apprehended attack on Wilmington. The next day Gen. G. W. Smith arrived, and then went on to Goldsboro. On the 16th I joined Gen. Smith at Goldsboro. Owing to information received on the 20th, I ordered Cook's Brigade to near South Washington, Ransom's to Kenonsville, and Pettigrew's intermediate, to support either. In the evening Smith went to Wilmington. On the 27th I received information that Gen. Smith had been ordered to Richmond, and a dispatch came for me from the War Department to repair to Goldsboro and assume command of all the troops. On the 3d of February I received orders to send reënforcements to Wilmington. I sent Evans's Brigade there. Orders also came to convene a court of inquiry on Gen. Evans. On the 8th forces were sent from Wilmington to Charleston, and on the 18th I examined the works around the city of Wilmington that I had constructed a year ago, and the next day visited the forts, Fisher, Caswell, etc. I returned to Petersburg on the 23d. Gen. D. H. Hill, having no troops, was put in command of those in North Carolina, leaving me Southern Virginia. I found in Petersburg Lieut. Gen. Longstreet.

In the summer of 1862 an estimable clergyman came to me and spoke of an opportunity of obtaining some supplies for the troops from Norfolk. I believed it feasible, and referred him to my chief quartermaster, Maj. J. B. Moray. It speedily was put into operation, and the plan was very simple. An Englishman, living some miles from Suffolk, having charge of or owning an estate on which he lived, had permission to pass the lines at will, and had a permit to purchase supplies for his place. Under this permit he procured for the reverend gentleman large supplies of sugar, coffee, clothes, shoes, medicines, surgical instruments, saddler's tools, bacon, etc. One day at Weldon, or Halifax, a trunk was sent to headquarters through this channel containing some coffee and the most costly pair of boots I have ever worn. The foot was calfskin and the tops of morocco, and came above the knee. They were worn long after the war ended. Who sent them I do not know. The only trouble I gave to this matter of obtaining supplies was to place a respectable and permanent guard that could be trusted, to let the boats land with the supplies.* When I went to Petersburg the ladies were

---

* By this arrangement my quartermaster, Maj. J. B. Moray, obtained bacon, sugar, coffee, blankets, shoes, cloth, saddlers' tools, medical supplies, etc., in no small quantities. He also had hay and fodder baled, by sending a hay press through the north counties of North Carolina to bale this forage, and obtain grain. On the arrival of Gens. D. H. Hill and Longstreet it terminated, for Longstreet took the teams.

The following letter from the Hon. James A. Sedden relates to this matter:

WAR DEPARTMENT, C. S. A.,
RICHMOND, February 20, 1863.

Gen. S. G. French, Commanding, Etc.

General: I have derived much satisfaction from your letter of the 12th, and am gratified to see how fully you have realized and understand the great needs of our army on the Rappahannock for supplies of forage and subsistence, and the difficulty of meeting them. The scarcity in this State is really great, and without distressing exactions from the people, and much consequent suffering, there is no prospect of drawing any large supplies from them.

Our great reliance must be on the large producing counties of North Carolina, and, unfortunately, the richest are in the hands of, or under the control of, the enemy. Great efforts must be made to draw all that can forced or tempted from that quarter, and there can be no better employment of our forces in North Carolina than in protecting and aiding such operations. Even illicit dealings with persons of doubtful position, or

somewhat "slipshod," for no ladies' shoes, toothbrushes, pins, needles, or materials for dresses were for sale. Through respectable men "running the blockade," I had the town supplied. All that I required of these men was that they should bring a few necessary articles for the government, then as much as they wished for sale, but the invoice must be submitted to the quartermaster to see if there were any other things useful for the army.

There was a large, tall woman named Johnston by whom hundreds of letters, with money in them, were sent by soldiers to their families in that part of Virginia, and in return she brought letters to Confederate soldiers. I detailed an intelligent man to read all letters going out and returning by the blockade runners; all letters, too, going *north* by, or received from, the flag of truce boats were examined before being delivered to the persons addressed. Only a few of these letters were referred to me. I never doubted Mrs. Johnston's integrity, but some of my staff endeavored to have me believe she was a spy on both sides. She always told me the truth about the enemy, for I could see it corroborated by the testimony of others. One time she was gone about six weeks, then returned and said Gen. Vielè had put a guard over her house in Norfolk and kept her a prisoner. When some years afterwards I met Gen. Vielè in New York he told me he could do nothing with her, she defied him, and he kept her at home that while. She gave him no truthful information, but was faithful in her reports to us.

There was a girl living in Norfolk that wanted to cross the lines and go to Richmond. Three prominent citizens, separately, informed me that she was a spy. Gen. J. J. Pettigrew, on the Blackwater, received like information, and asked me for instructions. I wrote: "Let her come, but send an officer to watch her." She arrived by train, in company with a "roach-backed" looking woman with a child in her arms, and went to the hotel. I directed the city marshal to arrest her if she attempt to leave for Richmond, and he arrested her at the Richmond depot the next morning and brought her to me. She swore she was a true

mercenary natures, might be encouraged to the extent of procuring supplies, particularly of meat. But with the clear views and convictions you have on this whole subject it is unnecessary to urge the adoption of special means. You will, I doubt not, adopt all that can be made available, and in so doing you will have the sanction of the department.

Very truly yours.   JAMES A. SEDDON, *Secretary of War.*

woman to the Confederacy, that she had a brother in the service. I asked her how she left Suffolk. She declared she passed the Federal lines with the woman now with her, who had a pass for two persons, that she brought the woman and child along with her lest the woman should be imprisoned for aiding her over the line of pickets, etc. Then I read to her several letters informing me "Fannie Cooper left this morning in a carriage with a Yankee officer to go to Richmond." She denied it all. I told her she would have to go to Salisbury a prisoner until I could inquire into her case further. She begged not to be imprisoned there, so I sent her back to Gen. Pettigrew, commanding on the Blackwater, to have her sent back to her home. Now, during the siege of Suffolk, many persons told me that "she did go out of Suffolk in the carriage with an officer," etc. In 1866 she wrote me a letter declaring all I heard about her was false, and wishing me all sorts of bad things. All in all it would have been an interesting case for Sherlock Holmes.

Petersburg was under martial law, and to keep the city in peace and order was no small task. Men who were regarded respectable would sell liquor to the soldiers. To fine the offenders was useless. To end it, the suggestion was made that a court-martial should condemn the next offender to have his head shaved and wear a "barrel shirt," and be marched through the city two hours every day for ten days. That ended selling whisky. How would a dude look with his head shaved and protruding through a hole in the head of a barrel? Would the sun affect *his* intellect? The doctors reported that no ordinary person could endure it, so I remitted a part of the sentence.

One day the provost marshal arrested a blockade runner for not obeying his instructions. His goods were placed in a rented store, and J. A. Shingleur, of Columbus, Ga., and Sidney Lanier, of my signal corps, were detailed to sell them. The money was deposited in bank to my order. After the war was ended I gave the owner the funds. I have often wondered if that quiet, gentle soldier-poet remembered his experience as a merchant in Petersburg? Often he and a friend would come to my quarters and pass the evening with us, where the "alarums of war" were lost in the soft notes of their flutes, for Lanier was an excellent musician. I believe his cantata was sung at the opening of the World's Exposition held in Philadelphia in 1876.

Another duty was the exchange of prisoners on arrival at City Point of the flag of truce steamer. Our men were sent out to a camp I had, and thence to their commands. I never went to the flag of truce boat in all this while but once, and then I did not go aboard of her. I dismounted and took a seat on a box. All was quiet. The staging from the main deck rested on the wharf. On this deck, by the staging, were posted two soldiers with arms aground. On the upper deck were three or four United States soldiers. Their clothing was clean, neat, and new, and they wore unsoiled white cotton gloves. The wharf was guarded by a lone Confederate soldier. On his head was a straw hat, his raiment was butternut in color, his shoes were low-quartered, his hair and beard long. In countenance he was dignified, and his eye bright. To protect himself from the cold north wind, a brown blanket was tied, or pinned, in front around his neck, and as he turned to the north, pacing to and fro in front of the stage, his blanket would swing now east, now west, and on returning wrap him in its folds. He heeded not the neat clad enemy on the steamer, but walked his post with the conscious conviction that he was their peer in every walk of life. None of the soldiers leaning over the railing and looking down on him were commenting on his garb, or laughing at him. Battle had taught them to respect him. Still the contrast in clothing and comfort was marked.

CHAPTER XII.

ON March 1, 1863, I received a telegram from the Secretary of War stating that he wished to see me in regard to a change of service. The day following I called at the office of the Secretary, Hon. J. A. Seddon, and he expressed a desire that I would go to the city of Vicksburg to assist in the defense of that place. I did not give my assent, preferring to consider the matter. On the 3d I rode around the line of defensive works that I had constructed around Petersburg with Gen. Longstreet, and did not get back until 3 P.M.

I have already stated that on my return from Wilmington on the 23d of February, 1863, I found Gen. Longstreet in Petersburg in command of the divisions of Gens. Hood and Pickett. The main object of his coming was to provision his troops and forage his animals (until active service commenced requiring him to join Gen. Lee or otherwise) from the supplies in the adjoining counties of Virginia and the counties of North Carolina in the northeastern portion of the State, and be in readiness to join Gen. Lee promptly, which he said was arranged before he left Fredericksburg. (See Longstreet's "Memoirs," page 329.)

That the trains might move in safety, it was necessary to confine the Federal forces in the works around Suffolk and Norfolk. Accordingly about the middle of April Longstreet moved with his two divisions and one of mine on Suffolk. The approach of our troops was not discovered until the advance was in open view of the defenses around the city. Their pickets were quietly captured, and the lookout sentinel in an observatory on a platform in the top of a large pine tree in front of the city might have been captured also had it not been for the desire of one of the Confederates to take a shot at him while he was in the top, before any one had been sent near the base of the pine.   The man came down as lively as a squirrel, and the alarm was given.

The circumvallation of the city, in part, was made by Pickett's division on the right, mine in the center, and Hood's on the left, and thus the siege of Suffolk began.

When Gen. Longstreet had been in Petersburg some time, he said to me one day that he purposed to attack Suffolk after his preparations were made, and to take the trains and send them down into the seaboard counties for provisions.

The next thing I knew, April 9, he put his command in motion, and took from me a division and a number of batteries, and was on his way to Suffolk without informing me in any way of his designs, or of his wishes.*   The next day I put a staff officer in charge of the department headquarters, and with my other staff officers rode to Suffolk and took command of my own troops there that had been removed without sending the order through my office as courtesy required.   No doubt the object of such proceedings was to give the command of a division to Gen. M. Jenkins, a worthy and gallant officer, who had distinguished himself in the seven days' fight around Richmond.   On the morning of the 13th I took command of my own troops, the brigades of Pettigrew, Jenkins, and Davis, and my batteries.   I found Gen. Longstreet down near the front, where there was considerable artillery firing and skirmishing on the advanced line.   Longstreet asked me to accept the command of all the artillery, which I refused to do.   I told him I did not intend to give up the command of my division to any one, but that I was willing to give all the assistance I could, personally and through the

---

*This was a violation of military usages that both Gens. Andrew Jackson and Z. Taylor denounced.   Here is an extract from the order of Gen. Jackson:

HEADQUARTERS DIVISION OF THE SOUTH, }
NASHVILLE, April 22, 1817.   }

The commanding general considers it due to the principles which ought and must exist in an army to prohibit the obedience of any order emanating from the *Department of War* to officers of this division   .   .   .   unless coming through him as the proper organ of communication.   The object of this is to prevent the recurrence, etc.

Here we see Jackson forbidding obedience to any order to troops or officer in his command unless it was communicated to him first for his action.

chief of my artillery, to place in position guns to prevent gunboats going up and down the river; and, although my diary does
not mention it, all the artillery was ordered to report to me.   I
assigned all the batteries belonging to them to the *command of
the respective divisions*, and thus it was scattered along the line
for several miles, leaving me some spare batteries and a few
siege guns in charge of my chief of artillery.   But I will copy
from my diary:

Tuesday, 14th. Heavy skirmishing; rode to Pickett's Division and to
the extreme right of the line, and met Gen. Armstead there.

Wednesday, 15th. Started down the river with some artillery to endeavor to destroy the gunboats; found but one in the river, and it was too
far below. After getting guns in position withdrew them. Day very
rainy.

Thursday, 16th. Rode down the river and examined it for positions for
defense; met Longstreet at Mr. Riddick's place; then went to Mr. Le
Compte's house. We were invited to stay for dinner, but before it was
ready a gunboat opened fire on the house while we were resting in the
yard behind it and while the family were in it. After the second shot,
which went through it, we rode out into the field by the side of the house
in open sight. They did not fire at us (myself and four of my staff), but
all the while continued the attack on the dwelling, and over the heads of
the little children, who were on the lawn in front waving white handkerchiefs. The dwelling was built of brick, and was riddled with large
holes. The wonder to me was how the children escaped. As we were
leaving the field and the doctor had his hands on the latch of the gate to
open it, it was opened by a three-hundred-pound shell striking the post
that the gate was hung to, demolishing it.

17th. Last night I gave my consent that two guns from Stribbling's
battery be put in an old work that was to be garrisoned by two companies of Gen. Law's Brigade, and some guns from Martin's battery were
put in another work. A gunboat came up and opened fire on the fort
where the two Alabama companies were, without damage.

18th. Passed all day down the river. Got the two thirty-two pounders in position, ready to open to-morrow.

19th. This forenoon the gunboats came up, and the thirty-two pound-
er fired on them and drove them back. They were also attacked by some
sharpshooters.

Just before sunset the gunboats and several batteries of artillery
opened a very severe cross fire on the *fort* and over the plain in the rear
of the fort, where the two guns from Stribbling's battery had been placed
to aid the garrison. Pending this attack the enemy landed a strong infantry force, under cover of some timber, on our side of the river, carried the place by a sudden assault, and captured the *garrison,* consisting
of Companies A and B, Forty-Fourth Alabama Regiment, and a squad of
artillerymen.

11

I heard the distant firing about sunset, and at 9 P.M. I heard in camp that one of the forts in Hood's command had been captured. I went over to Longstreet's headquarters, and he asked me to go down and take command. On arrival I found on the ground there Gens. Hood and Law with Robertson's Brigade and Connelly's Fifty-Fifth North Carolina Regiment, and took command as I was ordered. The Fifty-Fifth North Carolina Regiment was advanced, but it was driven back in the darkness by the cross fire of the gunboats and the enemy in the captured works. It was so plain to any one who had a knowledge of the art of war that the enemy would not hold an isolated work on our side of the river, that I was not inclined to make an assault which would have sacrificed so many lives uselessly. Yet such was the order given by Longstreet.

20th. Remained in position till morning, when Longstreet arrived. Both Gens. Hood and Law strenuously insisted that no attack should be made to capture the works while the troops would be subjected to the severe cross fire over the neck of land from the enemy's fleet of vessels and the troops in the redoubt and artillery opposite on the other side of the river.

At 1 P.M. I turned the command over to Hood, or rather left him in command of his own troops, advising him to wait and let the enemy abandon the place, which they did. Soon after this Capt. Cussons, commander of Law's scouts, with a few men and a loud "yell," ran in the enemy's pickets, and entered the works with them. They went on out, and left Cussons to hold the empty fort.

22d. If that redoubt, which gave support to our left flank (that otherwise would have been "in air"), was worth a great sacrifice of life to recapture it, as ordered by Longstreet, then certainly it was in accord with the science of war to place two guns on the works to strengthen and protect the left flank of his army.*

---

* Longstreet reiterates the story of the capture of the battery in his book, but is silent about the garrison or the capture of the redoubt. Therefore I will append a statement handed to me by George Reese, an honored citizen of Pensacola, Fla. My account is from my diary; his is from memory. He writes:

"I was a lieutenant in Company A, Forty-Fourth Alabama Infantry, Law's Brigade, Hood's Division, Longstreet's Corps, and was with my command at the investment of Suffolk in 1863. On the 18th day of April, while in line, Companies A and K received orders, about 8 P.M., to move. I think we numbered fifty men, all told. We were marched about two miles to the left of Longstreet's army.

We arrived at an old fort, or rather redoubt, exposed on the land side, but protected by a high embankment on the river side. In this fort we found two guns of Stribbling's battery, with their complement of gunners. This whole force, with the two guns, was captured on the 19th of April, near 6 P.M. About 1 P.M. the enemy opened a terrific fire on the fort from a great number of guns massed on the opposite side of the river and from the gunboats and infantry. Under cover of this fire a transport landed about a thousand men behind a point of land extending into the river just above the fort, concealed by thick undergrowth. They were within one hundred yards of the fort when discovered. It was natural that the infantry should blame Gen. Longstreet for thus placing so small a force so far away from support, and loud complaints were heard from both men and officers. We were taken to Suffolk the same night and next morning to Norfolk, and two weeks after exchanged.   GEORGE REESE, *Lieut. Co. A, Forty-Fourth Alabama.*

"Pensacola, Fla., March 1897."

I am tired of *volunteering* against gunboats any more, and declined having anything to do with the line defended by Gen. Hood because of a communication received from the general commanding saying I was "in charge of the river defenses." To have charge of the river defenses involves more or less the command of all the army. I really had officially nothing to do with the river defenses, only I *voluntarily placed* two large siege guns in position to be used in attacking any boats passing up or down the river. Connally's Regiment was a support for these two guns.

23d. Confined myself to the immediate command of my division, and took no more interest in Hood's line, and ordered Connally's Regiment to join his brigade.

24th and 25th. There was some skirmishing.

26th. Rode down with Gen. Longstreet to the Whitemarsh road. Gone all day. The line there is commanded by Gen. Armstead.

And now come the Richmond papers proclaiming: "From Suffolk—Gen. French lost Stribbling's battery." Mark you, no mention of the capture of the *fort;* no mention of the capture of the *two companies* that garrisoned it. It would not do to have it reported that the Yankees crossed the Nansemond yesterday and captured a fort on our side of the river by assault. The garrison, composed of two companies of the Forty-Fourth Alabama Regiment of Law's Brigade, Hood's Division, were taken prisoners and the two guns were lost. But it will not do to let this be known. No, no; write it down thus: "Yesterday Gen. French lost Stribbling's battery." The world is too busy to inquire, and the world will believe it. The truth is, I was never in the fort, *never saw it.* I had no authority over the garrison, and I was in no way responsible for the loss of the redoubt, the garrison, or guns.

The most remarkable feature of this little affair is the persistency with which headquarters proclaimed that "French lost Stribling's battery," and were silent about the infantry garrison captured, etc. I will give two letters here from the War Records:

HEADQUARTERS NEAR SUFFOLK, April 21, 1863.

Maj. Gen. D. H. Hill, Goldsboro.

Gen. Longstreet is closely engaged to-night, and he has asked me to write you briefly the particulars of the affair of Sunday night which resulted in the capture by the enemy of Stribbling's battery. Several batteries had been planted on the Nansemond to hold the river against the passage of gunboats and transports. Stribbling's occupied an old uninclosed work on Hill's Point, a tongue of land a little above the confluence of Western Branch and Nansemond. About dark on the evening of the 19th the enemy opened a severe fire from his field batteries planted opposite, and his gunboats above and below the fort, entirely sweeping with a cross fire the plain in the rear of the work. Under cover of this fire and darkness they landed a force, not more than one hundred and fifty strong, a very little distance from the fort, rushed upon its rear, and surprised and captured its garrison.

The artillery on the river was directly under the management of Maj. Gen. French. There were five guns, fifty-five artillerists, and seventy infantry (sharpshooters) in the fort, which all fell into the hands of the enemy.

The affair is regarded as a most remarkable and discreditable instance of an entire absence of vigilance. A regiment (Fifty-Fifth North Carolina and seven hundred strong) which Gen. Longstreet had particularly ordered to the vicinity for the protection of the battery was not posted in supporting distance. No official report of the affair has yet been received from Gen. French. The captured guns were carried across the river. It is some consolation that *only* the guns and ammunition chests were lost. The horses and ammunition carriages, being considerably in the rear of the battery, were saved. We are otherwise quite comfortable here. The quartermasters and commissaries are actively engaged in getting out supplies.

I am, General, very respectfully your obedient servant,

G. M. SORREL, *Assistant Adjutant General.**

This letter comes from the headquarters of Gen. Longstreet, and should be a careful account; whereas it contains errors in stating occurrences well known at the time it was written. I will point out some of the errors:

1. Only a small part of Stribbling's battery was captured by the enemy.

2. Stribbling's battery was not in the redoubt, as stated, in numbers.

3. The estimate that the enemy's force was not over one hundred and fifty differs very much from that of Lieut. George Reese, who was an officer of one of the companies forming the garrison that was captured, who writes it was near one thousand.

4. "The artillery on the river was directly under the command of Maj. Gen. French" is an error, as I declined it the day of my arrival, only I voluntarily offered to assist in checking the gunboats passing up or down the river.

5. It states that "there were *five guns*, fifty-five artillerists, and seventy infantry captured by the enemy;" whereas it was known to the entire army by the 21st, the date of this letter, that only *two guns and about eighteen artillerists* were lost when

---

*See Vol. LI., Part 11. Serial No. 108, War Records, page 692.

the redoubt fell by the capture of the garrison. No horses, caissons, harness, forge, etc., were in the fort. They were in camp.

6. Gen. Longstreet did not particularly order the Fifty-Fifth North Carolina Regiment to that vicinity for the protection of the battery. It was one of the regiments of my command, and I sent it down to support two thirty-two-pounders that Col. Cunningham had mounted at a place we had selected farther down the river. The "protection" to the two guns at the fort *was the garrison Hood sent to the fort* and such other as he directed. The better explanation is, the guns were asked of me to aid the garrison.

7. The statement that "no official report of the affair has yet been received from Gen. French" is misleading, and a report from me would have been supererogatory. The report of that "affair" was strictly a matter between the general commanding and Gen. Hood, who commanded the division and placed the garrison in the fort to protect his extreme left, then "in air."

8. When headquarters announced that "it was some little consolation that only five guns and ammunition chests were lost," it may have been joyous that *only* the garrison was lost instead of the whole of Hood's Division, of which it formed a part.

9. I must give Gen. Longstreet's adjutant general the manliness to be the only officer in Longstreet's Corps who has, in any manner or form, put on record the fact, directly or indirectly, that there was a garrison placed in that redoubt by order of Longstreet, or Hood, or both, and it was captured by the enemy, and with the garrison went the two guns. To the world has the publication gone that Gen. French lost Stribbling's battery.

10. If it be creditable for headquarters to publish that "this affair is regarded as a most remarkable and discreditable instance of an entire *absence* of vigilance" on my part, then I claim it is proper for me to remark that this effusion from the head of this army may be also "regarded as a most remarkable and discreditable instance of an entire *absence* of correctness in stating that affair."

There was no doubt a want of vigilance; and if Gen. Longstreet had desired, he could have learned whether the commander of the garrison put out pickets or not.   He could have ascertained *what orders* were given the commander by his colonel, or Gen. Law, or by Gen. Hood, and fixed the responsibility where it belonged.   Who put the garrison there, and what instructions were given the commander? embraces the question.   He says he "particularly ordered Col. Connally's regiment there himself for the protection of this battery," which is an error.

Like the ghost of Banquo, Stribbling's battery rises up again at headquarters and will not out.

HEAQUARTERS NEAR SUFFOLK, April 20, 1863, 7 P.M.

Br'g. Gen. H. L Benning, Commanding Brigade.

Your communication of 3 A.M. to-day has been received.   .   .   .   The cannonade that you heard last night arose from a successful effort of the enemy to capture one of our batteries on the river.   Under cover of darkness and the fire of his gunboats and land batteries he landed a force near Hill's Point, and *took possession of Stribbling's battery by a surprise.*

I am, General, very respectfully your obedient servant.

G. M. SORREL, *Assistant Adjutant General.**

I now will continue my diary:

27th, 28th, and 29th.   Passed most of the day examining the line between my right and Gen. Garnett.   Reported to Gen. Longstreet.   Spoke's Run is no barrier to infantry.   To-day, the 29th, orders came for *Gen. Longstreet to join Gen. Lee immediately*.   He sent for me and told me he was ordered to join Gen. Lee with his *two divisions;* but that he could not go, as his wagons sent for supplies had not returned.   I made no reply, but thought it strange, considering all the company wagons, etc., he required to move were in the camp.

30th.   "Waiting for the wagons" is still the song.   Terrible thunderstorm.   Lightning injured a number of men.

Friday, May 1.   This afternoon about 4 P.M. the enemy was found in line of battle.   One regiment, said to have been the Fifty-Ninth New York, advanced on my picket lines and were handsomely repulsed by Col. Connally's regiment.   In supporting his men in the pits he lost ten men.   The enemy shelled the plain furiously for an hour and a half in my front.   Courier came and said they were advancing on the Fifty-Fifth and fighting like h—l.   I rode over to Jenkins, and we galloped to the front.   Ordered Connally to send support to his pickets, and it was done valiantly.   The enemy lost over forty men.   By sunset all was quiet.   This was a demonstration in favor of Hooker, who was now at Chancellorsville.

May 2.   All was quiet last night, more so than usual, and now up to 6 P.M. all is still save an occasional gun and a little picket-firing, and this continued during the night.   Received to-day general instructions to withdraw to the Blackwater.

* From War Records, page 692, Serial No. 108.

May 3. This morning sent to the rear all spare articles, baggage, etc. At 11 A.M. Gen. Longstreet started for Franklin, and left me in command of the army to withdraw it. Heavy firing down the river, and the enemy is shelling the railroad crossing. Captured men report Gen. Dix in command in Suffolk. Some Yankees came over the river with sugar and coffee to trade.

The skirmishing on the left was very heavy, and I sent down one regiment to support Gen. Anderson, and moved Davis's Brigade to the left about a mile. I am now informed that Gen. Longstreet did not go at 11 A.M. as he expected to do. At sunset the firing on the left still continued, and the order to withdraw was countermanded. About 7 P.M. I received orders from Maj. Latrobe to withdraw in half an hour. I then ordered up the supports from the railroad, and directed the men in the advanced rifle pits to be withdrawn at 11:20. At 10 the column was in motion, and we marched steadily the distance of six miles. . . . Arriving at the junction of the South Quay and Summerton roads, I learned that all Maj. Mitchell's trains had crossed the Blackwater, and Pickett's wagons were now passing on to the river to cross. Being thus advised, the division was halted, and I rode on to look for a good position to form line of battle to defend the crossing in case the enemy should pursue. I found an admirable position, and disposed my forces accordingly. Pickett's Division came up, and I left Col. Bratten, with two regiments and a battery of artillery, *to remain with the cavalry* to guard the *South Quay road*. This was on the morning of the 4th.

4th. In the afternoon received orders to cross over the river, and that when all were over to ride up to see him (Longstreet). The orders of the General left me but two brigades for the defense of the line from the James river to the Chowan river.

5th. Started this morning for Ivor; posted Davis at the Blackwater bridge. . . . Rode on to Zuni. I found Longstreet was in Petersburg, and, as there were two trains ready to leave, I determined to ride up and ascertain why he wished to see me, and try and get a third brigade. I sent Feribee's regiment down to the Isle of Wight to find out where the enemy was. I left Zuni at 2 P.M., and reached Petersburg at 3:50 P.M. I called on Longstreet as directed. I could not induce him to leave me the third brigade. . . . I then asked of him permission to remain in Petersburg until the morning, which he granted. Soon after a communication was handed me in which the general commanding "expressed surprise that I was in the city, and asked me to explain what induced me to abandon my command." I had a locomotive waiting to take me back to Zuni, or Franklin, as occasioned required; but considering the General told me I could remain, and by reason of this artful note, I determined not to leave anyhow under such an imputation. He may have lost his temper at Lee's victory at Chancellorsville without him.

6th. Wrote this morning to the President and asked for a court of inquiry.

Now, while on this subject, I will state that the request was not granted. Gen. J. R. Davis informed me that the President said to him my course needed no vindication, and Gen. Davis knew all the facts, and I presume he stated them to the President. I wanted the court to investigate the cause of the surprise and capture of the garrison and Stribbling's two guns, and other matters named in my application for the court, if it were granted.

I will explain, although it is a trifling matter, why I went to Petersburg. First, Longstreet wrote me to call and *see* him as soon as my command crossed the Blackwater, but he left before I passed over. Next, when I got to Zuni I had posted my troops all in their old positions on the line of the Blackwater as they were before Longstreet moved them to Suffolk; no Longstreet was at Zuni.

Secondly, Petersburg was my headquarters, and from there I could communicate with Zuni and Franklin, on the Blackwater, by telegraph and railroad, and be in either place in a short time.

Thirdly, Longstreet left Franklin without turning the command of his two divisions over to me, and I presumed he was pressing forward with his command to the aid of Gen. Lee at Chancellorsville, who had called him to his assistance on the 27th of April, and so often afterwards. Continuing, my diary says:

Busy the balance of the day in my office with official business. I did not leave the city until 9 P.M., when I took the cars for Franklin. I arrived there after 11 P.M. Found all quiet. Whilst I was in Petersburg Gen. Hood was impressing horses for cavalry service. Carriages, wagons, carts, etc., from which the horses were unhitched, were left in the streets.

8th. Changed headquarters to-day to Ivor. . . .

9th. Arrived at Ivor at 10 A.M. Gen. J. R. Davis left to-day on leave.

13th. Went to Petersburg and remained there all day following.

15th. Started for Richmond. Saw Gens. Lee, Elzy, Cooper, Ransom, Ewell, and others. Dined with the Hon. Judge James Perkins. In the evening I went to the President's. I found him ill and suffering with a cough. I took tea with them. . . .

16th. Saw the Secretary of War this morning. Spoke to him about leave of absence. Said it could not be granted. . . .

23d. Went to the Blackwater bridge, where Jenkins's Brigade was. For exercise to the troops crossed over the river to feel the enemy, in force, on the other side. I took about three thousand men and four batteries of artillery. Col. Green, with two Mississippi regiments, advanced and drove in their pickets, and captured some property. Could not draw them out to attack us. After dark withdrew.

Wednesday, 27th. Went to Petersburg, intending to go to Fort Powhatan. Found there a dispatch informing me that I would be ordered on the day following to report to Gen. J. E. Johnston in Mississippi.

29th. No orders having been received, I went to Richmond to see about taking staff officers with me. Gen. Cooper could allow me only my aids. Finally the Secretary of War gave me permission to take my adjutant general, assistant adjutant general, quartermaster, and orderly. The Secretary of War told me that Gen. Joseph E. Johnston had applied for an officer of the rank of major general, and as they knew I was acquainted with the country, he had ordered me, etc.

As I had once been called on to submit a plan for the defense of the Mississippi river, and complied with the request, it might have had some influence on the action of the Secretary. Besides, I had once declined duty at Vicksburg. (See letters from the President to Gen. Lee, War Records, page 716, Vol. LI., No. 108 Serial, suggesting that I be sent to Mississippi.)

Before I take leave of the arduous duties I had been performing, of defending a line three hundred miles in length, of exchange of prisoners, examining correspondence, obtaining supplies, etc., I will refer to some matters again relating to the siege of Suffolk, about which I made no report. I have alluded to Gen. Longstreet taking my troops without consulting me, and his movements on to Suffolk, and his attempts to have Gen. Jenkins keep the command of them. I am quite sure it was Hood's chief of artillery who asked my artillery officer for guns to place in the works on the Nansemond river, and to which I gave my consent. It was not Gen. Law, because he protested when ordered to garrison the fort. But this matters not. The garrison and the guns formed a part of Hood's command, and yet (I am told) both Pollard and a clerk in the Rebel War Office state in their books that I lost "Stribbling's battery;" and yet, most erroneous of all, Longstreet in *his book* states "that a battery was put on a *neck of land* and captured by the enemy." He fails to state that the *fort and garrison therein* were captured, which of course includes the arms and the guns.

The great events of war often hinge on some small matter not obvious to an ordinary commander, but which, at a glance, would be visible to the eye of the great captain, and provided for in his plans for a victory. The commander of a remote supporting corps is presumed, when alone, to be able to consider carefully everything that might occur to prevent an immediate compliance with any expected order, especially that of a prompt and rapid movement to the aid of his chief, the moment the call is made; and *Longstreet awaited that call.*

Now from Suffolk to Zuni messages were passed rapidly by the best of signal men. Thence by telegraph to Petersburg, Richmond, and on to Gen. Lee. On the 21st of April Gen. Lee reported the enemy was at Kelly's Ford; that Hooker was putting his army in motion; the 28th they crossed the Rappahannock; the 29th they crossed the Rapidan, and skirmishing commenced near Chancellorsville. On the 30th the armies were face to face.

From this it will be seen that Gen. Lee sounded the notes of warning to Longstreet as early as the *21st of April*, and Norris on the 21st (as chief signal officer) informed him Hooker was moving with one hundred and fifty thousand men, nine days before he crossed the Rappahannock near Chancellorsville and was confronted by Lee. As soon as the plans or intentions of the enemy were further divined. Lee took measures to concentrate his forces. To Gen. Longstreet, with his army corps at Suffolk, he sent urgent dispatches, ten of which I copy from the War Department Records (Vol. 25, Part 2) as follows:

No. 1. PAGE 763.

GEN. COOPER TO GEN. LEE.

RICHMOND, May 1, 1863.

Gen. R. E. Lee, Fredericksburg. Va.

Orders were sent on Wednesday (the 29th of April) to Gen. Longstreet to move forward his command to reënforce you. He replied he would do so immediately, but expected to be a little delayed in gathering up his transportation train to prevent its falling into the hands of the enemy, then in sight.   S. COOPER, *Adjutant and Inspector General.*

No. 2. PAGE 752

R. E. LEE TO THE PRESIDENT.

HEADQUARTERS, ARMY OF NORTHERN VIRGINIA, *April 27, 1863.*

His Excellency, Jefferson Davis, President of the Confederate St tes.

Mr. President: I have written to Gen. Longstreet to expedite, as much as possible, his operations in North Carolina, as I may be obliged to call him back at any moment. . . .   R. E. LEE, *General.*

No. 3. PAGE 757.

GEN. S. COOPER TO GEN. D. H. HILL.

RICHMOND, VA., April 29. 1863.

Maj. Gen. D. H. Hill, Commanding, Goldsboro, N. C.

General: The following telegram has just been received from Gen. Lee:

ROBERT E. LEE

JAMES LONGSTREET

The enemy is crossing below Deep Run, about the same place as before. . . . Where his main efforts will be made I cannot say. Troops not wanted south of James river had better be moved in this direction, and all other necessary preparations made.

This renders it important that such forces as you deem judicious should be concentrated at Richmond, to be in supporting distance. Gen. Lee may telegraph you. . . . *A like dispatch has been sent to Lieut. Gen. Longstreet.*

I am, General, very respectfully, your obedient servant,

S. COOPER, *Adjutant and Inspector General.*

No. 4. PAGE 757.
GEN. COOPER TO GEN. LONGSTREET.

Gen. Longstreet.

The following dispatch has just been received from Gen. Lee:

FREDERICKSBURG, VA., April 29, 1863.

The enemy is in large force on the north bank of the Rappahannock opposite the railroad at Hamilton's crossing. He is crossing troops below the point at which he crossed in December. . . . I hear of no other point at which he is crossing except below Kelly's Ford, where Gen. Howard has crossed with his division, said to be fourteen thousand, six pieces of artillery, and some cavalry. . . . All available troops had better be sent forward as rapidly as possible.

S. COOPER, *Adjutant and Inspector General.*

No. 5. PAGE 758.
GEN. COOPER TO GEN. LONGSTREET.

ADJUTANT AND INSPECTOR GENERAL'S OFFICE, ⎫
RICHMOND, VA., April 29, 1863. ⎬

Lieut. Gen Longstreet.

The following telegram just received since the one already communicated to you:

If any troops can be sent by rail to Gordonsville, under a good officer, I recommend it. Longstreet's Division, if available, *had better come to me;* and the troops for Gordonsville and the protection of the railroad, from Richmond and North Carolina if practicable. Gen. Howard, of the enemy's forces making toward Gordonsville. . . .

The Secretary, in view of the above, *directs the return of your command,* or at least such portions of it as can be spared without serious risk; also any surplus force that can be spared from D. H. Hill. . . . These movements are required to be made with *the utmost dispatch.*

S. COOPER, *Adjutant and Inspector General.*

No. 6. PAGE 758.
SECRETARY SEDDON TO GEN. COOPER.

WAR DEPARTMENT, C. S. A., April 29, 1863.

Gen. Cooper.

Dear General: Gen. Lee telegraphs that all available force at our com-

mand be sent at once by rail or otherwise toward Gordonsville. . . .
Telegraph French at Petersburg to send all available force at his command. . . .   J. A. SEDDON, *Secretary of War.*

No. 7. Page 758.

SECRETARY OF WAR TO GEN. COOPER.

WAR OFFICE, RICHMOND, April 29, 1863.
Gen. Cooper.

Gen. Lee, by another telegram just sent the President, says: ". . .
Longstreet's Division, if available, had better come to me. . . ."

                                         J. A. SEDDON, *Secretary.*

No. 8. Page 760.

GEN. COOPER TO GEN. LONGSTREET.

RICHMOND, VA., April 30, 1863.
Lieut. Gen. James Longstreet, Suffolk, Va.

Move without delay your command to this place, to effect a junction
with Gen. Lee.   S. COOPER, *Adjutant and Inspector General.*

No. 9. Page 761.

GEN. LEE TO PRESIDENT DAVIS.

FREDERICKSBURG, April 30, 1863.
His Excellency, President Davis.

   . . . Enemy was still crossing the Rappahannock at 5 P.M. yesterday. . . . Object evidently to turn my left. . . . If I had Longstreet's Division, I would feel safe.   R. E. LEE, *General.*

No. 10. Page 765.

GEN. LONGSTREET TO GEN. COOPER.

SUFFOLK, VA., May 2, 1863.
Gen. Cooper.

   I cannot move unless the entire force is moved; and it would then take
several days to reach Fredericksburg. I will endeavor to move as soon as
possible.   JAMES LONGSTREET, *Lieutenant General Commanding.*

" Responsibility cannot exist without a name," or an object.

Perhaps Longstreet delayed to execute these orders for the
reason he states (page 329), that there was a " plan of battle
projected "—that is, " to *stand behind our intrenched lines and
await the return of my troops from Suffolk.*" "And my impression is that Gen. Lee, standing under his trenches, would
have been stronger against Hooker than he was in December
against Burnside, and he would have *grown stronger every*

hour of delay." "By the time the divisions of Pickett and Hood could have joined Gen. Lee, Hooker would have found that he must march to attack or make a retreat without battle. It *seems* probable that under *the original plan* the battle would have *given fruits worthy* of a general engagement."

Longstreet's first dispatch *disclosed his intentions to Lee*, and Lee wisely decided not to wait ten or twelve days for Longstreet to join him. Moreover, it is not probable that Lee thought Hooker would be so knightly as to await the arrival of the Suffolk troops before giving battle. Longstreet does not deal even in the conjectural, for it is not based on any evidence; he merely guesses.

But it is better to deal with the possible.

Two brigades could have been withdrawn from before Suffolk on the night of the 27th of April and sent to join Gen. Lee, then the main force on the night of the 28th. There is no doubt about this. In this event the enemy could have passed the 29th in discovering our intentions. Rather than crossing the Nansemond river and giving us battle, they would have awaited orders, and probably been sent to Fredericksburg to aid Hooker; but this is not important.

On the 28th he could have ordered Gen. D. H. Hill, then at Goldsboro, to have protected the train, called on Whiting at Wilmington for aid, while I had a division at Franklin on the Blackwater, and forces elsewhere which would no doubt have saved the train from the enemy. His first dispatch is very misleading, and does not convey the idea that he would sit down and wait six days for the wagons before he withdrew. While this was going on at Suffolk, the heroic "Stonewall" Jackson was marching to the right and rear of Hooker's army, and when it was announced to him that the enemy *was* capturing *his* wagon train, without checking the walk of his horse he said: "Do not let them capture any ammunition wagons." What value were his baggage wagons compared to the loss of even a few minutes in accomplishing the great object of his movement, on which victory depended. To his master mind before him was the enemy, the impending battle, the victory, and the reward due to genius of battle, with all the spoils of war strewn in the conqueror's path. And it was so. And thus it was that Longstreet, by not effecting a junction with Lee, "put the *cause* upon the hazard of a *die*, crippling it in resources and future progress." (See Longstreet, p. 330.)

Mark Antony, in his speech over the dead Cæsar, said: "Power in most men has brought their faults to light. Power in Cæsar brought into prominence his excellencies."

So power given Lee made known to the world the nobility of his character and greatness as a commander; while in others it disclosed a spirit of envy and a desire for detraction; and in all some peculiarities. Lee was not conscious of his strength, because his greatness of soul was derived from his goodness of heart, and it rested upon him with the ease and grace of a garment. His generosity induced him to overlook the frailty incident to humanity, and to forgive even disobedience in his lieutenants. He remembered what Job said about a book, and wrote none. He envied no one. He left no writings extant naming an enemy, and his harshest remark in reference to an officer of high rank was, in effect, that he was "slow to move."

The official reports show that Hooker had 161,491 men and 400 guns. Lee's forces numbered 58,100 men, with 170 guns. This was known to Lee's lieutenants.

The publication of the Official Record by Congress discloses the fact that Mr. Seddon induced Gen. Lee to send Gen. Longstreet with Hood's and Pickett's Divisions to cover Richmond, which he thought menaced from Fortress Monroe and Suffolk. Lee thought Pickett's Division sufficient. (Official Record, Vol. 22, p. 623.)

I had the name and reported strength of every regiment in both Suffolk and Norfolk, obtained from blockade runners and verified by prisoners. Suffolk had no strategic value to the enemy of any import, and none to us. In 1862 I designed the taking of Suffolk, and on an appointed day assembled some eight or nine thousand troops at Franklin, on the Blackwater. The only officers who had any knowledge of this were Gens. G. W. Smith, in Richmond, and J. J. Pettigrew. It was stopped, the morning the troops assembled, by Gen. G. W. Smith on strategic grounds and it not being a depot of supplies: and he was right. And when Secretary Seddon, against Lee's advice, joined with Longstreet in moving on Suffolk so late in the spring, he or Longstreet committed an error, the consequence of which was Lee had to fight Hooker with the force just stated, without the aid of his lieutenant general. Who was it, then, that put the "Confederacy on the hazard of a die?"

Hooker would never have embarked his great army on the Potomac at Aquia, and carried them back where they had once been under Gen. McClellan, and Richmond was not in danger, and Longstreet's expedition to Suffolk not in accordance with grand strategy; and but for Lee's audacity, and Stonewall Jackson's swift movements and vigorous blows at Chancellorsville, the Confederacy would have been there shattered into fragments, and all by one false movement to Suffolk.

"Fortune loves a daring suitor."

Lee threw down the iron glove, and the daring suitor won! It was the most remarkable victory of the war, but by the absence of those divisions, and the death of Stonewall Jackson, the large fruits of the victory were lost.

12

CHAPTER XIII.

ON Wednesday, June 3, 1863, I started in accordance with
orders from Petersburg to report to Gen. J. E. Johnston
in Mississippi. I arrived in Jackson on the 10th. Next day
reported for duty; but as I had not been home since I joined the
army, and the service was not pressing, got permission to visit my family. I went by stage to Yazoo City, and by chance
met my neighbor, F. A. Metcalf, there, and together we crossed
the Yazoo bottoms. Riding horseback, sixty-five miles the last
day, I reached my home on Deer Creek at 11 P.M., and found my
mother, sister, and little daughter, aged nearly eight years, all
well. I remained at home Monday, the 15th, and started back
on the 16th. Before I reached home Mr. Bowie, my agent, had
gone to Georgia with seventy-eight of my negro servants, leaving twenty-five here to cultivate a corn crop. I joined my division, composed of the brigades of Gens. Maxey, McNair, and
Evans, on the 24th, encamped at Mrs. Carraway's, in Madison
County, near Livingston; put Gen. Evans in arrest by order
of Gen. Johnston. I was in camp the 25th and the two days
following.

Before proceeding any further in reference to military matters
in Mississippi, I will give some rich correspondence that took
place between Gen. Johnston and President Davis and which I
knew nothing about until months after it occurred. Here it is.
(See page 195, War Records, Serial 36.)

JOSEPH E. JOHNSTON

WILLIAM T. SHERMAN

CANTON, MISS., June 9, 1863. }
Via Montgomery, June 10. }

His Excellency, President Davis.

It has been suggested to me that the troops in this department are very hostile to officers of Northern birth, and that on that account Maj. Gen. French's arrival will weaken instead of strengthening us. I beg you to consider that *all* the general officers of Northern birth are on duty in this department. There is now a want of major generals (discipline). It is important to avoid any cause of further discontent. J. E. JOHNSTON.

THE ANSWER.

RICHMOND, VA., June 11, 1863.

Gen. J. E. Johnston.

Your dispatch received. Those who suggest that the arrival of Gen. French will produce discontent among the troops because of his Northern birth are not probably aware that he is a citizen of Mississippi, was a wealthy planter until the Yankees robbed him; and, before the Confederate States had an army, was the chief of ordnance and artillery in the force Mississippi raised to maintain her right of secession. As soon as Mississippi could spare him he was appointed a brigadier general in the Provisional Army of the Confederate States, and has frequently been before the enemy where he was the senior officer. If malignity should undermine him, as it had another, you are authorized to notify him of the fact and to relieve him, communicating it to me by telegram.

Surprised by your remark as to the general officers of Northern birth, I turned to the register, and find that a large majority of the number are elsewhere than in the Department of Mississippi and eastern Louisiana.

JEFFERSON DAVIS.

Men of Northern birth who held high rank in the Confederacy: Samuel Cooper, general, New Jersey; Josiah Gorgas, chief of ordnance, Pennsylvania; John C. Pemberton, general, Pennsylvania; Charles Clark, general and Governor of Mississippi, Ohio; Daniel Ruggles, general, Massachusetts; Walter H. Stevens, general, New York; Julius A. DeLagnel, New Jersey; John R. Cooke, general, Missouri; R. S. Ripley, general, Ohio; Hoffman Stevens, general, Connecticut; Samuel G. French, general, New Jersey; Bushrod R. Johnson, general, Ohio; James L. Alcorn, general, Illinois (was Governor and United States Senator); Danville Leadbetter, general, Maine; Archibald Gracie, general, New York; William McComb, general, Pennsylvania; Otho French Strahl, general, Ohio; Daniel M. Frost, general, New York; Albert G. Blanchard, general, Massachusetts; Johnson K. Duncan, general, Pennsylvania; Albert Pike, general, Massachusetts; Daniel H. Reynolds, general, Ohio; Edward Aylesworth Perry, general, Massachusetts; Francis A.

Shoup, general, Indiana; Martin L. Smith, general, New York; Franklin Gardner, general, New York.

A brief sketch of these men was published in the *Atlanta Constitution* by Prof. J. T. Derry. The number is twenty-six, and twelve of them were educated at West Point. They believed in the right of States to secede, and, owing allegiance to the States where they lived or wished to reside, they cast their lot with the South.

July 1, 1863. Moved to some springs on the Vernon and Brownsville road.

2d. Moved at 4 A.M.; marched through Brownsville. I slept under a tree last night, but have an abandoned house to-night.

3d. Rode over to meet Gen. Johnston. There were present Gens. Loring, W. H. T. Walker, Jackson, and myself. If there be any one thing in this part of the country more difficult than all others, it is to find a person who knows the roads ten miles from his home. *Nine* hours were spent in vainly attempting to get accurate information from the citizens respecting the roads and streams. But little could be learned of the country on either side of the Big Black that was satisfactory, because it was so contradictory.

July 4. Anniversary of a declaration that was read eighty-seven years ago, and which awakened a benighted world to the fact that man was born with certain inalienable rights. All was still in the direction of Vicksburg. What does it portend? No firing there yet, and it is 12 M. But there is always something to mar one's pleasure or disturb his rest, for now came the news that the enemy had crossed Messenger's Ferry, on the Big Black. . . .

5th. Remained in camp. Some skirmishing on the Big Black. The order of Gen. Johnston to cross the Big Black and attack Grant's new line *was issued*. I soon after received news of the surrender of Vicksburg, and it was determined to fall back toward Jackson. The enemy's camp fires extend about three miles on the other side of the stream. . . .

6th. My division in advance. Moved by Queen's Hill Church to some ponds near Clinton. The day was very hot and the dust simply awful. I took breakfast with J. E. Davis, brother of the President. . . .

8th. We reached Jackson yesterday at 2 P.M. Enemy at Clinton. I rode around with Gen. Johnston to examine the line. It is miserably located and not half completed.

9th. This morning I was awakened at 2 A.M. to take my division to the trenches.

10th. All day there has been heavy fighting. In front of Gen. Evans the enemy has got so near that they render it difficult to man the guns. . . .

11th. The order of the divisions of the army that encircle Jackson, from the river above the city to the river below, is as follows, beginning on the right: Loring, Walker, French, and Breckinridge. Fighting commenced early this morning, and the firing was rapid all along the line. About 11

A.M. we drove the enemy from their lines and burned a number of houses that they occupied.

From now on to the 16th the usual occurrences of cannonading, dismounting pieces, fighting all the time, continued. Cotton bales were set on fire that were used for breastworks, flags of truce to bury the dead passed, shells are falling all over the town. The Governor of the State, Pettus, is in the city about the capitol. He goes over the river at night to prevent being captured. He believes the main object of the expedition is to capture *him*. Well, he has his early wishes gratified. The Yankees have set their feet on the sacred soil of his domain! Where are his double-barrel shotguns to ambuscade the Yankees?

16th. Met at Gen. Johnston's to consider the order of evacuating the town. At 10 P.M. troops were withdrawn from the trenches, and at 1 A.M. the advanced skirmishers. We reached Brandon at 8 A.M. Two of Evans's men were left, accidentally, on the skirmish line with some amateur soldiers, and in the morning when they awoke they found themselves alone. The enemy did not discover our departure until late.

While in camp near Brandon I was taken sick with remittent fever, and was granted a leave of absence and left for Columbus, Ga., and made my home with Judge G. E. Thomas. When my leave was out I received a dispatch from Gen. J. E. Johnston to remain in Columbus, as I would be required as a witness for him before a Court of Inquiry to be held in Atlanta.

I remained in Columbus and at the Warm Springs most of the month of September, and then went to Enterprise, Miss.

October 19. Received a dispatch to move to Meridian, prepared to take the field. Found the President at the hotel, and had an interview with him alone.

November 7. Moved my command to Meridian.

14th. Started to make a visit to my family at my home in Washington County. I took with me Lieut. James R. Yerger, one of my aids, and Levi, one of my servants.

16th. We left Canton with two cavalrymen as a guard; crossed the Yazoo at Yazoo City. About sunset we reached Col. Fall's plantation, on Deer Creek. The enemy had passed there the day previous. Crossing the creek at Judge Ruck's plantation (Judge Ruck is my aid's grandfather), we met an old negro man leading a pony over the bridge. Lieut. Yerger knew the old man, and asked what he was doing with the pony. He said the Yankees were on the creek about three miles below my house, and he was saving his pony. In the dark we were not recognized by the old servant.

But for meeting this old servant we should have ridden into the camp of the Yankees. After a while we recrossed the creek and rode on up to Eleck Yerger's, called him up, and slept in his parlor. He confirmed the negro's statement about the Yankees being on the other side of the creek. I got a cup of coffee, or something else (think it was the latter), and rode on up the creek till we got opposite my house.

It is the 19th of November. Indian summer: the sky hazy, and a drowsy sleepiness rested over the landscape. Seeing a crow resting himself on the front gatepost, I dismounted and crossed to my home. I found mother, sister, and my little Tillie all well. They were surprised and delighted to see us, and then they were frightened also. They said the Yankees were a mile or two above us, and two miles below us.

20th. I put a faithful male slave on the upper gallery to watch the roads, and especially to report if any dust was raised on the road, and then I was content for the day. However I thought the "Yanks" were too near, and that my being at home would be made known, so I ordered the horses to be at the door at 5 P.M. to ride down the creek to a neighbor's ten miles below, and the family to come down next day to where I was going. I was implored not to go, but I resisted entreaties. We rode across the plantation to Metcalf's house. My servant knocked at the door and received no response. Mrs. Metcalf came out by a side door and exclaimed: "Gen. French, you must not cross the creek. Look at the camp fires of the Yankees just in front of you!" I asked for Mr. Metcalf, and was told he had fled to the woods. His agent was on the fence watching for the "Yanks." It was now quite dark. Notwithstanding all this advice, we forded the creek and I went forward to reconnoiter. I found no pickets, so, it being late, we went into the woods and rested for the night.

21st. We mounted our horses and rode out to reconnoiter. We met Mr. Metcalf. I learned that two white Yankee officers and a company of colored soldiers surrounded my house about ten minutes after we left it. So as we were crossing the field east, this company was in the field coming up from the south. The negroes surrounded the dwelling, and the officers entered to capture me, They were told I had left. This did not satisfy them. My sister took a light and went with one officer and let him search all the rooms and closets upstairs. Then she told him where the steps were, and insisted that he should go up into the cockloft to be sure that I was not there. He declined, saying it was an unpleasant duty he was sent to perform, and apologized for the trouble he had given the family. When my sister returned to the sitting room the other officer had my United States army uniform coat in his hand. He told her it was a contraband article, and as such he would take it. She replied: "I know you are going to steal it, and to relieve your conscience from remorse I will give you the coat. It is my brother's, but he would scorn to wear it with those badges on it." He declined to accept it, but as a contraband article he would take it. She then asked him if contraband articles were the property of the individual, and he answered: "I shall make a report of my visit to the commanding officer." During these proceedings the "First Colored Native Mississippi Cavalry" stole two mules and a horse, all we had on the place. And I will here remark that my dear friend (classmate and roommate at West Point), Gen. Fred Steele, had in the spring carried off thirty-five fine mules for the benefit of the United States. He sincerely apologized to my mother for this act, but it was an order of Gen. Grant's that he had to execute. But more of this anon.

November 22. This is my birthday. After I learned that the blacks came so near capturing me I determined to let mother know that I was not captured, so I went back home and took breakfast with them. Bidding them good-by, I tried to console them, but it was with a bitter heart that I left them alone without a horse to send a servant in case of any necessity. During the night we saw a fire down the creek, and when I got back to where I left my aid I learned that the enemy set fire to Judge Shall Yerger's house while the family were asleep, and they barely escaped alive. The Yankees, colored ones, being mainly on the right bank, we traveled down the left, in the rear of the plantations, to Bogue Phalia. Away out in this wilderness of woods, at Dr. Harper's, we were treated to a bottle of champagne. We drank it on the banks of that meandering stream out of tin cups: it was good all the same. We went on to Mr. Heathman's, on Indian Bayou, to stay all night. My two guards, innocently going up Deer Creek, rode into a camp of negro troops and were fired at in the dark, and fled to this place. As we rode up to the house the two soldiers came out with their carbines, but Mr. Heathman (a feather bed ranger) jumped out the window and hid back in the rear, and no calling induced him to come back. About twelve o'clock at night he came up, peeped in the window, saw we were not Yankees, and came in. But his supper had vanished.   .   .   .

25th. I arrived at Jackson, or where Jackson once was, and found it in ruins, it having been burned down by '' childlike and bland '' Sherman. Now I first heard of the defeat of Bragg at Missionary Ridge yesterday, November 25, and felt very gloomy.

December 6. I received orders to move the brigades of Ector and McNair to Brandon with the batteries. Capt. C. D. Myers left to-night. He is a gentleman and a good officer. His home is in Wilmington, N. C.

13th. Gen. Johnston arrived yesterday. Gen. J. R. Lidell remained in camp with me Friday and Saturday.

14th. Capt. J. M. Baldwin left this morning for Columbus, Ga., taking with him my servant, John Sharp. He is not in the service now, and goes there as my agent to care for my servants taken out there.

17th to 22d. Gen. Johnston ordered to the command of the Army of Tennessee. Lieut. Gen. Polk in command of this department now. To-morrow Gen. Johnston will leave for the Army of Tennessee, much to my regret.

December 24. This morning Gen. Polk sent for me and told me that he would start for Enterprise at once, and we rode down to the depot together. The cars had left, and he took a locomotive and started after the train. During the ride he said he wished me to go to Jackson and put the railroad and the bridges in repair. In the afternoon we drove to Jackson. At Mrs. Ruck's we had tableau and charades. Women are never

suppressed, always cheerful. How many of the Yerger families were there?
There are five brothers, all lawyers, and good ones.

26th. Returned to Brandon. Nothing of note occurred between the
26th and 30th.

Judge Shall Yerger was a neighbor of mine on Deer Creek,
near Greenville, Miss. He was an eminent jurist and able judge.
He maintained almost absolute silence in his court. Except
those engaged in a case, no one was permitted to talk above
a whisper. He was fond of telling anecdotes to good and appreciative listeners. His aversion to the use of liquor was
marked, and he condemned playing cards for money.

Now it happened in some way that the grand jury of Washington County had indicted his nephew, who was sheriff of the
county, Dr. Finley, and some others for playing cards for money. At the meeting of the court, when the nephew's case was
called he pleaded guilty, and, after some good advice, the judge
imposed on him a fine of fifty dollars. When Dr. Finley's case
was before the court his attorney declared the witness was re-
vealing the secrets of the bedchamber. Yet he was found guilty
on two indictments. The Judge sat in a rocking-chair, and before he pronounced sentence he occupied about ten minutes in
delivering a homily on the impropriety of an accomplished gentleman, who by his profession had the entrée to all the best families, who should, while perhaps the shadow of death was hovering
over his patient, be so indifferent as to play cards and distress
the family, . . . ending in fining the Doctor fifty dollars in
each case in the most imperturbable manner, and saying the Doctor would stand committed until the fine was paid. To this the
Doctor observed: "May it please your honor, you know that we
all keep our funds in New Orleans, and I can only pay by a
draft." He was informed that was a matter between him and
the officers of the court. So he finally sat down, and as the
Judge was indebted to Finley for professional services, he drew
the check on *him*, and handed it to the sheriff, who gave it to
the clerk, who in turn passed it to the Judge. He glanced over
it, all the while rocking gently, and without a change of countenance handed it back to the clerk with the quiet remark: "*The
court remits the fine imposed on Dr. Finley.*"

On landing in Vicksburg one day, and when walking to the
hotel, he was met by a man to whom he owed a small bill, who,

after the usual salutations of the day, said to the Judge: "I have some debts to pay, and I wish you would hand me the small amount you owe me." "Sir," said the Judge, "have you the audacity to ask me to pay my debts while your own are unpaid? Go and pay your debts first, then you can with propriety ask me to pay mine," and left him to analyze the sophistry of his advice.

When Gen. Frederick Steele was sent to Deer Creek by Gen. Grant to destroy all mills that could supply the garrison in Vicksburg with flour, and bring away the live stock, he reached Judge Shall Yerger's about noon, and he and his staff were invited to dine with them. Steele gave positive orders only to break the machinery of the grain mill, and to burn nothing. While they were at dinner a servant woman rushed into the dining room and exclaimed: "O missus, the ginhouse is on fire." Mrs. Yerger rose from her seat in great excitement, but the Judge said in the most quiet manner: "Sit down, my dear, sit down; Gen. Steele's troops are doing this complimentary to us for the hospitality shown him." Gen. Steele left the table, and in every way tried to discover who set the building on fire, and failed. Steele was a gentleman always.

31st. This morning it was springlike, but after a while far distant thunder was heard. Nearer and nearer it came, until at last the storm burst on us in all its fury. The rain was violent, accompanied with hailstones as large as hen's eggs. Next, the wind veered around to the northwest, and it became very cold and snow fell. After dark two men brought to the office a benevolent man from Connecticut, a prisoner, and some papers that were found on his person. From these I discovered that he was cultivating some plantations in cotton on the banks of the Mississippi, near Red River. That he had permits from the Freedmen's Bureau to visit his plantation between certain gunboat stations at will, etc. He was, he argued, doing the work of a Christian in cultivating abandoned lands, bringing wealth out of the earth, giving employment to the idle, in making the slaves work, etc. I asked him whose place he was on, or made his home. He told me. I inquired if the owner was on the plantation. He replied in the affirmative. To another question he said that he occupied the dwelling and the proprietor the overseer's house, and then gave the details of working the crop and dividing the same. I did not agree with him, and told the guard, who had heard all, to put him in the guardhouse in the town. They wished to carry him to camp. I would not permit it. Next day I sent him to Gen. Polk. He was no doubt a charitable man, for he had left his New England home, and was kindly cultivating these plantations to prevent them from growing up in weeds and briers, but there were some *facts* that upset his *theory* of philanthropy.

January 1, 1864. It is very cold, and the ground is frozen hard. I dined at Mr. Proctor's. Among the guests were Drs. Langley and Thornton, Capt. Smith, and Mr. Whitfield. . . .

7th. Received orders to move my command to Meridian. For want of transportation, troops were not sent until the 9th. On the 10th, when I left Brandon, people were sliding, and some skating, on the pond near the depot. Ice two inches thick. During the remainder of January there is nothing in my diary worth recording here.

February 1. This morning I was directed to hold my division in readiness to move to Jackson. On the evening of the 2d I was sent for by Gen. Polk and told to move as soon as possible. I reached Jackson at 5 P.M. on the 4th. I found Gen. S. D. Lee about sixteen miles in front of Jackson skirmishing with the enemy, who were advancing on Jackson under Sherman. Telegraphed Gen. Polk that the enemy, 25,000 strong, was advancing, and their destination, *Meridian.* Also wrote him to the same effect. I had now in Jackson only 2,200 men, and I had no artillery horses, no wagons, no ambulances.

5th. In constant communication with Gen. S. D. Lee and Gen. Loring. I informed the latter that the enemy would be in Jackson before he could get here. So Loring went to Madison Station, and said he would cross the Pearl river at Culley's Ferry. All stores were now sent to Meridian, and stores from Brandon were ordered to be sent early. The enemy pressed Lee hard. By every telegram Lee said he wished to swing to the left and not cross the river, and remain west of the Pearl.

I telegraphed Gen. Forrest the strength and position of the enemy. In the evening I received a dispatch from Polk to continue labor on the railroad. Indiscreet order to execute to-day, and I will postpone it. At 4 P.M. I crossed the river and started the troops for Brandon, hastened the loading of the trains, and then myself and staff returned to the city. I found the Federal troops in possession of the western part of the town, so we turned round and had a race with their troops for the bridge (a pontoon bridge) and ordered it taken up. As the end was being cut loose one of Gen. Lee's staff officers (his doctor) sprung his horse on the bridge and cried out that Lee's force was in the city and would have to cross here. Replaced it. At this moment the enemy lined the high bank and opened fire on us. We soon threw some of the plank into the river and knocked the bottoms out of the boats. Lee got out of the city by the Canton road. Under fire of their batteries, in the dark, the infantry marched for Brandon. Maj. Storrs, my chief of artillery, a most gallant man, was left behind to get his horses out of the cars and bring on the guns, which he did under fire of the enemy. I left a squadron of cavalry to watch the enemy at the crossing. Next day I moved on toward Barrett's mills.

On my arrival in Jackson I telegraphed Lee that I would join him, and also sent to him my aid, Yerger, with the message that I would join him and risk a battle if he advised it. He thought it not proper to do so considering Loring had declined to give battle. On the 7th, moved on and encamped near Morton. I found Loring here with his division.

8th. This morning Loring placed the whole force present at my command to face about, form line of battle, and give the enemy a fight. I formed this line two miles from town. Some skirmishing ensued. We held a good position and the troops were in fine spirits, but the enemy would not attack us. At a council held it was deemed best to continue to fall back and await the arrival of Baldwin's Brigade and Lee with his cavalry, so we marched all night to Hillsboro. All this time the enemy spread the report that they were en route for Mobile.

9th. Gen. Polk arrived this morning. He had been at Mobile, caught the contagion, and ordered me at once to Newton Station with the brigades of Quarles, McNair, Ector, and Cockrell, there to take trains and proceed to Mobile, take command, and defend the city, as I outranked Gen. Maury. After a tedious march all night we reached the station, thirty miles distant, by daybreak. Here I found trains enough for the brigades of Quarles and McNair. These two brigades, after arriving at Meridian, were carried to Mobile. About noon Polk arrived and told me to remain, as Gen. Maury was sent there by the War Department. Loring marched by dirt road.

11th. This afternoon the brigades of Ector and Cockrell, and the remaining batteries left for Meridian, where we arrived before dark. These two brigades were detained, and did not go to Mobile.

14th. At 7 P.M. started for Almucha, and after a tedious march encamped beyond the town. Next day marched to Gaston.

16th. Started early this morning, my division in advance. Gen. Polk's headquarter wagons and *cows* took the road to Moscow, and we to Lewis's Ferry. Reached there at 11 A.M. Found the engineers there with three steamers and three (decked) scows, with which to make a pontoon bridge over the Tombigbee. It was apparent that they would not span the river. The steamer Admiral came down and "rounded to," and then started down the river at full speed. She was necessary for the bridge, so I sent the steamer Clipper after her, with Lieut. Freeman and a guard on board, to capture her. She was overtaken six miles below and brought back.

It was now 12 M., and nothing had been done to bridge the river. My advanced train had reached the river at 2 P.M. the day previous, and were crossing the wagons on scows, and by dusk had eighty on the other side. At 1:30 P.M., Gen. Polk arrived, and in his presence I remarked to the engineer officer that "it was time to go to work," when the General in an abrupt manner said: "If Gen. French pleases, I have given my orders." Be that as it may, nothing had been done by his orders to get the army over, and there would have been no bridge had I not caught the steamer Admiral. When at last the bridge was finished, all my division train had been ferried over save six wagons, and it was about 2 A.M. before it was all over. Then Loring's Division had to cross.

Gen. Polk had been an Episcopal bishop, and enjoyed the best the land afforded. The matin songs of the birds disturbed not his morning repose. The glorious sun rose too early for him to see it from the mountain top. It showed its face there at an unseemly hour. But when the "drowsy morn" was passed, and the milkmaid had drawn tribute from the cows, and the coffee-pot was steaming on the hearth, and the light rolls were hot by the fire, and the plump, fine capon, with sides well lined with fat, was broiling on the coals, sending a savory odor through the apartments, the Bishop would arise, his face radiant with joy. He was a valiant trencherman, but when the repast was over he threw aside the surplice. The priest became a warrior when he girded on his saber, and sallied forth a paladin in the strife.

During all the long retreat from Jackson to this place we have done but little fighting with the infantry. It has nearly all been done by the cavalry and artillery.

18th. Moved to Demopolis and encamped there. It is very cold and snow is falling. Mr. Fournier gave me rooms at his house. He came to Demopolis with Gen. Le Febre, who came to the United States after the abdication of Napoleon. I received letters from home.

21st. Went to Judge Dixon's, a neighbor of mine, and we attended divine service at the Episcopal Church. The Rt. Rev. Bishop Wilmer preached an eloquent sermon. The congregation is under the charge of Mr. Beckwith, who formerly resided on Deer Creek and was acquainted with my family. [He was afterwards Bishop of Georgia.]

26th. Left on a ten days' leave of absence to visit Columbus, Ga. On the cars were Gens. Hardee, Loring, Withers, and Walthall. On arrival in Columbus I went to Gen. A. Abercrombie's in Russell County, Ala.; remained there till Monday morning, and arrived in Demopolis on the 11th of March; remained in camp there until the 31st, when I started for Lauderdale with my division. In Demopolis I met many agreeable families. Among them were Mr. Lyons, Fournier, Glovers, Thornton, Lightfoot, Inges, Sheadwicks, and others. I remained at Lauderdale, Miss., until the 20th of April, when I received orders to move to Tuscaloosa. *En route* I passed through Gainesville, and entered Tuscaloosa on the 26th. I reviewed the troops one morning for Gen. Hodge, and the same day I reviewed the cadets at the University of Alabama. Among the pleasant people I met in Tuscaloosa were W. S. and C. M. Foster, Misses Annie Fiquet, Belle Woodruff, Cassady, Edden, Searcy, and others. I called to see J. E. Davis, brother of the President.

On the 4th of May Gen. Polk was ordered by Adj. Gen. Cooper, also by Gen. Johnston, to move Gen. Loring and all available force to Rome. A consequence of these orders was that I, being at Tuscaloosa, Ala., received from Polk, at Demopolis, at 9 A.M. on the 5th, orders to halt Sears's brigade, then near Selma, and send it to Montevallo, a station on the railroad to Rome, and concentrate my division at Montevallo.

At the time this order was received Cockrell's Brigade was partly away up in North Alabama in the counties of Marion,

LEONIDAS POLK

MATTHEW D. ECTOR

Walker, etc., by order of Gen. Polk. Ector's Brigade was with me in Tuscaloosa, and Sears's north of Selma. Immediately orders were given to concentrate, as may be found in "War Records," Vol. 38, Part IV., and in this volume will be found many orders and letters pertaining to this movement.

Gen. Sears's Brigade, on May 5, was nearer Rome than Loring at Demopolis, and was at Montevallo on the 9th when Gen. Polk arrived there, and *could have been sent with him to Resaca* had transportation been provided. My diary records these vexatious delays, and that the superintendent of the railroad received no orders to move my division until Tuesday, the 10th, and that he was to have the cars there on Thursday, the 12th. Polk's administrative ability was not largely developed so as to anticipate the plainest necessity for coming events if he were accountable for these delays and others.

May 7. We left Tuscaloosa for Montevallo. I found there the brigade of Mississippians, commanded by Gen. Sears, that is to form a part of my division. *On the 9th Gen. Polk arrived.* He directed that five days' rations be cooked at once, and that Sears's Brigade should leave that afternoon for Blue Mountain by railroad. How easy it is to talk about such things! There was no meal at the commissary's and no cars for the troops.

10th. No trains yet; raining hard; Ector's Brigade arrived. Sent all the artillery horses by wagon road.

11th. Rain, rain, and thunder, and no trains yet for the troops. I wonder if there is a commander of this department.

12th. No trains yet. I resolved to march the troops, but met Col. Sevier, of Polk's staff, and he assures me that he will have transportation. Some of my men got on a passing train. I am informed that no grain was sent up last night for the artillery horses. Can it be that Gen. Polk knows nothing about these matters?

13th. To-day I got the remainder of Sears's Brigade off; and through the night, Ector's troops. Cockrell arrived with his brigade. I had sent him, by order of Gen. Polk, north of Tuscaloosa on an important expedition.

Struck tents and left for Blue Mountain. Sears was thirty-six hours on a train. Such delays were distressing.

Rode this morning, the 16th, into Rome. Yesterday the enemy's cavalry was within two miles of the city. Gen. Sears arrived, and at 10 P.M. his brigade was sent on the cars to Kingston.

17th. Sent two batteries by dirt road, also by trains, to Kingston. About 1 P.M. to-day, as I was putting Ector's Brigade on the cars for Kingston, I was informed by Brigadier Davidson that the enemy was within two miles of the town, on the right bank of the Oostanoula river, and that he had but one hundred and fifty men (mounted) to check them.

13

That you may the better comprehend the situation of troops, Federal and Confederate, I will state that on the 13th Gen. Johnston, on his retreat from Dalton, had reached Resaca, a town on the right bank of the Oostanoula, and was there attacked by Gen. Sherman on the 14th and 15th. On the 15th Sherman's army began crossing the river, and our troops also. On the 16th both armies were south of the river, Johnston's force falling back on Kingston and the Federals in pursuit. Polk, with Loring's Division, was with Johnston at Resaca, and two brigades of mine would have been there only for the want of transportation at Montevallo as stated.

So when I found the enemy at Rome, no alternative presented itself but to put Ector in the trenches over the Oostanoula, and hold the town until Cockrell arrived, who was, in the morning, thirty-two miles distant. A strong line of skirmishers was advanced, which was soon engaged with the enemy. During the afternoon Gen. J. T. Morgan arrived and said that his command was en route to Rome from Adairsville, and that he and Gen. Furgerson were both hard pressed by the enemy. At 4 P.M. Gen. Ross (cavalry) arrived with two regiments. The men were dismounted and placed on the hills. Davidson, with a few cavalry, moved on the enemy's right. Then, at 6 P.M., Ross, with his men, charged their line of skirmishers and drove them back to the main line. Hoskins, with two guns and all the fragments of dismounted men and the like, was placed on the hill north of the town on the left bank of the river to at least intimidate the Federals. In this fight I did not lose over one hundred men, and they were mainly from Ross's Brigade.

During all this day constant communications passed between me and Gens. Polk and Johnston urging me not to fail to join the retreating army. Cockrell's Brigade arrived at dusk, having marched thirty-two miles, and were at once furnished cars and started for Kingston at 10 P.M. Ector's Brigade reached Kingston at 7:30 A.M. Before we left Rome I had all the horses, stores, sick, and wounded removed. When we reached Kingston, on the 18th, I found Gen. Johnston moving, with his army, to Cassville, and I marched my division there also, and joined Gen. Polk and encamped near headquarters.

It was an error to not have had Polk's Corps concentrated and well in hand to unite with Johnston to oppose Sherman's advance from Dalton, considering the month of May was passing and the time for active movements had arrived. As it was, they were widely separated. On the 4th of May Gen. Polk was ordered to concentrate his command at Rome. From causes noted in my diary the last brigade did not reach there until the 17th.

With Gen. W. T. Sherman, above Dalton, Ga., in command of a hundred thousand men, it behooved either the War Department at Richmond, or Gen. J. E. Johnston, in command of the Army of Tennessee, to have concentrated the Army of Mississippi under the command of Gen. Polk, and held it ready to join the Army of Tennessee; whereas it was widely separated. April 26, I was in Tuscaloosa, Ala., and ordered by Gen. Polk to send a brigade north to the counties as stated. The consequence of all this was only one division of the Army of Mississippi reached Johnston before the battle of Resaca was fought, on May 13–15.

CHAPTER XIV.

Cassville—The Line of Battle—Hood's Line Not Enfiladed—History of that
Conference—Two Lieutenant Generals Invite Their Commander to a
Council of War—Johnston Obliged to Fall Back—We Cross the Etowah
River—Dallas—New Hope Church—Constant Fighting—Rain, Rain—
Death of Lieut. Gen. Polk—Battle of the Latimer House—My Division
Occupies Little and Big Kennesaw Mountains—The Battle—Incidents
of the Battle—Confederates Save Wounded Union Soldiers from Burn-
ing—Kennesaw During Night Bombardment—Col. Martin's Noble Con-
duct—The Irony of Fate—Maj. Poten and French Soldier.

IT will be seen that of those troops under Hood that were
maneuvering to attack the enemy advancing on our right,
I was the last to leave the position east of Cassville, for the
whole line of battle was formed before I fell back, and I would
have been in reserve entirely had Hood, as he should have done,
extended his line to the left until it touched Canty's Division.

May 19, 1864. This morning the army was formed in line of battle. At
first I was on the extreme right, but soon after, by change of dispositions,
I occupied the line from the hills, on Loring's right, across the valley to
the top of the first hill on my right. Hood's Corps was on my right, maneuvering to attack the enemy, but from some cause no fight was made.
After this line was formed Cockrell, who was in reserve, was placed on a
range of hills *south* of Cassville, and behind the town. *At 4 P.M.*, I was
ordered to fall back and form *behind* the division of Gen. Canty and Cockrell's Brigade, which I did. But as there was an interval between Hood's
line and Canty without troops, I placed there in position Hoskin's Battery and half of Ector's Brigade. This left me Sears's Brigade and half of
Ector's Brigade in reserve. Then came an order adding to my command
the division of Canty, which was directly in front of me. Cockrell, on
Canty's left, was put, for the occasion, under the orders of Loring.

About 5 P.M. our pickets from the extreme front were driven in toward
the second line by the enemy's cavalry. Hoskin's Battery opened on the
cavalry and checked them. About 5:30 P.M. the Federals, having placed
some batteries in position on a ridge in front of Hood's right, opened fire
on our line, and the shells from their extreme left (in *front* of Hood's right)
enfiladed Hoskin's gun and the line that for a little while curved out to the
battery. Hood's line was not a prolongation of Polk's line, because it *fell
back* at the point of junction about twenty-five degrees. [See map in the
"War Records."]

After dark, as I was returning from dinner, I met Gen. Hood, who asked
me to ride over with him to see Gen. Johnston at Gen. Polk's headquarters, and take supper.

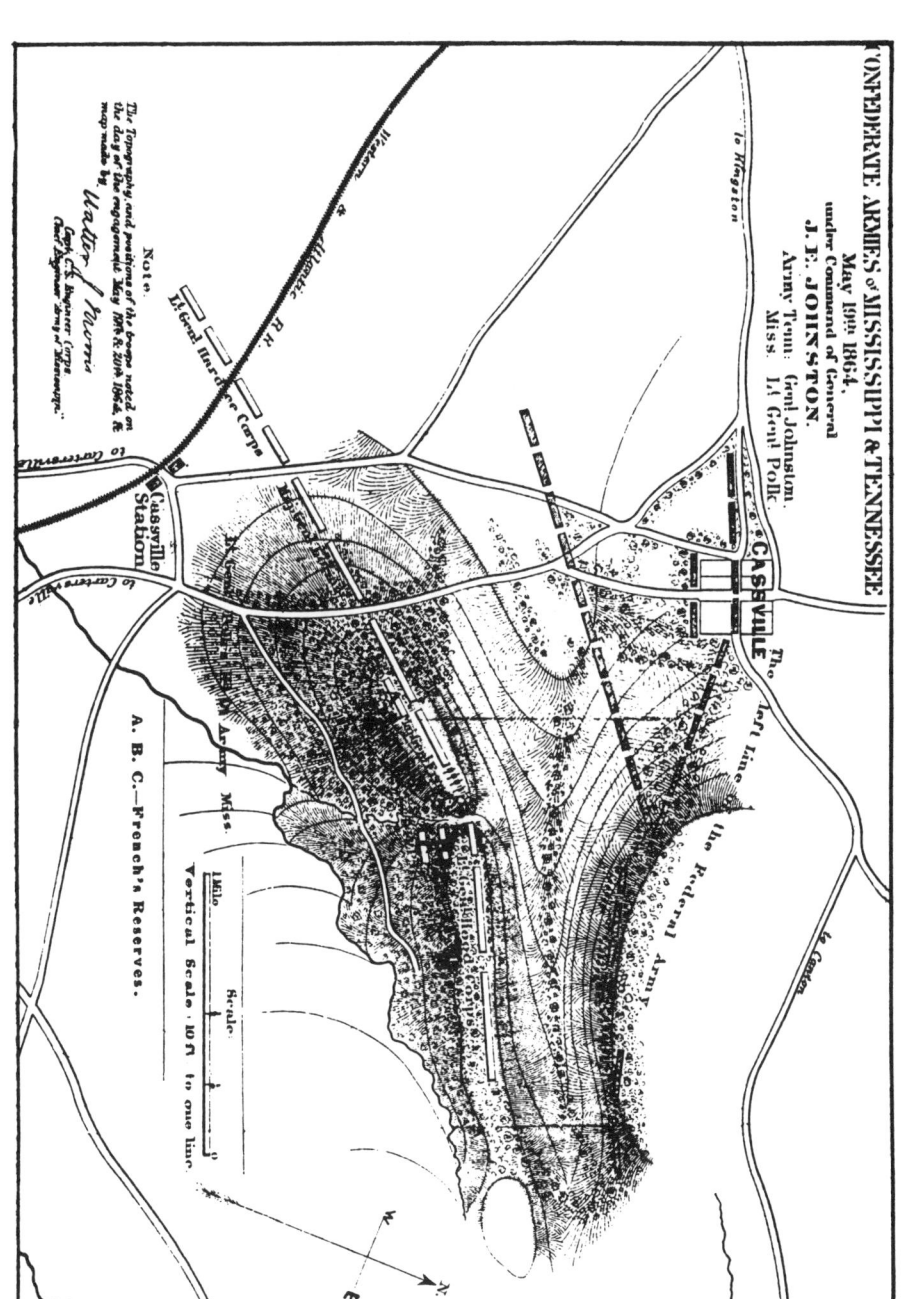

CONFEDERATE ARMIES of MISSISSIPPI & TENNESSEE
May 19th 1864.
under Command of General
J. E. JOHNSTON.
Army Tenn: Genl Johnston.
Miss. Lt Genl Polk.

Note.
The Topography and positions of the troops noted on
the day of the engagement May 19th & 20th 1864, &
map made by
Walter J. Morris
Capt C.S. Engineer Corps
Cont Engineer Army of Mississippi.

A. B. C. — French's Reserves.

Scale:
1 Mile
Vertical Scale : 10 ⅓ to one line

Lt Genl Hardee Corps

Cassville
Station

The Left Line

the Federal Army

CASSVILLE

to Kingston

to Kingston

to Centre

to Cartersville

to Cartersville

N
W
E
S

When supper was over Hood and Polk asked Johnston to a conference that they had previously arranged, and Johnston asked me to go with him. At the conference, at this time, Hardee *was not* present. Hood commenced by declaring that his line and Polk's line were so enfiladed by the Federal artillery that they could not be held. Polk was not so strenuous. Johnston insisted on fighting, and my diary says:

At 9 P.M. it was, I am sure, determined to fight at Cassville, and, after remaining at the conference sometime longer, I hastened to camp to entrench. Soon after it was intimated to me by an officer riding along past me that we would fall back, owing to the enemy moving so far on our left.

20th. At midnight we commenced to leave our position. Skirmishers were left, and a few men in the trenches were given axes to fell trees to deceive the enemy and drown the noise made in withdrawing the artillery.

I am obliged, before I proceed any further, to make a digression here in reference to the proceedings of this conference by reason of what has been published about it.

Johnston, in his "Narrative," gives his version of what occurred, and so far as what took place it is mainly correct. Hood, in his "Advance and Retreat," makes an incorrect statement of the condition of his line, and, whilst I was there, made no reference to being in a good position for acting on the aggressive and making an attack. His memory is defective, because in a letter of his, written to me ten years after, he had entirely forgotten that I was present at the conference. Then again, in October, 1894, there appeared in the New Orleans *Picayune* an anonymous article that endeavored to transfer Polk's concurrence with Hood to not fight on to my shoulders. It was so entirely erroneous—nay, purely imaginative—that it required me to notice it for the benefit of my children, and it can be found in the *Southern Historical Magazine*, Vol. XXII., pages 1 to 9, published in Richmond, Va., January–December, 1894.

I regret that this fabulous *Picayune* article, emanating in New Orleans, was ever written on account of Gen. Polk. It made him appear to be a weak man.

21st. Yesterday we crossed the Etowah river and encamped at an iron furnace in charge of Gen. G. W. Smith, who had resigned from the army. Remained in camp all day. There was some firing in the evening on the river below where we crossed. I received orders to be ready to move in any direction.

23d. Left Allatoona to-day at noon and marched until dusk, then encamped for the night.

24th. Started at 4 A.M. and marched westerly toward Dallas. Encamped in line of battle. Heard guns in the direction of Dallas.

25th. This morning I moved still farther toward Dallas. Enemy reported on the road from Rome, striking for, or below, Atlanta. In the evening I rode along our front. I met Gen. Johnston while riding toward New Hope Church. The enemy made an attack on Gen. Hood's front. I returned immediately to hasten up my command, and arrived about dark in the midst of a thunderstorm. After placing troop in position during the night, I slept by the roadside under shelter of a fence.

26th. Assumed line of battle and passed the day in intrenching. Cheatham is on my right and Canty on my left. During the night Cheatham moved to the left, and on the 27th I extended in that direction. In the afternoon there was an attack on Gen. Hood, which he repulsed. At midnight I received orders to move my division to the right to relieve the division of Gen. Stevenson, which was not completed until 4 A.M. I found the line a miserable one, and the enemy's sharpshooters within twenty yards of the lines. I relieved his skirmishers and his division left. The Yankees called this place "hell hole," because, among other things, we shot twenty-one of their men, one after the other, in one rifle pit. Soon after sunrise the Federals opened fire with infantry and artillery, and during the day it increased, and once I thought we had to repulse a charge on the line. A great many shells have passed overhead and some through the top of a little apple tree at the foot of which we are sitting. They come without invitation. During the night there was such firing that I got up to ascertain if they were driving Loring's picket line in, on my right over the valley. I will remember New Hope Church.

29th. Firing not so heavy to-day as yesterday. I rode over to Gen. Polk's at 5 A.M. Yesterday there was an attack on the left made by Gen. Bate, and on the right by Gen. Wheeler. My line is a hard one to defend. In the evening after dark I was sent for by Gen. Polk, and found him at Gen. Johnston's. While there the enemy made an attack on Canty and my left. The firing was severe. During the night there was continuous firing on the left, and after midnight heavy artillery firing. Owing to the condition of the atmosphere, the roar of the guns was increased, and the sound of bursting shells overhead was like near by thunder, while the glare makes night hideous, consequently I got no sleep. This is getting to be interesting now, but the play is too long, it takes all night.

30th. Col. Riley, a most gallant officer, is killed. There is trouble again on Canty's line. Some people are always in trouble. After dinner I went to Gen. Johnston's, and he sent me to examine Canty's line. There is not much firing to-night. The enemy's line is close to ours in front of Canty. We want engineers. [Next day nothing to relate.]

June 1. I wrote to headquarters for tubes for Enfield rifles. This morning there is an artillery duel going on between one of our batteries and

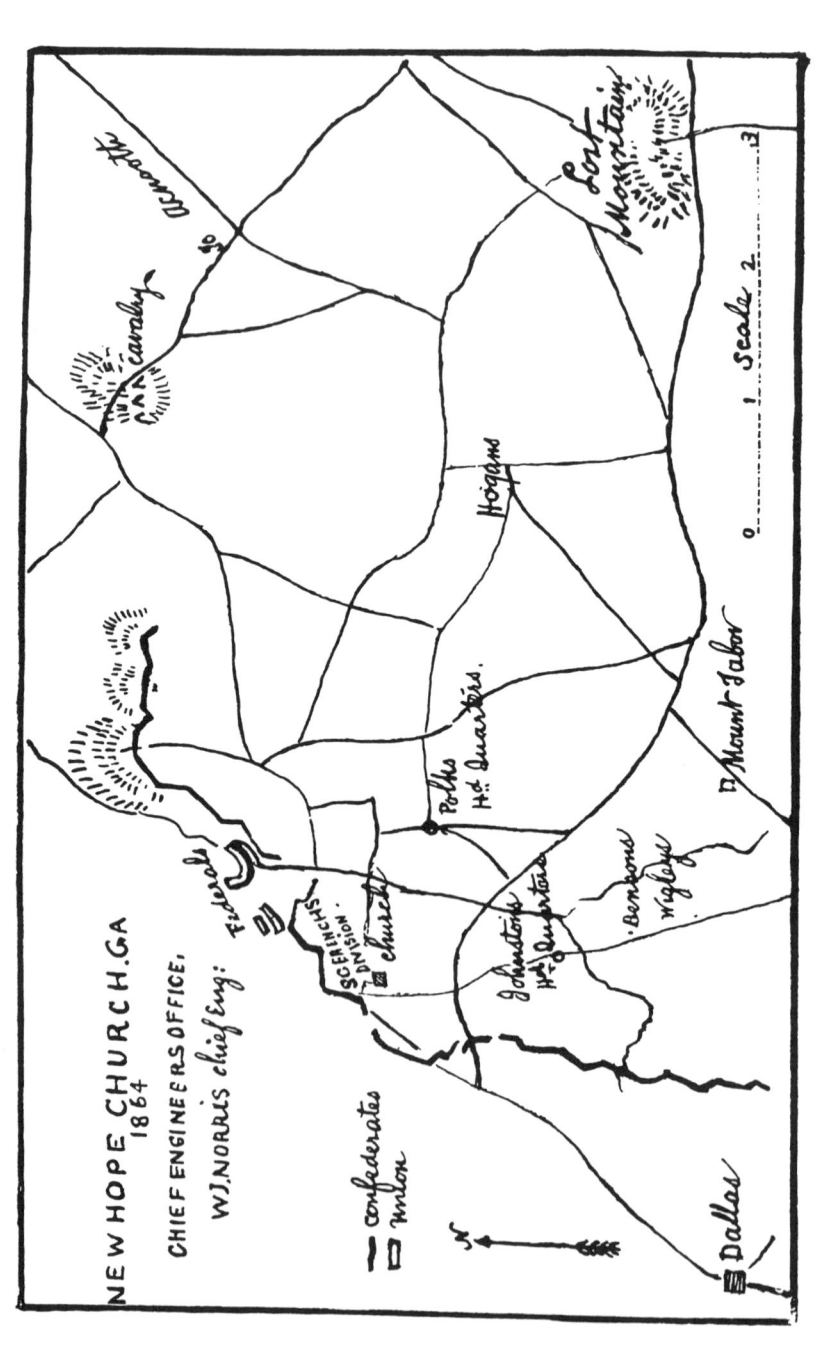

those of the enemy. Enormous trees are falling from the shot. I formed an engineer company, and put Capt. Venet in command of it. I examined the whole line. Canty withdrew his line last night, leaving mine to be maintained, now quite six hundred yards in advance, connected only by their cross line.

2d. Gen. Ector was wounded this afternoon. An awful thunderstorm came up, the peals of thunder were frightful, and the Yankee tried to drown it with mimic artillery, as if one at a time was not divertisement enough. Some people can't be satisfied. The ditch is filled up to some depth with water. Over this I sleep on one board with my face turned up to the glare of the shells that shine through the closed eyelids.

3d. Firing as usual, and the enemy moving to our right. Another heavy thunderstorm is in progress. The roar of artillery shakes the rain out of the clouds. We drove in the enemy's skirmish line. One consolation the staff says we have is that no one comes to see us; the ride is not interesting. We see no one, and get no orders. That there is good in everything, including shells, is their doctrine. This battle has now lasted ten days.

4th. Rain again this morning. It was a disagreeable night in the trenches. There is firing in front. I have good news from Virginia. At 4 P.M. I received orders to withdraw our lines. It is raining to-night. This, with previous rains, rendered the roads as bad as they can well be, and the night was very dark. Mud, mud everywhere, and the soldiers sink over their shoe tops at every step. It took seven hours to move six miles. At 7 A.M. on the morning of the 5th we were in line of battle on Lost Mountain.

6th. I obtained a good night's rest. This morning I had to change the line of battle. The view from this lone mountain top is beautiful. It is about nine miles east of Marietta. It swells from the plain solitary and lone to the height of six hundred feet, affording a fine bird's-eye view of the surrounding country. To the north the encampments of the enemy are spread out below, and from hundreds of campfires the blue smoke rises to float away as gently as though all were peaceful. Beneath this silver cloud that hangs around the mountain, there is an angry brow; the demons of war are there.

7th. I slept in camp in the rear of the mountain, and for once all is quietness. At 10 A.M. I was ordered to the extreme right, and to the left at 1 P.M. All the information I can deduce from a single equation, to which I have reduced *five orders* received verbally from Polk's staff, is: X equal to a line to be formed in a dense wood 73 degrees northeast. I found Loring plunging about in quest of some center that is movable, and as invisible as the North Pole. As I could not determine the value of X at dark, I concluded to sleep the matter over on the ground where I am.

8th. This morning Maj. Prestman, engineer, examined the ground for my line. It is a weak, faulty, miserable line. The engineer took all my tools yesterday, so to-day I am unable to construct any works. I have reported the matter to Gen. Polk, but he is so much engrossed with fine-spun theories that he fails to attend to things requiring prompt attention.

Well! just think of it! This staff of mine, unreasonable fellows, wish they were back in the trenches again, where, for about eight days, they were not troubled with orders. Judge Wright came to see me. I have a high regard for him, and have seen him several times lately. He is from Tennessee.

9th. Everything was quiet last night, and I heard no guns until 3 P.M. My division was ordered to follow Loring's toward the railroad. Contradictory orders again from Gen. Polk's staff. I got into position at dark, and was called up at 2 A.M. to change again by moving Ector's Brigade to the right.

10th. Some skirmishing and artillery firing this morning. At 1 P.M. a violent thunderstorm came up, and the rain fell until dark. I believe it has rained now nine days in succession. The enemy is reported advancing to-day, and the firing shows it. In the evening I rode on the picket line with Gen. Ector. Firing continued until dark.

11th. Rain.

12th. Rain once more, and everything is drenched. Enemy firing with artillery from my front toward Kennesaw Mountain.

13th. Terrible rain last night and all day to-day till noon. Eleven days' rain! If it keeps on, there will be a story told like unto that in the Bible, only it will read,

> It rained forty days and it rained forty nights,
> And the ark it rested on the Kennesaw heights;

For to that place we are floating, it seems to me.

14th. This morning, by written orders (I am glad they have found paper to write on), Loring went to the right, Canty from the left to the center, and I extended to the right. No rain! Telegram of Forrest's victory. During the morning I rode over to Gen. Polk's quarters and asked him (when Gen. Johnston rode with him to our left) to come down my line. He said probably he would do so. Alas! "man proposes, God disposes." I heard at 12 M. that he had been killed. I sent an officer to his headquarters, and he returned saying that the report was true. I then went immediately to his camp and found that his remains had been sent to Marietta. I was very much shocked at his untimely fate. A universal sadness seemed to rest on the countenance of every one. He had accompanied Johnston to the left and gone on Pine Mountain, and while in front of our lines the party was fired on by one of the enemy's batteries, and the third shot fired struck the General on the left side and killed him instantly. Thus died a gentleman and a high Church dignitary. As a soldier he was more theoretical than practical.

I was ordered last night to be in readiness for an advance of the enemy at 3 A.M. He came not.

15th. All quiet at sunrise. Soon after desultory firing commenced along the line and continued until 3 P.M., when it became quite heavy. Featherston had his skirmishers driven in to their ranks. At 9 P.M. my skirmish line was attacked unsuccessfully.

16th. Early this morning the enemy opened on my front with a battery, and at 10 A.M. they shelled the picket line and skirmish line very severely. At 3 p.m. they again shelled my line for an hour without serious damage. Cockrell is held in reserve for Gen. Hardee, and thus I am constantly holding a reserve for some one else; never yet has a brigade been held for me, and never, not once, have I asked for assistance.

17th. The now monotonous artillery awakened us this morning to reveille *before* we had made any parched —— for coffee, the unfeeling hirelings of *toute du monde!* Last night all the troops on my left swung back and took a new line that placed me in command of a salient with an angle of about eighty-five degrees, liable to be enfiladed and taken in reverse.

18th. Early this morning both pickets and skirmishers on my left (Walker's Division) gave way and let the Federals in behind Cockrell's skirmishers, and thus the enemy gained possession of the Latimar House in my front. Ector's Brigade skirmishers also came in. The way being clear, the enemy soon advanced in line of battle, and with many guns enfiladed my line all day. This constant firing never ceased, but I could not induce them to come out and make an assault on my front with infantry, and ere night came my loss was 215 men. Capt. Guibor's Battery has lost more men (13) to-day than it did during the entire siege of Vicksburg. Men became in time so familiar with danger and death that, Gallio-like, they "care for none of those things." Toward evening I was ordered to withdraw from this line and occupy Kennesaw Mountain. This was done during the night.

19th. Early this morning the enemy followed us, and soon the skirmishing commenced, and by noon the artillery fire was severe. It ranged up the slope and over the mountain with great fury, and wounded Gen. Cockrell, and thirty-five of his men were *hors du combat.*

The position of our army to-day is: Hood is on our right covering Marietta or the northwest. From his left Polk's Corps (now Loring's) extends over both Big and Little Kennesaw Mountains, with the left on the road from Gilgal Church to Marietta. From this road Hardee extends the line nearly south, covering Marietta on the west. The left of my division was established on the Marietta road; thence it ran up the spur, or incline, of the mountain called Little or West Kennesaw, and thence to the top of the same; thence on up to the *top of Big Kennesaw,* where it connected with Gen. Walthall's troops. Featherston was on the right of Walthall and joined Gen. Hood. Walker, of Hardee's Corps, was on my left. Then in order, Bate, Cleburne, and Cheatham came.

Kennesaw Mountain is about four miles northwest of Marietta. It is over two and a half miles in length, and rises abruptly from the plain, solitary and alone, to the height of perhaps seven hundred feet. Its northwestern side is rocky and abrupt. On the northerly and southerly extremities it can be gained on horseback. Little Kennesaw, being bald and destitute of timber, affords a commanding view of all the surrounding country as far as the eye can reach, except where the view is hidden by the higher peak. The view from this elevation embraces Lost Mountain, Pine Mountain, and all the beautiful cultivated plain, dotted here and there with farmhouses, extending to the Allatoona Mountains, a spur of the Great Smoky Mountains of North Carolina.

20th. Busy this morning in establishing batteries to command the road,

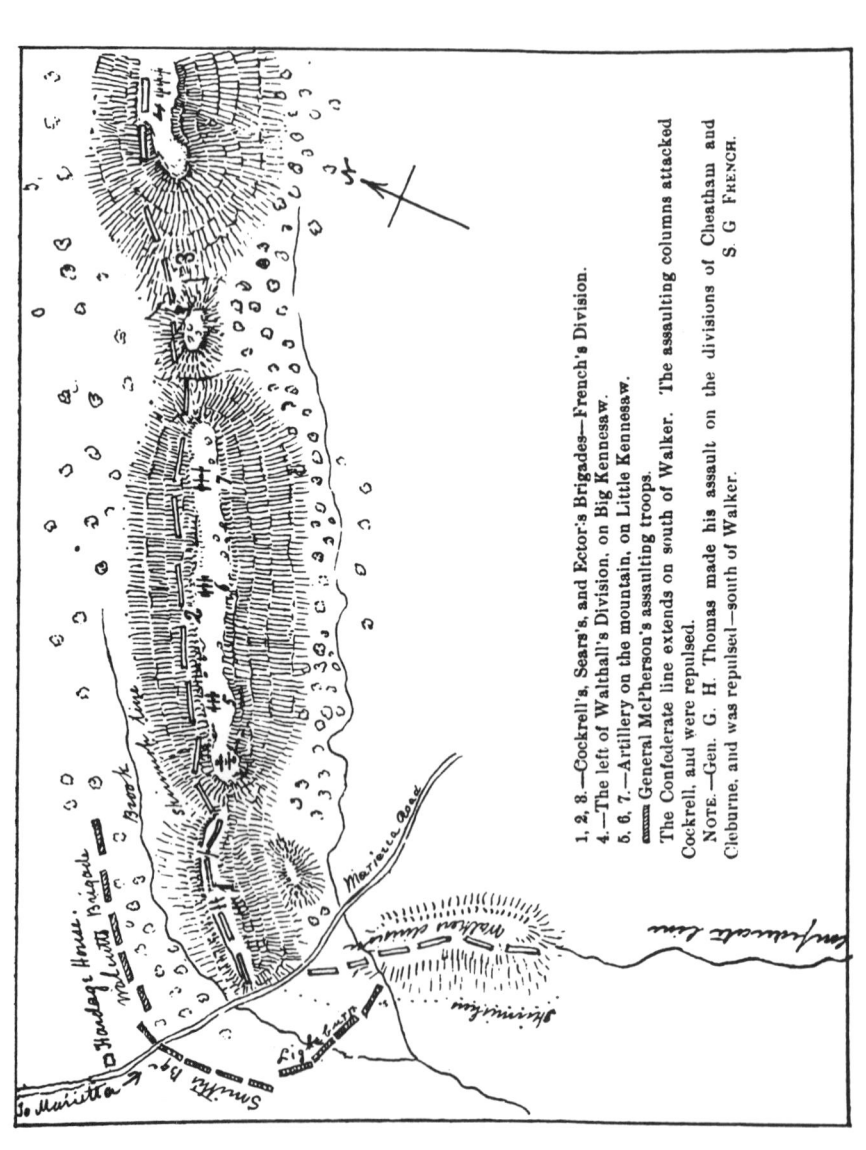

1, 2, 8.—Cockrell's, Sears's, and Ector's Brigades—French's Division.
4.—The left of Walthall's Division, on Big Kennesaw.
5, 6, 7.—Artillery on the mountain, on Little Kennesaw.
▭▭▭ General McPherson's assaulting troops.

The Confederate line extends on south of Walker. The assaulting columns attacked Cockrell, and were repulsed.

NOTE.—Gen. G. H. Thomas made his assault on the divisions of Cheatham and Cleburne, and was repulsed—south of Walker.
S. G FRENCH.

BATTLE OF KENNESAW MOUNTAIN, JUNE 27, 1864.

and others on the line extending up the mountain and on the top of Little Kennesaw. I changed the line of infantry lower down the side of the mountain fronting the enemy, so as to command the ascent down as far as possible. Lost ten horses and a few men killed and wounded to-day.

21st. I went to the top of the mountain this morning, and while there witnessed an artillery duel between the batteries on Hardee's lines and those of the enemy in front of it. Rather interesting to look down upon, and more exciting than a grand display of fireworks.

22d. The constant rains have ceased, the sky is clear, and the sun, so long hid, now shines out brightly. Skirmishing (I am tired of that word) on my line last night. I rode to the top of the mountain quite early, to where I had placed nine guns in position. During the night the enemy had moved a camp close to the base of the mountain. It was the headquarters of some general officers. Tent walls were raised, officers sitting around on camp stools, orderlies coming and going, wagons parked, soldiers idling about or resting in the shade of the trees, and from the cook fires arose the odors of breakfast, and all this at our very feet. It was tantalizing, that breakfast, not to be tolerated. So I directed the powder in a number of cartridges for the guns to be reduced, so as to drop the shells into the camp below us. I left them in their fancied security—for no doubt they believed that we could not place artillery on the height above them, and they were not visible to our infantry on the mountain side by reason of the timber. How comfortable they appeared, resting in the shade and smoking! At length the gunners, impatient of delay, were permitted to open fire on them. Thunder from the clear, blue sky could not have surprised them more. They sprang to their feet, and stood not on the order of their going, but left quickly, every man for himself, and soon " their tents were all silent, their banners alone," like Sennacherib's of old, and there was a deserted camp all this day.

The enemy appeared this morning to be moving permanently to our left, and the firing in the afternoon extended farther in that direction, Toward dark I opened fire on the enemy's batteries; also again at 11 P.M.

23d. Yesterday Gen. Cockrell had fourteen men wounded. During the night the enemy removed their tents, wagons, etc., from their abandoned encampment that was shelled yesterday, and the place looks desolate. At 10 A.M., when all was quiet on the mountain, the enemy commenced a rapid fire from guns put in position during the night, and concentrated it on our guns on the point of the mountain. Yesterday we had it all our own way; to-day they are repaying us, and the cannonade is "fast and furious." Last night there was fighting on our left, but so different are the reports received that I cannot get at the truth.

24th. There has been but little fighting during the day.

25th. The everlasting " pop," " pop " on the skirmish line is all that breaks the stillness of the morning. I went early to the left of my line, but could not ride in the rear of Hoskin's Battery on account of the trees and limbs felled by the shells. From the top of the mountain the vast panorama is ever changing. There are now large trains to the left of Lost Mountain and at Big Shanty, and the wagons are moving to and fro everywhere. Encampments of hospitals, quartermasters, commissaries, cavalry, and infantry whiten the plain here and there as far as the eye can reach. Look at our side of the long line of battle! It is narrow, poor, and quiet, save at the front where the men are, and contrasts, with here and there some spots of canvas amidst the green foliage, strangely with that of the enemy.

The usual extension is going on. Troops of the enemy are moving to the left, our left, to outflank us, and we lengthen out correspondingly; and now the blue smoke of the musket discloses the line by day trending away, far away south toward the Chattahoochee, and by night it is marked, at times, by the red glow of the artillery amidst the sparklike flashes of small arms that look in the distance like innumerable fireflies.

At 10 A.M. I opened fire on the enemy from the guns on Kennesaw. The enemy replied furiously, and for an hour the firing was incessant. I received an order to hold Ector's Brigade in reserve. In the afternoon there was considerable firing, and all the chests of one of my caissons were blown up by shell from the enemy, and by the explosion of a shell in one of the chests a gunner was killed. They have now about forty guns in front of me, and when they concentrate their fire on the mountain at any one point it is pretty severe, but, owing to our great height, nearly harmless. Thousands of their Parrott shells pass high over the mountain, and, exploding at a great elevation, the after part of the shell is arrested in its flight and, falling perpendicularly, comes down into camp, and they have injured our tents. Last night I heard a peculiar "thud" on my tent and a rattle of tin pans by the side of my cot, and this morning my negro boy cook put his head into my tent with the pans in his hands and said: "See here, master Sam, them 'fernal Yanks done shot my pans last night. What am I going to do 'bout it?" A rifle ball, coming over the mountain, had fallen from a great height and perforated the pans and penetrated deep into the earth.

26th. This is Sunday, and all is comparatively quiet on the lines up to this 4 P.M., except one artillery duel, but now cannon are heard on our extreme left.

27th. This morning there appeared great activity among the Federal staff officers and generals all along my front and up and down the lines. The better to observe what it portended I and my staff seated ourselves on the brow of the mountain, sheltered by a large rock that rested *between* our guns and those of the enemy, while my infantry line was farther in front, but low down the mountain sides.

Artillery-firing was common at all times on the line, but now it swelled in volume and extended down to the extreme left, and then from fifty guns burst out simultaneously in my front, while battery after battery, following on the right, disclosed a general attack on our entire line. Presently, and as if by magic, there sprang from the earth a host of men, and in one long, waving line of blue the infantry advanced and the battle of Kennesaw Mountain began.

I could see no infantry of the enemy on my immediate front, owing to the woods at the base of the mountain, and therefore directed the guns

BIG KENNESAW

LITTLE KENNESAW

BATTLE OF KENNESAW MOUNTAIN — DEFEAT OF McPHERSON'S ASSAULT

from their elevated position to enfilade the blue line advancing, on Walker's front, in full view. In a short time this flank fire down their line drove them back, and Walker was relieved from the attack.

We sat there perhaps an hour enjoying a bird's-eye view of one of the most magnificent sights ever allotted to man, to look down upon a hundred and fifty thousand men arrayed in the strife of battle below. 'Twere worth ten years of peaceful life, one glance at their array!

> Better an hour on this mountain top
> Than an age on a peaceful plain.

As the infantry closed in, the blue smoke of the musket marked out the line of battle, while over it rose in cumulilike clouds the white smoke of the artillery. So many were the guns concentrated to silence those three guns of ours on the mountain brow behind us, and so incessant was the roar of cannon and explosion of shells passing over our heads or crashing on the rocks around us, that naught else could be heard; and so, with a roar as constant as Niagara and as sharp as the crash of thunder with lightning yet in the eye, we sat in silence watching the changing scenes of this great panorama.

Through the rifts of smoke, or as it was wafted aside by the wind, we could see the assault made on Cheatham. There the struggle was hard, and there it lasted longest. From the fact that I had seen no infantry in my front, and heard no musketry near, I thought I was exempted from the general infantry attack. I was therefore surprised and awakened from my dream when a courier came to me, about 9 o'clock, and said that Gen. Cockrell wanted assistance, that his line had been attacked in force. Gen. Ector was at once directed to send two regiments to report to him. Soon after a second courier came and reported an assault made on the left of my line. I went immediately with the remainder of Ector's Brigade to Cockrell's assistance, but on reaching him I found the Federal assault had been repulsed. The assaulting column had struck Cockrell's works near the center, recoiled under the fire, swung around into a steep valley where, exposed to the fire of the Missourians in the front and right and of Sears's Mississippians on their left, it seemed to melt away, or sink to the earth, to rise no more.

The assault on my line repulsed, I returned to the mountain top. The intensity of the fire had slackened, and no movement of troops was visible, and, although the din of arms yet resounded far and near, the battle was virtually ended.

From prisoners, and from papers and diaries found in their possession, I learned that my line, from its position, had been selected for assault by Gen. McPherson, as that of Cheatham's and Cleburn's had by Gen. Thomas.

Gen. McPherson was a distinguished officer, and it would be a reflection on his judgment and skill as a general to infer that he did not, under the eye of his commander, with ample men and means, make what he deemed adequate preparations for its accomplishment; but owing to the ground and the determined resistance encountered, his men by intuitive perception, awakened by action, realized that the contest was hopeless, and, where persistence was only death, very properly abandoned the field.

Gen. Cheatham's loss was 195; mine (French's), 186; all other Confederate losses, 141. Being a total of 552. What the Federal loss was I do not know, but it was estimated at from *five to eight thousand.*

The following orders of Gen. Sherman will explain the attack clearly; and the telegrams the result of the battle.

HEADQUARTERS MILITARY DIVISION OF THE MISSISSIPPI,
IN THE FIELD NEAR KENNESAW MOUNTAIN, June 24, 1864.

The army commanders will make full reconnoissances and preparations to attack the enemy in force on the 27th inst., at 8 A.M. precisely.

The commanding general will be on Signal Hill, and will have telegraphic communication with all the army commanders.

1. Maj. Gen. Thomas will assault the enemy at any front near his center, to be selected by himself, and will make any changes in his troops necessary, by night, so as not to attract the attention of the enemy.

2. Maj. Gen. McPherson will feign, by a movement of his cavalry and one division of his infantry, on his extreme left, approaching Marietta from the north, and using artillery freely, but will make his *real attack* at a point south and west of Kennesaw.

3. Maj. Gen. Schofield will feel to his extreme right and threaten that flank of the enemy, etc.

4. Each attacking column will endeavor to break a single point of the enemy's line and make a secure lodgment beyond, and be prepared for following it up toward Marietta and the railroad in case of success.

By order of Maj. Gen. W. T. Sherman.   L. M. DAYTON,
                                                                        Aid de Camp.

HEADQUARTERS MILITARY DIVISION OF THE MISSISSIPPI,
IN THE FIELD, June 27, 1864, 11:45 A.M.

Gen. Schofield: Neither McPherson nor Thomas has succeeded in breaking through, but each has made substantial progress at some cost. Push your operations on the flank and keep me advised. W. T. SHERMAN,
                                                                        Major General Commanding.

HEADQUARTERS MILITARY DIVISION OF THE MISSISSIPPI,
IN THE FIELD NEAR KENNESAW, June 27, 1864, 11:45 A.M.

Gen. Thomas: McPherson's column marched near the top of the hill, through very tangled brush, but *was repulsed.* It is found impossible to deploy, but they hold their ground. I wish you to study well the positions, and if possible to break through the lines to do it. It is easier now than it will be hereafter. I hear Leggitt's guns well behind the mountain.
                              W. T. SHERMAN, *Major General Commanding.*

As nothing decisive was obtained by Sherman's attack, the fire slackened, except on the skirmish line. After dark the ene-

14

my withdrew to their main trenches, the roar of guns died gradually away, and the morning of the 28th dawned on both armies in their former positions. The battle of Kennesaw, then, was a display of force and an attack on the entire length of our line by artillery and infantry, under cover of which two grand attacks were made by assaulting columns, the one on my line and the other on Cheatham's.

28th. After the battle of yesterday there is less activity in front, and the enemy move about in a subdued manner and less lordly style, and yet they resent defeat by a cannonade this afternoon.

29th. Everything is quiet this morning, and so continued till 5: 30 P.M., when they opened on our guns on Kennesaw with a new battery to aid the previous ones. Perhaps they design attacking my line again. A great number of shells fell in camp, or rather they were fragments of shells bursting high over the mountain. At dusk cannonading burst out again.

30th. Rather quiet this morning. At 2:30 A.M. last night we were all aroused by a severe rattle of musketry on the left. We got up and saddled our horses, but after about twenty minutes the firing ceased and all was quiet till morning. It appears that this night attack was caused by a false alarm. This morning I rode to Marietta, it being the first time I have left my line. This afternoon I went to the batteries on the mountain with Gen. Mackell, and then again with Gen. Stevens. There has been but little firing to-day.

July 1. After lying down last night I was aroused by some shells passing overhead, and then again by some sharp musketry on my left. The awful lies found in the newspapers, manufactured by correspondents, lauding certain generals and magnifying their victories, should ruin them.

This afternoon the enemy turned fifty-two pieces of artillery on the three guns I have on the west brow of Little Kennesaw, and continued the fire until long after dark. Seldom in war have there been instances where so many guns have been trained on a single spot. But it was only in the darkness of the night that the magnificence of the scene was displayed— grand beyond imagination, beautiful beyond description. Kennesaw, usually invisible from a distance at night, now resembles Vesuvius in the beginning of an eruption. The innumerable curling rings of smoke from the incessant bursting of shells over the mountain top, added to the volumes belching forth from our guns, wreathed Kennesaw in a golden thundercloud in the still sky, from which came incessant flashes of iridescent light from shells, like bursting stars. The canopy of clouds rolling around the peak looked softer than the downy cotton, but ever changing in color. One moment they were as crimson as the evening clouds painted by the rays of the summer setting sun, and the next, brighter than if lit by the lightning's flash, or bursting meteors. However brilliant and varied and beautiful to the sight, it was not one of pure delight, because it was not a grand display in the clouds for amusement, and when it died away, when silence came, and night threw her dark mantle over the scene, there was no feeling of joy, only one of relief from the excitement of hope and fear ever incident to the wager of battle.

The good people of Marietta, who often watched from house tops these scenes of excitement, will never forget them.

It was during this battle that one of the noblest deeds of humanity was performed the world has ever witnessed. We have the Bible account of the man who, "going from Jerusalem to Jericho, fell among thieves," and the good Samaritan who "had compassion on him and bound up his wounds;" we have Sir Philip Sidney, and the generous conduct of a French cuirassier at Waterloo who, seeing Maj. Poten, of the King's German Legion, had lost his right arm, when about to cut him down, dropped the point of his sword to the salute and rode away. The French soldier was happily discovered, and received the cross of the Legion of Honor. But here *we* have "Col. W. H. Martin, of the First Arkansas Regiment, of Cleburne's Division, who, seeing the woods in front of him on fire burning the wounded Federals, tied a handkerchief to a ramrod and amidst the danger of battle mounted the parapet and shouted to the enemy: 'Come and remove your wounded; they are burning to death; we won't fire a gun till you get them away. Be quick!' And with his own men he leaped over our works and helped to remove them. When this work of humanity was ended a noble Federal major was so impressed by such magnanimity that he pulled from his belt a brace of fine pistols and presented them to Col. Martin with the remark: 'Accept them with my appreciation of the nobility of this deed. It deserves to be perpetuated to the deathless honor of every one of you concerned in it; and should you fight a thousand other battles, and win a thousand other victories, you will never win another so noble as this.' Alas! alas! The noble Col. Martin lived to return to his home. His lovely wife died, leaving an only child. Broken-hearted, he sailed to Honduras, as he said, to make a fortune for his little girl, and there, one day when sailing in a small boat on the —— river, with only a boy to help him, the boom struck him on the head, knocking him overboard, where he was drowned. Such is the irony of fate." *

---

* Mr. Joseph M. Brown, of Marietta, Ga., has a letter from Col. Martin's brother, who was aware of his conduct at the battle of Kennesaw, and relates the circumstances of his death as above written by Mr. Brown.

CHAPTER XV.

I LEFT Kennesaw with regret. From its slopes we repelled the assaults of the enemy, and from its top, where I loved to sit and witness the almost daily conflicts, and hear the "Rebel yell" from away down the throat, and the Federal cheer from the lips. The "Rebel yell" was born amidst the roar of cannon, the flash of the musket, the deadly conflict, comrades falling, and death in front—then, when rushing forward, that unearthly yell rose from a thousand Confederate throats, loud, above "the thunder of the captains and the shoutings," and with the force of a tornado they swept on over the field to death or victory. O how the heart throbs and the eye glares! As that yell is the offspring of the tempest of the battle and death, it cannot be heard in peace, no, never, never! The Federal cheer lives on, and is heard daily in the land. That Confederate yell was never, as far as I know, made when standing still. It was really an inspiration arising from facing danger and death which, as brave men, they resolved to meet. Ye children of peace can never hear it; wherefore I write of a sound that was produced by environment ye will never have. It died with the cause that produced it. The yell produced *awe;* the cheer indicated *joy.*

July 2. Not content with the waste of ammunition last evening, the enemy commenced again at 4:15 this morning—the heathens—and kept it up until 6 A.M. from every battery, and from some guns until 11 A.M. I went up the mountain early in the morning. The fire was not confined to my guns on the mountain, but extended some distance down the line. All this was intended, no doubt, to hold Johnston's main force on his own

ALEXANDER P. STEWART

WILLIAM W. LORING

right while they moved to our left, flanking as usual. At 1 P.M. I received orders to withdraw my division to-night, and did so at 10 P.M.

3d. The regiments left in the trenches and the skirmishers did not leave until 3 A.M. Owing to detention of the trains, etc., we did not reach our new position until after daylight. I went to work intrenching our line—and it is a bad one. Soon in the morning the enemy drove in our cavalry, and by noon had out his skirmishers and artillery to the front. It is wonderful how well our soldiers understand this falling back. Never before did an army constantly fight and fall back for seven weeks without demoralization, and it plainly establishes the intelligence and individuality of the men.

4th. The shelling this morning was very severe. This caused the Mississippi Brigade to seek protection in this way: They used the shingles from a house for spades, and bayonets for picks, and thus in a few minutes the men were in a shallow ditch. My men in rifle pits were shelled out and driven in. We were ordered to fall back to-night, which was done with much difficulty.

5th. At 3 A.M. we were on the retreat, and it was well executed by the troops, and we came into Vining Station ahead of the other divisions. Some sharpshooters with Whitworth rifles and a lieutenant of Hoslin's Battery were left in camp asleep, and they barely escaped capture. We were now on the right bank of the Chattahoochee river. The right of my line was a small redoubt east of the railroad (Western and Atlantic), thence it crossed it, thence across the Marietta dirt road, etc. At 10 A.M. the enemy swept the whole plain with shells down to the river. I established headquarters with Gen. Walthall in an old log house by the roadside.

6th. The enemy is quiet this morning. Yesterday the impolite followers of Sherman came near spoiling our dinner as we sat on the ground eating, by sending a twenty-pound Parrott shell near enough to throw the sand about and over it.

7th. This morning I rode along the lines with Gens. Loring and Shoup. Gen. A. P. Stewart, having been promoted to a lieutenant general, assumed command of the Army of Mississippi. After the death of Gen. Polk I unhesitatingly said that Gen. Stewart would be promoted. I rode along the whole of his command with him.

8th. The enemy keep up a sharp fire on our skirmish line at night. They evidently are apprehensive that we will cross the river at night, for during the day they are quiet.

As we have no tools for throwing up breastworks, Gen. Ector came to me for permission to move a regiment to his front in the woods, from where he had swung back, so as to attack the enemy when they came out to establish a picket line. This he did successfully, and returned with good picks, spades, and steel axes (ours were cast iron) that will cut wood. Shingleur, Robinson, and Yerger, aids, are all sick.

9th. About 9 A.M. the enemy attacked the line of skirmishers in front of Sears's Brigade with force and drove them from their pits. Col. Barry advanced the Thirty-Sixth Mississippi Regiment, under command of Maj. Parton, and forced them back, captured their line, and drove them nearly to their main works, and reëstablished ours. Prisoners were captured from five different regiments. Our loss was fifty-two men in all. After this they shelled my line for hours. About 2 P.M. the enemy commenced a slow cannonade on my front, and continued it till dark. The twenty-pound Parrotts passed over our quarters constantly and exploded in the road.

This P.M. I was sent for by Gen. Stewart, and received orders to withdraw my command across the river by the railroad bridge. After all were crossed both the railroad and dirt road bridges were burned. We moved on toward Paces' Ferry, and bivouacked by the wayside.

10th. The morning has been quiet, and the wearied troops have rested. This retrograde movement was caused by the enemy crossing the river above, near Roswell. The works of Gen. Shoup, with its stockades, did not give Johnston spare troops enough to prevent this movement of the enemy. Thus we are constantly outflanked by a superior force not disposed to attack us behind any kind of works. At 4 P.M. it commenced raining, and then artillery firing began at the railroad crossing and farther down the river. Now for nearly two months we have had daily firing, save only one day when on Lost Mountain. Gen. Ector was left to guard the railroad crossing and the river, above and below. This was on the 11th.

12th and 13th. The camp is filled with rumors. The enemy is reported to have crossed the river and then gone back. I rode to Stewart's headquarters, and thence to Atlanta. I saw Capt. Maupin in the hospital. Poor fellow; he was shot, at the Latimar House, through the breast. I went to see Gen. Johnston, and found Gen. Braxton Bragg there. He comes from Richmond. What is his mission? Who knows? Is Sherman on this side of the river? Has Grant's failures in Virginia, and Early's invasion of Pennsylvania, affected movements down here? A few days will determine. O for brighter days for the Confederacy! I have been obliged to order the guards to fire on the cavalry when they go in the river to bathe with the Federal cavalry. Federals never venture in unless our men are bathing. Our men are not seeking fords; they are. This is what they are looking for.

14th, 15th, 16th. We remained in bivouac, and nothing unusual occurred. We are still anxious to learn more about Early in Maryland. There is the usual amount of firing on our front.

Sunday, 17th. The enemy commenced a more rapid and continued fire from their batteries near the railroad bridge, where I have pickets. This, as usual, presages some movement. And here it is: "Hold your command ready for a movement." It does seem strange that we cannot have one quiet Sabbath. Sherman has no regard for the Fourth Commandment. I wish a Bible society would send him a prayer book, instead of shipping them all to the more remote heathen: but it would be the same in either case. The one is wicked by nature; the other, I fear, is becoming so from habit. Perhaps "Tecumseh" has something to do with it. There is much in a name.

18th. I moved into a position where my left rested on the Marietta road, and commenced intrenching at night. Gen. Johnston was relieved on yesterday from the command of this army, and Gen. J. B. Hood assumed command by orders from Richmond. Early this morning I rode down to army headquarters and bade Johnston good-by.

And here I will state the conversation that occurred between Hood and me. I told him that I was sorry Johnston had been relieved; that I had often, when in Mississippi, talked with him concerning the manner of conducting the war; but " now that you are in command, I assure you I will serve under you as faithfully and cheerfully as with him." Although he took my hand and thanked me, I was ever afterwards impressed with the belief that he never forgave me for what I said.

Now, since I have alluded to it, I will state that in our conversation I agreed with Johnston that our success mainly depended on breaking the enemy down financially, by procrastinating the war; that to do this the strength of the army in the East and in the West should be maintained; that the armies upheld the government, and a great defeat would be disastrous.

It was because we could obtain no more recruits that Grant refused to exchange prisoners and receive the Andersonville prisoners and return a like number to increase the ranks of Lee's army. Here is Grant's letter on exchange of prisoners:

CITY POINT, August 18, 1864.

To Gen. Butler.

On the subject of exchange, however, I differ from Gen. Hitchcock. It is hard on our men held in Southern prisons not to exchange them, but it is humanity to those left in the ranks to fight our battles. Every man released, on parole on otherwise, becomes an active soldier against us at once, either directly or indirectly.

If we commence a system of exchange, which liberates all prisoners taken, we will have to fight on until the whole South is exterminated. If we hold those caught, they amount to no more than dead men. At this particular time to release Rebel prisoners North would insure Sherman's defeat, and would compromise our safety here.

As Gen. Grant discusses the humanity of his acts, I will compare it with what other distinguished men have written on the subject of exchange of prisoners.

Carthage, dispirited by her losses, wished for peace. For this purpose ambassadors were dispatched to Rome. Regulus (a prisoner in Carthage) was sent with the ambassadors to further the exchange, bound by an oath to return to Carthage in case of a failure to make peace or exchange of prisoners. He dissuaded his countrymen from agreeing to either proposition, and, bound by his oath, returned to Carthage, where he well knew torture and death awaited him.

Cicero applauds Regulus in both particulars in returning to Carthage. Sir Walter Raleigh commends Regulus in maintaining the obligation of his oath, but in dissuading the Senate not to agree to exchange of prisoners he condemns his inhumanity, which no good reasons of state could justify.

However, be this as it may, one thing is certain, and that is that the inhumanity, if there were any, was assumed by the act of the United States (the North) in refusing to mitigate their sufferings on both sides by not exchanging prisoners, and it releases the South from the charge of all suffering incident, al ways, to prison life.*

O! had the gifted Senator from Georgia, Benjamin H. Hill, known of the existence of this letter defining the policy of the North in the treatment of prisoners of war, he would have vanquished his antagonist, Hon. J. G. Blaine, and silenced the jingoes and stopped the waving of the bloody shirt to fire the Northern heart against the South.

In a private conversation with President Davis he told me that so great was the pressure made on him by deputations, committees, individuals, officials, and the press demanding to know if Atlanta and the State of Georgia were to be given up without a battle for its preservation, that he was reluctantly obliged to relieve Gen. Johnston to satisfy the clamorous demands made for a halt and a battle in defense of the State while the army was in the mountainous region, and so he yielded to the cry of the people.

20th. This morning it was resolved to attack the three corps of the enemy that were on the Peachtree creek and separated from the corps that were near Decatur. Sears's Brigade being on duty on the river and creek, I moved with the brigades of Cockrell and Ector to the right and formed line of battle in front of the Ragdale House. This position was the extreme left of the army.

The plan of battle was a good one. Hardee was to gain the enemy's rear, swing to the left, taking their line in flank, while we attacked the line in front in echelon of brigades as the battle swept down the creek. Walthall was on my right, and I was to keep within about three hundred yards of him. In advancing I came to an open field in front of the ene-

---

my. Their line was fortified, with two field batteries in position that kept up a continuous fire on my line. Gen. Loring's troops broke through the enemy's line of works. Reynolds and Featherston had to abandon the captured line by reason of the flank fire on them. The failure of Hardee deranged the plan of battle. After dark we withdrew.

22d. I had a slight skirmish with the enemy yesterday. We got twenty-four of them. Last night the army occupied Atlanta. My division formed the extreme left of the army. My headquarters are at Mr. Jennings's house, and the line crosses the road to Turner's Ferry and runs toward the Western and Atlantic railroad. Preparations are being made to attack the enemy's left wing over toward Decatur. Noon has passed, and there has been no infantry-firing yet, only the booming of artillery; but about 4 P.M. the volleys of musketry fell on the ear, died away, and then burst out anew, and did not cease until dark, when they receded in the distance, indicating the advance of our troops. The fruits of the victory are reported to be twenty-four pieces of artillery and three thousand one hundred prisoners. With it comes sad regrets for the death of Gen. W. A. T. Walker on our side, and Gen. McPherson, United States army, on their side.

27th. Nothing has occurred, save the usual siege firing, since the 22d. This morning when I was at Ward's Battery there was some artillery-firing, and a shell exploded overhead, striking Gen. Ector above the knee, requiring amputation, and Capt. Ward, mortally wounding him. I sent them to my quarters and thence to our hospital. Ward was an accomplished gentleman and a brave soldier. I wrote to Mrs. Ward, trying to console her in her bereavement. Gen. Ector in due time was walking by the aid of crutches. Gen. S. D. Lee to-day was assigned to the command of Hood's Corps.

28th. I rode to Gen. Stewart's and heard that the enemy was moving to our left. I then went to Hood's. Knowing that four divisions had been moved to my left, I felt assured that a battle was pending. S. D. Lee was in command. About 1 P.M. it began, and continued four hours. By request of Walthall I sent them Guibor's guns and Ector's Brigade. The attack was a failure because it was fought by weak detailed attacks instead of a consolidated force. Gen. Stewart was struck by a partly spent ball in the forehead, and Loring was wounded. As soon as I learned the position of the enemy I opened fire on them from my rifled thirty-two pounders and continued the fire slowly all night.

29th. All is quiet this morning. I rode to corps headquarters, and found that both Stewart and Loring had left, which made me commander of the corps, but to my surprise I found that Hood had placed Cheatham in command. I wrote to Hood in regard to the matter. Hood's act was in keeping with the intriguing so ruinous to this army, and I asked to be relieved from serving in it any longer.

31st. Nothing unusual happened yesterday. To-day is Sunday, and it dawned as though peace had spread her white wings over the land, for not a gun has yet been heard, and so it continued most of the day. Divine service was held in the brigades, and in the pond in front of my quarters a baptism took place.

August 1. My command was extended to cover Walthall's original front. I made a call on Gens. G. W. Smith and R. Toombs, and wrote to Richmond. This P.M. the enemy commenced artillery fire on the redoubt in front of my house. One shell killed a mule in the yard, another broke my wagon tongue, while a third knocked the pipe from Hedrick's (my orderly) mouth, etc. My application to be relieved from duty was returned disapproved, and I was informed that I would not be relieved. So on August 2 I wrote to the Adjutant General to be relieved from command in or serving with this army.

2d, 3d, 4th, 5th. [To transcribe my diary for these days would only be a reiteration of daily siege attacks.]

6th. I made a demonstration on the enemy this morning in his works in my front to aid Lee on our left. I moved my left over a mile to the front and attacked the enemy on his skirmish line and then their main line, but it was done at the expense of Lieut. Motherhead killed, Maj. Redwine wounded, and forty-three men killed and wounded. I was directed to make this demonstration; ordinarily they do but little good against old soldiers, because they know so well that they would not be attacked behind their works seriously unless by massed troops. Neither will they attack ours. In the afternoon they shelled my line complimentary to my attack in the morning. How polite they are in returning attentions! Bad news received from Mobile. It is reported that the United States fleet has passed Fort Morgan and is now in the bay.

8th, 9th. I gave my large map of the Yazoo Valley to Gen. M. L. Smith, who sent it to Macon to be copied, one copy for the commander of the Department of Mississippi, and the other for the War Department. I rode along the lines with Gen. Sears, who has returned. Cockrell also got back yesterday. While I was at Col. Young's the enemy commenced shelling, and it has continued ever since, full seven hours. So far it has done but little damage. Very many shells have fallen close by, and exploded over the house, and it has become anything but a pleasant residence, and at night disturbs pleasant dreams.

I sent a letter to the President on the matter of Gen. Hood's conduct in the assignment of Cheatham to Stewart's Corps during his absence.

10th and 11th. I rode out to our hospital this morning. The enemy seems disposed to get possession of my vidette line, which I have maintained up to this time. When the siege began I sent for my principal officers and told them all that I did not intend my camp should be rendered unpleasant from rifle balls, that the vidette line away in front must be held; that the picket line five hundred yards in front should be strong, and on it the fighting should be to the last extremity. The result of this course has been that my men are entirely free from annoyance, except from some artillery fire, and that is foolishly directed at our redoubts. I use artillery on their infantry camps and lines so as to destroy their rest both day and night. See the difference While we sleep in safety, in some parts of the lines around the city no one can move without drawing the fire of the Yankees on themselves, so near are the lines together.

12th to 17th. [The diary is too full of detail to record here, so I will merely remark that the everlasting fire continues on my picket line, and their guns shell my redoubts.]

17th. Gen. Stewart came to my quarters early this morning, at 6 A.M., and we went along the line. We returned and had breakfast. Then the artillery, as usual, began at the redoubt in front of the house. As the shells crossed the road on both sides of the house, it was dangerous to leave, and he remained an hour or more.

In the evening I was sitting on the fence enjoying my pipe while watching the explosion of the shells, when who should ride up but Gen. M. Jeff. Thompson, and he was invited to our quarters. I could not keep from laughing. I have an illustrated copy of the illustrious Don Quixote, and here was a duplicate picture, or rather here before me was the Don himself, in form and features, and if Sancho had seen Jeff he would have called him "Master." He passed the night with us, entertaining us with his adventures in the West. In the morning he went to see his Missouri friends.

18th. The Yankees must be angry. Because my batteries dared to wake them up with a few shells they raised—well—(I begin it with a "w") and never ceased until 2 P.M., and they threw not less than two thousand shot at us, and accomplished nothing, only one shell went by accident through our house.

19th, 20th, 21st, 22d. These days witnessed the usual expenditure of ammunition. On the 21st Lieut. Col. McDowell was killed in the rear of our second skirmish line. What an excellent man and gallant officer gave his life for the Confederacy! Peace to him and his friends!

23d. Firing as usual.

24th. The enemy fired hot shot on the city all last night, and to-day they set on fire some cotton, and burned a few houses.

25th. I wrote to Judge Ould. Firing as usual.

26th. This morning at daylight I was informed that the enemy had abandoned their works on my right and front nearly to my left. I found everything in their works horribly filthy, and alive with "dog" flies to such an extent that our horses could not be managed. The clothing, new and old, was covered with vermin. My servant boys carried some jackets home that had to be buried. Their line of works was very strong. I found the brick furnace where they made "shot red hot" to fire day and night at intervals to burn the city. At first little "niggers" got their fingers burned picking them up to sell to the ordnance department. Again on my skirmish line this evening was another good officer killed. Lieut. Col. Samuels fell from a rifle ball. From Decatur all the way around to the Turner's Ferry road the enemy has moved to our left. . . . There are no flies or vermin in our camp—strange but true.

27th. I made a reconnoissance with two brigades and artillery to Turner's Ferry over the Chattahoochee river. We had a fight there and captured some prisoners. They told me that the place, as I could see, was strongly fortified; that the Twentieth Corps (Hooker's) occupied the work; that Hooker had gone and Slocum was in command. I think they told me this, although not named in my diary. We slept in peace.

28th. I rode through the city. To give you an idea of the terrible musketry fire, in an open field between their picket line and mine one brigade picked up about five thousand pounds of lead balls that had been fired on the lines. The ground was literally covered with them—oxidized white like hailstones. Trees three and four inches in diameter in front of my line were cut down by balls. The lead was sold to the ordnance officers, and the weight was thus known.

29th, 30th. Our troops are moving to the left. Six of our men crossed the river and captured nine men and two wagons.

31st. Featherston and Walthall have been withdrawn from the city. My division and some State troops under the charge of Gen. G. W. Smith alone are in the city to-day. Some cavalry scouts followed my scouts nearly into the city. Firing is heard on our left. The railroad to Macon was cut to-day. This is unpleasant news.

September 1. This morning the news is that Hardee had failed to dislodge Sherman from his position. Everything indicates that Atlanta is to be abandoned, and before noon the order came. I became the rear guard. There is confusion in the city, and some of the soldiers in the town are drunk. Common sense is wanted. The five heavy guns that I had ordered to be spiked by the rear guard at 11 P.M. were burned by order of the chief of ordnance at 5 P.M., a proclamation to the enemy in my front that we were evacuating the place. As soon as I started to leave the works some of Hood's officers fired the ordnance trains. This should have been done the last of all, when the rear guard or pickets were withdrawn. Who would extinguish an ordnance train of bursting shells? So lighted by the glare of fires. flashes of powder. and bursting shells, I slowly left Atlanta. and at daylight on the morning of the 2d we were not five miles out of the city. I started soon after for Lovejoy's Station.

3d. Featherston took the advance. Last evening artillery was heard at Lovejoy's Station. Hardee was holding in check all of Sherman's army except the Twentieth Corps. and we are marching to his assistance. I passed S. D. Lee's Corps on the road. It was yesterday at Rough and Ready. This is attacking *in detail* as usual. On arrival my division was ordered to relieve Gen. Brown's. After dark I was ordered to move to my left and Gen. Guist to his right to exchange positions. This was a deliberately planned *trick* of Hardee's to put me in one side of a salient angle that was subject to a reverse fire of artillery from the enemy.

4th. This morning cannonading was not so rapid.

5th. Last night I made a change of position. Firing as usual. While I was on the line Capt. Kennerly (Mrs. Bowen's brother) and four others were killed and five wounded. During the day I lost forty men.

6th. It was now discovered that the enemy were falling back to take possession of Atlanta. now abandoned. Gave Cockrell permission to pursue them. and he skirmished with their rear guard and killed many of them and returned with over twenty prisoners.

7th. 8th. and 9th. [Diary records no important events.]

10th. A communication from Sherman to Hood was received stating that the citizens of Atlanta must leave. Those who so elect will be sent to the North. The remainder will be sent South. The work is to commence on Monday. There are about eighteen thousand people in the city. I am told that he also offers to exchange prisoners, provided he should receive only men who have yet two years to serve in the United States army. Prisoners who have served out the period of their enlistment, or have only a short time to serve, will not be received. Gen. Loring returned to-day.

CHAPTER XVI.

THE BATTLE OF ALLATOONA.

From Lovejoy's to Lost Mountain—Big Shanty—Acworth—Destroying
Railroad—In the Rear of Sherman—Situation of the Two Armies—Or-
ders to Destroy the Etowah River Bridge—To Fill Up the Railroad Cut
at Allatoona—Hood Not Aware that Allatoona Was Fortified and Garri-
soned—March to Allatoona—Summons to Surrender—No Answer—Gen.
Corse's Report Erroneous—The Fortifications—Strength of Forces—
Equalization of Forces—Some Federal Dispatches—The Battle—Corse's
Account—Col. Ludlow's Description—Desperate Fighting—The Main
Line Captured—Enemy Driven into an Interior Fort—Dispatches from
Gen. Armstrong Respecting Movements of the Enemy at Big Shanty—
Withdraw to Avoid Being Surrounded by Converging Forces—Corse's
Dispatch to Sherman—Provisions—Confederates Three Days and Nights
without Rest or Sleep—Pass by the Enemy—Evangelist P. P. Bliss
Writes the (Gospel) Hymn, "Hold the Fort"—Hood and His Erroneous
Publications in His Book—His Admiration for Corse—My Admiration
for the Confederates—The Soldier's Grave—The Lone Grave—Lieut.
Gen. A. P. Stewart's Note in Regard to This Account of the Battle.

September 29. This morning Loring's, Walthall's, and my divisions
moved on the Pumpkinton road and *crossed the Chattahoochee river* and encamped beyond Villa Rica. The following day we marched to near Brownsville Post Office.

Saturday, October 1. I remained in camp. At 10 A.M. all the division
commanders were invited to Gen. Hood's headquarters, and the object of
the move was discussed. I found in the room on my arrival Gens. Stewart, S. D. Lee, Loring, Walthall, Stevenson, and Clayton. As soon as I
entered the room Hood said to me: "Gen. French, what do you think Gen.
Sherman will do now?" I replied: "I suppose he will turn southwest and
move on to Mobile; or he may go to Augusta to destroy our powder mills,
and then make for Charleston or Savannah." "In that event do you believe he can sustain his troops on the march if our cavalry lay waste the
country before him?" I answered: "He will find all he wants as he moves
on." To this Hood replied: "Well, I have nothing to do with that, as the
President has promised to attend to that matter." Every officer present
disagreed with me save Gen. S. D. Lee. He thought all would have difficulty to subsist except the cavalry.

On the subject of destroying Sherman's communications my
diary says:

I was in favor of an immediate move on the railroad above Kennesaw
with the *whole army*, and expressed my regrets at the delay.

I received orders to move to-morrow. We were requested to inform

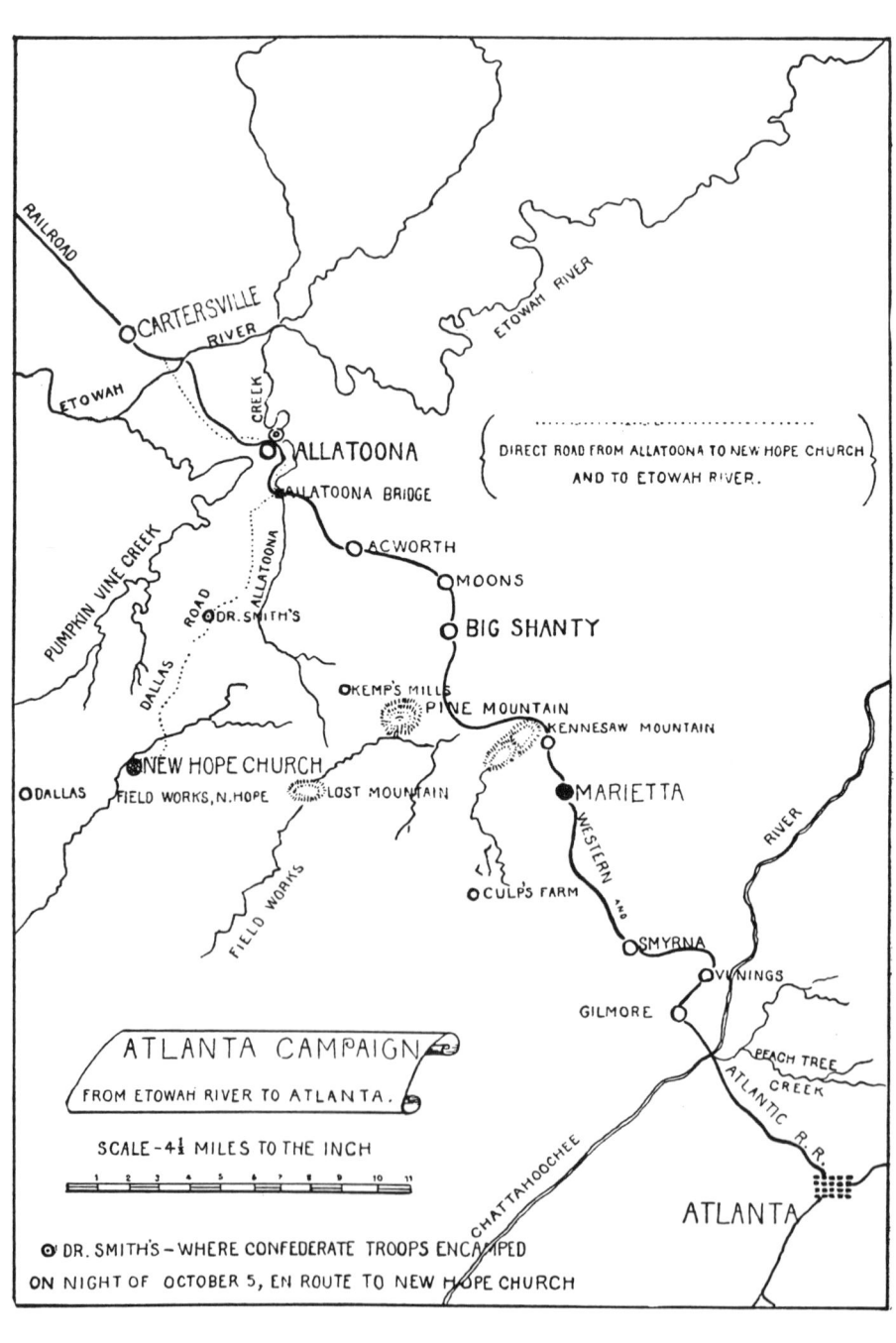

RAILROAD

CARTERSVILLE
RIVER
ETOWAH

ETOWAH RIVER

CREEK

ALLATOONA

ALLATOONA BRIDGE

DIRECT ROAD FROM ALLATOONA TO NEW HOPE CHURCH
AND TO ETOWAH RIVER.

PUMPKIN VINE CREEK

ACWORTH

MOONS

BIG SHANTY

DALLAS ROAD

ALLATOONA

DR. SMITH'S

KEMP'S MILLS

PINE MOUNTAIN

KENNESAW MOUNTAIN

NEW HOPE CHURCH

DALLAS

FIELD WORKS, N. HOPE

LOST MOUNTAIN

MARIETTA

RIVER

WESTERN AND

CULP'S FARM

FIELD WORKS

SMYRNA

VININGS

GILMORE

PEACH TREE CREEK

ATLANTIC R.R.

ATLANTA CAMPAIGN

FROM ETOWAH RIVER TO ATLANTA.

SCALE-4½ MILES TO THE INCH

1 2 3 4 5 6 7 8 9 10 11

CHATTAHOOCHEE

ATLANTA

⊙ DR. SMITH'S — WHERE CONFEDERATE TROOPS ENCAMPED
ON NIGHT OF OCTOBER 5, EN ROUTE TO NEW HOPE CHURCH

the brigade commanders of the object of moving in the rear of Sherman's army, and they were to inform the regimental and company officers.

2d. I left camp and marched to Moon's, and this brought us to the same ground we occupied on the 24th of May.

3d. When Sherman discovered that Hood had crossed the Chattahoochee and was marching to obtain possession of his line of communication, he immediately adopted measures to defeat Hood's plans and give him battle.

The general situation of the two armies to-day is: Sherman's main body of troops is at Atlanta, with garrisons at the Chattahoochee, Vining's, Marietta, Kennesaw, Big Shanty, Moon's, Acworth, Allatoona Creek, Allatoona fortifications garrisoned by just about one thousand men, Gen. Elliott, chief of cavalry, with his command at Kennesaw, Gen. J. E. Smith, with his division, at Cartersville, Gen. J. M. Corse at Rome with a division, and the garrisons at important places on up to Chattanooga, as disclosed by the movements of troops, dispatches sent directing their movements, and subsequent information.

Hood's army marched to Lost Mountain, where he remained with two corps, while Stewart's Corps went thence in the rear of the enemy's line of fortifications to Big Shanty. Gen. Featherston captured some forty prisoners at Big Shanty, and commenced destroying the railroad. Loring, sent to Acworth (near Allatoona), captured about two hundred prisoners, and Walthall took seventy prisoners at Moon Station. All night every one was hard at work destroying the railroad, and the next day by noon we had about eight miles of the track taken up and the rails twisted.

4th. At noon, when filling up the railroad cuts at Big Shanty, I received orders to fill up the deep cut of the railroad at Allatoona, and then, if possible, destroy the railroad bridge over the Etowah river. About this time some one living near by told us that the enemy had fortifications at Allatoona, well garrisoned and commissary stores there. Under these peculiar orders (which will be given in full hereafter in my report) I left Big Shanty with my division at 3 P.M. for Acworth and thence to Allatoona, while Loring and Walthall were ordered in the direction of New Hope Church. I was now entering the zone of active movements of the Federals, and away from all support, and all support from me, and the enemy converging on Allatoona from all directions. I reached Acworth about dark, and was detained there till 11 P.M., awaiting rations and getting some one for a guide. I saw camp fires of the enemy east of the railroad and north of Kennesaw, and night signals from Allatoona to Kennesaw. From two young ladies, who to-day had visited Allatoona, I obtained the name of the commander there, and the probable strength of the enemy in the several works. I also succeeded, through some of the citizens, in getting a boy for a guide. I moved from Acworth about 11 P.M., and on arriving at Allatoona Creek I left there the Fourth Mississippi Regiment and one piece of artillery, with instructions to burn the bridge and capture the garrison of one hundred men in the blockhouse. When at Acworth I sent fifteen men from a Capt. Taylor's company of cavalry, Pinson's Regiment, to strike the railroad near the Etowah river and

15

tear up the track to prevent reënforcements from reaching Allatoona. I moved on then from the creek, and arrived before Allatoona about 3 A.M. All was darkness; nothing could be seen except occasional lights flitting about the place. I put the artillery, eleven guns, in position, or rather left them in what the guide said was a good place, and also left two regiments of Ector's Brigade under Col. Andrews as a support to them. With the guide directing, I moved the division to gain the flank and rear of the line of works. There were five detached works on the high ridge through which the Western and Atlantic railroad runs. No road leads to this ridge except the Cartersville road, that ascends the ridge by a winding ascent, and enters the works, passing within a few feet of the main redoubt, under its guns, and then runs on the crest of the ridge for two hundred and fifty yards to where it passes out through the fortifications. So the guide directed us through the dark *woods* and up the steep, rugged, rocky *hills*, and down into deep *valleys* until we were lost, and the guide acknowledged that he could not find the way. This determined me to stop and rest till daylight. The pickets had been driven in, and now and then shots were exchanged. Starting again at dawn, I reached the high ridge on which the redoubts were at 7:30 A.M. with the leading brigade. I halted Cockrell's and Ector's Brigades on the ridge, and sent Gen. Sears to gain the rear of the works. The artillery opened fire on the forts (one on either side of the railroad) about 7 A.M., and when we gained the ridge appeared to keep the enemy quiet.

These dispositions being made, about 8 A.M. I summoned the commander to surrender the place. I then supposed the garrison consisted of only about nine hundred men, as reported to me at Acworth. Maj. D. W. Sanders was instructed to allow about twenty minutes for the officer to whom he delivered the message to go and return with the reply. After waiting longer than the specified time, he returned without an answer. Believing Sears was now well around on the north side, and having waited to hear his attack so long, I put Cockrell's Brigade in motion, supported by Ector's Brigade (of four regiments), to make the attack, as it was now 10:20 A.M.

The three companies of the Ninety-Third Illinois that were in the two extreme west redoubts abandoned them without making much resistance, and fell back to a very strong line of defense protected by all the entanglements of modern warfare. Through the center of this work ran the Cartersville road. This part of the defensive work was occupied by the Thirty-Ninth Iowa, Seventh Illinois, and seven companies of the Ninety-Third Illinois, making, in officers and men, a total of just about nine hundred. Against this force, placed in carefully constructed works, I could send only the Missouri brigade and four regiments of the Texas brigade, in all one thousand three hundred and fifty. I had been informed by Gen. Armstrong that the enemy's cavalry was moving up east of the railroad. Then again I received from him a second dispatch informing me that the Federal infantry was passing through Big Shanty and moving up the railroad. This dispatch was dated 9 A.M. Knowing that this column could reach the junction of the Sandtown and Dallas roads before I could, I determined to withdraw, trusting to arrive there first.

FRANCIS M. COCKRELL

But as all these matters are more fully referred to in my report, I will here quit, for the present, further extracts from my diary, and give the report.

In Volume 39, Series 1, page 814, will be found in the " War Records " the following report:

HEADQUARTERS FRENCH'S DIVISION,
TUSCUMBIA, ALA., November 5, 1864.

General: Sometime since I had the honor to submit to you a brief preliminary report of the battle of Allatoona. As the report of the brigade commanders are now in, I have the honor to forward one embracing some of the details of the battle.

About noon on the 4th of October, when at Big Shanty, the following order was handed me by Lieut. Gen. Stewart, it being a copy of one to him:

HEADQUARTERS ARMY OF TENNESSEE, October 4, 1864, 7:30 A.M.

Lieut. Gen. A. P. Stewart, Commanding Corps.

General: Gen. Hood directs that later in the evening you move Stevenson back to Davis's Cross Roads, and that you bring two of your divisions back to Adams's and between Adams's and Davis's Cross Roads, placing them in such a way as to cover the position at Adams's now occupied by Stevenson, and that your third division (say French) shall move up the railroad and fill up the deep cut at Allatoona with logs, brush, rails, dirt, etc. To-morrow morning at daylight he desires Stevenson to be moved to Lieut. Gen. Lee's actual left, that two of your divisions at that time at Adams's shall draw back, with your left in the neighborhood of Davis's Cross Roads, and your right in the neighborhood of Lost Mountain, and the division that will have gone to Allatoona to march thence to New Hope Church and on the position occupied by your other troops—that is, that the division shall rejoin your command by making this march out from the railroad and via New Hope. Gen. Hood thinks that it is probable that the guard at the railroad bridge on Etowah is small, and when French goes to Allatoona, if he can get such information as would justify him, if possible move to that bridge and destroy it. Gen. Hood considers its destruction would be a great advantage to the army and the country. Should he be able to destroy the bridge, in coming out he could move, as has been heretofore indicated, via New Hope.

Yours respectfully,
A. P. MASON,
Assistant Adjutant General.

Soon after an order, of which the following is a copy, was sent me:

HEADQUARTERS ARMY OF TENNESSEE,
OFFICE OF THE CHIEF OF STAFF, October 4, 1864, 11:30 A.M.

Lieut. Gen. Stewart, Commanding.

General: Gen. Hood directs me to say that it is of the greatest importance to destroy the Etowah railroad bridge. if such a thing is possible. From the best information we have now he thinks the enemy cannot disturb us before *to-morrow*, and by *that time* your main body will be near the remainder of our army. He suggests that if it be considered practicable to destroy the bridge when the division goes there and the artillery is placed in position the commanding officer shall call for volunteers to go to the bridge with lightwood and other combustible material that can be obtained, and set fire to it.

Yours respectfully,
A. P. MASON,
Major and Assistant Adjutant General.

Gen. Stewart's Corps had struck the railroad at Big Shanty on the evening of the 3d, and all three of his divisions had worked all night destroying the railroad from near Kennesaw up to Acworth Station. As we had been informed at Big Shanty that the Allatoona pass or cut was fortified, and that the enemy had a garrison there of three regiments, and had accumulated a considerable amount of provisions, it was considered a matter of importance that the place should be captured, and after the orders were handed me, at my request, Gen. Stewart sent me (with Maj. Myrick) four additional pieces of artillery. *It would appear, however, from these orders that the general in chief was not aware that the pass was fortified and garrisoned that I was sent to have filled up.* Under these orders I left Big Shanty about 3:30 P.M., and marched to Acworth, a distance of six miles, arriving there before sunset. There I was detained, awaiting the arrival of rations and cooking them, until 11 P.M.

As I knew nothing of the roads, the enemy's works or position, it was important to procure a guide, and at last a young man, or rather boy, was found who knew the roads, and had seen the position of the fortifications at Allatoona, he being a member of a cavalry company. At Acworth Capt. Taylor, of Pinson's Regiment of cavalry, with twenty-five men, reported to me for duty. He was immediately directed to send fifteen men under a trusty officer to strike the railroad as near the Etowah railroad bridge as possible, and take up the rails and hide or destroy them, to prevent trains from reaching Allatoona with reënforcements, as well as to prevent any trains that might be there from escaping. From an eminence near Acworth the enemy could be seen communicating messages by their night signals from Allatoona with the station on Kennesaw; and to the east of us were the fires of a large encampment of the Federals and apparently opposite Moon's Station. Citizens residing here informed me that there was a blockhouse with a garrison of about one hundred men at the Allatoona bridge; that at Allatoona there were two small redoubts with outworks, defended with four pieces of artillery and garrisoned with three and a half regiments of infantry. About 11 P.M. the march was resumed. The night was very dark, and the roads bad. After crossing Allatoona creek, Col. Adaire, with his Fourth Regiment, Mississippi Volunteers, and one piece of artillery, was left near the blockhouse with instructions to surround it, capture the garrison, and destroy the bridge over the creek. Continuing the march, the division arrived before Allatoona about 3 A.M. Nothing could be seen but one or two twinkling lights on the opposite heights, and nothing was heard except the occasional interchange of shots between our advanced guards and the pickets of the garrison in the valley below. All was darkness. I had no knowledge of the place, and it was important to attack at the break of day. Taking the guide and lights, I placed the artillery in position on the hills south and east of the railroad, and the Thirty-Ninth North Carolina Regiment, under Col. Coleman, and the Thirty-Second Texas were left as a supporting force, both under command of Col. J. A. Andrews, commanding the latter regiment. This being done, I proceeded with the guide to gain the heights, or ridge, crowned by the works of the enemy. Without roads or paths the head of the line

CAPTURE OF BLOCKHOUSE, ALLATOONA CREEK, OCTOBER 5, 1864

reached the railroad, crossed it, and began ascending and descending the high, steep, and densely timbered spurs of the mountains, and after about an hour's march it was found that we were directly in front of the works, and not on the main ridge. The guide made a second effort to gain the ridge, and failed, so dark was it in the woods. I therefore determined to rest where we were and await daylight. With the dawn the march was resumed, and finally, by 7:30 A.M., the head of the column was on the ridge about six hundred yards west of the main fortifications, and between those he occupied and an abandoned redoubt on our left.

Here the fortifications, for the first time, were seen, and instead of two redoubts there were disclosed to us three redoubts on the west of the railroad cut, and a star fort on the east with outer works and approaches defended to a great distance by abatis, and nearer the works by stockades and other obstructions. The railroad emerges from the Allatoona Mountain by crossing this ridge through a cut sixty-five feet deep. Dispositions for the assault were now made by sending Gen. Sears's Brigade to the north side or rear of the works, Gen. F. M. Cockrell's (Missouri) Brigade to rest with its center on the ridge, while Gen. W. H. Young, with the four Texas regiments, was found in the rear of Gen. Cockrell.

Maj. Myrick had opened on the works with his artillery, and was ordered to continue his fire until the attacking force should interfere, or until he heard the volleys of musketry.

Gen. Sears was to commence the assault on the rear, and when musketry was heard Gen. Cockrell was to move down the ridge, supported by Gen. Young, and carry the works by (as it were) a flank attack. So rugged and abrupt were the hills that the troops could not be gotten into position until about 9 A.M., when I sent a summons to surrender. The flag was met by a Federal staff officer, and he was allowed seventeen minutes to return an answer. The time expired without any answer being received, whereupon Maj. D. W. Sanders, impatient at the delay, broke off the interview and returned. No reply being sent me, the order was given for the assault by directing the advance of Cockrell's Brigade. Emerging from the woods and passing over a long distance of abatis formed of felled timber, and under a severe fire of musketry and artillery, nobly did it press forward, followed by the gallant Texans. The enemy's outer line and one redoubt soon fell. Resting to gather strength and survey the work before them, again they rushed forward in column, and in a murderous hand-to-hand conflict that left the ditches filled with the dead they became masters of the second redoubt.

The third and main redoubt, now filled by those driven from the captured works on the west side of the railroad, was further crowded by those that were coming out of the fort on the east side of the road, from the attack of Gen. Sears. They had to cross the deep cut, through which our artillery poured a steady and deadly fire. The Federal forces were now confined to one redoubt, and we occupied the ditch and almost entirely silenced their fire, and were preparing for the final attack.

Pending the progress of these events I had received a note from Gen. F. C. Armstrong, dated 7 A.M., asking me at what time I would move toward

New Hope, and informing me also that the enemy had moved up east of the railroad above Kennesaw and encamped there last night. I had observed this movement when at Acworth, but at 12 M. I received another dispatch from him, written at 9 A.M., saying: "My scouts report the enemy's infantry advancing up the railroad. They are now entering Big Shanty. They have a cavalry force east of the railroad."

On the receipt of this second note from Gen. Armstrong I took my guide aside and particularly asked him if, after the capture of the place, I could move to New Hope Church by any other route than the one by the blockhouse at Allatoona creek and thence by the Sandtown road to the Acworth and Dallas road, and he said I could not. Here, then, was Gen. Sherman's whole army close behind me, and the advance of his infantry moving on Acworth, which changed the whole condition of affairs. Ammunition had to be carried from the wagons, a mile distant at the base of the hills, by men, and I was satisfied that it would take two hours to get it up and distribute it under fire before the final assault. I had learned from prisoners that before daylight the place had been reënforced by a brigade under Gen. Corse. I knew the enemy was at Big Shanty at 9 A.M. By noon he could reach Acworth and be within two miles of the road on which I was to reach New Hope Church. I knew Gen. Stewart had been ordered to near Lost Mountain. My men had marched all day on the 3d; worked all the night of the 3d destroying the railroad; that they had worked and marched all day on the 4th; marched to Allatoona on the night of the 4th; had fought up to the afternoon of the 5th; and could they pass the entire third day and night without rest or sleep if we remained to assault the remaining works? I did not doubt that the enemy would endeavor to get in my rear to intercept my return.

He was, in the morning, but three hours distant, and had been signaled to repeatedly during the battle. Under these circumstances I determined to withdraw, however depressing the idea of not capturing the place after so many had fallen, and when in all probability we could force a surrender before night. Yet, however desirous I was of remaining before the last work and forcing a capitulation, or of carrying this interior work by assault, I deemed it of more importance not to permit the enemy to cut my division off from the army. After deliberately surveying matters as they presented themselves to me. I sent to Gen. Sears to withdraw his men at once, moving by the route he went in, and directed Gen. Cockrell to commence withdrawing at 1:30 P.M.

Before the action commenced it was foreseen that it would be impossible to carry any wounded, on litters, to the road where the ambulances were placed, owing to the steepness of the hills, the ravines, and the dense woods. Accordingly the wounded were brought to the springs near the ridge. All who could be moved without the use of litters were taken to the ambulances. The others were left in charge of surgeons detailed to remain with them.

The troops re-formed on the original ground, west of the works, and marched to the south side near the artillery, and at 3:30 P.M. commenced the move toward New Hope. After the troops left I rode on down to Col.

Andrews's position in front of the works and directed him to remain until 5 P.M., and then withdraw and move on in our rear.

Before I commenced to withdraw the infantry from the captured works (but after the guide said I would have to return by the way I came) I sent orders to Maj. Myrick to send two batteries and caissons to a point beyond the blockhouse on the Sandtown road, to act in concert with the troops left there. Having been informed by Col. Andrews that the blockhouse at the Allatoona bridge had not been captured, I directed Capt. Kolb, with his battery that had remained with Col. Andrews, to move on and report to Gen. Cockrell for the purpose of taking the blockhouse.

Shortly after 4 P.M., and when not a person could be seen in or around the forts, I left the command of Col. Andrews and overtook the division near the blockhouse. Col. Adaire had burned the railroad bridge over Allatoona creek (over two hundred feet long), and also the duplicate of the bridge, which had been already framed to replace the old structure. Under the increased artillery fire the garrison of the blockhouse surrendered.

We captured two hundred and five prisoners, one United States flag, and the colors of the Ninety-Third Regiment of Illinois, a number of horses, arms, etc., and killed and wounded seven hundred and fifty of the enemy, being, with the garrison of the blockhouse, over one thousand.

History will record the battle of Allatoona one of the most sanguinary of the war; and when it is remembered that the enemy fought from within their strong redoubts the desperate deeds of daring performed by our troops in overcoming so many of the foe will win a meed of praise for their heroic valor.

The artillery opened about 7 A.M., and, except when the flag of truce was sent in, continued until 2 P.M.

The attack, commencing about 10 A.M., continued unremittingly until 1:30 P.M., and the rattle of musketry did not cease entirely until 3 P.M., when it died away, and a silence like the pall of death rested over the scene, contrasting strangely with the previous din of battle.

I cannot do justice to the gallantry of the troops. No one faltered in his duty, and all withdrew from the place with the regret that Gen. Sherman's movements—closing up behind us—forbade our remaining longer to force a surrender of the last work.

After leaving out the three regiments that formed no part of the assaulting force, I had but little over two thousand men.

My entire loss in killed, wounded, and missing was 799, as follows: Cockrell's Brigade: Killed, 42; wounded, 182; missing, 22. Sears's Brigade: Killed, 37; wounded, 114; missing, 200. Ector's Brigade: Killed, 43; wounded, 147; missing, 11. Staff: Captured, 1. Total: Killed, 122; wounded, 443; missing, 233; captured, 1. Grand total, 799.

Among the killed from Sears's Brigade is Col. W. H. Clark, Forty-Sixth Mississippi. He fell in the advance, near the enemy's works, with the battle flag in his hands. He was an excellent and a gallant officer. Also, were killed Capt. B. Davidson and Lieuts. G. C. Edwards, J. R. Henry, and J. D. Davis. Col. W. S. Barry, Thirty-Fifth Mississippi, and Maj.

MAJ. D. W. SANDERS

GEN. S.G. FRENCH'S UNIFORM COAT

Partin, Thirty-Sixth Mississippi, were wounded, together with Capts. R. G. Yates and A. J. Farmer and Lieuts. J. N. McCoy, G. H. Bannerman, J. M. Chadwick, J. Copewood, R. E. Jones, E. W. Brown, G. H. Moore, and Ensigns G. W. Cannon and A. Scarborough.

Texas will mourn for the death of some of her bravest and best men. Capt. Somerville, Thirty-Second Texas, was killed after vainly endeavoring to enter the last work, where his conspicuous gallantry had carried him and his little band. Capts. Gibson, Tenth Texas, Bates, Ninth Texas, Lieuts. Alexander, Twenty-Ninth North Carolina, and Dixon E. Wetzel, Ninth Texas, were killed while gallantly leading their men.

Brig. Gen. W. H. Young, commanding the Texas Brigade, was wounded. Most gallantly he bore his part in the action. Col. Camp, Fourteenth Texas, one of the best officers in the service, was seriously wounded. Also Majs. McReynolds, Ninth Texas, and Purdy, Fourteenth Texas. Of the captains wounded were Wright, Lyles, Russell, Vannoy, and Ridley, and Lieuts. Tunnell, Haynes, Gibbons, Agee, Morris, O'Brien, Irwin, Reeves, and Robertson.

In the Missouri Brigade were killed or mortally wounded Majs. W. F. Carter and O. A. Waddell, Capts. A. J. Byrne, A. C. Patton, John S. Holland, Lieuts. Thomas S. Shelly, Joel F. Yancey, G. R. Elliott, R. J. Lamb, G. T. Duvall, and W. H. Dunnica, and Ensign H. W. De Jarnette—men who had behaved well and nobly during the whole campaign.

Among the wounded are Maj. R. J. Williams, Capts. Thompson Alvord, G. McChristian, G. W. Covell, and A. F. Burns, Lieuts. Joseph Boyce, Silas H. F. Hornback, J. L. Mitchell, A. H. Todd, and H. Y. Anderson, and Ensign William A. Byrd.

I have named the killed and wounded officers in this report. The names of the private soldiers who fell or were wounded will also be filed with this as soon as they are received. It is due to the dead, it is just to the living, that they who have no hopes of being heralded by fame, and who have but little incentive except the love of country and the consciousness of a just cause to impel them to deeds of daring, and who have shed their blood for a just cause, should have this little tribute paid them by me, whose joy it was to be with them.

For the noble dead the army mourns, a nation mourns. For the living, honor and respect will await them wherever they shall be known, as faithful soldiers, who, for their dearest rights, have so often gone through the fires of battle and the baptism of blood. It would perhaps be an invidious distinction to name individual officers or men for marked or special services or distinguished gallantry where all behaved so well, for earth never yielded to the tread of nobler soldiers.

I am indebted to Gens. Cockrell, Sears, and Young for bravery, skill, and unflinching firmness.

To Col. Earp, on whom the command of the gallant Texans devolved, and to Col. Andrews, who commanded on the south side, and Maj. Myrick, commanding the artillery, I return thanks for services. Maj. D. W. Sanders, assistant adjutant general, Lieut. Wiley Abercrombie, aid, Capt. W. H. Cain, volunteer aid, Capt. Porter and Lieut. Mosby, engineers, were zealous in the performance of their duties, and E. T. Freeman, assistant inspector general, was conspicuous for his gallant conduct. I commend the last-named to the government for promotion.

Col. E. Gates, First and Third Missouri, Maj. E. H. Hampton, Twenty-Ninth North Carolina, and W. J. Sparks, Tenth Texas, and Lieut. Cahal, of Gen. Stewart's staff, are named for gallant services.

Lieut. M. W. Armstrong, Tenth Texas, seized the United States standard from the Federals, and after a struggle brought it and the bearer of it off in triumph.

In the inclosed reports of brigade commanders will be found the names of many officers and soldiers that I know are entitled to commendation and all marks of distinction that the government can award.

The cavalry officer who was sent to cut the railroad (early in the afternoon of the 4th) and failed to perform that duty is, in my opinion, much to blame. Had he taken up the rails (and there was nothing to prevent it), reënforcements could not have been thrown in the works, and the result would have been different. After events showed that a cavalry force and *Corse's other brigade arrived just three hours after we left Allatoona*, and reënforced the garrison in the fort.

Very respectfully submitted.   S. G. French,
                                      Major General Commanding.

You have now my official report of the battle of Allatoona as it was written soon after the event, and I will say here that, had I known it would have been so incorrectly reported by Gen. Corse, it would have embraced much matter of detail elucidating what occurred. I shall now proceed to copy some part of Gen. Corse's report, after which its errors will be pointed out as substantiated by facts not then known, and some that were not regarded. So, with my report, unintentional errors have been made known, as shown by subsequent information.

Gen. Corse's Report.

. . . I directed Col. Rowett to hold the spur on which the Thirty-Ninth Iowa and the Seventh Illinois were formed, . . . and taking two companies of the Ninety-Third Illinois down a spur parallel with the railroad and along the bank of the cut, so disposed them as to hold the north side as long as possible. Three companies of the Ninety-Third, which had been driven from the west end of the ridge, were distributed in the ditch south of the redoubt, with instructions to keep the town well covered by their fire, and to watch the depot where the rations were stored. The remaining battalion of the Ninety-Third, under Maj. Fisher, lay between the redoubt and Rowett's line, ready to reënforce wherever most needed.

I had barely issued the orders when the storm broke in all its fury on the Thirty-Ninth Iowa and the Seventh Illinois. Young's Brigade of Texans had gained the west end of the ridge, and moved with great impetuosity along its crest till they struck Rowett's command, when they received a severe check, but, undaunted, came again and again. Rowett, reënforced by the gallant Redfield, encouraged me to hope that we were safe here, when I observed Gen. Sears's Brigade moving from the north, its left extending across the railroad (opposite Tourtellotte): I rushed to the two companies of the Ninety-Third Illinois, which were on the brink of the crest running north from the redoubt, they having been reënforced by the retreating pickets, and urged them to hold on to the spur; but it was of no avail; the enemy's line of battle swept us back like so much chaff, and struck the Thirty-Ninth Iowa in flank, threatening to ingulf our little band without further ado. Fortunately for us, Col. Tourtellotte's fire caught Sears in flank, and broke him so badly as to enable me to get a staff officer over the cut with orders to bring the Fiftieth Illinois over to reënforce Rowett, who had lost very heavily. However, before the regiment sent for could arrive, Sears and Young both rallied, and made their assaults in front and on the flank with so much vigor and in such force as to break Rowett's line, and had not the Thirty-Ninth Iowa fought with the desperation it did, I never should have been able to get a man back inside the redoubt; as it was, their hand-to-hand conflict broke the enemy to that extent that he must stop and re-form before undertaking the assault on the *fort.* Under cover of the blows they gave the enemy the Seventh and Ninety-Third Illinois, and what remained of the Thirty-Ninth Iowa, fell back into the *fort.*

The fighting up to this time, about 11 A.M., was of the most extraordinary character. Attacked from the north, from the west, and from the south, these three regiments (the Thirty-Ninth Iowa and the Seventh and Ninety Third Illinois) held Young's and a portion of Sears's and Cockrell's Brigades at bay for nearly two hours and a half. The gallant Col. Redfield, of the Thirty-Ninth Iowa, fell shot in four places, and the extraordinary valor of the men and officers of this regiment and the Seventh Illinois saved to us Allatoona.

So completely disorganized were the enemy that no regular assault could be made on the fort till I had the trenches all filled and the parapets lined with men. The Twelfth and Fiftieth Illinois, arriving from the east hill, enabled us to occupy every foot of trench, and keep up a line of fire that, as long as our ammunition lasted, would render our little fort impregnable. The broken pieces of the enemy enabled them to fill every hollow, and take every advantage of the rough ground surrounding the fort, filling every hole and trench, seeking shelter behind every stump and log that lay within musket range of the fort. We received their fire from the north, south, and west of the redoubt, completely enfilading our ditches and rendering it almost impracticable for a man to expose his person above the parapet. An effort was made to carry our works by assault; but the battery (Twelfth Missouri) was so ably manned, and so gallantly fought, as to render it impossible for a column to live within a hundred yards of the work. Officers labored constantly to stimulate the men to expose themselves above the parapet, and nobly set them the example.

The enemy kept a constant and intense fire, gradually closing around

us, and rapidly filling our little fort with the dead and dying. About 1
P.M. I was wounded by a rifle ball that rendered me insensible for some
thirty or forty minutes, but managed to rally on hearing some persons
cry "Cease firing!" which conveyed to me the impression that they were
trying to surrender the fort.

Again I urged my staff, the few officers unhurt, and the men around me
to renewed exertions, *assuring them that Sherman would soon be here with
reënforcements.* The gallant fellows struggled to keep their heads above
the ditch and parapets in the face of the murderous fire of the enemy now
concentrated upon us. The artillery was silent, and a brave fellow, whose
name I regret having forgotten, volunteered to cross the railway cut,
which was under fire of the enemy, and go to the *fort* on the east hill to
procure ammunition. Having executed his mission successfully, he returned in a short time with an arm load of canister and case shot. About
2:30 P.M. the enemy were observed massing a force behind a small house
and the ridge on which the house was located, distant northwest from the
fort about one hundred and fifty yards. The dead and wounded were
moved aside so as to enable us to move a piece of artillery to an embrasure
commanding the house and ridge. A few shots from the gun threw the
enemy's column into great confusion, which, being observed by our men,
caused them to rush to the parapet and open such a fire that it was impossible for the enemy to rally. From this time until near 4 P.M. we had the
advantage of the enemy, and maintained it with such success that they
were driven from every position, and finally fled in great confusion, leaving their dead and wounded, and our little garrison in possession of the
field. [See War Records.]

The above extracts *from Gen. Corse's report* are taken from
an address made by Col. William Ludlow, United States army,
to the Michigan Commandery, at Detroit, April 2, 1891, and I
desire it to be borne in mind that he is a graduate of the Military Academy and was with Gen. Corse at Allatoona during the
battle, for I shall have cause to refer to his address after a while.

There have been so many erroneous accounts given to the public of this battle, impugning of motives, *guessing* at the controll-
ing objects that influence action, falsifying of numbers, glorify-
ing dispatches, and complimentary orders, that won the admiration even of a Confederate lieutenant general, that I purpose,
as well as I am able, to give an impartial account of it.

To do justice to the troops engaged on either side in the conflict, it will be necessary: 1. To have a knowledge of the ground
or topography of the field of action. 2. The strength of the
fortifications, and the time and labor bestowed on them. 3. The
strength of the respective forces. 4. The ratio of inequality between men in strong fortifications and men attacking from with-

out, immediately on arrival. 5. The inspiring inducement to the garrison *not to surrender* when relief is at hand; and the advantage to be gained, if successful, compared with the risk of remaining after ascertaining that the enemy was converging on the place from every point.

1. If an examination of this topographical map be made in connection with the photographic views of the railroad cut, the star fort, and the view from the sally port, it will give you an idea of the rough mountain spurs over which we had to pass.

2. These forts and redoubts were built by a distinguished engineer in the United States army, and, with their mutual defensive relation the one to the other, form a remarkably strong line of fortifications on every side. Sherman wrote to Gen. Blair, June 1, 1864, "Order the brigade left at Allatoona to be provided with tools, and to intrench both ends of the pass very strong," and frequently he speaks of Allatoona as a "natural fortress," etc.

Beginning at the east, we have a fort about fifty feet in diameter in the interior (marked "T" on the map), near three hundred yards east of the railroad, with a deep ditch around it. Walls twelve feet thick, and having embrasures for artillery, for which it was mainly designed. This fort was connected with a line of heavy intrenchments extending to the railroad cut, and along the cut to defend the star fort "C" by a flank fire, and also the redoubt "R." Again, there are intrenchments on the east side of the railroad near the depot that sweep with a flank fire the south front of the star fort "C," the Cartersville road, depot, etc. There was also protection given by inundating the country north by a dam across the creek.

Crossing the railroad to the west, on the summit of the ridge and on the verge of the deep cut, you will find the star fort "C" surrounded by a wide ditch six feet deep. The interior is seventy-five feet in diameter, and has eight embrasures for large guns. It dominates, from its elevation, all the surrounding country, and commands the approach in every direction, completely sweeping the ridge both east and west, protecting the redoubt "R" from any force attacking it. The Cartersville *road* passes under the muzzle of its guns, and then runs west on the ridge, through redoubt "R."

The two forts, "T" and "C," are interior isolated *works for*

16

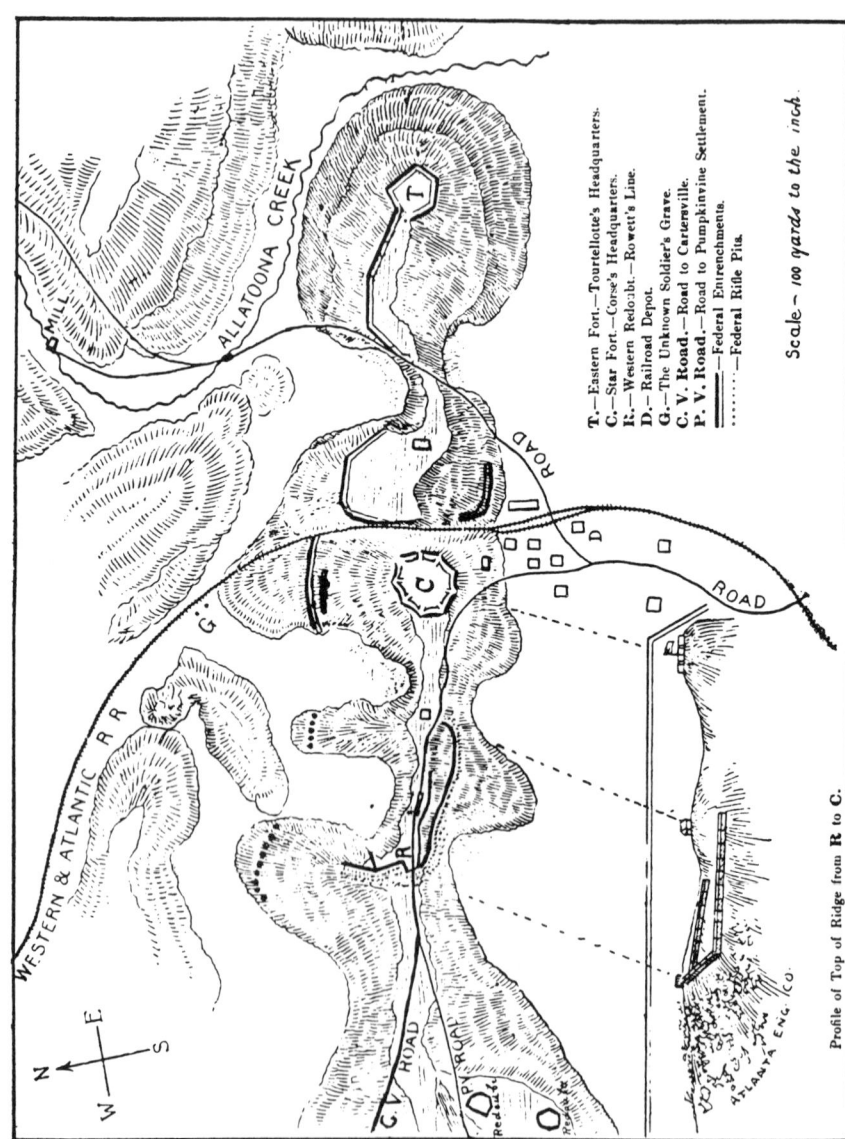

T.—Eastern Fort.—Tourtellotte's Headquarters.
C.—Star Fort.—Corse's Headquarters.
R.—Western Redoubt.—Rowett's Line.
D.—Railroad Depot.
G.—The Unknown Soldier's Grave.
C. V. Road.—Road to Cartersville.
P. V. Road.—Road to Pumpkinvine Settlement.
——————Federal Entrenchments.
............—Federal Rifle Pits.

Scale — 100 yards to the inch.

Profile of Top of Ridge from R to C.

FORTIFICATIONS—ALLATOONA, GA.

artillery, and the fire from each swept all the other works both inside and externally.   Both were surrounded by ditches six feet deep, making their parapets about *twelve feet* high.   Consequently they could not be taken by assault without *scaling ladders*, or otherwise, usual in sieges, unless by the sally port.   In fact these two inside forts could be used as citadels, or a place of *refuge* when the long exterior lines of defense were captured. And this was the case with fort "C" in the battle of Allatoona. The whole formed a mountain fortress.

The Federals call the intrenchments at "R" "rifle pits," to which they bear about as much relation, in regard to strength, as a battleship does to a dispatch boat.   Commencing about one hundred and twenty-five yards west of the fort "C," and on the south side of the Cartersville road, are two lines of intrenchments running nearly parallel with that road.   These two, or double, lines of defense converge and meet below the crest of the ridge, then, turning north, cross the road (with angles for flanking fire) and continue north down the slope.   From this north line an intrenchment runs due east toward the main fort.   The parapet is revetted with timber, and the interior ditch is very wide.   On the parapet are large chestnut *head logs* to protect the persons of the soldiers.   In front were immense entanglements of abatis, stockades, stakes, etc., to check any assault on the works.   So well was the work done that in 1890, when I was there, time had not defaced them, and the revetments and "head logs" are today as round as when placed there.   I am the more particular about this redoubt because here happened, perhaps, the bloodiest tragedy in the history of the war.

3. *The strength of the respective forces.*

Col. Tourtellotte's command was composed of the Ninety-Third Illinois, officers and men, 294; the Eighteenth Wisconsin, guns, 150; Fourth Minnesota, guns, 450; the Fifth Ohio Cavalry, men, 16; giving an apparent total of 910.   To this must yet be added the force for the six pieces of artillery, not less than 60.   If we add the company officers not enumerated, it will be found that Tourtellotte had about 1,000 officers and men.   The above numbers are official.

Corse's official statement is that he brought with him to Allatoona the Thirty-Ninth Iowa, 280 men; Seventh Illinois, 267 men; Fiftieth Illinois, 267 men; Fifty-Seventh Illinois, 61 men;

Twelfth Illinois, 155 men; or 1,030 *men.* To this must be added (say) 107 regimental and company officers, making the force that he brought with him 1,137 officers and men. So with Tourtellotte's troops the aggregate is 2,137 instead of 1,944 as reported by him, which excluded himself and officers.

As regards the strength of my division at Allatoona, the War Records show that on September 20, at inspection, I had present for duty 331 officers and 2,945 men. Total, 3,276.

Cockrell's Brigade was composed of eight small regiments consolidated into four, Ector's Brigade of six regiments, and Sears's Brigade of six regiments, and two batteries, 8 guns.

To this force add one four-gun battery sent with me, and deduct one gun and one regiment left at Allatoona creek bridge, and my entire force present was *3,197.*

And thus officially we have Federals, 2,132; Confederates, as above.

4. *Equalization of forces.*

The ratio of inequality between a force *within ordinary* intrenchments in line of battle and the attacking force *without* is well known.

Gen. Cox in his "Atlanta Campaign," page 129, says: "One man in the trench is equal to five in front." Gen. O. O. Howard, in reference to the battle of Kennesaw Mountain, says: "My experience is that a line of works thoroughly constructed, with the front well covered with abatis and other entanglements, well manned with infantry, whether with our own or that of the enemy, *cannot be carried by direct assault.*" Gen. R. S. Granger informs Gen. G. H. Thomas that the fort at Athens, manned by 700 men, can hold out an enemy 10,000 strong. (War Records, V. 39, Part 3, page 519.) Vicksburg, Jackson, Cold Harbor, Kennesaw, Petersburg, Atlanta, Knoxville, and other lines repelled the assaults. Now Allatoona was, without doubt, thrice as strong as these, and the attacking force was only *one and a half to one inside.* Then, too, we should consider that the works on the *hills* were almost inaccessible.

Battery Wagner, a sand fort on a level plain on Morris Island, Charleston, S. C., was garrisoned by only 740 men, who successfully defended it *fifty-eight days and nights* against the assaults and continuous fire of 11,500 men, with forty-seven cannon, aided by ships—the Ironsides, eight monitors, and five gunboats.

And Fort Sumter never was taken by assault. It was quietly abandoned February 18, 1865.

On Sunday, April 16, 1865, seven days after the surrender at Appomattox, a small redoubt or fort, of weak construction, garrisoned by an unorganized force hastily collected, at West Point, Ga., near Atlanta, consisting of 64 men under Gen. Tyler and Col. J. H. Fannan, held the fort all day against 3,750 men of Gen. J. M. Wilson's command, and surrendered only for want of ammunition and loss of men. Col. O. H. LaGrange, of Wisconsin, commanded the Federals. Ratio, 1 to 62.

5. The *inspiring hopes* given the garrison will be discovered in the following dispatches informing them aid was at hand, begging them to hold out until reënforcements arrived. In these dispatches bear in mind that Gen. Stanley was in temporary command of the Army of the Cumberland, and Gen. Elliott was the commander in chief of Sherman's cavalry. I give only a few of the many dispatches in the War Records.

No. 1. VOLUME 39, PART 3, PAGE 53.

SHERMAN TO COMMANDING OFFICER AT ALLATOONA.

October 3, 1864.

Hood might slip up to Acworth and Allatoona. I want the utmost vigilance there. If he goes to Allatoona, I want him only delayed long enough for me to reach his rear. . . . If he moves up to Allatoona, I will surely come in force.

No. 2. VOLUME 39, PAGE 65.

SHERMAN TO STANLEY.

IN THE FIELD, October 4, 1864.

I heard from Gen. Elliott to-night. He was on the Sandtown and Allatoona road. . . . I will be up to-day and move to Kennesaw.

No. 3. VOLUME 39, PAGE 66.

SHERMAN TO STANLEY.

October 4, 1864. Received 10 A.M.

Yes, move to Little Kennesaw and west of it. Tell Elliott in my name to interpose with his whole force between Dallas and Allatoona, and strike for any force in the direction of Acworth.

No. 4. VOLUME 39, PAGE 71.

SHERMAN TO ELLIOTT.

October 4, 1864, 11 P.M.

Don't risk the safety of your cavalry until I get up with my whole force, but make bold reconnoissances in connection with Gen. Stanley. My chief object is to prevent the enemy from making an attack on Allatoona to-morrow.

No. 5. Volume 39, Page 71.
SHERMAN TO COMMANDING OFFICERS AT ALLATOONA, KINGSTON, AND ROME.

October 4, 1864.

The enemy is moving on Allatoona, thence to Rome.

No. 6. Volume 39, Page 52.
SHERMAN TO GEN. VANDEVER.

October 3, 1864.

Sherman wants the force at Big Shanty cleaned out, and wants it done to-night if possible.

No. 7. Volume 39, Page 75.
CORSE TO GEN. J. E. SMITH.

Rome, October 4, 1864.

I will move my entire command to Cartersville and unite with Gen. Raum in attacking the enemy from Allatoona direct.

No. 8. Volume 39, Page 75.
CORSE TO RAUM.

Rome, October 4, 1864.

I am expecting a train every moment; as soon as I can get ready I will move 3,000 to 4,000 men.

No. 9. Volume 39, Page 77.
VANDEVER TO SHERMAN.

Near Kennesaw, October 4, 1864.

Elliott is between Big Shanty and Kennesaw on our left. I am skirmishing with the enemy now.

No. 10. Volume 39, Page 77.
VANDEVER TO SHERMAN.

Near Kennesaw, October 4, 1864.

Gen. Elliott has all his force near the west base of the mountain. Gens. Kilpatrick and Garrard are both with him, so couriers report.

No. 11. Volume 39, Page 78.
VANDEVER TO COMMANDING OFFICER AT ALLATOONA.

Kennesaw Mountain, October 4, 1864, 2 p.m.

Sherman is moving in force. Hold out.

No. 12. Volume 39, Page 78.
VANDEVER TO COMMANDING OFFICER AT ALLATOONA.

Near Kennesaw Mountain, October 4, 6:39 p.m.

Gen. Sherman says hold fast, we are coming.

No. 13. Volume 39, Page 88.
SIGNAL OFFICER AT ALLATOONA TO SIGNAL OFFICER AT KENNESAW.

Allatoona, October 5, 1864.

Gen. Corse is here with one brigade. Where is Sherman?

No. 14. Volume 39, Page 89.

SHERMAN TO STANLEY.

Kennesaw Mountain, October 5, 1864, 11:15 a.m.

No news by signal from Allatoona. Heavy firing, indicating an assault and repulse. Occasional shots now, but too smoky to see signals. Can see the field about Lost Mountain. No large force of Rebels there. Can see Kilpatrick's cavalry massed in a big field this side, but no skirmishing.

No. 15. Volume 39, Page 89.

SHERMAN TO STANLEY.

Kennesaw Mountain, October 5, 1864. Received 2:30 p.m.

Throw forward pickets on the Sandtown road. Take strong position and hold it.

No. 16. Volume 39, Page 90.

STANLEY TO SHERMAN.

Pine Top, October 5, 1864, 3:10 p.m.

I am on Pine Top. . . . I saw our cavalry about two miles in advance of Kemp's Mills.

No. 17. Volume 39, Page 90.

SHERMAN TO STANLEY.

In the Field, October 5, 1864.

I want to control the Sandtown road back to Allatoona.*

No. 18. Volume 39, Page 91.

SHERMAN TO ELLIOTT.

In the Field, October 5, 1864.

Dispatch Garrard to-night to Allatoona, making a circuit to the right, and to learn if possible the state of affairs there. . . . The day was so hazy that we could get but *few* messages. Corse is there with his division.

No. 19. Volume 39, Page 92.

SHERMAN TO ELLIOTT.

In the Field, October 5, 1864.

I have heard from Allatoona. All right. Corse is there, but wounded. You need not send Garrard's cavalry, but send a squadron.

No. 20. Volume 39, Page 92.

SHERMAN TO ELLIOTT.

In the Field, October 5, 1864.

I have been up on Kennesaw all day watching the attack. Since it ceased I have a signal, O. K. Corse wounded. . . . I want to establish communication with Allatoona.

No. 21. Volume 39, Page 96.

TOURTELLOTTE TO SHERMAN.

Allatoona, Ga., October 5, 1864.

Gen. Sherman: Corse is here.

---

* This is the road to New Hope Church over which we marched.

No. 22.   VOLUME 39, PAGE 96.

TO COMMANDING OFFICER, ALLATOONA.

KENNESAW MOUNTAIN, October 5, 1864.

Near you.

No. 23.   VOLUME 39, PAGE 96.

SIGNAL DISPATCHES FROM AND TO KENNESAW MOUNTAIN.

At 8 A.M. I called Allatoona for two hours and a half. I asked for news, and at 10:30 A.M. received the following message: "We hold out. Gen. Corse here."   ADAMS, *Signal Officer.*

At 4 P.M. I again called Allatoona, and at 4:15 got the following: "We still hold out. Gen. Corse is wounded."

No. 24.   VOLUME 39, PAGE 97.

KENNESAW MOUNTAIN, October 5, 1864.

Tell Allatoona to hold on. Gen. Sherman says he is working hard for you.

No. 25.   VOLUME 39, PAGE 97.

GEN. G. B. RAUM TO GEN. J. E. SMITH.

CARTERSVILLE, GA., October 5, 1864.

We have won a great victory at Allatoona to-day. *I am just from there.* Gen. Corse is slightly wounded in the cheek; Col. Tourtellotte slightly in the left thigh.

No. 26.   VOLUME 39, PAGES 111, 112.

LIEUT. W. H. SHERFY, CHIEF SIGNAL OFFICER, KENNESAW, REPORTS.

October 4, 1864.

I called Allatoona and sent the messages received last night. I saw the enemy hard at work destroying the railroad on both sides of Big Shanty.
. . At 5 P.M. the enemy began to move off on the Acworth road, and at *6 P.M. our army moved into camp at the foot of Little Kennesaw Mountain.*

October 5.

To-day the battle of Allatoona was fought. I could see the smoke of guns and shells. Gen. Sherman was with me all day sending and receiving messages.

Having now given you some knowledge of the ground, the strength of the fortifications, the numbers engaged on either side, the ratio of inequality between troops inside and those outside ordinary works, and the many inspiring hopes sent to the garrison to hold out, you can better comprehend

THE BATTLE.

The day dawned beautiful and bright, and as the sun rose higher and higher in the mellow autumnal sky, and lit up the forest-clad heights, it turned into a quiet Indian summer day of hazy, drowsy appearance inducive of rest. All nature seemed at variance with the active preparations being made for the impending conflict of arms.

Gen. Corse had placed in redoubt "R" the Seventh Illinois, the Thirty-Ninth Iowa, and the Ninety-Third Illinois. He had some companies in advance of "R," and the remainder in reserve in the rear of "R." These three regiments for the defense of this redoubt (called rifle pits) numbered nine hundred and four officers and men.

Tourtellotte, in fort "T" and the intrenchments, had for the defense east of the railroad the Fourth Minnesota, Eighteenth Wisconsin, and the Fiftieth and Twelfth Illinois Regiments. Soon, however, the Fiftieth and Twelfth Illinois were ordered over by Corse to the west side of the railroad.

I made the following disposition of my division of infantry present on the ridge. Sears's Brigade was ordered to the north side of the ridge and *east* of the railroad. Cockrell's Brigade and the four regiments of Ector's Brigade were on the ridge west of the enemy's works.

About 9 A.M. the artillery ceased firing, and, under a flag of truce, I sent a summons to the commander of the garrison to surrender, supposing the forces were small or to be the same as reported to me when I was in Acworth. The summons was carried by Maj. D. W. Sanders, Adjutant General. He waited about twenty minutes for a reply; receiving none, he returned. I had no idea that the garrison had been reënforced by the arrival of Gen. Corse with one of his brigades.

It was now near 10 A.M. when, impatient at the delay of Sears not getting in position, I ordered Cockrell to make the attack on the redoubt "R" with his brigade of nine hundred and fifty strong, supported by four regiments of Ector's Texas Brigade of about four hundred men. The ridge was so narrow that when deployed the wings were in the woods on the steep sides of a rocky ridge. As Cockrell neared the line he was subjected to the fire of the artillery from the two forts "T" and "C," and the musketry from "R," and the troops in the intrenchments on the east side of the railroad, near the deep cut, that swept his approach on every side. Arriving near the redoubt, the troops were stopped by the formidable abatis and other entanglements.

BATTLE OF ALLATOONA

In this picture the timber is omitted in order to show the ridge on which the fortress was constructed. All the troops visible are Confederates.

There for an hour, under this searching fire, they worked to make a way through the abatis. When passages had been made they rushed to the assault, and, after a terrible hand-to-hand conflict, the redoubt was carried, and the survivors fled to fort "C," followed by our men, and in a few minutes every Union soldier west of the railroad, including the Fiftieth and Twelfth Illinois, sought refuge in fort "C" and the ditch surrounding it, crowding them beyond measure.

Thus did 1,350 Confederates carry the redoubt defended by 904 brave Union veterans, although subjected all this time to the fire of forts "T" and "C," and other flanking works. But I will let Gen. Corse tell the story himself, as found on pages 761–766, Volume 39, War Records, only I will correct the errors in names and figures in some instances:

I had hardly issued these incipient orders when the storm broke in all its fury on the Thirty-Ninth Iowa and Seventh Illinois. Young's [Cockrell's] Brigade of Texans, 1,900 strong, had gained the west end of the ridge, and moved with great impetuosity along its crest till they struck Rowett's command, where they received a severe check, but, undaunted, they came again and again. Rowett, *reënforced by the Ninety-Third Illinois*, and aided by the gallant Redfield, encouraged me to hope we were all safe here, when I observed a brigade of the enemy under command of Gen. Sears moving from the north, its left extending across the railroad. I rushed to the two companies of the Ninety-Third Illinois, which were on the brink of the cut running north from the redoubt [fort "C"] and parallel with the railroad, they having been reënforced by the retreating pickets, and urged them to hold on to the spur, but it was of no avail. The enemy's line of battle swept us back like so much chaff, and struck the Thirty-Ninth Iowa in flank, threatening to ingulf our little band without further ado. Fortunately for us, Col. Tourtellotte's fire caught Sears in the flank and broke him so badly as to enable me to get a staff officer over the cut with orders to bring the Fiftieth Illinois over to reënforce Rowett, who had lost very heavily. However, before the regiment sent for could arrive, Sears and Young [Cockrell and Young] both rallied and made their assaults in front and on the flank with so much vigor and in such force as to break Rowett's line, and had not the Thirty-Ninth Iowa fought with the desperation it did I never would have been able to have brought a man back into the redoubt [fort "C"]. As it was, their hand-to-hand struggle and stubborn stand broke the enemy to that extent that he must stop to re-form before undertaking the assault on the fort. Under cover of the blow they gave the enemy the Seventh and Ninety-Third Illinois and what remained of the Thirty-Ninth Iowa fell back into the fort. The fighting up to this time—about 11 A.M.—was of a most extraordinary character. Attacked from the north, from the west, and from the south, these three regiments, Thirty-Ninth Iowa, Seventh Illinois, and Ninety-Third

Illinois infantry, held Young's and a portion of Sears's and Cockrell's [should be Cockrell's and Young's] Brigades at bay for nearly two hours and a half. [We were delayed about an hour, and that by the entanglements that prevented us from reaching the parapet; besides, we were un der fire from guns everywhere.] The gallant Col. Redfield, of the Thirty-Ninth Iowa, fell, shot in four places, and the extraordinary valor of the men and officers of this regiment and the Seventh Illinois saved to us Allatoona.

The capture of the redoubt by Cockrell and Young under the fire of six pieces of artillery, two in fort "C" and one in a battery in advance of the fort, three in fort "T," and musketry fire from every place, besides the 904 men in the redoubt, ends the first act of the tragedy.

It is proper here to give a description of this scene by quoting from an address made by Col. William Ludlow, Corps of Engineers, United States Army, who was with Gen. Corse during the battle, to the Michigan Commandery, Loyal Legion, at Detroit, April 2, 1891. In referring to the capture of redoubt "R," he said:

But the appalling center of the tragedy was the pit in which lay the heroes of the Thirty-Ninth Iowa and the Seventh Illinois. Such a sight probably was never presented to the eye of heaven. There is no language to describe it. With all the glad reaction of feeling after the prolonged strain of that mortal day, and the exultant surge of victory that swelled our hearts, it was difficult to stand on the verge of that open grave without a rush of tears to the eye and a spasm of pity clutching at the throat. The trench was crowded with the dead, blue and homespun, "Yank" and "Johnny," inextricably mingled in the last ditch. Our heroes, ordered to hold the place to the last, with supreme fidelity, had died at their posts. As the Rebel line ran over them they struck up with their bayonets as the foe struck down, and, rolling together in the embrace of death, we found them, in some cases, mutually transfixed. The theme cannot be dwelt upon.

I will now go on with Corse's report, and let him tell his story of the battle in his own way.

So completely disorganized were the enemy that no regular assault could be made on the fort until I had the trenches all filled and the parapets lined with men. The Twelfth Illinois and the Fiftieth Illinois, arriving from the east hill, enabled us to occupy every foot of trench, and keep up a line of fire that as long as our ammunition lasted would render our little fort impregnable. The broken forces of the enemy enabled them to fill every hollow and take every advantage of the rough ground surrounding the fort, filling every hole and trench, seeking shelter behind every stump and log that lay within musket range of the fort. We received fire from the north, south, and west face of the fort, completely enfilading our ditches, and rendering it almost impracticable for a man to expose his person above the parapet. An effort was made to carry our works by assault [This is an error. We had no scaling ladders, besides the ditch was *solid full* of Corse's men who found shelter there], but the battery, Twelfth Wisconsin, was so ably managed and so gallantly fought as to render it impossible for a column to live within one hundred yards of the works. Officers labored constantly to stimulate the men to exertion, and almost all that were killed or wounded in the fort met this fate while trying to get the men to expose themselves above the parapet, and nobly setting them the example.

The enemy kept up a constant and intense fire, gradually closing around us, and rapidly filling our little fort with the dead and the dying. About 1 P.M. I was wounded by a rifle ball, which rendered me insensible for some thirty or forty minutes, but managed to rally on hearing some persons cry, "*Cease firing,*" which conveyed to me the impression that they were trying to surrender the fort. Again I urged my staff, the few officers left unhurt, and the men around me to renewed exertions, assuring them that *Sherman would soon be here with reënforcements.* The gallant fellows struggled hard to keep their heads above the ditch and parapet in the face of the murderous fire of the enemy now concentrated upon us.

Here we have the astonishing official statement that his men would not expose themselves enough to fire over the parapet or out of the ditch, and that most of the officers lost their lives in "nobly setting them the example;" and this is also established by Col. Ludlow in his address, where he says:

Rowett's order to "*c ase firing*" had, of course, nothing to do with the cry of "*surrender.*" It is true that there were men in the fort ready to surrender or to do anything else in order to get out of it alive. Happily these were few, and most of them lay prone, close under the parapet, *playing dead,* with the combatants and wounded standing and sitting upon them. If I mistake not, *Corse himself,* at least for a time. *was holding down one of these living corpses,* who preferred to endure all the pain and discomfort of his position rather than get up and face the deadly music that filled the air with leaden notes. . . . It was absolutely necessary to keep room for the fighting force along the parapet, so the wounded were drawn back, and in some cases shot over and over again. The dead were disposed of in the same way, except that as the ground became covered with them they were let lie as they fell, and were stood or sat upon by the fighters. . . . The slaughter had been frightful.

One of our guns was disabled from the jamming of a shot, and we were out of ammunition for the other two. . . . I recall distinctly the fact that a regimental flagstaff on the parapet, which had been *several times* shot away, fell again at a critical moment toward the end of the action. There was a mad yell from our friends outside, and a few cries of "sur-

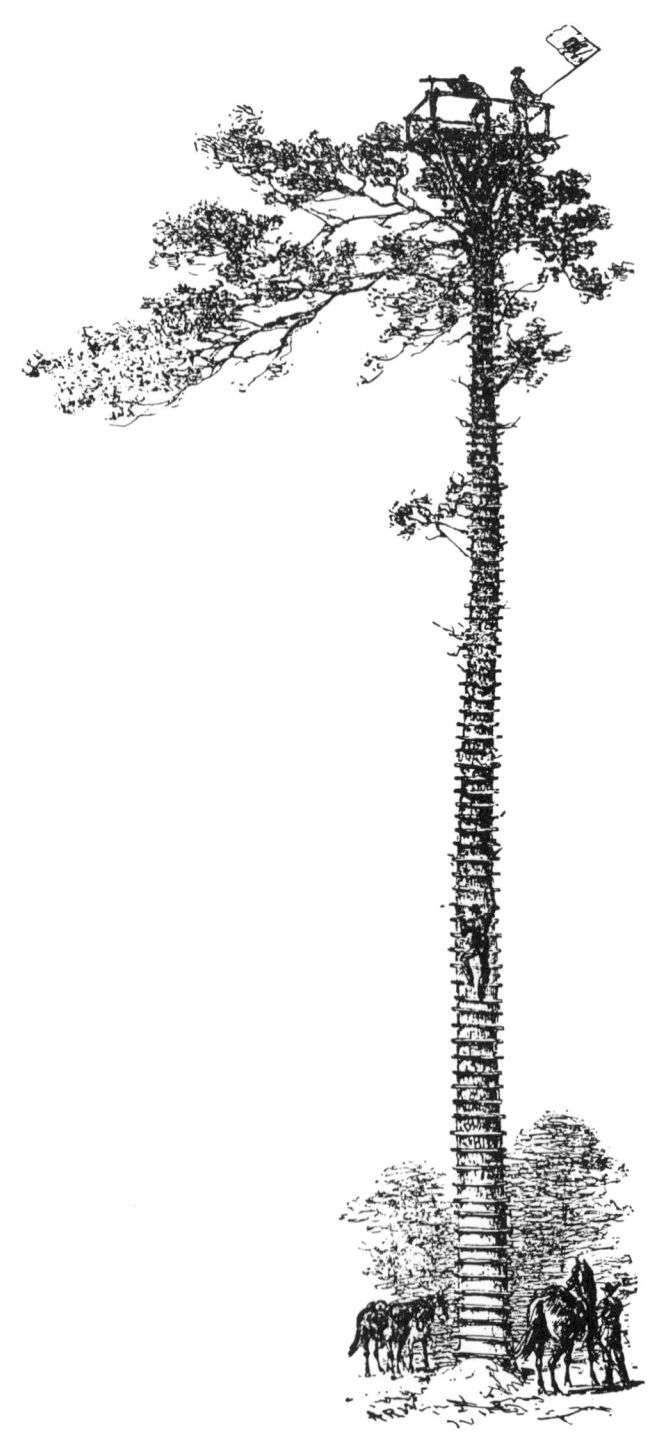

SIGNAL TREE, ALLATOONA, OCT. 5, 1864.

render " among our own people, but a brave fellow leaped to the summit of the parapet, where it did not seem possible to live for a single second, grasped the flagstaff, waved it, drove the stump into the parapet, and dropped back again unhurt. His action restored confidence; a great Yankee cheer drowned the tumult, and no cry of " surrender " was afterwards heard.

Here now is presented the testimony of Corse himself, and of Col. Ludlow, that the men would not expose themselves, and that they cried "cease firing," and "surrender." I know, as do hundreds of others now living, that the fire of the fort was silenced, because our men were close up; and if any one inside the fort or in the ditch exposed his head, instantly it became the target for several Confederates. Confederates moved about with impunity, and I called the attention of my staff to Johnson (Cockrell's flag bearer) riding up to the north side of the fort, sitting quietly on his horse, and listening to what was going on in the fort. In a recent letter from him he writes to J. M. Brown, of Atlanta: "I remember riding up very close to the fort. The distance was short, as I was close enough to tell what the Federals were doing in there." After 12 m. the Confederates merely watched for any person exposing his head above the parapet, and so I am sure that the fire described was not so severe as related by Gen. Corse, but it was very fatal.

Gen. Corse goes on with his report, and writes that about 2:30 p.m. the enemy massed a force (behind a small house) which he threw into great confusion, and that "from this time on until 4 p.m. we had the advantage of the enemy, and maintained it with such success that they were driven from every position, and finally fled in great confusion, leaving their dead and wounded, and our little garrison in possession of the field."

It is hardly possible to crowd into a short paragraph more errors than are found in the four lines above, and most of them he well knew to be false. It is true, no doubt, that he was not aware of the information sent me that induced me to withdraw my troops. That dispatch was received at 12:15 p.m. The Cartersville road, running north, passes within a few yards of fort "C," and then continues some two hundred and fifty yards on through the captured works. It was open to my infantry, but was there not life enough in the two forts, "C" and "T," to shoot down some of the horses and mules passing by within short pistol shot if I attempted to move the artillery, baggage wagons, and ambulances and block the road if I decided to move *north* to avoid Sherman's troops marching from the south to the relief of Allatoona?

So I resolved to obtain possession of the Acworth and Dallas road before it was occupied in force by the Federals, trusting to their slow and cautious movements. To this end, I first ordered all the artillery except one battery to start at once to the Allatoona Creek bridge to join the Mississippi regiment left there, and hold that position. Next, Sears was directed to withdraw immediately from the north side in front of fort "T," and Cockrell to commence at 1:30 P.M.; and, owing to the rough hillsides, *to come out in squads, or individually*. Although Sears began the movement over an hour before Cockrell and Young did, the latter were all collected on the ridge first, and sat there under the shade of the trees, within sight and easy rifle range of fort " C," until about 3 P.M., waiting for Sears, who had to go around the pond made by the Yankees damming up Allatoona Creek. During all this time but few shots were fired by the enemy. One, however, was fired at us, and it killed a man who had appropriated a fine pair of cavalry boots from the stores, and he fell dead at my feet where we were sitting. In the meantime I went among the wounded men who could not walk over the rocky hills to our ambulances, and explained to them why they would have to be left, and that surgeons had been detailed to remain with them. They gave me thanks without complaint.

After I showed Gens. Cockrell and Young the dispatches I had received, and informed them of my intention not to remain and make an assault on fort " C," lest reënforcements for the garrison should arrive before we could leave the place, they demurred, and said their men were mad, and wanted to remain and capture the place. Col. Gates, of the Missouri Brigade, declared that he would capture fort "C" in twenty minutes after the arrival and distribution of our ammunition, by way of the sally port. He asserted that they were so crowded inside that but few men could fire.

I adhered to my decision to withdraw, because the men had already been three days and two nights without rest or sleep, and that they could not pass a third night without sleep, and risk having to fight reënforcements momentarily expected; and the subsequent arrival of troops from Cartersville at 8 P.M. proved the correctness of my judgment; also Martin's Brigade reached Allatoona next morning.

About 3 P.M. the last of Sears's men arrived on the ridge near the fort where we rested awaiting them, and we then left the ridge and moved to the Cartersville road, where the wagons were left. Cockrell was now ordered to proceed with the infantry force to the Allatoona Creek bridge, and join the Mississippi regiment and artillery already there on the Dallas road. I rode down to the battery still in position on Moore's Hill to give instructions, and remained there sometime, not a little astonished at the scene presented to my view. The declining sun, seen through the calm, hazy atmosphere, shone red, like the rising of the full-orbed moon, on the fortifications before us. All was silent now where the battle raged so long, and the mellow light gleamed so gently down on the wounded and the dead that I remarked to the officers and men around me: "Silence, like the pall of death, rests over Allatoona; it is as lifeless as a graveyard at midnight." I even went up an inclined tree and used my glasses in vain to discover a human being. And so Corse's statement that we "were driven from every position, and finally fled in great confusion," leaps over the bombastic and loses its force in ridiculous excess of inaccuracy.

Corse, in his report, says that he brought with him 165,000 rounds of ammunition, and Ludlow states that "it was all expended except two hundred and fifty rounds." All the artillery ammunition Corse had in fort "C" was expended, and he got a man to go after some from fort "T," and he returned safely with an armful. See his report.

I will pause here awhile, that you may make a survey of the field of battle at 1:30 P.M.

For over two hours there had been pent up in fort "C," inside and in the ditch outside, the Thirty-Ninth Iowa, the Seventh Illinois, the Fiftieth Illinois, the Ninety-Third Illinois, the Twelfth Illinois, two companies of the Fifty-Seventh Illinois, and their artillery, 1,453 in number, less the killed, badly wounded, and prisoners resulting from their defense of the redoubt " R."

The fort, built for artillery mainly, had but seventy-seven yards of parapet, which made it so dangerous for any one to expose his head above the parapet that their men would not fire

17

voluntarily, "and most of their officers were killed or wounded in setting the men an example;" and they passed the word to "cease firing." They cried "surrender." Some "played dead," and the combatants stood on the "living corpses." Others sat down on them. Even Corse himself used one for a seat after he was wounded (Ludlow). They were out of water. Their ammunition was nearly all expended. Their firing had slackened to a musket shot at intervals. They let us withdraw without molestation, and we sat in the shade of the trees in full view of the fort, within musket range, from 1:30 P.M. until 3 P.M. awaiting Sears. They saw us all leave the ridge at the last named hour. At 4 P.M. Corse sent dispatch No. 23: "We still hold out." So they were in the fort then, and did not come out until the Confederates were all out of sight. The officers tried to keep up the spirits of their men by assuring them that "Sherman will soon come" (Corse's report). The hope of speedy relief prevented utter despondency, and they waited and waited, hoped and hoped for the fulfillment of the encouraging promises implied in the dispatches sent them by Sherman, as: "Hold fast, we are coming;" "Sherman moving in force, hold out;" "Sherman working hard for you;" "Near you." With his troops in this condition, and in the face of all these facts, Corse officially publishes to his commander and to the world, in a vainglorious manner, that the Confederates "were driven from every position, and finally fled in great confusion, leaving their dead and wounded, and our little garrison in possession of the field!!!" It is a beautiful description of an event that never happened.

It must have been pretty soon after we left Allatoona that Gen. Green B. Raum, commanding a division of cavalry that was hovering around *between* the Etowah bridge and the Allatoona, arrived and made a social call on Corse, and sympathized with him in his afflictions; but he must have left at an early hour, for he went to Cartersville that evening and sent a dispatch, which will be found, No. 25, dated October 5.

Soon Sherman was informed that the Confederates had retreated, and had taken the road to Dallas. So *he checked his troops that were marching on Allatoona*. However, Corse's train, expected *every hour during the battle*, returned to Allatoona at 8 P.M. with the remainder of *Rowett's Brigade*. Some cavalry

also arrived, and the next morning came *Martin's Brigade*. With him the condition of affairs was very much changed now.

During this time the weary Confederates, after capturing the blockhouse with a garrison of one hundred and ten men at Allatoona Creek bridge, marched on till midnight of the 5th, and the next morning were at New Hope Church, far away from Allatoona. Corse was now resting in the bosom of his friends, who no doubt congratulated him on his happy deliverance from the distress of the day previous; and as there were no Confederates near to distress him any more, he wrote Sherman, AT 2 P.M. ON THE 6TH, his (so-called) famous dispatch, which for CHEEK is unequaled:

I am short a cheek bone and an ear, but can whip all h-ll yet!!

Now the adverb "yet" in this case implies conditions unchanged. But, as they were then entirely changed, he was not justified in sending such a dispatch. It is a vainglorious, self-laudatory dispatch, no doubt sent to divert attention from the real condition in which his command had been placed; or it may be that the joy he felt the day after the battle, on being reënforced and rescued from the "slaughter pen" (in which he was pent up), by Sherman's movements to save him, caused him to write it; if so, it is not excusable. If, however, intoxicated at the mess table by the congratulations of friends and the usual accompaniments required for his condition, he was inspired to send that dispatch (as a postprandial speech is made), to mean nothing, then he may be forgiven.

But the unbought grace of life, the trained veracity, the chivalrous respect for foemen his equal in valor, whose daring he had witnessed, whose prowess he had felt, and from whose presence he so longed to be delivered, should have restrained him, at a much later date, from writing in his official report the fabricated story of how he "drove the Confederates from every position until finally they fled in great confusion," because he well knew this statement was not true.

In connection with Gen. Corse's visit with Joseph M. Brown to the battle ground at Allatoona, I have a letter from Mr. Brown giving me other information of what was said during his visit to Atlanta. As a guest of Senator Brown this conversation grew frank and friendly.

ATLANTA, GA., August 31, 1900.

Gen. S. G. French, Pensacola, Fla.

My Dear General: Answering your inquiry as to Mr. De Thulstrup's picture of the battle of Allatoona, I will state that in 1886 Gen. John M. Corse came to Georgia with the above well-known battle artist. I went with them to Allatoona, where we spent almost a day going over the various points of the ridge on both sides of the railroad, where there were fortifications.

Returning to Atlanta, these two gentlemen were my guests at my father's home. That night, after some social conversation, Gen. Corse and Mr. De Thulstrup went upstairs to their sleeping apartments. Within probably an hour afterwards I also went up to my sleeping room. The hall door leading from my room to Gen. Corse's being open, I was unintentionally made a hearer of conversation going on. Gen. Corse was quite animated in giving instructions to the artist as to how to draw the picture. I very distinctly heard him use the following expression: "*Be sure* you have the Rebels running." He repeated this in very positive tones.

Any one looking at the picture will see that the artist faithfully complied with the General's instructions.

Very truly yours. JOSEPH M. BROWN.

When J. M. Brown told Corse that French never received his reply to his summons to surrender, he answered: "This is the first information I have to that effect, that my answer never reached him." Then Corse told him he was in great haste in examining the lines and disposing of his troops. "When one of his staff officers hailed me with advice that he had a note from the enemy's commander, which he supposed was a summons to surrender, . . . I took the note and read it; it made me mad, because, from what I could *see* of his forces, and what I knew of mine, I believed that I had about as big a force as he had, hence considered the summons a superfluous piece of bravado. I sat down on a log, and, pulling my notebook out of my pocket, wrote the reply across the face of one of its pages, which I tore out and handed to my staff officer with instructions to take it to the bearer of the summons. . . . I never knew whether my answer reached French or not."

There is something in this statement which must be regarded as very remarkable, for in the ordinary affairs of life, if even a servant be sent to deliver a letter, and does not find the person to whom he was to deliver it, would he throw it away and never mention it, or would he return with it and report that he did not find the man to whom he was to hand it? And does not common

sense tell us that on such a momentous matter as this, involving
the lives of hundreds of men, his staff officer would have reported
that the flag of truce could not be found, and have returned the
dispatch given him?   And, furthermore, can any person of intelligence believe that Gen. Corse and the said staff officer did
not speak about this pretentious answer to the summons at any
time, which is published to the world in facsimile, of which Julius
E. Brown, of Atlanta, has one copy.   If he published the "facsimile" of the dispatch sent me, where did he get it?   It seems
to me the General "doth protest too much."   And further he
says: "Being in great pain from my wound, I took the train the
night of the 5th for Rome."   If this be true, how could he
have issued his "famous" dispatch from Allatoona on the afternoon of the 6th, for it gives the place, date, and the hour?

I am inclined to the belief that he did not leave Allatoona
until after the 6th, or on the second day after the fight.

I would not detract anything from the well-earned reputation
of Gen. Corse—and more especially so, as he is not living—yet
it is a duty incumbent on me, a duty I owe to my children, and
particularly to the noble Confederate soldiers who were with
me, to protect them against the statement of being "driven
away" by the garrison.   The demands of impartial history require of me—an actor therein, a living witness—to transcribe
from my diary the facts as there recorded at the time, so that
the world may know to what extent the many reported incidents of the battle have truth for their foundation as we now
find them related in nursery tales to children, taught in
schools, narrated in story, and sung in the gospel hymn of
"Hold the Fort" wherever the cross is seen and Christianity
prevails.

But in the current literature of the North derived from the
exaggerated bulletins daily sent from the seat of war there is a
wonderful admixture of truth and error, and I am trying to
separate them so far as they are found in the ordinary versions
of this battle, and emphatically to declare that the Confederate
troops were *not* repulsed as stated in the light publications of
the day, or as written in Corse's report.

If any further testimony be desired, I would refer you to the
following letter from a publication made by Joseph M. Brown,
son of the late Senator Joseph E. Brown, of Georgia.

ALLATOONA, GA., November 10, 1890.

Mr. Joseph M. Brown.

Dear Sir: In reply to the inquiries contained in your letter of October 31, I will state that, with my brother, I was in Allatoona on the night of October 4, 1864, when the place was surrounded by Confederates under Gen. French.

Early the next morning, for safety, we went into the fort on the west side of the railroad, and were there during the battle that day. Gen. Corse commanded on the west side of the railroad, and was in the fort all the latter part of the fight. The Federals fought desperately, and after they lost fort "R"* across the Cartersville road they were very much disheartened. They could get no water without exposing themselves to a deadly fire; and it was very much needed, especially for the wounded.

During the latter part of the engagement I frequently heard it said they were nearly out of ammunition. They were on the point of giving up the fight several times. The command "Cease firing" was given by somebody and passed around the fort, but then some of the officers rallied the men a little.

If the attack had been kept up a little while longer, the fort would have certainly been taken; but to the surprise of the Federals, their enemy's fire slackened and the Confederates retired from the front of the fort. The Federals at this time were at a loss to understand this movement, when they themselves were nearly ready to surrender. They seemed momentarily to expect a renewal of the attack from some other quarter. They remained quietly in the fort for nearly or quite three-quarters of an hour after the Confederates retired. But when they found that the Confederates would not renew the fighting there was a great rally in the fort. Then there was some desultory firing at the Confederates on the south of the fort near the depot and station. The Federals did not sally out of the fort until the Confederates were gone entirely out of sight.

W. M. DENTON.

As regards the arms captured by Corse, I will simple remark they were inferior muskets exchanged on the field for Springfield rifles, and Henry repeating rifles (16 shooters), one of which I turned over, by my Aid Yerger, to the United States Ordnance officer at the close of the war. Had Corse gone to the blockhouse at Allatoona creek, he would have captured there eighty-five muskets (thrown away) in the road, in exchange for those we captured there, which would have augmented his list of arms captured.

---

* It is proper that I should here state that my official report (page 816, War Records, Vol. 39) contains an error. When I saw the Fiftieth and Twelfth Illinois leave the east side of the railroad and join the force on the west side, I believed that all were on that side, and wrote, "The Federal forces were now confined to one redoubt (fort 'C'), and we occupied the ditch." I did not discover this error until after it was too late to correct it. It must be remembered that the battle was fought on a mountain ridge, some of the sides inaccessibly steep, and covered with timber obstructing the view.

PROVISIONS.

There were about one million rations of bread at Allatoona, and two million seven hundred thousand in Atlanta, and *not* two million seven hundred thousand in Allatoona as stated by Col. Ludlow. (Sherman's letter to Corse, page 134, Vol. 39.) The rations in Allatoona in no way affected the "march to the sea." They were ordered to Rome on the 11th, for use above. (See page 207.)

"I propose breaking up the railroad from Chattanooga and striking out with wagons. . . . Until we can *depopulate* Georgia it is useless to occupy it. . . . The utter destruction of the *roads, houses, and people* cripple their resources. . . . I can make Georgia *howl*. . . . I have eight thousand cattle and three million rations of bread." (Page 162, Vol. 39.)

The destruction of the stores at Allatoona, had it been done, would not have interfered with the "march to the sea."

The stores in Allatoona were in our possession, and they were not set on fire by our men because they wanted some themselves, and much was appropriated. But I had no knowledge of there being a large depot there until I withdrew Cockrell and Young; and while waiting for Sears I heard the men speak about them. On obtaining this information a party of men were sent there to burn them. It is a singular fact that only three matches could be found, and Gen. Cockrell had them, and when the party reached the stores the matches failed to ignite.

Gen. Sherman left Atlanta November 15, 1864, and arrived at Savannah on the 10th of December. He writes that he had sixty-five thousand men. To supply these men the twenty-seven days they were on the march would require one million seven hundred and fifty-five thousand rations. They averaged eight miles per day—for the distance is about two hundred and twenty miles. I have related to you how I made a march (with a large wagon train, through a desolate country, heavily laden) of ninety-six miles in fifty-two hours; and this without water.

This much vaunted "march to the sea" was a pleasure excursion, through a well-cultivated country, and is a mere bagatelle compared with that made by the Mormons from Illinois to Utah, or the many expeditions made overland to California during the gold excitement. The distance to California is ten times greater than the distance from Atlanta to Savannah.

Sherman boastfully writes that he "destroyed two hundred and sixty-five miles of railroad, carried off ten thousand mules, and countless slaves; th..t he did damage to the amount of $100,000,-000.   Of this, his army got $20,000,000, and the $80,000,000 was waste," as they went "looting" through Georgia.

But not content with this, when "this cruel war was over," he presented the delectable spectacle of "how we went thieving through Georgia" at the grand review of *his* army in Washington, by mounting his bummers on mules laden with chickens, ducks, geese, lambs, pigs, and other farm productions, unblushingly displayed, to cover up the concealed money, jewelry, and plate taken from the helpless women—to delight the President, to edify the loyal people, to gratify the hatred of the populace to the South, to popularize the thirst for plundering made by his troops, to be an object lesson to the present generation, to instill a broader view of moral right, to heighten modest sensibilities, to refine the delicate tastes of young ladies, to humiliate a conquered people; or wherefore was this unwise "Punch and Judy" show given?

During the revolutionary war, when the British fleet ascended the Potomac river, one ship sailed up to Mount Vernon—the residence of the arch rebel, Washington—and made a requisition for provisions which his agent filled.   The English commander must have been a gentleman because he did not burn the dwelling, insult the family, nor commit robbery!!!

Gen. Bradley T. Johnston, in his life of Gen. J. E. Johnston, quotes that, "Abubekr in the year 634 gave his chiefs of the army of Syria orders as follows: 'Remember that you are always in the presence of God, on the verge of death, in the assurance of judgment and the hope of paradise.   Avoid injustice and oppression. . . .   When you fight the battles of the Lord acquit yourselves like men, without turning your backs; but let not your victory be stained with the blood of women or children.   *Destroy* no *palm tree*, nor burn any *fields* of *corn*.   Cut down no *fruit trees*, nor do any *mischief to cattle*, only such as you *kill to eat*.   When you make any covenant or article, stand to it and be as good as your word.   As you go on, you will find some religious persons who live retired in monasteries, and purpose themselves to serve God in that way.   Let them alone, and neither kill them nor destroy their *monasteries*.'

"Judged by the laws given Moses on Sinai, or the teachings of Him who stilled the waves on Galilee, or the Koran, the principles of morality, or feelings of humanity; were not the gates of Paradise open to Abubekr?

"Owing to the barbarities that were practiced by the English soldiers and sailors, and the refusal to exchange prisoners, Capt. John Paul Jones, when in command of the Continental ship, Ranger, on April 23, 1778, landed on the Isle of St. Mary, Scotland, with a small force and surrounded the house of the Earl of Shetland, to carry the earl away, and have him detained until through his means a general and fair exchange of prisoners, in Europe as well as in America, could be effected.

"The earl was not at home, and Jones permitted his men to take silverware from the castle as fair plunder and a just revenge for the acts of British sailors in America, who had not only looted the homes of the rich, but had driven off *one* cow and *one* pig of the laborer.

"The silver taken was of the real value of £500 pounds, but when sold for the benefit of the crew, Jones bought it and returned it (at his own expense) at a cost of £1,000 pounds, all told, to the noble lord." (Spear's "History of Our Navy," pages 142–148, Vol. I.)

Was not England fighting the colonies then in rebellion?

It is not I who charge Sherman with destroying cornfields, cutting down fruit trees, or "driving off *one* cow and *one* pig;" he himself boasts of having done it. If he did take the "*one* cow and the *one* pig," he kindly left the poor women their tears and their memory.

SHERMAN.

The dispatches numbered 1, 2, 3, 5, 6, 9, 10, 11, 12, 15, 17, 18, 19, 20, 23, and 26, which I have given, will show Gen. Sherman's untiring efforts to save Allatoona, and to prevent my division from joining Hood. No. 26 shows that on the 4th his force went into camp at the foot of Little Kennesaw. Nos. 15 and 16 show that Stanley, with a part of the army of the Cumberland, was on Pine Mountain at 2:10 P.M. on the 5th. At that hour we were sitting under the shade of the trees at Allatoona, waiting for Sears's men, and on the ridge by the fortifications.

My diary, written on the spot, says we left with the wagons

at 4:30 P.M. Next, we were detained an hour in capturing the blockhouse at the creek. If Stanley had moved promptly, he could have occupied the Dallas road, moving northwest, at some point many hours in advance of me. No. 17 informs Stanley: "I want to control the Sandtown road back to Allatoona." That is the road I marched over from the blockhouse to New Hope Church *on the 5th, and morning of the 6th.*

Sherman's cavalry was ordered several times to hold that road. They were two miles in advance of Kemp's Mill at 3:10 P.M. on the 5th (see No. 16), and not four miles from the road. We were then at Allatoona.

In Sherman's "Memoirs," Vol. II., page 147, you will find these words: "From Kennesaw I ordered the Twenty-Third Corps to march due west on the Burnt Hickory road, and to burn houses or piles of brush as it progressed to indicate the head of column, hoping to interpose this corps between Hood's main army at Dallas and the detachment *then* assailing Allatoona."

The *rest* of the army was directed straight to Allatoona, eighteen miles distant.

By the map, Allatoona (in a direct line) is thirteen miles from Kennesaw, ten miles from Pine Mountain, twelve miles from New Hope Church, eight miles from Big Shanty, eleven miles from Lost Mountain; and from Pine Mountain, where Gen. Stanley was on the 5th with part of the army of the Cumberland, to the road over which I passed on the 6th, *it is only five miles.* Also the cavalry that was at Kemp's Mill at 3:10 P.M. on the 5th was within five miles of the residence of *Dr. Smith, where I encamped on the night of the 5th.*

For these facts, read again the Federal dispatches that I have given. It is therefore manifest that only by tardy and cautious movements, or no movements, as Sherman ordered, arising from Hood's fighting qualities, they failed to place a powerful force across our road before I left the bridge across Allatoona creek or at any time on the 6th, the day following.

Sherman at first, or "for a time, attributed this result" (my withdrawing my troops) "to the effect of Gen. Cox's march" (see page 147, Vol. II., of his "Memoirs"), which, in truth, was mainly the cause; but he generously gave—however erroneously—all the credit to his lieutenant, with whom he was well pleased for "holding on" and "holding out" through faith in "his promises to come to his relief," and then complimented him in a general order that Corse must have felt as being a little ironical, save only as relates to "holding out" with a *faith* in Sherman which can be found in St. Paul's Epistle to the Hebrews, where he writes that "faith is the substance of things hoped for, the evidence of things not seen."

Sherman's signal dispatches to Corse before and during the battle to "hold the fort," intended only for their encouragement, has now become a world-wide inspiration in the form of a gospel song written by the evangelist P. P. Bliss.

Mr. Joseph M. Brown writes that "the circumstances of the messages and the battle being narrated to the evangelist, he caught from them the idea for the stirring words :

> Ho! my comrades, see the signal
> Waving in the sky!
> Reënforcements now appearing,
> Victory is nigh.
>
> *Chorus.*—Hold the fort, for I am coming!
> Jesus signals still:
> Wave the answer back to heaven:
> "By thy grace we will!"

"He wrote this song on the night that he first heard the story, and sung it in the Tabernacle in Chicago next day. It was caught up by the voices of thousands, and from that day to this has been a standard gospel lyric."

HOOD.

On the afternoon of October 4, 1864, when I was at Big Shanty, on the railroad near Kennesaw, Gen. A. P. Stewart, my corps commander, handed to me two orders from Gen. Hood. The first one is dated October 4, 7:30 A.M., and the second at 11:30 A.M. These two orders may be found in my official report of the battle of Allatoona on a preceding page.

The purport of these two orders is : that I will take my division to Allatoona and fill up the deep cut there (a photograph of a *part* of this cut is here given), and then go on to the Etowah river bridge and burn it, if possible ; and thence march to New Hope Church by taking roads running south to New Hope

RAILROAD CUT, ALLATOONA. FORT "C" ON THE LEFT, FORT "T" ON THE RIGHT.

Church, and join my corps there; the destruction of the bridge being the more important duty; and I was expected to join the army on the 6th.

If this cut be critically examined, it will be perceived that the order to "fill it up" in an hour or so, and then go on to the bridge, does not evince a profound knowledge of engineering. A little boy builds sand forts and castles on the seashore with wooden paddles, and believes he is a Vauban or an Inigo Jones.* He knew we had but a few spades, and directed Gen. Stewart to borrow for me tools from Gen. Armstrong; and he had none.

In 1880, sixteen years after he wrote those orders, Gen. Hood published a work called "Advance and Retreat," in which the following words are written (page 257):

"I had received information—and Gen. Shoupe records the same in his diary—that the enemy had in store, at Allatoona, large supplies which were *guarded* by two or three regiments. As one of the main objects of *the campaign* was to deprive the enemy of provisions, Maj. Gen. French was ordered to move with his division, to capture the garrison, if practicable, and *gain possession* of the *supplies.* Accordingly on the 5th, at 10 A.M., after a refusal to surrender, he attacked the Federal forces at Allatoona, and succeeded in capturing a portion of the works; at that juncture he received intelligence that large reënforcements were advancing in support of the enemy, and, fearing he would be cut off from the main body of the army, he retired and abandoned the attempt. Maj. L. Perot, adjutant of Ector's Brigade, had informed me by letter that our troops were in possession of these stores during several hours, and could easily have destroyed them. If this assertion be correct, I presume Maj. Gen. French forbade their destruction, in the conviction of his ability to successfully remove them for the use of the Confederate army."

Now, if any intelligent person will carefully scrutinize the orders given me, and then ponder over what Hood published, he can arrive at no other conclusion than that the account published is erroneous. They cannot both be true!

And further, when I made my official report I copied my orders that he gave me, and I stated in my report: "It would ap-

---

* Vauban—A French marshal, the greatest of military engineers; born 1633. Inigo Jones—An eminent architect; born in London 1572.

pear, however, from these orders, that the general in chief was not aware that the pass was fortified and garrisoned that I was sent to have filled up."

This report was, by Gen. Stewart, delivered to Gen. Hood, and by him forwarded to the War Department in Richmond; thence it went to the War Department in Washington. And although I therein state that Hood had no knowledge of the place being garrisoned, or fortified, he forwarded it without comment. He could not do otherwise. There were the originals copied in his own order book.

"Gain possession of the supplies!" under all the environments, is only a vague expression of a glittering generality and signifies nothing particular, and is a mere platitude and nothing more. What was I to do with them? Bring them away? remove them without a wagon, when about six hundred were required!

But let us suppose that Hood actually did know that Allatoona was fortified, garrisoned, and a depot for army rations. If so, then he should have imparted to either Gen. Stewart or me that information.

Again: Gen. Hood having declared that the main object of the campaign was "to deprive the enemy of provisions," here was the desired opportunity; nay, more—to appropriate them to his own use. He wrote the first order to me at 7:30 A.M. on the 4th. At that time I was at Big Shanty, Walthall at Moon's, and Loring at Acworth, only two hours' (daylight) march from Allatoona!

Now I ask in the name of common sense, Can it be possible that, with Gen. Stewart's army corps so near those much needed army supplies, he should order Gen. Stewart's Corps to remain there close by them "till late in the evening," and then march him away and order me, the most distant, to go there and "take possession of them?"

Had he known what he says he did, undoubtedly he would have ordered, at daylight on the 4th, every available wagon to Acworth, and (instead of the utterly impractical one of putting a mountain in a deep cut) ordered Gen. Stewart with his three divisions to Allatoona in all haste. Loring could have reached Allatoona by *11 a.m. on the 4th*, and the others soon after. The battle would have been fought on the 4th, and before the arrival of Corse at midnight. No! for the want of information, this was not to be.

And so I went all alone into the land occupied by the enemy, and Gen. Hood moved farther and farther away, leaving me isolated beyond all support or assistance.

Gen. Hood could not have had a good knowledge of the topography of the country, because when my dispatch to Stewart— that I would withdraw from Allatoona to avoid being shut up in a *cul de sac*—was received Hood tells Stewart that he does not understand "how Gen. French could be cut off, as he should have moved directly away from the railroad to the west." (Page 791, War Records, Vol. 39.) I am quite sure Gen. Armstrong, when (at 9 A.M.) he sent me his dispatch, also sent a copy of it to Gen. Stewart or Hood, because Hood at 1:15 P.M. tells Armstrong he "must prevent my being surprised, and enable me to get out safely."

I will state here again that it was about noon on the 4th, when some citizens, living on the line of the railroad above, remarked that we "could not tear up the track to Allatoona, because that place was fortified and garrisoned, and that it was a depot for supplies." Therefore it was that Gen. Stewart and myself, in discussing the order, were convinced that Hood did not know the condition of affairs at Allatoona, and at my request he gave me some additional artillery; and so there is ample evidence that Hood had no knowledge that the enemy occupied the Allatoona Pass.

Gen. Hood was indeed a brave man, if not a courageous one, and he couched his lance at the enemy wherever he met him, whether in the guise of a windmill or the helmet of Mambrino; but at last, in after days, he went over to the enemy, for on page 257 of his volume he writes: "Gen. Corse won my admiration by his gallant resistance, and not without reason the Federal commander complimented this officer, through a general order, for his handsome conduct in the defense of Allatoona!"

It is a pertinent question to ask from what source Gen. Hood derived his information. If he had read Gen. Corse's report, he would have discovered that his men would not expose themselves enough to fire over the parapet, and that they merely "held out" for the hourly promised assistance, etc., as I have narrated. Is it pleasing to learn from his pen his rapturous love for the Federals and contempt for the Confederates and his standard of admiration? Mine is different; and I am free to state that it was the Confederates with whom I was present, who by their death,

> "by their painful service,
> The extreme danger, and the drops of blood
> Shed,"

by their gallantry and perseverance won my admiration. And this is no reflection on the enemy they met. Hood's want of admiration for the soldiers he commanded in 1864 and 1865 is the highest meed to their intelligence.

Perhaps it was natural, in after years, that Gen. Hood should select some Federal officer on whom to bestow his admiration, and when they passed in review before him Gen. Corse was awarded this honor. I trow he must have forgotten Col. Clark R. Weaver, U. S. A.

Seven days after Allatoona, Gen. Hood with his entire army was at Resaca. It was garrisoned by about five hundred men commanded by Col. Weaver. Hood summoned Weaver to surrender in unmistakable terms, ending as follows:

> If the place is carried by assault, no prisoners will be taken.
> > Most respectfully, your obedient servant,
> > > J. B. HOOD, *General.*

To this Col. Weaver replied:

> In my opinion I can hold this post. If you want it, come and take it.
> > CLARK R. WEAVER, *Com'd'g Officer.*

(See Sherman's "Memoirs," Vol. II., page 155.)

Nevertheless, on page 257, "Advance and Retreat," Hood writes, "Gen. Corse won my admiration by his gallant resistance," etc., and further on—page 326 of his book—he writes, "The information I received that the enemy was moving to cut me off proved to be false," which is refuted by the arrival of reenforcements, as I have stated, and Sherman's dispatches that I have given.

It is singular that so many laudatory statements should have been made by Gen. J. M. Corse and admirers about the battle of Allatoona, which were not necessary to sustain his character as a soldier.

I have before me a book of nearly five hundred pages, written

18

by F. Y. Hedley, adjutant of the Thirty-Second Illinois Regiment, which is entitled "Pen Pictures of Everyday Life in Gen. Sherman's Army, from Atlanta to the Close of the War." This includes the battle of Allatoona, and as he makes the story to be palatable to the tastes of those who enjoy the marvelous, at the expense of the Confederate soldiers and myself, I feel obliged to expose more of the legerdemain used to deceive the public by juggling tricks.

I will state that on page 219 there is a facsimile of my summons to the commanding officer of the garrison to surrender. It was sent, as I have stated, because it was then supposed that the garrison was small in numbers. It reads:

AROUND ALLATOONA, October 5, 8:15 A.M., 1864.
Commanding Officer U. S. Forces, Allatoona:

Sir: I have placed the forces under my command in such positions that you are surrounded; and to avoid a needless effusion of blood, I call on you to surrender your forces at once, and unconditionally. Five minutes will be allowed you to decide. Should you accede to this, you will be treated in the most honorable manner as prisoners of war.

I have the honor to be very respectfully yours,

S. G. FRENCH,
Major General Commanding Forces C. S.

On the same leaf is a facsimile of Gen. Corse's reply to my note, and it reads:

HEADQUARTERS FOURTH DIVISION,
FIFTEENTH ARMY CORPS, 8:30 A.M., October 5, 1864.
Maj. Gen. G. S. French, C. S. A.:

Your communication demanding surrender of my command I acknowledge receipt of, and respectfully reply that we are prepared for the "needless effusion of blood" whenever it is agreeable to you.

I am very respectfully, your obedient servant.

JOHN M. CORSE,
Major General Commanding Forces U. S.

Let us investigate this matter.

The facsimile of my letter is true, no doubt about that; but we have also the facsimile of the reply made by Corse which was sent me, and by me never received; and in the face of that Corse "declared he never knew that I did not receive it, or that it was not delivered to Maj. Sanders, the bearer of the flag of truce," until so informed by Joseph M. Brown, whose guest he was when he came to Atlanta with the artist De Thulstrup to have the battle painted; and he further told him: "I took the note (French's) and read it. It made me mad, because from what I could see of his forces, and what I knew of mine, I believed that I had about as big a force as he ; hence considered the summons a superfluous piece of bravado. I sat down on a log, and pulling my note-book out of my pocket, wrote the reply across the face of one of the pages, which I tore out and handed to my staff officer with instructions to take it back to the bearer of the summons."

Not finding Maj. Sanders, of course he returned in a few minutes and gave Corse the note.

Next William Ludlow (now a general in the United States army), in his address to the Michigan Commandery, Loyal Legion, at Detroit, on April 2, 1891 (page 20), says: "Corse did reply; he wrote his answer on the top of a neighboring stump."

Then Hedley (page 223) says of Corse: "His every pound of flesh and blood was that of a hero: his eye flashed as if lighted with a Promethean spark; and his chest swelled with angry defiance to the hideous threat implied in the summons to surrender! 'Capt. Flint,' said he, 'answer this!' so Capt. Flint seated himself upon a tree stump and wrote the reply."

I care not who wrote the reply to my note; I only desire to know who kept it concealed for over twenty years, and then produced it, and, together with mine, authoritatively gave them to Hedley to photograph and publish side by side.

If Corse had it hid away, or knew where it was, then he must have been mistaken when he declared to Joseph M. Brown that he never knew that I had not received it. Besides, that I received no reply was reported officially and well known.

As regards the "hideous threat implied" in my note, it has been left to the hero of Allatoona to discover it for the first time, although the like and similar expressions have been used by many commanders in the years long past, and escaped the critical acumen of those to whom they were sent to find an implied threat therein.

No one except Ludlow, so far as I am aware, has ever published that Maj. Sanders was fired on by Corse's soldiers when approaching under a flag of truce. I made it known on an inclosure in my official report.

Adjutant Hedley says "the heroic *defense* of Allatoona is almost as famous as the 'charge of the Light Brigade,' and far more momentous in its results."

There was nothing momentous pending on it. It was Hood's ignorance of the enemy's position that caused the battle; it should never have been made. We had nothing to gain; we would not remain there, nor had I any means to carry stores away with me. It is well known what Hood ordered us to do: "fill up the Allatoona cut, and burn the bridge over the Etowah river," and join him on the 6th.

I here repeat that the one million rations of bread in Allatoona were not a factor in Sherman's march to Savannah. He refused to repair the railroad we had destroyed, and sent the rations north of the Etowah. Subsequently, however, he did put the road in condition so as to send the sick and wounded, etc., north from Atlanta. The war records show he had in Atlanta 3,000,000 rations and eight thousand beeves. For 65,000 men eighteen days were required 1,170,000 rations. On the march the most difficult problem Sherman had to solve was *what to do with his superabundant rations.*

Let us examine Hedley on this question. He writes, first: The regular commissaries and quartermasters foraged for the regular commands off the country; but "under the color of the *license* given by Sherman's orders *every* regiment in the army sent out an independent foraging party, whose duty it was to see that its particular command was furnished with all the DELICACIES the country afforded. These men were the most venturesome in the army;" they "took great risks and experienced startling adventures. . . . If the negroes told the bummers stories of cruelty they had suffered, or hostility to the Union, etc., the injury was avenged by the torch." So on the twaddle of negroes these bummers, acting as judges, without appeal, executed their own sentences.

The rehearsal of these scenes afforded amusement in Washington, and "Marching through Georgia" is still a favorite hymn to the sanctimonious people who delight in cruelty to innocent women and little children.

"The bummer was a wily diplomat and learned all that was to be known of the neighbor farther down the road whom he expected to raid the next day. . . . The bummer drew a line between the rich and the poor."

Speaking of one bummer, as an example of others, he writes: "About midnight his voice was heard arousing the camp; he had six animals, horses and mules, strung together with a motley improvised harness made of odds and ends. . . . He bestrode one of the wheelers, and swayed in the saddle from the effects of apple-jack; his wagon was an immense box of the Tennessee pattern, high at each end, low in the middle, similar to an old Dutch galiot, loaded to the guards with the choicest of wines and liquors; and by chance there was in the cargo a box of glass goblets. . . . Samples of the wines were sent to corps headquarters, pronounced excellent, with the intimation that a further supply would be acceptable, etc.," and so on the chapter reads to the end.

The bummers generally obliged the negroes to improvise teams, and in wagons brought their stealings into camp. "They ranged over a section between sixty to eighty miles in breadth." (Page 272.) The writer pursues a middle line: he tells us nothing about the distress of the thousands of women and children left homeless by these cruel wretches, nor does he see any of watches, plate, and jewelry stolen; and now here we are, in the last years of the century, told by the "Grand Army of the Republic" that we must not tell any of these matters to our children in our school histories.

I am now about to close my account of this battle and the false statements regarding it. I have written it because of Gen. Corse's willfully making an erroneous statement toward the close of his report about driving the division away, and because of his (so-called) famous dispatch, the gospel hymn, and the shouts of victory, congratulatory orders and admiration parties; because of Hood's statement about orders given me—all of which have thrown a glamour over the conflict, making things seem to be what they were not.

I have endeavored to dispel the illusion, remove the glamour, uncover the hidden truth to him who will seek it.

The "holding on" power of the Federal soldier in this battle was remarkable, and his faith commendable. From 11 A.M. to near the close of day they were pent up inside and around in the ditch of a small fort in such numbers that they lay on one another, sat on each other, stood on others dead or alive, praying for relief. There they stayed till, in the silence of the gloaming, they ventured out and "had the advantage of the enemy and maintained it"—without opposition, for the enemy had long been gone away!

In what I have written respecting this battle I have made no charge against the Union soldier of the want of courage or the desire to surrender.

It is they who furnish the evidence of their distress, refusal to man the parapets, and desire to surrender under the long delay and disappointments of the so-often-promised aid. Amidst all their environments, let none condemn them without cause.

The Soldiers' Grave.

BY JOSEPH M. BROWN.

[In Allatoona Pass, by the Western and Atlantic railroad, is the grave of an unknown soldier who fell in the battle there October 5, 1864.]

In the railroad cut there's a lonely grave
　Which the trackmen hold sacred to care;
They have piled round it stones, and for it they save
　Every flower, when their task calls them there.

Away from the home of his love,
　Away from his sweetheart or wife,
Away from his mother, whose prayers went above,
　He gave for his country his life.

We know not if, wearing the blue, he came
　'Neath the "bright, starry banner" arrayed,
And, dying, that it o'er the mountains of fame
　Might forever in triumph wave prayed;

Or we know not if, 'neath the "bonnie blue flag,"
　He rushed forth, his country's defender,
Valiant, smote those who her cause down would drag.
　And only to death did surrender.

That God only knows; and so in his hand
　Let the secret unfathomed e'er rest;
But this we know, that he died for his land,
　And the banner he thought was the best.

Heav'n pity the dear ones who prayed his return,
　Heav'n bless them, and shield them from woes,
Heav'n grant o'er his grave to melt anger stern,
　And make brothers of those who were foes!

JOSEPH M. BROWN

JOHN BELL HOOD

The Lone Grave.

BY PAUL DRESSER.

["The Lone Grave" is situated on the Western and Atlantic railroad between Chattanooga, Tenn., and Atlanta, Ga. A plain board marked the resting place of a soldier. Name "unknown." None could tell whether he had been a Federal or Confederate. The section hands, when laying the track, discovered the grave, sodded it over beautifully, and placed a headstone over it bearing the above inscription. The traveler's attention is always called to this spot, and the trains "slow up" in order to give all an opportunity to see it. Let this be an olive branch to the North and South to be again a united people.—AUTHOR.]

A story I am going to tell of a grave
    In the South where a brave soldier fell.
For his cause he now sleeps by the side of a track—
    What his colors none able to tell.
A plain, simple board, rudely carved, that was all
    That was left to remind one of that sacred spot.
The words, as we traced them, were simple enough:
    "A soldier sleeps here; O! forget me not."

Chorus.—The lone grave is there by the side of the track;
    It contains a wanderer who never came back:
    And when he appears on the great judgment day,
    Our Father'll not ask: "Was your suit blue or gray?"

There's a mother that sits by a fireside to-night.
    She is thinking of days long gone by:
And she pictures "a loved one who went to the war.
    But returned not," she says with a sigh.
If the mother could know that her boy calmly sleeps.
    Undisturbed by the march or the progress of time.
What feelings would haunt her, what thoughts would she have.
    Sobs, tears, and heartaches, what sadness sublime!

Joseph M. Brown, who was for many years engaged in collecting facts relating to this battle, and which he privately published some years ago, states that the remains of Col. W. H. Clark, of Mississippi, rest in this grave. He fell, with the colors of his regiment in his hands, leading his men in the attack. That is an error.

These now deserved tributes to a brave soldier were made "To an Unknown Hero." For it is not known whether he was in the United States or Confederate service. As the last resting place of a man who gave his life for his country, it was regarded a sacred spot, and it is hoped it will always be reverently

THE LONE GRAVE.

cared for out of respect to the dead. It is an honored grave. Millions of travelers pass by and do it reverence.

And now, in conclusion, I have shown:

1. That the remarkable orders I received from Gen. Hood were given before he had any knowledge of there being a garrison at Allatoona; and that his later statements may be erroneous.

2. That I was not aware that the garrison in the fortress had been reënforced (two hours before my arrival) by Gen. Corse and troops, when I summoned the commander to surrender; and that I never received any reply to my summons.

3. That when the outer line of the fortress was gained, and Gen. Corse with all his troops west of the railroad were driven into the "slaughter pen," the battle was lost to him; his troops would not face their assailants; would have surrendered, only their officers implored them to "hold out" longer, as relief was momentarily expected to end "the prolonged strain of that mortal day."

4. That when I received the dispatch from Gen. Armstrong informing me that the advance infantry of Sherman's army from Atlanta had passed Gen. Hood at Lost Mountain, and were at Big Shanty, I deemed it best to forego the gratification of a complete victory for myself and troops, which, if won, must still result in further fight (by my exhausted troops) with the reënforcements hourly expected. And so I would not yield to the importunity of both officers and men, who were mad, and wanted, also, to "hold on" until they captured the entire works. I weighed their promises to capture the last work when ammunition was obtained with the after probable consequences, and pointed them out, and adhered to my decision; deeming it best for the "Confederate cause" not to lose more men for the mere eclat of a victory of doubtful compensating utility. We could not remain an hour if the place were taken.

5. Considering the number of urgent dispatches that Sherman sent to his general officers to take possession of the road over which I passed (on the 5th and 6th) on my way to New Hope Church, it is left for them to account for permitting the Confederates to pass by them without any serious skirmishing, because dispatch No. 15, received by Gen. Stanley at 2:30 P.M. on the 5th (when I was at Allatoona), gave him seventeen hours to

occupy and hold the Sand Town road, as ordered, before I moved over it to join Hood at New Hope Church.

Lastly. Gen Corse's "famous" dispatch, originally, "I can lick all h---l yet," has not the merit of the excitement or inspiration of the battlefield. It loses its significance entirely for the want of applicability. He had "whipped" no one; his command was now doubled in numbers; no enemy was within twenty miles of him; an entire day (lacking an hour) had passed since the last shot was fired, when he deliberately and thoughtfully prepared that dispatch, perhaps to divert attention from the real, actual occurrences of the battle the day previous and tickle the public ear.

The testimony of hundreds of witnesses now living has been *recorded* to substantiate what I have written. For the Union soldier in this battle I have tried to

> nothing extenuate.
> Nor set down aught in malice,

and in after years, I trust, to the noble Confederates who fought this battle the impartial historian will

> Give them the honors they won in the strife,
> Give them the laurels they lost with their life.

CHICKAMAUGA, GA., April 12, 1897.

Gen. S. G. French, Pensacola, Fla.

My Dear General: The manuscript history of the battle of Allatoona which you recently sent me has been read over twice, very carefully. It was exceedingly interesting to me and must be correct in every particular. Those facts and circumstances which fell within my personal knowledge are stated correctly, according to my recollections: and your unswerving fidelity to the truth and careful attention to details are well remembered. Moreover, the account given of the conduct of your troops is just what every one who knew them, as I did, would expect of Cockrell's Missourians, of Young's (Ector's) Texans, of Sears's Mississippians, and of Coleman's North Carolinians. Do you not owe it to these men as well as to yourself and the truth of history to publish this account of that battle? I hope you will do so, and would suggest, in the event you do, that the route taken by Sears to reach the north side and rear of the Federal position, and the positions of your three brigades, be indicated on the topographical map (page 339). Very sincerely yours,

ALEX P. STEWART.

CHAPTER XVII.

Return from Allatoona—Hood's Deportment—Cross the Coosa River—
Devastation around Rome—Rome Burned—Garrison of Resaca Refuses
to Surrender—Capture of the Seventeenth Iowa Regiment at Tilton—
Dalton Taken—Dug Gap—Dinner of Roasting Ears—Supper—Captured
Officers are Jolly Good Fellows—Gadsden—Encampment at Mrs. San-
som's—Her Daughter a Guide for Gen. Forrest when He Captured Gen.
Streight—Cross the Black Warrior River and Sand Mountains—Deca-
tur—Some Fighting at Decatur—Gen. Beauregard with Hood—Beauti-
ful Valley of the Tennessee made Desolate by War—Tuscumbia—Dreary
March to Columbia, Rain and Snow—Stewart's and Cheatham's Corps
Cross Duck River *en Route* to .Spring Hill—Hood Slept—Schofield
Passed By—Pursue Schofield to Franklin—Battle of Franklin—Inci-
dents—Remarkable Order for a Second Assault at Night—Losses in My
Two Brigades—Exchange of Prisoners Stopped.

THE battle of Allatoona having been fought as I have described it, the blockhouse at Allatoona creek with a garrison of 110 men captured, we marched on toward New Hope
Church, and near midnight encamped at the residence of Dr.
Smith, in the midst of an awful rainstorm, and within three
miles of Federal forces.

October 6, 1864. The rain is still falling in torrents, and it continued
until we reached New Hope Church and joined the other two divisions.
When I called at headquarters, Hood reminded me of a disheartened
man. His countenance was sad and his voice doleful. He received me
with a melancholy air, and asked no questions; did *not refer to the battle*,
"told me where my corps was, and said he would leave next day." He
seemed much depressed in spirits. Perhaps he experienced a feeling of
remorse that his want of information had induced him to send me to burn
the Etowah bridge, stopping an hour or two *en route* at the Allatoona cut,
"fill it up and obtain information." Encamped on Pumpkinvine creek.

7th. Marched early this morning to Van Wirt, by a road leading along
a high ridge. Was invited to the house of Dr. Pearce for the night.

8th. Started at dawn and marched to Cedartown, and encamped near
there.

9th. Remained in camp till 12 M. Left the sick and lame-footed men
with the baggage wagons to move on to J, and took up the line of march
from . . . toward Rome. Struck the road over which we marched May
17, last. Encamped at Cunningham's, on the road from Cave Springs to
Rome, Gen. Beauregard arrived at Cave Springs; he was heartily cheered
by Cheatham's Corps.

10th. Moved by a wood road to near a ferry over the Coosa river. Arrived there at noon, but could not cross on the pontoon until the corps of Hardee had passed over. When my division was across we marched about three miles to Robinson's, at the gorge of the Texas Valley road. All over the country within a radius of ten or twelve miles of Rome the citizens have been robbed by the enemy of everything. Bureaus broken, women's clothing torn to pieces, children left in rags, mirrors broken, books torn, feather beds emptied in the road. stock driven off; and no effort left untried to distress the families.

On the 8th of this month Gen. John M. Corse, from Cartersville, near here, wrote Gen. Sherman that he could not *now burn* or abandon Rome because there were one thousand four hundred sick there. (War Records, page 150, Vol. 39, Part III.) I mention this to show that it was saved for a while but afterwards destroyed.

11th. This morning we crossed into Texas Valley, and marched to Amuch post office, where we encamped.

12th. Started this morning at 4 A.M., and after a tedious march all day struck the railroad one mile above Resaca. Gen. S. D. Lee took a position in front of the works at Resaca. It was garrisoned by five hundred men. Hood summoned the garrison to surrender. It refused to do so. Here Hood showed his good sense not to make the attack even with twenty thousand men. We did not want the place nor the garrison, and had no men to spare or lose in a useless fight. Allatoona was a warning to him. Stewart's Corps moved up the railroad about three and a half miles, and captured a blockhouse and a construction camp, and burned an immense amount of lumber. There was one company captured in the blockhouse, which, however, was a temporary structure of hewn timber. Worked all night destroying railroad.

13th. Moved my division up the railroad, and surrounded a very large and strong blockhouse at Tilton. It was garrisoned by the Seventeenth Iowa Regiment, commanded by Col. Archer. He refused to surrender. As it was, from its oaken walls, impregnable to field artillery, it resisted a long time. Gen. Stewart, hearing the firing, came on the field and also called on the commander to surrender. Again he declined. I had placed a field battery in position, and directing shells to be fired at the narrow loopholes, we succeeded in driving shells through them, which, exploding inside, filled the structure with a dense, suffocating smoke, and soon the white flag was waved. Seventy shells were fired. The garrison consisted of three hundred and fifty men. Col. Archer, not being well, was paroled. The plundering of the stores, especially the sutler's, was the work of a few minutes, and our hungry men obtained some articles not found in the Confederate commissary department. The sutler came to me with his books and begged me to keep them for him, as he had no other evidence of what was due him from the regiment. I introduced him to my quartermaster, and asked him to keep them for the sutler. To add to the quick confusion, Loring's division was passing by at the time and tried to obtain some of the sutler's stores. Burned everything but the transportation, arms, stores, etc., and then moved on to Dalton. I had now four hundred and fifty prisoners. Dalton was captured by Cheatham. It was garrisoned by negro troops.

14th. My division became the rear guard. We crossed the mountain at Dug Gap and encamped near Villanow. When I crossed the mountain ridge I found a large field of corn by the roadside. The roasting ears were fine. I halted the division; called the brigade commanders, and gave them half an hour to get dinner out of the cornfield. Wonderfully quick were the fires made, and the corn roasted and fried. The prisoners and men dined indiscriminately. The Yankees made themselves useful, and knew how to rob a cornfield. Encamped in an orchard, and had some cows driven up and shot for supper and breakfast in the morning.

15th. Cheatham in advance. Loring, Walthall, and I were in the rear. During the march most of the field and staff officers of the Seventeenth Iowa walked along with me. They were jolly, good fellows, and laughed heartily at their dinner of green corn, and warm cow beef for supper and breakfast, and one of them presented me with a silk sash. He insisted on my accepting it. He told me "that much stress was placed on starving us out, but from the experience they had in the past two days they did not think we could be starved out at all, and that they would write home and tell their friends that the starvation game was played out." They made no complaint, for they messed with our men.

16th. Left Treadway's Gap this morning. Gen. Sears's Brigade and Kolb's battery remained to defend the Gap. I moved on through Summerville and encamped at Rhinehart's. Ordered to move to Lafayette at 2 A.M. Pigeon Mountain looms up in sight, and the scenery is beautiful.

17th. Started to Lafayette. as ordered, but returned and went to the junction of the road from Lafayette and Rome with the Alpine road. Here Sears's Brigade joined the division. Encamped at Mr. Mosteller's.

18th. Took the road at 5:30 P.M., passing through Gaylesville, and encamped four miles beyond the town. There are some good farms on the Chattooga river, which is here about twenty-five yards wide, with rocky bottom.

19th. Started at 6 A.M., intending to go to Blue Pond, but left the road and marched across to the Rome and Gadsden road, thence to Gadsden. Crossed Little River. Encamped near the Jacksonville and Gadsden roads. Cheatham's Corps near by. I hear various rumors in regard to Sherman's movements. The main question is, has he transportation with him to enable his command to move far away from the railroad? I am sure he will find all he wants in the country as he proceeds. I *think* we do not leave much in the way of rations behind us. Received letters from home to-night.

20th. Marched about two miles beyond Gadsden and encamped at Mrs. Sansom's. Her daughter, Miss Emma, was at home. When Federal Gen. Streight with two thousand men from Rome was captured by Gen. Forrest, he was under many obligations to Miss Sansom, who during the fight mounted Forrest's horse, sat behind him, and piloted him across Black Creek, which contributed much to enable him to capture the enemy. Out of compliment to Miss Sansom, I got Gen. Cockrell's band to play for her and her mother. While we were honoring Miss Sansom, a hungry soldier was skinning one of the Madam's hogs, and, *apropos*, I had the skin secured to the soldier's back, and thus he was marched about camp, a warning to others not to plunder. There is a waterfall on Black Creek, near here, reported to be one hundred feet high.

The Legislature of Alabama has granted to Miss Sansom a section of land. If she had betrayed Forrest, she might perhaps now be in receipt of a pension from the United States treasury, because the pension roll is a Roll of Honor, and so comprehensive that it embraces deserters from our army who enlisted in theirs. I have not inquired if substitutes receive pensions, but it is fair to presume they do. Were they not patriots? What is a patriot? What is patriotism? Dr. Sam Johnson, the great lexicographer, declared it to be "the last refuge of a consummate scoundrel."

21st. Remained in camp. Next day marched nineteen miles. Crossed the Black Warrior river, and crossed over Sand Mountain. On the 25th we passed the dividing ridge between the waters of the Tennessee and Coosa rivers. Heard artillery firing all the morning, apparently at Decatur. This sounds natural, as I have heard big guns almost daily for three years. It must have been inspiriting, for we marched twenty miles to-day. I am to-night within seven miles of Summerville, and six miles in advance of Walthall.

25th. I had to wait until noon for Walthall to pass on in advance, consequently I marched only four miles. Rain is falling fast. It rained all day on the 26th. In the afternoon reached Decatur. Loring's division took position near the defensive works and commenced firing with his batteries on a fort in front. Went into bivouac in columns of brigades within easy cannon range of the guns of the enemy. At dusk sent Ector's Brigade to the Danville road to guard it until Cheatham's Corps arrived by that road. And still it rains.

27th. Here we all are in front of Decatur. Will Hood attack the defensive works of the town? I can see nothing to be gained by it to compensate for the loss of men. We do not want the position. This afternoon I received orders to move over west of the Danville road. Reached the position at sunset. Relieved Gen. Guist, and went into line not far in front of Mr. Garth's residence. Rode down to the skirmish line; found Gen. Brown there. I relieved his men on the line with three of my regiments, and drove in the Federal skirmishers. There was firing all round, but most on Loring's line. I believe some negro troops made an attack on him. Gen. Beauregard is at the residence of Mr. Garth.

28th. Remained in camp. Cheatham's pickets formed a line in front of my division pickets and Gen. Brown's also during the night. Had to send Cockrell's Brigade to report to Gen. Loring, who generally magnifies the forces of the enemy. Received orders to move my command to Court-land in the morning. The nights are cold and the frosts very heavy.

29th. Started this morning by the railroad, but *not* in the cars. The line of the railroad crosses from the right to the left bank of the Tennessee river at Decatur, and I am marching down the left bank. The country is beautiful, and the soil rich; but what a desolation everywhere! The dreamy silence, the absence of life, the smoky atmosphere, the abandoned dwellings, the uncultivated fields, the destruction of fences—everything, everywhere mark the ravages of war that has changed this once beautiful valley of the Tennessee into a desert in all save the rich soil. Here the tide of war has ebbed and flowed; and far and wide have the raiding parties roamed until almost every means of subsistence has been consumed or destroyed. The only signs of life are here and there a rabbit startled from ambush, and now and then a solitary crow perched on a dead limb of a tree. Made my camp on a farm belonging to Mr. Swoope, but now occupied by Mr. Watkins. Cheatham's Corps and some cavalry were left at Decatur.

The Federal forces in Decatur were commanded by Gen. R. S. Granger, an old friend of mine, and he was brevetted for his gallant defense of the town. Dear me! I did not think there was a skirmish there, and no effort was made to take the place, although the forces were, in strength, less than those at Alla-toona. Gen. Granger told me, when I met him after the war, what his numbers were.

30th. Left Courtland this morning, moving along the track of the rail-road toward Tuscumbia. Stopped at Col. Saunders's for dinner. They have a beautiful and costly residence. There were present for dinner Mrs. and Miss Saunders, Miss Sherod, Gen. Cheatham, Col. Shotwell, Col. Brown, Mr. Foster, and others. Encamped at Leighton, near the house of Dr. Kompy. Took tea with the family.

31st. Arrived at Tuscumbia. Encamped on the creek. Stopped at Mrs. Chadwick's. Gen. S. D. Lee had crossed the two divisions of his corps over the Tennessee river. I was surprised at this because of the width of the river, and the apprehension of the pontoons giving way or being broken. The day is bright and beautiful. Rode up to see the spring. The volume of water gushing out of rocks, from far below, is sufficient to form a large creek. The town is old, and now dilapidated. Most of the dwellings from Leighton to this place have been burned by the enemy.

The houses of absentees were always destroyed in that way, it being a crime to leave home.

November 1. Busy arranging transportation. I am told that the pontoons do not reach to the other shore. From to-day to the 13th we remained in Tuscumbia because of the heavy rains that delayed the arrival

19

of supplies. During this period the Yankees made two attempts to cut the ropes of the pontoons; once they went down the wrong channel; next day they cut the rope, but their boat upset and they were captured. Rumor reports that Sherman, with a large force, is between Chattanooga and Atlanta. I remained at or near Tuscumbia until the 20th, when I prepared to cross the river. For three weeks it has rained almost continuously, making the roads very bad. I remonstrated with Gen Hood, at a meeting of his officers, against taking so many pieces of artillery with the army unless we had a *full* supply of horses for the guns. But he insisted that, once in Tennessee, men would join us, horses could be obtained, and the men be supplied with shoes and clothing.

20th. I passed over the Tennessee river by the pontoon bridge *en route* to Nashville. To-day we learned that Sherman's advance had reached Griffin on the 16th. Here are two armies that have been fighting each other from about the first of May to the first of November, six months—parted—the one heading for the Atlantic ocean, two hundred and ten miles from Atlanta, and the other marching from Tuscumbia, Ala., for Nashville, Tenn., one hundred and fifteen miles distant. The one is a strategic move against the army of R. E. Lee, in Virginia, and the other appears a military error, because it must meet accumulative forces as it advances into the enemy's zone. Winter is near and the army not clothed.

21st. Having crossed the river yesterday, and moved out on the Lawrenceburg road five miles, we started this morning through mud from four to twenty inches deep, and through snow that the keen wind blew in our faces. In the afternoon we encamped by the roadside, near a deserted habitation. The weather is bitterly cold, and the snow falling. Sleeping on the ground covered with snow.

22d. Resumed the march. Roads miserable. Encamped seven miles beyond Priwit's Mills. Lee's Corps is on our left and Cheatham's on the right. Stewart's is the central column. Snowed some to-day, and the ground was frozen so hard that it bore the wagons. Artillery delayed everything, and some of it did not reach camp until daylight, just as I told Gen. Hood it would be; in fact, men had to haul their guns over bad places. In the conference, I told Hood he would take the guns to Nashville only to turn some of them over to the enemy for want of horses. This is my birthday. What a delightful time I have had!

23d. This morning I was ordered to remain in camp and await the arrival of the supply train. Artillery went on under charge of Col. Williams. Bushwhackers reported on the road. Continued the march to Mt. Pleasant. Remained all night with Mr. Granbury. The roads still in very bad condition. Started on the morrow amidst the rain and mud. Passed through a beautiful country. Passed the home of Gen. G. J. Pillow. Reached Columbia. Encircled the town with troops, and some skirmishing ensued. The enemy left the place last night, and early this morning we entered the town. Gen. Schofield with his army is now on the north side of Duck river, offering a strong resistance to our crossing. I was invited to the house of Mr. Mathews. In the afternoon I moved my division up the river to cross it: but as the bridge was not ready, I turned back.

29th. This morning Cheatham's Corps, Johnston's Division, and Stewart's Corps, and one battery of artillery (the cavalry in advance) moved up the river to near Hewey's ferry and crossed it on a pontoon bridge; Gen. S. D. Lee, with the remainder of the army, remained in Columbia, making a strong demonstration to hold the enemy there.

This was a strategic movement of Hood's to gain the Franklin pike in rear of the enemy. We marched rapidly for Spring Hill by a country road. Hearing the cannonading all the time at Columbia, we were encouraged and hopeful of reaching Spring Hill before the enemy did. Schofield, no doubt, was informed that we were crossing, and, having a shorter and better road to travel, got Gen. Stanley with a division and much artillery at Spring Hill and in position before Hood arrived there at the head of Cheatham's Corps. Perhaps, apprehensive that the enemy might move on the Murfreesboro road, he halted Stewart's Corps and Johnston's Division at Rutherford creek, some four miles from the pike. Our corps was kept here until dark, when it was ordered to move on toward the pike.

When Hood arrived in view of the pike and saw the road filled with United States wagons in hasty retreat to Franklin, what orders he gave Cheatham I know not, for *his* version differs from what Hood says were given *him*. But Hood was on the ground present, and that settles the question. The sun went down, darkness came, and later we went into bivouac. The head of our army reached the pike about 3 P.M. and we were halted. As but little musketry was heard, officers naturally asked: "What did we come here for?" There was a house near by my headquarters, and about 9 P.M. I walked over to it. In the drawing room I found Gen. James R. Chalmers and other cavalry officers. Chalmers said they were short or out of ammunition. On inquiry as to the cartridges they used, Maj. Storrs, my ordnance officer, said he could supply them with ammunition, and I ordered him to issue them cartridges at once. Occasionally we heard some picket firing toward the north. It was Gen. Ross's men on the road to Franklin. Cheatham's Corps went into bivouac near the pike, and so in comparative silence the long night wore away. Hood slept. The head and the eyes and ears of the army, all dead from sleeping. Ye gods! will no geese give them warning as they did in ancient Rome?

30th. We were up before the morning star. My division was ordered to take the advance to Franklin in *pursuit* of Schofield, for now every one knew he passed by us while we were dreaming. Artillery and wagons, infantry and horse, all gone on to Franklin! When I reached the pike I met Gen. Hood, and he exclaimed; "Well, Gen. French, we have missed the great opportunity of the war!" "Yes," I replied, "I am told the Yankees passed along all night and lit their pipes at our camp fires." Of course my answer was a *little* figurative, but some soldiers heard it, and, taking it literally, it soon spread through the ranks.

The idea of a commanding general reaching his objective point, that required prompt and immediate action and skillful tactics, to turn away and go to bed surpasses the understanding. The truth is, Hood had been outgeneraled, and Stanley with the Federal troops got to Spring Hill before Hood did. What information Hood received of the enemy, when he reached the pike, if any, no one will ever know. Why did he not in person form his line of battle and attack the enemy at Spring Hill? Although we yielded the right of way, the enemy must have been a little nervous, because the slight firing done by Ross's men caused the enemy to abandon about thirty wagons, and I could not but observe what a number of *desks* containing official vouchers had been *thrown* from the wagons by the roadside. Had there been a cavalry force with artillery north of Spring Hill and near the pike to have shelled the road, there would no doubt have been a stampede and a wreck of wagons.

My division overtook the enemy near Franklin, drawn up on a range of hills about two miles from the town, and when I began to deploy my troops, to advance a line on their flank and rear, they fell back to the town.

I rode with some members of my staff to the top of a high wooded hill, from which I could look down on the surrounding country. Before me were the town, the green plains around it; the line of defensive works, the forts and parks of artillery on the heights across the river, long lines of blue-clad infantry strengthening their lines, and trains moving over the river. While I sat at the root of a giant tree a long time surveying the scene before me, I called to mind that *never* yet had any one seen the Confederates assigned to me driven from any position, much less from defensive works, by assault, and I inferred that it would require a great sacrifice of life to drive the veteran Federals from their lines, and thought if Hood could only ride up

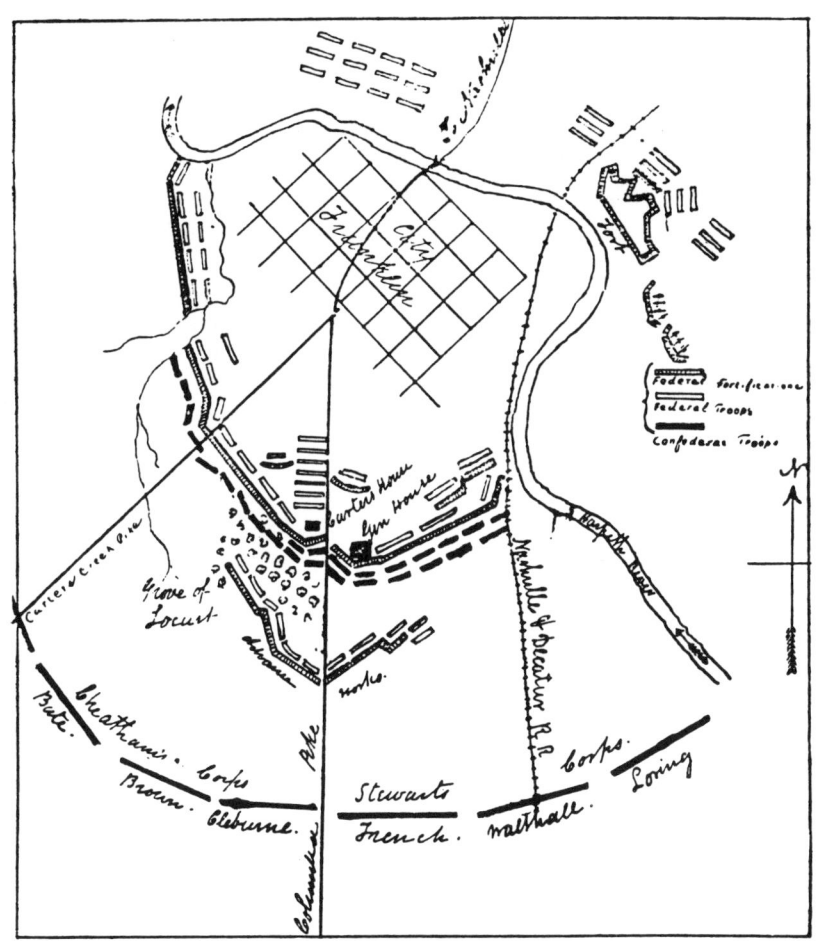

BATTLE OF FRANKLIN.

here and look calmly down on the battle array before him he would not try to take the town by assault. But the offspring of Hood's conception at Columbia came stillborn at Spring Hill, caused by an oversleep. Chagrin at this mishap and awakened at the consequences, without duly considering the whole field of war and deducing therefrom what was best for the *cause*, he impatiently formed line with the two corps with him and prepared to assault the town. Perhaps he forgot to call to mind the well-acknowledged fact that *one* man behind an intrenched line is equal to *five* in front. Now Schofield had at Franklin, by report in the War Records, 25,420 men, exclusive of cavalry; and Hood had 21,874 men, exclusive of a part of Lee's Corps, the cavalry and Ector's Brigade detached. So any one can compute what Hood's strength, or numbers, should be to make a fair fight. Therefore, it is probable that Hood, by disappointment at Spring Hill, inconsiderately, and without careful reconnoissance, determined immediately to attack the fortified city with 21,874 men, without any artillery, except two guns brought with him.

The sketch of the field of Franklin will show that the Harpeth river in its meandering covers three of the four sides of the town. The line of intrenchments extended from the Nashville and Decatur railroad around the southern and western parts of the town to the Harpeth river, with an advanced line extending to some distance on either side of the Columbia pike. Also I saw rifle pits inside the works from which a fire was opened on our troops after they scaled the main line.

THE BATTLE.

My division, as I have told you, was the van of the army, and as we neared Franklin it left the pike, turning to the right or east, and halted near the river. Here Gen. Stewart formed his corps in order of battle by placing Loring on the right, Walthall in the center, and French on the left. This brought me nearest to the Columbia pike, as will be shown. Cheatham's Corps was formed with his right resting on or near the pike, which brought Cleburne's right a half mile distant on my left. We were thus formed, as it were, in a circle like the fellies of a wheel; and each division marching to one common center caused them to overlap before reaching the enemy, because the circle became smaller and smaller. My division consisted of only two brigades, Cockrell's and Sears's. Ector's Brigade was on detached duty. Stewart's Corps, being in advance, was first formed, and we rested. The sun was sinking in the west, the day was drawing to its close, the tumult and excitement had ceased. The winds were in their caves, the silence that precedes the storm was *felt;* the calm before the earthquake which by some *law* of nature forewarns fowls to seek the fields, birds to fly away, and cattle to run to the hills, although withheld from man, seemed to presage an impending calamity, as painful in suspense as the disclosure of any reality. From this feeling of anxiety, sometimes incident to men when held in readiness to engage in a great battle, there came relief by a signal. And what a change! Twenty thousand gallant Confederates at the word of command moved proudly over the open plain to the attack. It was a glorious and imposing sight, and one so seldom witnessed, as all were in full view. Soon my division came under the artillery fire of both the guns in front and those in position in the forts across the river, undaunted by the crash of shells, all moved gallantly on and met the fire of the enemy in the outer line of defense. It was only the work of a few minutes to crush the outer line, and when it broke and tried to gain the main works they were so closely followed by our men that friends and foe, pursuer and pursued, in one mass, rushed over the parapet into the town. During this time the fire from the enemy on this part of the line ceased so as to admit their own troops. But the Confederates now inside were confronted with a reserve force and either killed or captured.

As our division overlapped, immediately another line made the assault, and again the smoke cloud of battle so obscured the plain that I could see only beneath the cloud an incessant sheet of flame rolling on the ground, in which the combatants flitted about like the pictures of demons in Tophet. The shock was too violent to last. Its force was soon spent. The fire slackened, and as the smoke was wafted away in broken clouds, the sight was appalling! What a ghastly scene was in front of the gin-house! The dead and wounded were visible for a moment, only to be again enveloped in the cloud of battle beneath which the Angel of Death garnered his harvest. "On! on! forward! forward!" was the cry. It was death to stop, and safety was in a measure found in the ditch beneath the fire from the parapet. There thousands remained all night; others were repulsed and driven back. My division was re-formed beyond the range of musketry, but exposed to artillery in front and from the fort across the river.

Gen. Sears's men, those that were repulsed, fell back with some order, but Cockrell's Brigade had nearly all disappeared. Now and then a few came out. Cockrell was wounded. Col. E. Gates came out riding with his bridle reins in his mouth, being wounded in both hands. I was on foot. My horse, during the continued shelling at Kennesaw Mountain, took a dislike to shells, and manifested it on this occasion by using only his hind feet when walking. I had to give him to the orderly to lead.

Gen. Walthall came out at the time we did. He rode up to me, and as I put my hand on his horse's shoulder to talk with him, the animal reared up, plunged violently forward, and fell dead, throwing the General far over his head. The horse had been shot and that was the death struggle. We fell back, and bivouacked just out of range of fire. It was now growing dark; but still the battle raged furiously at intervals till near midnight, especially on the west side of the pike, mainly between our troops in the ditch, and on the captured parapet, with the enemy on inside lines; and the bright glare of musketry with the flashes of artillery lit up the surroundings with seemingly fitful volcanic fires, presenting a night scene frightfully wild and weird.

Gen. S. D. Lee's Corps and the artillery had arrived, and after dark orders were given by Gen. Hood that after midnight or near dawn one hundred rounds would be fired by every piece of artillery, and then the troops *would assault the works again* over the same ground. Festus assigned a reason for St. Paul's madness, but no one attributed Hood's madness to that cause when *this* order was given.* However, when no reply was made to our guns it was discovered that Schofield had, with the main body of his army, abandoned Franklin and was on his way to Nashville.

It was a terrible battle. One of my brigades, Cockrell's, made

---

* See S. P. Lee's "Brief History of the United States." It confirms my diary. Also book of Gen. J. D. Cox, United States army, and War Records, and Maj. Sanders's letter, on page 340. Also letter of Rev. Thomas R. Harkham, page 342.

the assault with 696 officers and men, and when it was over he had 277 men in his brigade. His loss was, killed, 19 officers and 79 men; wounded, 31 officers and 198 men; missing, 13 officers and 79 men; total, 419, which was over sixty per cent. The missing were captured inside the works, as stated by some who escaped. Sears's Brigade met with less loss, because it stopped a few minutes in the exterior line before moving to the main line. There were twelve general officers killed and wounded and one taken prisoner. *

Hood's official report puts our loss at 4,500. I believe that this grand charge of 21,800 men, for a mile or more over an open plain, all in full view, was grander than any charge at Gettysburg.

After the fall of Vicksburg, and the battle of Gettysburg had been fought, and enlistments in the Confederate service had practically ceased, and the exchange of prisoners stopped, as I have stated, it certainly behooved the government and the generals in command of the armies in the East and in the West to husband their *men* and resources. I know this was the opinion of Gen. J. E. Johnston, and it was perhaps, in a measure, attributable to this that Gen. Hood superseded him in command of the army then at Atlanta, for he had the reputation of being a "fighter," and when put in command had to sustain that reputation. Gen. Grant was intrusted with the exchange of prisoners and (to take the ignominy off the government) discontinued the exchange, †

---

* Gen. John Adams, of Loring's Division, was killed about two hundred yards east of the ginhouse, and his body was removed to near the ginhouse by order of Col. Casement, United States army, who put a guard over it. So after the battle it was not found where he fell. This led to the belief that Loring's Division extended to near the ginhouse.

It has been a source of regret to me that I was unable to write an official report of the battle of Franklin immediately after it was ended, but on account of the condition of my eyes it was put off; and now I wonder why I did not have my chief of staff write it under my dictation, but so it is: amidst the confusion following the battle it was neglected. I might add here that it was years before my eyes were well, though treated by a specialist.

† The following is an extract from a letter dated August 18, 1864, written at City Point by Gen. U. S. Grant to Gen. B. F. Butler, agent of exchange at Fortress Monroe, Va.:

"It is hard on our men held in Southern prisons not to exchange them, but it is humanity to those left in the ranks to fight our battles. Every

and thus all increase of our fighting force ceased. Therefore the men in the army had become *the Confederacy*, and to them the power was virtually transmitted, and the commanders of armies held the destiny of the nation in their hands. No dictator appeared! Wisdom called for the Fabian policy; heedless of her voice, the *third* day after being in command he fought the battle of Peach Tree Creek. Two days after this (on the 22d) he fought the battle of Atlanta; and on the 28th, a third battle, without a victory, and all the time the siege of the city continued. The men he lost diminished his power. The loss to the enemy was nothing. Men cost nothing, and they could get all they wanted. Next came Jonesboro, and then Allatoona, both reducing his strength. And now came the battle of Franklin, where he lost about 5,000 more men. Why were the lines of the enemy assaulted at Franklin? Was it a strategical point? No. Were there in the town magazines or army stores? No. Was there anything of such value as to justify 21,874 men assaulting a town defended by 25,420 veteran troops? No! Schofield was crossing his teams as rapidly as possible to join Gen. Thomas at Nashville.

I was asked by Gen. T. J. Wood, U. S. A. (in 1865), who was at Franklin: "Why did you fight us at Franklin, when we were getting away from there as fast as we could?" He said: "The order directing the operation of withdrawing the troops had been issued, and the officers were assembled in Schofield's office, when, to our astonishment, a cannon shot was heard, and, looking out, we saw your troops advancing. That order for evacuating the place was not changed. Our apprehension was that you would cross the river and outflank us, as you did at Spring Hill."

I thought when we arrived at Franklin that Hood, who had declined to attack a garrison of 500 men at Resaca with his

---

man released on parole or otherwise becomes an active soldier against us at once, either directly or indirectly. If we commence a system of exchange which liberates all prisoners taken, we will have to fight on until the whole South is exterminated. If we hold those caught, they amount to no more than dead men. At this particular time to release all Rebel prisoners North would insure Sherman's defeat, and would compromise our safety here." (See War Records, page 606, Series II., Vol. VII., Serial No. 120.)

whole army present, and did not risk an attack on the works at Decatur when garrisoned by 2,000 men, would surely not assault the town garrisoned by an army of 25,000 men, with the two army corps and one division he had with him numbering only 21,800 men. Why he gave battle when so little could be gained, except some eclat, I cannot tell. I only know that he said to Gen. A. P. Stewart that "captured dispatches told him the time had come to fight."

An army belongs to the nation that made it, and not to the general commanding it. Therefore he has no right to sacrifice it.*

---

*Gen. J. D. Cox, Union army, who commanded most of the troops engaged in the battle of Franklin, in his volume published describing this battle (on page 15) states that *our killed*—1,750—exceeded "Grant's at Shiloh, McClellan's in the seven days' battle, Burnside's at Fredericksburg, Rosecrans's at Stone's river or at Chickamauga, Hooker's at Chancellorsville, and were almost as many as Grant's at Cold Harbor, and nine less than the British loss at Waterloo out of 43,000 men." The killed, as I have shown at Buena Vista, is very great compared with the wounded; more than at Franklin.

Comparisons often surprise us. An examination of the "United States Army Dictionary," by C. K. Gardner, Adjutant General U. S. A., brought down to 1853, shows also that the number of the killed and wounded in the United States forces during the war with Great Britain from 1812 to 1815 were: killed, 1,045; wounded, 2,656; total *3,701*. (The Creek Indian war in Georgia and Alabama omitted.)

Again, the whole number of killed and wounded, from the firing of the first gun on the banks of the Rio Grande to Buena Vista, from Vera Cruz to the City of Mexico, thence to the shore of the Pacific and in California, was only 4,808.

And so the facts of history show that out of the 21,800 Confederate soldiers engaged in the battle of Franklin more were killed, in a few hours, than during either of the two preceding wars. In the Confederate war the United States lost, killed, 99,183, and from disease, 171,806.

The dispatch that Hood captured just before the battle, dated November 29, 1864, 3.30 A.M., will be found in Gen. Cox's book (page 25). There is no information in it to justify Hood in making the assault. Thomas merely "tells Schofield to fall back from Columbia to Franklin, and that Gen. A. J. Smith's command had *not* arrived in Nashville," etc.

MAJ. D. W. SANDERS'S LETTER.

May 6, 1897.

Gen. S. G. French, Pensacola, Fla.

My Dear General: In answer to your letter of the 29th ult., in which you say that in recent correspondence with Gen. A. P. Stewart he says that he

Mrs. S. P. Lee states (on page 493) that "orders were given to carry the inner fortifications at daylight."

---

has no recollection of Gen. Hood's order for the artillery at Franklin to be put in position, and to open on the enemy about midnight, and when it ceased the infantry was to charge the lines over the same ground that they did in the first attack. In this letter you also ask me to give my recollections about this matter, and if I remember the order.

I remember very distinctly that the order was given, and you communicated it to me as the adjutant general of your division upon your return that night—to wit, November 30, 1864—from Gen. A. P. Stewart's headquarters. This order I delivered to the officers in command of two of your brigades; your third brigade, which was Ector's Brigade, at that time was on detached service guarding the trains in the rear of the two corps which charged the enemy's works November 30, 1864, at Franklin, Tenn.

The artillery had arrived from Columbia, Tenn., and was placed in position to execute this order of Gen. Hood's. Lieut. Col. Llewellyn Hoxton was in command of the battalions of artillery. At the time indicated in the order Col. Hoxton's artillery opened on Franklin with a heavy cannonade, to which there was no response, and it was therefore evident that Schofield had successfully withdrawn his forces and retreated to Nashville.

In September, 1886, I met Col. Hoxton at the Episcopalian school, four or five miles from Alexandria, Va., and had a conversation with him, and he said to me that I was entirely correct in my recollection of this particular order, and that he was in command of the artillery, and in the execution of his order opened upon Franklin, and no reply from the enemy satisfied him that Schofield had retreated, and he ceased firing, and scouts were sent to the works, which they found abandoned, and penetrated the village of Franklin to the crossing of the Harpeth river; and immediately thereafter a great many soldiers, under the command of their officers, went through the streets and alleys of Franklin, and it was thus ascertained to be a fact that the enemy had retreated.

I remember distinctly the comments of the officers of your division upon the delivery of Gen. Hood's order to them, that they would obey promptly and cheerfully, but that it looked to them as the highest desperation to undertake to charge the works under cover of this artillery fire, and carry them at the point of the bayonet. The fact that this order was given, and the circumstances surrounding Hood's troops at that time, are indelibly impressed upon my memory, and I have no hesitancy whatever in saying distinctly and unequivocally that the order was given, and that it was communicated by me to the commanders of the brigades of your division.*

Yours sincerely,

D. W. Sanders.

---

*The only official report I know of, which in any manner refers to this order, and this inferentially, is that of Gen. C. L. Stevenson, in which he says:

" During the night (November 30, 1864) this division was put in position preparatory to an assault which it was announced was to be made by the entire army at daybreak." (See War Records, Battle of Franklin.)   D. W. S.

The Rev. Thomas B. Markham, chaplain to Featherstone's Brigade, writes: "Our artillery was moved to within point-blank range of the enemy's works, . . . to open fire on them at earliest daybreak, after which a general assault, was to be made by the infantry," etc. (Page 272, *Confederate Veteran*, June Number, 1899.)

Note.

It has been a source of much regret to me that I was unable to write an official report of the battle of Franklin immediately after it occurred; but on account of the condition of my eyes it was put off from time to time, and now I wonder why I did not have my adjutant general do it for me. But so it was, under the sorrow for lost friends and comrades, and the immediate pursuit of the enemy to Nashville, it was neglected. Besides, as is usual, no report was called for by the commander of the army; and so with many it has become only a memory of a great and uncalled-for disaster to the Confederate cause—a battle fought against great odds, without any compensating value if successful.

CHAPTER XVIII.

March to Nashville—Cold Weather—Partial Investment of the City—Leave of Absence—Turn the Command Over to Brig. Gen. C. W. Sears—Battle of Nashville—Hood Not Physically Able for the Duties of a Commander in Want of All Supplies—Marshal Saxe—Mulai Malek—Going to Nashville a Failure; Could Not Be Otherwise—Leave for Columbus, Ga.—Marriage to Mary Fontaine Abercrombie—Go to Meriwether County to Avoid Wilson's Raid—Robbing in Columbus—Adventures of My Orderly—Yankees Raid the Houses—Gen. A. Had No Pies—Gens. Lee and Johnston Surrender—Terms Thereof—War with the Musket Ends.

DECEMBER 2, 1864, Hood in his impetuosity rushed in pursuit of Schofield's army, that was securely at rest behind the fortifications at Nashville, where he formed a junction with the troops there under Gen. G. H. Thomas. Hood formed his line close as he could in front of their works. My division was on the left of the Granny White turnpike, and ran north of the dwelling of E. Montgomery, who was a cotton planter and neighbor of mine in Mississippi. Owing to the condition of my eyes, I could write no more in my diary. The weather was cold, the ground frozen, and covered with snow.

I remained there suffering with my eyes until the 13th, when I was granted a leave of absence, and I turned the command over to Gen. C. W. Sears. I remained there the 14th, intending to leave the next day, but, observing a movement of the enemy's troops on the 15th, remained there to ascertain his intentions. Instead of a demonstration, it proved to be a real attack. I remained on the field all day, and by night our left was forced back parallel to the Granny White pike. By noon on the 16th it was plain that the battle was lost, and in the afternoon I was advised to leave to avoid confusion of the retreat. So, with my two aids, we started for the Tennessee river, and crossed it at Tuscumbia. The horses were given the servants to ride to Columbus, Ga., and we left by train for the same city.

The history of the Army of Tennessee from this time to its surrender on April 25, 1865, by Gen. J. E. Johnston in North Carolina may be found in the War Records. Johnston was placed in command of this army again at the request of the Confederate Congress by a joint resolution that was passed.

As I shall here probably take my leave of Gen. Hood, I desire to say that, had he not made erroneous statements in his reports and in his book, and perverted facts, and cast reflections on me and the men I had the honor to command at Allatoona, I would have kept silent, and this biography would never have been written; but he and Gen. Corse have obliged me to vindicate the truth of history for my children and myself, and the Confederate soldiers that I had the honor to command.

Gen. Hood was a noble commander of a division, for he was indeed a brave man; but as the commander of an army, circumstanced as the Confederate States were, he was too impulsive. As well try to catch all the fish in the ocean as to kill all the men that the United States could obtain, or recruit, from the nations of the earth, including our slaves, for the bounty offered. Constant conflicts entailed losses on both sides, and we had no men to sacrifice. The misfortune in part was that he had condemned Johnston's policy, and obeyed him reluctantly, and felt bound when he superseded him to carry on an aggressive war, and in doing so wrecked the Army of Tennessee.

The influence of personal valor in an officer on his men is generally limited to a small body of troops that witness it; whereas, victory for an army depends on the *skill* and the *art* with which the impulsive force of the masses is united on the field of battle, quickly to accomplish an object and destroy the plans of the enemy. By the art of skillful maneuvering an army may be obliged to abandon an advanced position without being driven out at the expense of life. Hood was a fighter; but he was not able by reason of his wounds to undergo the labor devolving on a commander constantly marching and fighting, often without supplies.

It is true that Marshal Saxe, carried on a litter, won the battle of Fontenoy; that Mulai Malek, Emperor of Morocco, in a dying condition, planned his last battle, and was carried on a litter through the ranks to animate the men. With anguish of mind he saw some of his troops giving way. In his last agonies he collected strength of life enough to throw himself from the litter, and rallied them, and led them to the charge. Exhausted, he fell on the field. When placed again on the litter, he laid his finger on his mouth to enjoin secrecy on his officers, and in a moment expired; but he won the victory. These, and others I remember, are exceptions, but it is not safe to make exceptions the rule.*

Hood's physical condition should have been considered by the authorities before he was placed in command, and the question asked: "Has he ever been thrown on his own resources to *provide for* and *direct* an independent command?" To command a corps is a small matter compared with directing a campaign (against a superior force) often without supplies. I have no desire to criticise Hood's movements, and will only remark that I am not able to see why he interrupted Gen. Schofield from leaving Franklin when he was getting away as fast as he could. That interference cost us the loss of nearly 5,000 men, the flower of the army, without any compensating object in view or result likely to be obtained under the environments.

Then came Nashville. We went there for recruits and army supplies. The presence of our poor, worn-out, and badly clothed troops that had survived the late battles of Peach Tree Creek of July 22 and 28 outside of Atlanta, and the siege of that city, Jonesboro, Allatoona, Franklin and many smaller conflicts consolidated the stream of reënforcements sent to Thomas at Nashville until it became a formidable army.

As a river on its course when stopped by a dam must overflow the obstruction or sweep it away, so Thomas's army was gathering force to overwhelm ours, which received no additional strength, but on the contrary lost some at Murfreesboro. On the walls of Hood's tent were now written: "*An army that can obtain no recruits must eventually surrender.*" And that he could not interpret. Then the tempest came! And the best reason I can give that the remnant of the grand Army of Tennessee so successfully crossed the Tennessee river is that Gen. Thomas always rode his horse at a walk. This is no reflection on the defense of our rear guard.

I remained in Columbus, Ga., and on the 12th of January,

---

*The battle of Alcazar, called the "Battle of the Three Kings," fought about three hundred years ago between Mulai, the emperor of Morocco, on the one side, and his nephew, king of Fez, on the other, assisted by Don Sebastian, king of Portugal, under whose standard had flocked the nobility of Christian Europe. Mulai Malek had 40,000 Moorish cavalry. Fifteen thousand of the allies were left dead on the field, and the river Machassan ran red with blood.

1865, married Miss Mary F. Abercrombie, daughter of Gen. Anderson Abercrombie, a planter in Russell County, Ala.*

Sherman had now captured Savannah, and was marching to join Grant. Then came the surrender of Gen. Lee. And now Gen. J. H. Wilson was nearing Columbus. To escape his thieving crowd, I started on Saturday, April 15, in a carriage with my wife to take her to Mrs. Campbell's, in Meriwether County, Ga., some twenty-five miles above Columbus. We remained that night in town with Judge G. E. Thomas, and started next morning. Gen. Howell Cobb was in command of the troops in Columbus, and he asked me to remain and take the command of the forces. This I declined, but I promised to return Monday morning and aid him. About 10 A.M. we heard cannon at Columbus, and knew that Wilson had attacked the town. The next morning at the dawn of day fugitives from Columbus were passing by, and told us that the town was in possession of the Federals. So I did not go to join Gen. Cobb. However, being anxious to know the condition of affairs, I asked my orderly, Hedrick, if he would next morning ride down in the direction of the city, and ascertain the condition of affairs, and he said: "Yes, General."

Now it chanced, soon after he started, that Hedrick met a Con-

---

*Gen. Anderson Abercrombie was adjutant of Maj. Freeman's battalion of Georgia volunteers, U. S. army, in the war of 1812. Again under the command of Brig. Gen. John Floyd, U. S. A., and was wounded in the battle with the Creek Indians at Camp Defiance, Ala., January 27, 1814.

In an engagement on the 14th of July, 1864, between the Confederate troops under Gen. J. H. Clanton and the Federal forces under Gen. Rousseau, Miss Abercrombie's brother, Capt. Robert S. Abercrombie, was mortally wounded. He stood in the road alone, whence all had fled, save one friend beside him (Albert Hyer), whose life he had saved in battle, and when surrounded and *begged* to surrender refused. To capture him they shot him, designedly in his leg, and then through thoughtlessness let him bleed to death, notwithstanding there was a tourniquet in his pocket, and Mr. Hyer had another. He was buried under a red oak on Mr. D. Carroll's place on the Talladega road, Calhoun County, Ala., one and three-quarter miles from Greensport, within a half mile of Ten Island P. O., on the beautiful Coosa river. He received from the United States officers every attention to save his life, except the all-important one of stopping the flow of blood from the wound, which was *below* the knee. The great loss of blood was not noticed by reason of so much water poured on the wound. Thus perished a brave man whose life might have been saved.

20

federate soldier who told him that the Yankees had taken the
fort at West Point, Ga., and gave him the name of the Federal
officer who commanded the expedition, and Hedrick's sagacity
applied the information to the accomplishment of his purposes.
Riding on, just below the town of Hamilton, he suddenly encountered a regiment of Federal cavalry. Without hesitation he
rode up to the leading officer, and inquired for Gen. Wilson,
saying he was a messenger from the Federal commanding officer
at West Point, sent to meet Gen. Wilson.* He was directed to
go on to Columbus. About a mile farther on two cavalrymen in
a skirt of wood cried out "Halt," and said: "You are a prisoner." He told them the story of his having been sent to find
Gen. Wilson. They were doubtful, and one said: "If you please,
none of your blarney to us, for we are from Ould Ireland itself,
and you are a Johnnie Rebel, and are after daceiven' us, you are.
Look at the stripe on your jacket." Hedrick explained that he
could not ride through the country with his United States uniform on, and that his clothing was taken from a prisoner, etc.
"Mike," said one of them, "of course he could not wear his own
coat, and I am sure he is a gentleman; and did not the colonel
himself let him pass?" So Pat agreed with Mike, and Hedrick
rode on. Next, after crossing a stream, he came to a dwelling
by the roadside: the owner was sitting on the fence by the front
gate, watching for more Yankees to pass by, when Hedrick rode
up to him and asked if he could have dinner. The farmer inquired who he was; and he varied the story of being a messenger to suit the occasion, by saying he was a Yankee, and as so
many Yankees had just passed, he invited him into his house.
His daughters hastily prepared a dinner. Hedrick was gracious,
told them to come down to Columbus—send down chickens and
butter, and get coffee, sugar, and nice dresses—and with thanks
departed. About a mile farther on he was stopped by a number
of men armed with shotguns (in quest of stragglers), farmers in
the neighborhood, who also inquired who he was and where he
was going. He said that he was my orderly, "sent to Columbus in
quest of information." They did not believe him until one of the
party, who was a lieutenant in the Confederate army, asked

*The name of the Federal commander. and also that of the Confederate
officer who so nobly defended the fort. have been given in a previous
chapter.

him, "How long have you been with Gen. French? were you with him at Suffolk? where did he have his headquarters?" etc., to all of which he gave true answers. The lieutenant, who had been at Suffolk, said, "Gentlemen, he is all right, I know, for I was there;" and so Hedrick journeyed on. Near Columbus he encountered the videttes, rode up, and asked that one of them should be sent with him to Gen. Wilson's headquarters. The corporal refused, telling him, however, where he would find the commanding officer. It was dark when he entered the city. He rode to Judge Thomas's, remained there all night, and saw Gen. Wilson leave the town next morning riding in the carriage taken from J. C. Cook. After the troops left the city for Macon, Hedrick rode back to Mrs. Campbell's and related to me his adventures.

Two days after we started for Columbus, and below Hamilton, we found that lieutenant and a squad of men still guarding the road. He asked me if I had sent my orderly to Columbus. On my answering that I did send him, the maddest man in the crowd was the one who, when he sat on the fence, had bidden his daughters to give the Yankee a dinner. He swore he "would shoot Hedrick for deceiving him;" and while I was remonstrating with him Hedrick, who was behind, rode over the hill and was recognized by the irate man, who exclaimed: "Yonder the rascal comes." He was warned by his party to be quiet. Hedrick passed us, raising his cap to the crowd, bowed smilingly, and passed on. Poor Hedrick, without occasion, and for mere adventure, ran the risk of being captured as a spy in Columbus.

When we were at Mrs. Campbell's the Federal cavalry several times was near by and kept the ladies alarmed, and as for myself I was not inclined to be captured and carried off, if it could be avoided. Our horses were kept saddled to leave, and several times word was sent us that raiding parties were on the road. Tired of these alarms, we were at dinner, when some one rode by and said: "The Yankees are coming." One of the ladies went to the front door, and came back screaming. I went to the gate, and like a whirlwind came a cloud of dust, and beneath it I thought I saw the feet of cavalry horses; but in half a minute, at full run, passed by about forty loose mules driven by negro men at their heels wildly shouting. For three days Hedrick and the servants were camped out in the woods lest our

horses should be stolen at night. It was so demoralizing that I
returned to Columbus, where there was a Federal garrison,
passed through the town, and returned to Gen. Abercrombie's.

While we were gone—as I anticipated—nine of Wilson's bummers quietly surrounded the dwelling of Gen. Abercrombie
(near Columbus), and entered the grounds from different directions. The General was sitting in a chair on the front gallery
by the door, and the first intimation he had that the thieves were
at work was a hand from behind him passed, snakelike, over
his shoulder and down to his vest pocket to get his watch; fortunately, he had placed it where it was safe. In a few minutes
those in the house went *through* every wardrobe, bureau, closet,
etc. They took all the silverware and jewelry. While this was
being done the two guards in the rear entered the large out
kitchen, where "old Aunty Minty," the negro cook, had presided for fifty years, and screamed out: "Get us something for
dinner, quick." The good old soul was scared half out of her
wits, and raised her hands, pleading for mercy. "Get some
ham and eggs for us quick, quick, you old dunce." The stove
was hot, and she cooked some with the turn of a hand. In a
minute the platter was empty, and they demanded of her to
"bring on the *pies*." She called on all the saints to witness that
she had no *pies;* the rascals swore they "never saw a house as
big as that was that did not have *pies* in it." However, the pie
question was settled by the captain of the band shouting "Come
on," and they mounted their horses with their plunder, and left
for other fields. Then "Aunty" came into the house and told
her mistress: "Them is the meanest people I ever did see."

When my overseer left the plantation with the negroes for
Columbus, he packed up my Brussels linen and best China, and
took them with him, and left them at Judge Thomas's house.
The evening Columbus was taken, Mrs. Thomas was sitting by
a parlor window, and seeing some men in the yard, she asked,
"Who are you there?" and the reply was, "Yanks; you did
not expect us so soon, did you?" They *went through* everything in the house in a jiffy, Judge Thomas with them. By his
engaging manners he got them by the baggage room, and saved
things there. But they carried my chest of crockery out of the
basement, thinking they had a prize; but when they found only
China they commenced breaking it, but desisted at Mrs. Thom-

as's request. These men became experts from long practice, and generally knew where to look for hidden treasures. "As the hart panteth after the water brooks," so the hearts of these hirelings panted for plunder.

When the Yankees first went to my plantation, in five minutes a company of about thirty men marched into the garden, formed line, fixed bayonets, and, marching abreast, probed the ground until they struck a box that was buried there containing silver tableware. But in this case I am sure "old Aaron," a house servant who buried it for mother, betrayed her confidence in him and told the Yanks where it was. These are small matters, but I mention them to show how the men, by the connivance of officers, if not by participation, became an army of thieves generally.

In a day or two authenticated information was received that both Lee's and Johnston's armies had been surrendered on terms of agreement, and as I was included in the latter army, I went to Columbus and obtained my parole. The terms of the surrender were that we were not to be molested by the *United States authorities* so long as we obeyed the laws which were in force previous to January, 1861, where we resided.

On my part, I was sworn "not to bear arms against the United States of America, or give any information, or do any military duty or act in hostility to the United States, or inimical to a permanent peace," etc., and thus the war *with the musket* ended.

On reading my parole I discovered what seemed to me a *petty trick*, for it read "not to be disturbed by the *United States military authorities*," leaving me at the mercy of the civil authorities to be indicted. I was informed those were the paroles sent them to be used in Columbus. It must have been a misprint.

CHAPTER XIX.

IF a man had ascended one of the lofty peaks of the Southern Appalachian chain of mountains at the termination of the war, and been endowed with telescopic powers of vision extending for hundreds of miles in every direction, he would have beheld the wreck of " the storm-cradled nation" that fell in defense of the rights that they possessed under the constitution of 1787–88, which was shaped, and established, and agreed to, by the States forming the convention. As far as such vision could extend, that once beautiful country was almost desolate and silent; the busy hum of industry had ceased, the daily smoke of burning buildings, the marching of armies, and the dull sound of distant cannon terminated; railroads had been destroyed, bridges were burned, many wagon roads were impassable; agriculture had nearly ceased, draft animals had been taken for war purposes; the flower of the South, with its pride of ancestors, had "fallen foremost in the fight;" the noble women were almost paralyzed in mind, ready to doubt the existence of a just God who seemingly had been deaf to their prayers, and made fatherless their little children; four million slaves sat idle around their decaying cabins, impressed with the prevailing idea that freedom meant to do as they pleased, and not work any more; provisions were scarce, and the whole scene was a picture of war's desolation and misery.

I can call to mind the delight I experienced when reading that wonderful description by Burke of the desolation of the Carnatic, in India, by the butcher Hyder Ali, in years long passed; or with sorrowful heart the desolation of the Palatinate by the French troops by order of Louvois, but I am not aware of any Northern pen having told the story of the destruction of the beautiful Valley of the Shenandoah* in Virginia by Gen. P. H. Sheridan, though it be a theme as sad as the one immortalized by the genius of Burke.

Hyder Ali left nothing in the Carnatic that drew the breath of life; Sheridan left nothing in the Valley for a crow to feed on—as stated in his official report, wherein he writes that "a crow could not cross the Valley without carrying his provisions with him."

It is true, however, that you can find in some of the Northern schoolbooks a beautiful poem entitled "Sheridan's Ride," as mythical as Barbara Frietchie; still there are in the true story some incidents not unlike those in Burns's "Tam O'Shanter" that kept "Sheridan far away."

And now the surviving Confederate soldier returned to what was once his happy home. He had faith in the terms of his *parole*, that he was "not to be molested by the United States authorities as long as he obeyed the laws of 1861." Inured to hardships incident to a soldier's life, he was well equipped to become an industrious, peaceful citizen; he had stormed fortifications, captured batteries, marched up to the cannon's deadly mouth without tremor, passed days without rest and nights without sleep, subsisted on parched corn, been frost-bitten by cold, and burned by the torrid sun. His bare feet had left their prints in blood on the rocks, and crimsoned the snow on many a wintry march; he had stopped the marauder in his path, and turned the enemy from his course; he had tempted the ocean in its wrath, and driven off its waters the enemy's commercial sails. All that man dares he had done. And now in adversity, almost naked, with unending toil before him, he commenced life anew, and went manfully to work with hope for the joy of peace, little thinking of the degradation, insults, humiliations, oppressions, robbery, extortions he and his family would be

---

*Shen-an-do-ah means the "Bright Daughter of the Stars."

subjected to during the coming years, caused by revengeful legislation. And now behold him even greater in peace than in war!

The plunder obtained by the soldiers of the Union army had so whetted the avaricious spirit of those who had furnished substitutes for themselves, that they were bent on having their share of the spoils; and the politicians, anxious to ride into place and power, to that end resorted to more machinations than Machiavelli ever dreamed of in his advice to the prince.

By the daily trains came men, generally from the Eastern States, in every garb, and they walked along the streets in single file in quest of cheap hotels and boarding houses, and the *insignia* of their *order* was a carpetbag, and their interests and tastes—not their sympathy—prompted them to associate with the freedmen, considering themselves just as good and honorable as the "Wards of the Nation."

You must not deem it out of place if I here make mention of some incidents that occurred pretty early in the war.

In the Bible we read how Jephthah vowed a vow unto the Lord that if he would deliver the children of Ammon into his hands he would do certain things. So Lincoln made a solemn vow before God that if Gen. Lee were driven back from Maryland he would set the *slaves free*. After "Antietam" he announced his *intention* of issuing, and on September 22, 1862, he did issue, a proclamation setting free, by *his military authority*, all the slaves in the rebel States. He still founded his action on "policy and the Constitution." * As the Confederate States did not return to the Union as required in his September proclamation, on January 1, 1863, he issued his emancipation proclamation, the slaves having been confiscated by Act of Congress in 1862.

The act of confiscation and the President's proclamation emancipating the slaves in the Confederacy could not abolish slavery, because it existed under the *laws of the States*. It could alter no State law, still it did affect slavery in this way: it caused slaves to leave their owners, and to this extent diminished their property and their wealth, but under the laws they could purchase others.

The great undefined latent power of the Constitution is em-

* Goldwin Smith.

bodied in Article I., Section 8: "To provide for the common
defense and general welfare." Under this section almost all the
outrages of the war were committed, restrained only by international rules of war; but these were ignored under the plea
that the war was only a rebellion—quite a family affair, and
would soon be settled. Under this article also is found the
power to tax to any amount " for the common defense and public welfare."

The confiscation act of Congress was unconstitutional. Ed
Burke, in the Warren Hastings trial, said: "I do not know the
method of drawing up the indictment against a whole people."
The Constitution *declares* that the "trial of all crimes, except in
cases of impeachment, shall be by jury." But this confiscation
act punished a "whole people" without indictment, trial by jury,
or conviction.

As the slave owners were called the only *privileged class* in
the United States, it is pertinent to inquire if this class of people did not exist in all the States when the Union was formed,
and if they of the North did not sell their claim to a privileged
class for a "mess of pottage" and then howled at the purchasers for being a privileged class! Who demanded the enlargement of slavery by making it legal to steal or purchase negroes
from Africa until the year 1808, to give employment to the six
hundred slave ships owned in the North—in New York and New
England. We know the town of Newport, R. I.—now the
abode of wealth—in the year 1750 had one hundred and seventy
ships engaged in the slave trade for "the love of money."

A question presents itself here—and it is a pertinent one,
for it commences at the beginning of this whole matter of
modern slavery in this country: Who *first owned* these slaves,
how did they obtain them, how did they treat them, and to whom
did they sell these human beings for money, and then with the
price of blood in their pockets soon began to howl against the
sin of slavery, and thank the God they served that they were not
slaveholders any longer?*

It has been said by a Northern writer that "indirectly, and

---

*I commend to you an article published in the September (year 1900)
number of *Scribner's Magazine*, page 303, giving an account of the treatment of slaves by their owners North; also an account of the last slave
ship captured by the United States navy (*Century Magazine* for May, 1894).

for the purpose of a more equal distribution of direct taxes, the framers of the Constitution *tolerated*, while they condemned, slavery, but they tolerated it because they believed it would soon disappear. They even refused to allow the charter of their own liberties to be polluted by the mention of the word ' slave.' " But take heed: did not this convention give ear to the clamor of the owners of slave ships and slaves theron to continue for twenty years longer to increase slavery and increase their wealth by enslaving free people in Africa?

No, "they could not, consistently with honor or self-respect, transmit to future ages the evidence that some of them had trampled on the inalienable rights of others."

"Though slavery was tolerated by being ignored, we should not dishonor the memory of those who organized that government to suppose that they did not intend to bestow upon it the power to maintain its own authority—the right to overthrow or remove slavery or *whatever* might prove fatal to its permanence or destroy its usefulness."

To this the answer is yes. But the proper mode of removing it is the real question. It should not be by making war, laying waste the country, burning all public buildings and dwelling houses, sinking ships, blockading ports, killing, wounding, and capturing soldiers, creating debts, levying taxes, exposing our soldiers to deadly battle and all the horrors of war—but by removing the evil by compensation "for the term of service" of the slaves to their owners.

This government is under obligation to compensate, and does compensate, parents, masters of apprentices, masters of slaves, for service and labor of those subjects who are enlisted in the army and navy, for the Constitution recognizes slaves as "persons held to labor or service." Removal by compensation might have prevented the war.

England compelled the abolition of slavery in her colonies, and she paid in compensation for services, to the slave owners, the sum of one hundred million dollars. Out of this, for instance, Cape Colony obtained fifteen million dollars, which was about four hundred dollars per slave.

If slavery was believed to be fatal to the permanence of the Union, it could have been removed by compensation, as in the case of England, and not by hatred and fanaticism.

View it as we may, the fact exists that the confiscation act, although unconstitutional, did, in effect, rob the Southern people of about two thousand million dollars ($2,000,000,000), computing four million slaves at five hundred dollars each, which is only about half their value; and this was done as a punishment for secession. In law it was void; but the property was of such a character that it became useless to the owners, because it was enticed away. So this act and Lincoln's proclamation caused the slaves to leave their owners. And so without a crime, without an indictment, without a trial by jury or conviction, this property was taken from the owners. It was the largest steal ever committed by a nation; and, furthermore, they stole from the South slaves that they had sold the South. Call it by what name you will, it was robbery. It exceeds in magnitude, in money value, any of the invasions of India, from Genghis Khan down to the English East India Company; or the robbery of the proconsuls of Rome; or the wealth Spain derived from Mexico and Peru by the infamous acts of Cortez and Pizarro. And, after all, the loss from confiscating the "labor" of the slaves, great as it is, becomes but one item of loss to which the Southern people were subjected.

It would perhaps be unjust for me to assign the inducements that moved Mr. Lincoln to issue this proclamation, considering Congress had already confiscated them. I do not know if possession of property is, or is not, necessary before it can be *sold* by confiscation.* If a slave not in possession of the United

---

*The question of confiscating property, especially slaves, and setting them free will be found in the War Records, Series 2, Vol. I., Serial No. 114, from page 749 to page 822. This correspondence, and orders, show that in 1861 and part of 1862 "*confiscation by act of Congress limited the penalty to property actually employed* in the service of the rebellion with the knowledge and *consent* of its owners, and instead of emancipating slaves thus employed left their *status* to be determined either by the courts of the United States or by subsequent legislation." (See Holt's opinion to President Lincoln, page 768, etc.) This was legitimate war. However, the want of success changed all this, and the proclamation of May 19, 1862, not being complied with, the war ceased to be confined to the troops in the field, and degenerated into one of robbery, plunder, destruction of private property to reduce the South to subjugation. To this end slaves were told they were free, and 178,975 were mustered into the United States army, armed, and, thus encouraged, employed to fight their owners. The

States marshal, being in the interior of the Confederacy, can be confiscated, then also could all property be confiscated by a paper bulletin posted on the wall. But in that proclamation there was a sinister object in view, and that was to array against the Confederate States the sympathies of the Christian world, by trying to make it appear that we made the war in defense of, and to perpetuate, slavery. Others there are who think that the "loyal governors" who met at Altoona, Pa., obtained it by insidious threats. But, be this as it may, the proclamation, as a legal paper, was worthless. The slaves were afterwards legally emancipated by the several States, by the thirteenth amendment to the Constitution, and by taking the oath prescribed in the President's proclamation, dated May 29, 1865; and all the owners of slaves who were worth twenty thousand dollars, being disfranchised, had to make oath "not hereafter, at any time, to acquire any property whatever in slaves, or make use of slave labor, or make claim for slaves liberated." The numerous oaths and various proceedings required to set the negro legally free, and make it binding, remind me of many loyal friends in the North going before some judicial officer and renewing their oaths of allegiance every new moon, to make it sure and clear by accumulated recorded evidence.

When Jephthah made his vow there was no power to restrain him from fulfilling it. Lincoln could not perform his; he was not an abolitionist from principle, and there is very much evidence that he was not in favor of emancipation; his proclamation set free (on paper) only the slaves in a part of the *Confederate States*, leaving slavery untouched in the *United States*. That is, the Yankees retained slavery in Delaware, Maryland, Kentucky, and Missouri, and part of Louisiana and the *North*, and tried to abolish it where they could not, and maintained it where they *could have abolished it*. At this malignant confiscation of the slaves *only in the Confederacy*, Fanueil Hall went wild with delight, and Exeter Hall, England, was jubilant.

I have no desire to discuss annexation (reconstruction) here, and hasten on, only to relate some of my experiences under it, so that you may know the patience, forbearance, and charity of

South did not arm a slave to kill white men. There was a marked parallel between the treatment of the noncombatants of the *South* and that of the noncombatants of *Cuba* by the Spaniards.

the Southern people under persecution. No one possessing knowledge has a right to withhold it from his fellow-men, if it will be valuable to them; and so I write.

And now came reconstruction (annexation), with all its evils. President Abraham Lincoln had been foully murdered, and Vice President "Andy" Johnson reigned in his stead.

It is stated that he disliked the refined and best class of people in the South; and now, in authority, he thirsted for vengeance against them. He declared that "treason should be made odious," and would have arrested Gen. R. E. Lee and other Confederate army officers and punished them if possible, had not Gen. Grant declared that they could not be molested without violating the paroles he had given them, and so prosecution was abandoned and persecution substituted, as will be shown after a while.

Having surrendered and signed a written agreement, and made oath to the same, I desired to go to my home in Mississippi, as stipulated in the parole.

Gen. Grant's declaration that his paroles could not be violated seems to have been, with him, an after thought, as the following telegram will show:

WASHINGTON CITY, April 15, 1865, 4 P.M.

Maj. Gen. Ord, Richmond, Va.

Arrest J. A. Campbell, Mayor Mayo, and the members of the old council of Richmond who have not yet taken the oath of allegiance, and put them in Libby prison. Hold them guarded beyond the possibility of escape until further orders. Also arrest all *paroled officers* and surgeons until they can be sent beyond our lines, unless they take the oath of allegiance. The oath need not be received from any one who you have not good reasons to believe will observe it, and from none who are excluded by the President's proclamation, without authority to do so. Extreme vigor will have to be observed while assassination remains the order of the day with the Rebels.   U. S. GRANT, *Lieutenant General.*

Here is Ord's manly answer:

RICHMOND, VA., April 15, 1865.

Gen. U. S. Grant.

Cipher dispatch directing certain parties to be arrested is received. The two citizens I have seen. They are old, nearly helpless, and I think incapable of harm. Lee and staff are in town among the paroled prisoners. Should I arrest them under the circumstances, I think the rebellion here would be opened.

I will risk my life that the present paroles will be kept, and, if you will allow me to do so, trust the people here, who, I believe, are ignorant of the assassination done by some insane Brutus with but few accomplices.

Campbell and Hunter pressed me earnestly yesterday to send them to Washington to see the President. Would they have done so if guilty? Please answer.   E. O. C. Ord, *Major General.*

HEADQUARTERS ARMY OF THE UNITED STATES, }
WASHINGTON, April 15, 1865, 8 P.M.   }

Maj. Gen. Ord, Richmond, Va.

On reflection I will withdraw my dispatch of this date directing the arrest of Campbell, Mayo, and others, and leave it in the light of a suggestion, to be executed only so far as you may judge the good of the service demands.   U. S. GRANT, *Lieutenant General.*

RICHMOND, VA., April 15, 1865, 9:30 P.M.
[Received at 10:20 P.M.]

Lieut. Gen. U. S. Grant.

Second telegram, leaving the subject of arrests in my hands, is received.
E. O. C. ORD, *Major General.**

It was after this date that Grant, on reflection, turned around and informed the President that the paroles he gave at Appomattox should not be broken; that he would defend them. All honor to him for this! And greater honor to Gen. Ord, who pledged *his life* for the honor of the Southern men who were paroled!

The first matter to claim consideration was money. I had in gold a five-dollar piece and in Confederate notes a few thousand dollars. The purchasing power of the latter may be ascertained from a bill made by Miss Abercrombie, now my wife, of which the following is a true copy:

Miss Abercrombie.
                         To Goodrich & Co.

September 23.	½ yd. Crape	$ 20 00
October	7.	1 Hoop Skirt	100 00
"	7.	14 yds. French Merino (Blk.) @ $87.50	1,225 00
"	7.	14 yds. Blk. Rep @ $25	350 00
"	14.	20 Blk. Calico @ $10	200 00
		1 Blk. Crape	40 00
	Total		$1,935 00

Columbus, Ga., October 14, 1864.

As I had no means to purchase tickets over the railroads, I applied to the Quartermaster, U. S. A., for transportation for myself, two servants, and two horses, which was furnished me. It was sometime in May that we started for home via Mont-

*See War Records, Vol. XLVI., Series 1, pages 762, 763, Part 3.

gomery, Mobile, and New Orleans. As I had to call at the headquarters of the commanders in these cities for passes and permits, I will here remark in regard to my reception by these my late enemies: Gen. A. J. Smith was crabbed and petulant when I showed him the order for transportation for the negroes. Gen. Sturgis was kind and did all that was desirable for our comfort. In New Orleans Gen. Canby was very polite to us, as he was to every one. He sent me up the Mississippi river on a chartered steamer. The trip up the river was pleasant. There were only two other passengers—Father Livingston, a priest, and a sick boy. Livingston—may God bless him!—had but one change of linen, and he gave that to the sick boy, who was a stranger to him, and nursed the lad attentively.

I was forcibly struck with the amount of the most costly second-hand *furniture* sent by express to small towns in Illinois and Ohio, put up in oat sacks.* But furniture in New Orleans, you know, like "Butler's" spoons, belonged to the victors. The captain of the steamer put me on shore at Argyle Landing, near my home. I mounted my horse, and the first man I saw was "Tom Shelby" sitting on the fence looking at some negro men plowing a large field of corn. He hailed me, but I paid no attention to him. He was a "rampant" war man before the war began, but he stayed at home. Indeed, every one of my immediate neighbors—ten in number—were not in the army; and all, except one, able-bodied men and younger than I was. The

---

* Col. Augustus Choate Hamlin, U. S. A., in his "Battle of Chancellorsville" (Bangor, Me., published by the author), says (page 27), speaking of Blenker's Division: "The men justly complained of their treatment, and also of the abuse bestowed upon them during the march across the Shenandoah Valley for alleged acts of pillage on the way. From what the inspector saw he was of the opinion that the stories had been overestimated, and he has thought since that the Second Corps put in the breastworks at North Anna more valuables, in the shape of pianos, scientific apparatus, and choice furniture, than Blenker's Division stole or destroyed during their march over the mountains to Northern Virginia. Their booty and destruction, even as exaggerated, was infinitesimal as compared to that of the army of the Potomac at the capture of Fredericksburg."

After Gen. Payne, U. S. A., who was stationed at Paducah, Ky., had been court-martialed, he was relieved, and among the papers left behind him was one saying: "Don't send any more pianos, or plated silver, or pictures: all the kin are supplied: but you can send bed linen and solid silverware."

Scott boys and Calhoun Hale and his brother were good and faithful soldiers, living outside the belt around me.

When I dismounted at my door, God only knows my agony of heart. None to welcome me, none to greet me!

> "Desolate the hearth,
> And wild weeds gathering on the wall."

Where were the laurels that were to crown my brow? Willows! Fences burned, bridges destroyed; the plantation a forest of tall weeds; horses, mules, cattle, sheep, poultry, provisions, wagons, implements of every kind—all gone; wealth, servants, comforts—all means of support for my family gone; all lost save honor. I sat down and surveyed the desolation around me. Fortunately my house was not burned, and I had a shelter for my family, should they come here. I knew the noble women of the South, who for years had labored hard and cheerfully, trusting in God and the justice of their cause, would not despond. Lord Byron makes the beautiful daughters of

> The tribes of the wandering foot and weary breast

sit down by the rivers of Babylon and weep, but never would they string a harp for their foe. The beautiful daughters of the South had wept no bitter tears of repentance, nor sung pæans for their foe; they had proved themselves equal to adversity in war, and would they not help build up lost fortunes in peace? So resolve took the place of despondency, and I returned to Columbus for my family.

Sherman—the fell destroyer—had burned the city of Jackson, Miss., and the ruins reminded me of Pompeii. In walking one of the streets I passed a canvas shanty, from which I was hailed by an Israelite with "Good morning, General; come in." He had been in the army and knew me; he had some goods and groceries for sale. When I was leaving, he asked: "General, can't I do something for you? Here are fifty dollars, just take them; maybe you can pay me back sometime." I thought the angel of mercy was looking down on us, and I thought of Portia's address to Shylock on the quality of mercy. I thanked him kindly, and the day came when I had the pleasure of repaying the debt. In a few days I arrived in Columbus, and there I found a letter from my cousin, Clayton French, of Philadelphia, Pa., containing a check for a thousand dollars. I had written to him to send me some money, and this was his liberal response.

The servants I had in Columbus had been nominally "confiscated" and set free; so they came to me, almost daily, begging me to take them back to the plantation in Mississippi. As I was not able to do this, I applied to some "bureau," that had charge of "refugees," for transportation for these negroes, and to my surprise it was granted. As soon as possible they were put on the cars and started for the plantation.*

On the 17th of September, 1865, Mrs. French and I left Gen. Abercrombie's for Greenville, Miss., via Montgomery, Mobile, and New Orleans, on some box cars, furnished with wooden benches for seats—such was the condition of the railroads at that time.

When we reached home we found most of my old servants there awaiting our arrival. To feed and clothe about a hundred of these people, and to plant a crop of cotton in the spring, clothing, provisions, mules, wagons, farming implements, harness, etc., had to be procured.

To obtain funds to purchase the articles enumerated—to com-

---

* When Maj. Wiley Abercrombie, Mrs. French's brother, left college to join the Confederate army, his father sent Rica, his carriage driver, to wait on him—Wiley being a youth.

Now Rica had never worked on the plantation; from childhood he had assisted in taking care of the family horses and carriages, and in due time became the driver of the family carriage.

At the battle of Gettysburg Rica was captured and carried nearly to Philadelphia, Pa. One night, however, he made his escape, traveled on foot to the Potomac, crossed that river, and finally reached Richmond, Va. Thence the authorities gave him transportation to Columbus, Ga. When Wiley became a member of my staff Rica came with him, and continued with us till the war ended. He and his wife remained in my family in Columbus; thence they went with us to Winter Park, Fla.

In 1884 Rica made a visit to Columbus, and on his journey home, becoming short of money to purchase a ticket from Jacksonville to Winter Park, he obtained work on a railroad. While thus employed he was accidentally killed by a tree felled on him by one of the hands.

Poor Rica! His fate was a sad one. A slave in name, he fled from freedom given him at Gettysburg, and wandered back to be a bondsman; and next when freedom was imposed on him by legislative enactment he spurned it, desiring only a home for life with the family that had treated him almost as one of their own children. I had almost similar experience with my own servants before and after the war.

21

mence again—I went to Philadelphia and New York (by special permission of the government) in November.

My clothing was not very tidy; it had seen service; and I concluded after I left St. Louis to travel through the enemy's country incognito so as to avoid war talks. I got along very well until I reached Philadelphia. I had been advised to go to the Lafayette Hotel; and, too proud to present myself there in my present garb, I entered a large clothing establishment and arrayed myself in a suit of black broadcloth, and told the attendant to wrap the old suit up. When I paid the bill, judge of my astonishment to have him say: "To what hotel, General, shall I send the package?" "Why do you call me general?" I asked. "Because I saw your rank and name in full written on the inside of your vest; that is all right; call and see us again." Next I entered the hotel, and went to register my name. As the clerk threw the book around, he exclaimed: "How do you do, Gen. French!" I was surprised; he replied: "I was in the Confederate army, and knew you in Virginia; I am employed here because we want Southern patronage." Here was my incognito discovered twice in one hour. But that is not all. The next day I took the train from Camden, N. J., for Woodbury, where my mother, sister, and daughter had been refugeeing since they left Mississippi until they joined me at the plantation in November, 1865. I knew many people in the city, and had the honor to have been *hung* there once in effigy by its fanatical people in the beginning of the war, for some reason, or no reason, save they did a foolish thing and repented of it; and as the "bitter war feeling" raged there yet, like the billows of the ocean after the storm has passed, I took the last seat in the rear car as a quiet place. Now it so happened that the seat opposite me was occupied by a genteel-looking fellow, who evidently had been indulging too freely in whisky and wanted to make himself companionable. I answered his questions briefly, but he persisted in talking, desirous to know who I was. Finally I told him my name was French, at which he exclaimed, "Are you Gen. French?" in such a loud voice as to draw the attention of many of the passengers to me; and, rising, he proffered his hand and said: "Going to your mother's, I reckon; I am a Union soldier, and when we reach Woodbury I will get my musket and be your escort." He walked up the street with me to the corner, where we parted; and his parting words were: "If any one troubles you, send for me. My name is Paul." * Such was my experience in trying to travel incognito. I gave it up, and, when necessary, fought square out for Confederate rights. As I went North on business, I avoided all controversy about the war as far as possible.

I must now make a digression. In the autumn of 1864 my mother, sister, and child, owing to illness, engaged passage on a steamer at Greenville, Miss., and started for our summer home in Woodbury, N. J. On arriving at the Girard House, in Philadelphia, Mr. Edward Cooper, a relation of mother's, called on her and asked her where she was going, and she said: "Down home." He then informed her that the property had been *confiscated* and *sold*, and that he had bought it, and rented it. He asked her also about funds, and, finding she had near a thousand dollars in Confederate money (valueless), under the pretense of exchange he replaced it with "greenbacks"—a kind act delicately done. Besides, a few years later he voluntarily deeded the property back to me. This was in striking contrast with others who bought my personal property, valuable mainly as *mementos*. It is always pleasant to find a gentleman. They are seldom found to the manor born,

"Where commerce long prevails."

Mother went down to Woodbury and engaged board there, and returned to the hotel. Next day when they arrived by train in that town, the baggage wagon, the express, the porters—no one would take their trunks to the house; nothing could induce these *loyal* people to *touch* the trunks of a Rebel—unless to confiscate them. And so my mother—an old woman, alone, in the town in sight of which she was born and where she lived, among her kindred—had to walk away and leave the baggage. Now, happily, a man—a Quaker—heard of their *loyal* proceedings, and went to my mother and said, "Well, Aunt Rebecca, if no one will bring thy trunks from the depot for thee, I will do it;" and in his own wagon this Friend came with the baggage. Gomorrah would have been saved had it contained ten men like this one. The new dispensation saved Woodbury. The family

---

* How noble the conduct of this man who had been in the army contrasted with the citizens who remained at home crying for vengeance!

lived in exile until autumn, when they went down to the plantation.

I will refer to the main object of my visit to the North. I made a visit to New York and failed to obtain funds, returned to Philadelphia, and there made the best contract I could; and the spirit of liberality shown by my friend will commend itself to you by the terms of the contract, which I now have:

PHILADELPHIA, PA., December 9, 1865.

Borrowed of —— eight thousand dollars ($8,000), payable within one year from the date of this instrument. In consideration of this money being furnished me without interest, I agree to furnish or ship him, at such point as he may direct, thirty commercial bales of cotton of four hundred pounds each, of average quality, out of the crop raised by me on my plantation during the year eighteen hundred and sixty-six (1866). The cotton thus shipped to be the *sole property* of ——.

[Signed]   S. G. FRENCH.

As cotton was selling at, or over, forty cents per pound, the bonus was (in lieu of legal interest—$30 \times 400 \times 40 = \$4,800$) at least four thousand eight hundred dollars, which is only sixty per cent interest.

When in Venice, I visited the Rialto a number of times, and curiosity prompted me to seek the shop near by where Shylock studied finance and made that loan to Antonio; and you will remember that when "Tom Walker sold himself to the devil he agreed to use the money in the *service* of the devil by turning *usurer*." * My friend obtained his knowledge of thrift, I know not where. But which of these three was the most benevolent I will leave you to decide. I only care to observe that they all knew that "the poor man's necessity was the rich man's opportunity." With me it was Hobson's choice.

While North I met in New York City and Washington many Federal army officers, with whom I had been associated in years gone by, and they were kind, especially Gens. Ingalls, Quinby, Grant, Steele, Wright, and others. I could not but observe about Philadelphia that people were distrustful of each other, as though under surveillance. Gen. Robert P. invited me to come to his house after dark, and evidently, from what he said, did not wish it known that I had been there. Mr. Bayard, whose son, Gen. G. D. Bayard, was killed at Fredericksburg,

---

* Washington Irving.

sent me a message that he would like to meet me, but that it would not be prudent for him to have me visit him at his home. These and other friends were timid about their loyalty being challenged if seen with a so-called "Rebel."

To this general timidity so prevalent Clayton French was an exception. He took me to church, theaters, clubs, and wherever inclination led, in contempt of the crowd that were afraid their loyalty might not be above suspicion. Samuel H. French, his brother, forgot his intense prejudice against the South, for he was one of the best men that ever lived, and forgave *all* the "Rebels" except Jeff Davis. In evidence of the purity of his character he told me just before his death that he had never been guilty of an act or said anything that he desired to conceal from his family. There will be no charges against him when the judgment book is opened.

I arrived in St. Louis on my way home on the 16th of December, and saw the floe of ice crush the steamers at the landing like eggshells. The next morning I walked across the river on the ice, and got home on Christmas day and found the weather balmy and warm. And now I longed for rest, but the curse of the freedmen's bureau was here, to instruct even the cooks when to prepare meals and regulate household affairs, and approve all contracts for labor on the plantation.

In connection with my visit North in 1865 it will not perhaps be out of place to give here an account of a conversation that related to an important contemplated movement. Now, whilst I was in Philadelphia, a friend of mine, and late member of the United States Senate, called to see me. During a long conversation on matters pertaining to the war, he asked me "if in 1862 there was any feeling among the Confederate troops that there would be an armistice, and peace made during the truce by the fraternization of the opposing forces." I told him that in the summer of 1862, when I was in Petersburg, Va., there was a vague idea floating around relating to a peace being near at hand, and, although it could not be explained, it was felt to be more than a fairy tale, and yet could be traced to no source. He then informed me that "a few prominent men in the North desired the war should be stopped, and to obtain this end, soon after the battle of Antietam, I think it was, a particular friend and relation of Gen. McClellan's was sent to him to obtain his

views, and ascertain if he would *agree to the proposed plan.*"
When the agent had unfolded the plan, McClellan denounced it.
Soon after he was removed, and Burnside put in command of
the army, which looks as if there was something that they could
feel in the air there too.

It is useless to speculate on the results of such a bold undertaking. The actors of the movement are all dead, and I pause
in silence at the brink of their graves. They wished to end the
war, and restore the Union in that way. Of course McClellan
would have been made dictator for the time. He would not be-
tray his trust.

This incident induces me to remark that war is the most uncertain of all undertakings of a nation, and, like the tempest,
cannot be controlled, and seldom or never ends as predicted.
The North proclaimed that this "little rebellion" would end in
sixty days! It lasted four years, and ended as no one had foreseen. It had to suppress rebellions caused by people who entertained Southern opinions in New York, Chicago, Cincinnati, and
other cities; muzzle the press, prohibit freedom of speech, ban-
ish prominent individuals, arrest men without warrant, and im-
prison them without charges made known to them; and violated
nearly every resolution and pledge made in the beginning relating to the South; they cast aside constitutional law, and substituted martial law, under which the South became a scene of desolation and starvation.

Much has been said about firing the first gun, "firing on the
flag." The crime rests on them who made it obligatory to fire
the first gun. Northern writers are in error when they state
that "firing on the flag" fired the Northern hearts with unanimi-
ty of purpose. On the contrary, as I have stated, it produced
dissension, even to rebellion, until suppressed by arms and in-
timidation from suspension of the writ of *habeas corpus.*

This firing the first gun is made a veritable "humbug." It
reminds me of an occurrence in the grand jury room in Greenville, Miss., in reconstruction days. A man, whom I will call
"A," sent a message to "B," giving him notice that he intended
to kill him on sight should he meet him. Warned in this way,
"B" armed himself with a shotgun. They met. "A" raised his
gun to his shoulder, and aimed at "B." Seeing this, "B" fired
instantly, and killed "A." The grand jury investigated the mat-

ter, and only one member voted to find a true bill against "B," and he did it on the grounds that "B" should have waited to see if "A" was really going to kill him.

Now the government of the United States was in the position of "A," only it was not honest enough to inform the Confederate States that it was going to reënforce Fort Sumter; but really made false statements about it, for it secretly sent eight warships for that very purpose, which were then at the bar off the harbor of Charleston.

The Confederate government was in the position of "B," and was it to wait to see what the eight ships of war would do, to see if "A" would reënforce the garrison, which it pledged itself not to do, or fire to prevent it? This is all well known now.

My own opinion is that the *first gun* was fired, at the instigation of a number of prominent men North, by John Brown at Harper's Ferry, and for which he was apotheosized and numbered among the saints.

Mr. Lincoln said: "The dogmas of the quiet past are inadequate to the stormy present. The occasion is piled high with difficulty, and we must rise with the occasion. Our case is new. We must think anew, and act anew. We must disenthrall ourselves, and then we shall save the country." (Joel Parker Lecture at Harvard College.)

These words indicate that the powers of the Constitution were inadequate to the conduct of the war, and henceforth the war must be conducted as occasion deemed expedient. In other words, the executive power must be declared greater than the power that made it, or the creature greater than the Creator, and with dictatorial methods the war was conducted. Avaunt, Constitution, avaunt! We are fighting for the Union, for dominion over the Southern territory again, and so the Constitution was folded up, etc.

CHAPTER XX.

WHEN I commenced writing the narrative of my observations in early life and the incidents of service in the
United States army and my diary of the civil war, I did it to
preserve for my children the record of these events, but in volume it has increased more than at first intended; and as it may
perhaps some day be made public, I feel it incumbent on me to
give *my experience* under the workings of reconstruction as being of more value than a description by any historian of a later
age who would have no enlightenment by living under its arbi-
trary rule.

An act creating the Freedmen's Bureau was passed March 3,
1865. The commissioner was authorized to set apart for the use
of loyal refugees and freedmen abandoned lands, also confiscated
lands, and assign forty acres for three years, etc., to families.

In 1866 a supplementary bill was passed over a veto to extend
the act. "Among other things the bill subjected any white person, who might be charged with depriving a freedman of civil
rights or immunities to imprisonment or fine or both, without
defining the meaning of "*civil rights or immunities*." The jurisdiction of the agents extended to all contracts, and without a
written contract and the agent's approval no freedman could be
employed. No indictment by a grand jury nor a trial by a
jury was necessary. The *ipse dixit* of an ignorant negro was
cause for fine or imprisonment without appeal.

Gen. O. O. Howard, noted for exuberant piety, was made
Commissioner, and his career, his establishing of the Howard
University in Washington for the higher culture of the negro,

the cottages he built for them, the aid he gave the Church, the land he bought, and the Freedman's Bank he established, which blew up or burst, can be found in a report of a congressional committee. Under this bill the annual expenditure was $11,-750,000.

An article published in the *Atlantic Monthly* for August, 1865, sounded the keynote for the action of the United States government in legislation for the "rebels," wherein it is stated: "We are placed by events in that strange condition in which the *safety* of the republican form of government we desire to insure the Southern States has more safeguards in the INSTINCTS OF THE IGNORANT than in the INTELLIGENCE OF THE EDUCATED." And furthermore it is declared that "the highest requirements of abstract justice coincide with the LOWEST REQUIREMENTS of political prudence, and the LARGEST JUSTICE to the loyal blacks is the real condition of the WIDEST CLEMENCY to the rebel whites."

This declaration proclaims that the Southern States would be safer if their governments were established on the ignorance of the blacks than on the intelligence of the whites. Could malignity go any farther? On this degrading plane were the State governments established.

They had called for blood, and got none, save in the case of Wirz, who was given to the mob as a "sop." As they could not indict a whole nation, they arrested President Davis, and, discovering no grounds for conviction, he was released, because a failure to convict would establish legally the right of secession, and thus prove the North to be the aggressor. Failing on this line, the human passions and human prejudices of the people arrayed under the higher law of conscience swayed them like a mob, and, failing to find any lawful means to spill blood, sought vengeance in the enacting of partisan laws for plunder of wealth, and the humiliation of the whites. To this end the Freedmen's Bureau was created, and President Johnson's proclamation was issued disfranchising the whites on fourteen different counts: among them was one that made the possession of twenty thousand dollars' worth of *property a crime* that disfranchised the owner. Then came the ironclad oath, which debarred all persons from taking it "who had ever borne arms against the United States since they have been citizens thereof, or who have voluntarily given *aid, countenance, counsel,* or *encouragement* to *persons engaged* in armed hostility thereto; that they have never sought, nor accepted, nor attempted to exercise the functions of any office whatsoever under any authority, or pretended authority, in hostility to the United States," etc.

All men above twenty-one years of age who could take *this oath* could vote, and *no others.* As there were very few white men who could take this oath, the elections fell, as intended, into the hands of the negroes, carpetbaggers, and the United States troops on duty South.

The enactment of the fourteenth amendment to the Constitution of the United States was regarded in the North as a magnanimous exhibition of philanthropy toward the untutored slaves, and it was so accepted by nations; but in reality it was an insidious mode of punishing the Southern people.

The white people who owned the land and paid quite nine-tenths of all the taxes were now disfranchised, and the amendment was intended as a punishment by denying them a voice in legislation.

Senator Morton and Thaddeus Stevens, like the Roman augurs, could not look in each other's face without laughing at the success of their machinations.

Two years later (in 1870) the fifteenth amendment to the Constitution was passed. These last three articles placed the Anglo-Saxon people in the South under the rule of their former slaves! This was the *Sin* that started the race problem. The freedmen, left to themselves, would have settled the labor question, and their social position and the race issue; but for aggrandizement of power and acquisition of wealth he was dragged into the halls of legislation and flattered into the belief that also socially he was on an equality with the whites. From this sprung unmentionable crimes, and daily lynchings followed as a remedy.

What a change! As a slave he was the faithful protector of his mistress and her family; his children the terror now of unprotected women!

And here I will tell you how the voting was done. The negroes had, previously, been required to take the oath. At my home a table was placed on the gallery, and there the registrars were seated. The negroes were called up; as many as could touch the Bible were asked if they "had ever held office under the United States or given aid," etc. Some said "No," some said "Yes," and some were silent. At last they were told to say "No," and registration papers were given them, with the charge not to lose them. There I sat, no more a citizen than if I had been born in China, while my negroes were made eligible to almost any office in the country.

It is now generally acknowledged that all the negro received was by the force of environments; and now he has discovered that he has been grateful to the radical party, and payed them for a debt of love that had no foundation except in hypocrisy. They were told that they were now American citizens, endowed with all their moral and civil rights.

"The *natural rights* of a solitary individual have no connection whatever with the *moral and civil rights* of the man who has entered into association with others." (Huxley.)

The dominant party entertained the belief that the slaves would politically always belong to the party that "confiscated"* them; and confounding natural rights with civil rights, they forced the Southern States to pass the fourteenth amendment to the Constitution, which made them citizens of the United States and the State wherein they reside.

As vultures sail in long lines from their roost (countless in numbers) to where the carcass is, so came the harpies and political adventurers to the carcass (the South) to embrace the colored citizens; and, hand in hand, cheek by jowl, they entered the political arena, and filled the capitols of the South. Every officer in the State from governor to coroner was dismissed, and new appointments made. The Legislatures became bacchanalian feasts to divide the spoils of office and increase the debts of the States by selling State bonds to the amount of countless millions. They subsidized everything they could; in short, they ate up or took possession of all that was left after the war ceased; and at last departed with stolen wealth, and the execrations of all the honest people. Negroes were appointed or elected to such offices as Senator, Governor, members of Congress,† and the judiciary of the States and county officers.

---

*The confiscation of the slaves by act of Congress is an acknowledgment of the just decision made by Chief Justice Taney in the Dred Scott case, that a slave was chattel, or personal property.

†I know a man North who paid $6,000 to a Congressman for his son's

June 13, 1865, William A. Sharkey was appointed provisional governor of the State of Mississippi, and he ordered an election of delegates to the convention, and here is the way the members were elected:

On the appointed day the new-made citizens went to the precincts to vote. When they came home I asked my servant Levi, who had been with me through the war, how many persons were at the polls, and he said "about two hundred, that only two white men were there, and they were inside the house." When asked who he voted for, he replied "he voted for that thing, you know, called *invention*," and the way they voted was this: "You remember the paper we had [registration]; I handed it to two white men inside the room, through a window; they looked at it, handed it back to me, and said open your hand; I did so, and one of the men then put a little folded paper in my hand, then took it out and put it in a box and said, 'Move on.'" This was a Republican free election, peaceful, quiet, and decisive, based on ignorance. The complexion of the convention was dark, of course. This ungenerous revenge taken against a conquered people will ever remain a dark shadow over the generosity and Christian spirit of the Northern people. It, however, must be attributed to uncultured minds and want of knowledge of history. The masses did not know that New England's ablest statesmen always claimed their right of secession, as the debates in Congress show. Besides, they were unmindful that opinion at the North was about equally divided on this question.

When the revolutionary war was ended, and the cry for persecution, and confiscation of property of the *Tories* was raised, our Minister to France, Ben Franklin, put that as a trump card in his pocket to win against England; and Gens. Alexander Hamilton and Nathanael Greene and other liberal gentlemen declared it would be "an outrage to punish them for holding the *same opinion* that we all held only a few years ago, before the war commenced." What a contrast between the age of honor and the age thirsting for gold!

Perhaps in all the wide world never again will be seen such malignant legislation, and maladministration of law, such trials

---

appointment. This was excluding the South from positions in the army and navy.

in the courts, speeches in legislative halls, preaching by illiterate negroes, mode of getting religion, idleness of the laborers, immorality taught by men from the slums of Northern cities, thirst for money, howling for office, insolence in office, with upheaval of society, creating constant anxiety of mind as to what a day might bring forth.

Add to these the formation of loyal league societies of negroes, by politicians swearing them to obedience to orders, bands of brothers and sisters, composed of blacks under white villains, to burn our towns, and murder the whites; the Kuklux Klan of the whites for protection, and other kindred vexations and trials that made the South the home of the spirits of pandemonium; so one could truly exclaim with Ariel,

"Hell is empty and all the devils are here." *

As I have said, they came like vultures to the carcass to devour the substance of the helpless South, and they were unblushingly successful. Under the Freedmen's Bureau and the military governors, those who could not take the ironclad oath were helpless.

The agent of the Freedmen's Bureau in our county (Washington, Miss.) who came first was desirous to aid the planters and freedmen to make a crop; and as this required reliable labor, the planters in the neighborhood agreed to give him cotton to the value of $5,000 if he would visit the plantations, when necessary or convenient, to encourage the hands to work faithfully, under the contracts that he had *approved*, and I will most cheerfully say that without this aid and influence the negroes would have been unprofitable producers.

The agents were changed, and in 1867 an Irishman came, who could handle the shillalah, drink whisky without the smell of peat, sing the "Irish Dragoon" or the "Widow Malone," and run the Freedmen's Bureau. And here is a little of my own experience under it with him.

In renting out the land on shares, among the squads was one squad of thirteen hands, with two negroes named Miles and Derry as head men. They had about eighty acres put in cotton. The recorded contract required them to work under my direction, and I was to furnish means to raise the crop, and their

---

* Shakespeare's "Tempest," Act I.

share was half the cotton. Owing to the almost constant spring rains, their crop became hopelessly overgrown with weeds and grass. I vainly tried to induce them to abandon the lowest part of the land and save about sixty acres; they refused. I then wrote a note to the agent. He came out late in the evening with the deputy sheriff and sent for Miles and Derry, heard what they had to say; then severely reprimanded them; took Miles by the ears and backed him against the side of the house and pounded his head against the wall vigorously; then taking Derry by the ears, he pounded his head as he did Miles's. By this time near a hundred negroes were on the lawn peeping up over the gallery, which was the arena of the acts.

Then he made a five minutes' talk to the people, giving them some good advice. He then took Miles and Derry through the the same enlivening bout, ordering them to be at his office the next day at 10 a.m. Again he spoke to the crowd, telling them how he had "fought, bled, and *died* that they might be free," etc.

While this was going on, to stop such proceedings, I took the deputy sheriff, Wilson, into the dining room, put a decanter of whisky on the sideboard, and told him to get the agent in there, give him a glass to sober him, and, when he came out, take his arm and go direct for the horses. Much to my relief, he got him on his horse and they returned to Greenville. Miles and Derry went to Greenville next day, as ordered. The former came back much subdued and Derry went to an adjoining plantation to work. Ridiculous as the performance was, which lasted over an hour, it had a good effect on the deportment of all the hands on the place.

The military governor had commissioned a man from the North named Webber as sheriff of the county. Bolton, an Irishman, Harris, an educated negro from Ohio, and Horton, a cotton field negro without education, were appointed justices of the peace in Greenville. I will very briefly give you an idea of the administration of justice in a few cases out of many brought before them.

Ed Chamberlain, who had been a negro soldier in the United States army, occupied a house at the southern gate of the plantation, and he was instructed to keep the gate shut on account of cattle. Twice *without cause* he had told H. N. Hood, a neigh-

boring planter, in an insolent manner: "Shut the gate after you."
On a third occasion he repeated the remarks, whereupon Hood
and a friend with him gave him a trouncing. They then went to
Justice Harris, told him what they had done, and settled the
case by each giving him five dollars. On trial day Chamberlain
went to court, and when the court adjourned he asked the justice
why he did not try his case, and the answer was: "Go home; I
tried your complaint long ago."

Another freedman on the place named Nelson one morning got
into a triangular fight with his wife and a colored girl. They
all started for Greenville to lay their respective grievances before Judge Harris. However, they met Harris on horseback
on the road running through the plantation, and he accosted
them: "Good morning, ladies and gentleman; where are you
going?" They told him that they were going to see him in
Greenville, and all made complaint to him there in the road;
whereupon he fined each the sum of five dollars, and I had to
advance the money or they would have left the plantation. That
was summary justice, and an examination of the books by the
grand jury showed that he had credited the county with the fifteen dollars.

A third case worthy of notice as illustrating the vigilance of
the colored brethren as magistrates is the trial of what may be
termed "State of Mississippi vs. S. G. French." John Dixon,
a freedman, about Christmas stole two bales of cotton from the
ginhouse in open daylight, and being pursued by my manager,
threw the bales off his wagon, and they were recovered. I went
to Greenville, and before Bolton, the justice of the peace, swore
out a warrant for the arrest of Dixon. A number of days passed
and he was not arrested. So I sent for Dixon, and settled *money
accounts* with him, and told him to leave the plantation.

Some days after this a deputy negro constable was sent to arrest Dixon; but, meeting one of my hands on the road and making known to him the purport of his visit, he was told: "Go
home, nigger; de ginneral done gone *settled* with John long ago,
and John have left the place." So the deputy returned and reported accordingly.

Perhaps it was a week after this that a negro constable came
to my house with a warrant to arrest me issued by the cotton-
field justice, Horton, charging me with having compounded a

felony. Who prompted Horton to issue the warrant I never knew; but, as he employed a "jack-leg" lawyer to keep his docket and act as legal adviser, he may have induced Horton to act in the matter. I asked Frank Valliant, a distinguished lawyer, to take my case and defend me. He said that he had resolved not to argue any case where a negro presided, for he disliked to say, "May it please your honor," to an illiterate negro. However, out of friendship, he said that he would appear for me if I would pay any fine imposed upon him for contempt of court.

Some two weeks after this the trial day came. Valliant and I went to the room where Horton dispensed justice, and found him behind a railing seated at a small table with the Mississippi code in his hand. John Dixon and "Jack-leg" were there, but no lookers-on. After turning the code first one end up and then the other several times, he announced: "Dis court am assembled to hear the case of Gen. French for *composing* a felony with John Dixon."

Valliant seemed to be swallowing something that was swelling in his throat, but he rose and went near the table and said: "Will your honor let me have the papers in this case?"

"What papers you want? I am done hab none."

"Where is the affidavit made against Gen. French?"

"I just told you, Mr. Valliant, I done hab none."

"Well, how could you arrest a person without charge being made?"

"Sir, dis court has been informed dat Gen. French swore John Dixon stole two bales ob his cotton, which am an offense, and then done settled and composed it, which am a crime against the law, and an insult to the majesty ob de State of Mississippi."

Here the "jack-leg" injected a remark to the judge, when Valliant asked him: "Are you engaged as an attorney in this case?"

He replied: "I am."

"Then I wish to see your license."

At this Horton said: "De gentleman wants to see your license. Go and get it, sir."

While he was absent in quest of the paper Valliant read the law to the court, showing his honor that the license must be granted by the Circuit Court.

When the license was handed to Valliant he read it to the court, and, it being one granted by the Chancellor, was of no authority. At this information Horton rose from his seat, and in a loud voice said: "Sir, you will stand aside. You have imposed on dis court, and am no more a lawyer in any case in court here."

When this incident was over, and the indignant court had composed itself, Valliant tried again to satisfy the judge that there was no case before the court; but he insisted that I had *composed* a felony, and that his court was bound to "'vestigate what am a crime in de eye of de law." Under the argument and showing of my attorney, however, the judge began to weaken, especially when told that he would be held responsible for this unwarrantable arrest.

Valliant now whispered to me: "We will have to buy out of this."

"All right," was the reply.

Then my attorney went to the table, and quietly whispered to Horton: "Will ten dollars settle expenses?"

A ten-dollar bill was handed the judge, and that sum *composed* the felony, the feelings of the court, and the offended majesty of the State.

Valliant was the wit of the Greenville bar, and a true friend. Some years ago he was called from his field of usefulness and sorrowing friends to

Sleep the sleep that knows no breaking.

These are not a tithe of my personal experience with the Bureau and the courts. They were almost daily annoyances to all.

One day I received a note from the agent of the Freedmen's Bureau to come to his office if convenient. I went as requested; found there one of my hands, who had no common sense, and was told he complained that I had not settled with him agreeably to the contract; and when the agent asked him what complaint he had to make he said that I had paid him only a *half*, whereas I had promised him a *fourth*, and insisted that four was more than two.

But I pass from the recital of these petty annoyances to larger ones. The circuit judge *appointed* was named S——, and in political parlance he was a "scallywag." It would seem that,

22

to make his loyalty apparent, he imposed harsh sentences or punishments on nearly every white person convicted, and he committed personally some criminal offenses.

It was, I believe, in the winter of 1876 or 1877 that I was a member of the grand jury of Washington County. All those who were summoned—twelve whites and six negroes—answered to their names. The judge excused one member, and accepted another person, who was sworn in. The matter of a murder was among other things brought to the notice of the grand jury. All voted against finding a true bill except two other members and myself. This same day (Saturday) we were about to find an indictment against the judge for falsely representing himself as surety on the bond of the notorious Bolton, who was appointed county treasurer, the facts in the case being that the judge did not sign his name to the bond, but told his clerk of the court to sign it for him. To this the clerk made oath, but excused himself by informing us that "it is common practice now."

On Sunday Bolton gave a champagne dinner to the judge, and it was there arranged that the judge should dismiss the grand jury on Monday morning to prevent indictments being found against *himself and Bolton.* The excuse offered was that putting a juror on in the place of one excused was irregular, and their findings would be void, and also we had failed to find a true bill against a certain man. And so we were all discharged without retaining *the three* who voted to find a true bill, and a new jury was empaneled. That night the negroes called a mass meeting to condemn these proceedings of the judge; but the meeting was captured through the influence of two negroes—Gray, the state senator, and Ross, a negro from Kentucky—and resolutions passed complimenting the judge. The fine hand of Bolton was seen in this. Some months after, the judge called on me, and said he wished to say that he discharged that grand jury because they did not find an indictment against S——, who had killed a man in an altercation. I replied: "Judge, no person in Greenville believes that to be true."

The judge was afterwards petitioned by the members of the bar to resign. The list was headed by the distinguished attorney, William A. Percy. *Six* months after this a person appeared in Greenville with a challenge for Col. Percy. For amusement Percy said: "The judge has had six months to practice at a target, and I also want a little time to practice; then I will accommodate him." After worrying the bearer of the cartel some time he accepted the challenge, the fight to take place on an island in the Mississippi river. Nothing further was heard from the challenger, and he died soon after, it is reported, from mortification.

Before the judge had dismissed the grand jury it had found a number of indictments against persons who belonged to a secret association of freedmen, known as the "Band of Brothers and Sisters," bound by oaths to rob, burn the town, and murder the whites. The day these disclosures were made the witnesses were shot at in the night, and claimed protection.

Bolton, who had been an officer in the United States volunteers during the war, was president of the band; Gray, negro state senator, vice president; and a scallywag named Brentlinger, from Kentucky, was treasurer. He was also postmaster, through Bolton's influence. Bolton spent most of his time in the post office, and induced Brentlinger to lend him public funds to the amount of about $3,000. An effort was made to destroy the post office books by setting fire to the office, but a man fortunately saved the books. Bolton, however, got them from the office as a package purporting to have come by mail, and destroyed them.

Then came a United States post office inspector, who discovered the loss of funds, books, etc., and removed or suspended the postmaster. Bolton went on Brentlinger's bond, and accompanied him to Jackson, Miss., where he was tried before Judge Hill. Bolton told Brentlinger that he had arranged it with the judge. If he would remain silent, and make no disclosures, he would be acquitted. He was found guilty, and sent to the penitentiary at Albany, N. Y.

In hope of convicting some of these scoundrels, I wrote to President Grant for permission to visit the penitentiary and obtain Brentlinger's testimony, and the attorney-general, Alphonso Taft, to whom the request was referred, gave permission.

In due time I made the visit to Albany, and with the keeper, Pillsbury, saw Brentlinger. He wrote out what he knew about the society, acknowledged that he was treasurer; but from timidity would give but little testimony of his own knowledge, and made it mostly hearsay evidence. It corroborated exactly what we learned in the jury room. No use was made of this testimony, because all who were implicated agreed to quit the State and never come back. I have this testimony and the attorney-general's letter.

The military governor appointed one T. L. Webber sheriff of the county. Without the knowledge of any one, he falsely reported thousands of acres of plantation lands, and other sections of land, sold for taxes. This he did for two years. Not a name of any delinquent taxpayer was ever published, and *no one* attended any sale. Planters continued paying their taxes regularly. At last it was discovered that the reported list of taxable lands did not embrace half the lands on which taxes were paid. A list was obtained for the grand jury. I found that six hundred and forty acres out of the heart of my plantation had been reported sold; Bourge's plantation of two thousand acres, all sold, and so on; yet we were paying taxes all the same.

Next year I know of but two planters who paid any taxes in the county. Had Gov. A—— remained, there would not have been any taxes paid in the State. He wrote to Bolton to know how he was to get any salary, or any courts could be held, or Legislatures meet, etc., and was told that the services of all such were not required, etc.

The *auditor* had been receiving from the sheriff only the money received from lands *on the tax list*, while he (the sheriff) pocketed all money paid on lands that he pretended were sold and not taxable—by "sold" meaning forfeited to the government. To escape perjury, Webber's *reports* of taxable lands were not signed by him, but by his brother, a worthless fellow.

When the people elected a negro sheriff over Webber, he bought the office of sheriff from him for $1,000 and the negro sheriff (O. Winslow) appointed him his deputy. Webber, when detected, turned into the bank $40,000 out of perhaps $150,000 stolen, and went to Florida. The ablest lawyers said he could not be convicted under the existing condition of affairs.

Those who would not pay taxes were permitted to redeem their lands by act of the Legislature, by paying back taxes, the title coming from the State. The $40,000 was distributed among the owners of the forfeited lands, and used in part payment of the taxes. O reconstruction, what a curse thou wast!

Had Ames remained, there would have been presented a singular revolution—the people of the State peacefully pursuing their avocations without a government; every function of state government would have been suspended. When the governor applied to Grant for troops he was refused. Grant telegraphed that "the public was tired of the annual autumnal outbreaks in the South."

Another source of annoyance to the planters—nay, it was ruinous—was the want of reliable labor. Capital could not command labor in the rich Yazoo bottoms, and it had to be obtained from a distance.

I went to Wytheville, Franklin, and Danville, Va., for labor. In Danville I made a contract with a man named Wilson to bring me some thirty hands. About the middle of February he arrived with the negroes. I paid him $1,040 for transportation and services. One pleasant noon in May a servant came in and told me a certain negro was leaving the place; he was the last of the men that Wilson brought, except a Spanish negro, who was painting my house.

My neighbor Jackson went to Richmond, Va., and obtained some forty hands; paid their way to Greenville. Their contract made was that they were to raise a crop of cotton and corn, and out of their share of the crop they were to repay expenses of transportation, provisions, etc. Gradually they began to leave him, and went into the employment of negroes who had rented land. They were hired for two bales of cotton. By this proceeding they escaped paying transportation.

One day in May the last of Jackson's hands (on Monday) went to the smokehouse and obtained their rations for the week, and then quit the plantation. They were arrested for breach of contract and obtaining supplies under false pretenses, and were tried before the notorious Judge Bolton. Whilst the trial was going on, Bolton asked my views of the matter. I told him if they were acquitted every contract recorded in court would be worthless, and it would damage the planting interest in the county perhaps two hundred thousand dollars. Nevertheless, he decided that there was no evidence to prove that the hands had any intention of leaving *when* they drew their rations, although they had a place engaged and left as soon as they got the provisions. For months I never retired to rest without apprehension that some of my hands would leave during the night, at the persuasions of visiting spies.

Another trouble was to check the thoughtless extravagance of the freedmen. If they were largely in debt, when fall came, they would not gather their cotton, believing it mortgaged to the merchants for all it would bring, but quit, and pick cotton on some other place, by the hundred, for cash. Of these things there was no end.

The counties of Bolivar, Washington, and Issaquena composed a levee district in Mississippi, and had for years protected the lands from overflow by constructing levees. Funds were obtained by tax on lands and by sales of bonds. When the war ended, I was elected president of the board. Gen. Alvan C. Gillem was military governor, and gave me all the aid he could to rebuild the levees. I negotiated the bonds in New York City at par, and repaired the levees and saved the plantations from overflow. When Ames * became military governor, he one day sent a man to Greenville with an order dismissing us, and required the office to be turned over to the bearer, etc.; and this, too, when the river was at its highest stage. I went to Jackson to see him. I demanded the grounds for his action in the matter, and was refused. At this time the river was out of its banks everywhere, except in our district. I wrote to President Grant, and he answered: "You should have telegraphed at once." Gen. Sherman wrote, "Yours is not a public office, and Ames is wrong, etc., meddling with private corporations," or words to that effect.

Whilst in Jackson, the capital of Mississippi, I was offered the opportunity of seeing the legislators who made our laws, composed mainly of carpetbaggers and negroes. For this purpose I obtained a seat by the sidewalk on the main street leading to the capitol.

As the hour to meet had arrived, down this street could be seen the members approaching. Generally they came two together, arm in arm, a carpetbagger and a negro in close confab. The whites were clothed in garments of various makes and colors; the negroes rejoiced in black clothing, with Prince Albert coats and silk hats and gold-headed canes. Down the ave-

---

* Appointed June 15, 1868.

nue and far away could be seen the white of their eyes, teeth, shirts, and enormous collars.

The carpetbagger was generally holding on to the arm of his colored brother, and engaged in conversation; and, judging from the gestures, they were advocating some benevolent measure for the benefit of the "wards of the nation," and their own prosperity. One other observation I made: there were no small feet, and not an arched instep; flap, flap, came down their flat feet. I had seen enough; I thought the negro had the more honest face.

Thence I went into the House. Ye gods, what a sight! The floor was dirty, the many spittoons were all filthy—filled with quids of tobacco, stumps of cigars, pieces of paper around them were cemented to the floor by dried tobacco juice; fumes of tobacco filled the house, so that the air was foul and unpleasant.

The members were seated, black and white side by side, all over the house, perhaps to guide them in voting; and they lolled on the desks and chairs. A negro would lay his head on the desk of his white neighbor, look him in the face, and laugh with great glee at what was told him; the conversation was so loud and the laughter so boisterous that the Speaker could not command silence: he pounded with the gavel, and shouted "Order! order!" till his voice was drowned by the cries of "Master Speakyar!" from the negroes, while the whites shouted and waved their arms frantically to catch the Speaker's eye for recognition. The whole scene was one of confusion not unlike the Gold Exchange, New York, in days of yore, or the Stock Exchange.

I then went to the Senate chamber. It was cleaner than the House, and better order was preserved; but what a travesty on intelligence and decorum, and shame on the government of the United States, North, that made this not only possible but common, and laughed at it with joyous hearts; and wherefore? It was an assembly of mostly dishonest white men influencing the uneducated negro members to enact laws whereby the State was, by bonded indebtedness, plundered of millions of dollars. Their reign is ended.

"I myself have seen the ungodly in great power and flourishing like a green bay tree: I went by again, and lo, he was gone." Adieu! The royal Bengal tiger, when he once tastes human blood, will depopulate a village; so the loyal carpetbagger, having tasted Southern plunder, went home and devised a scheme of trust companies now in operation.

Then came taxation. On this matter I will merely remark that on realty it was about ten per cent. Government tax on cotton, in the aggregate, was sixty-seven million dollars. On cotton it was (all told), including charges by the government, about twenty dollars per bale. There should now be on file in the Department of Agriculture a letter written by me to Mr. Isaac Newton, commissioner, telling him that, were it practical, I would deed to the United States the land planted in cotton, if it were exempted from taxation one year, which meant—the market value of the land was twenty dollars per acre; and as one acre would produce a bale of cotton, and the tax on the bale was twenty dollars, the tax was equal to the value of the land—that was confiscation. An acre in cotton, if it produced a bale, was taxed, as I have related; but if planted in corn or sown in wheat, the produce was free. All these legal pilferings, vexations, insults, arrogance, and trials to our families were in silence and poverty submitted to, that our children might have food and clothing. Our patience in adversity, amidst trials and sufferings, gives greater evidence of elevation and dignity of character than did matchless achievements in arms. In the tented field we found redress for wrongs; in reconstruction years we lived in expectancy, as the Christians lived in the years of Nero, not knowing what would befall us next.

The negroes, when set free, became very pious, and gave more time to their devotions than to the crops. After the Freedmen's Bureau agents took their departure, nearly all of them "got religion" and wanted to preach. Their protracted ("distracted" they called them) meetings continued all night long, for five and six weeks continuously. Men and women would leave the church (I had one on the plantation) after sunrise, go to the field direct, and sleep leaning on their hoes. I found one sleeping on the creek bank, and on asking him what was the matter, he said: "O, I have got religion in me as big as a yearling calf." And thus piety impaired industry to an alarming extent, without improving morality.

Bishop Wilmer (Episcopal), during the war, had omitted the usual prayer "for the President of the United States and all others in authority," and this continued after the surrender. For this offense Maj. Gen. George H. Thomas was so distressed that he, by orders, caused the bishop and the clergy in the diocese to cease from preaching; and this gave rise to a discussion, which was terminated by the President denouncing the silly order and revoking it. I have no doubt of Gen. Thomas's sincerity, for he was prudent and cautious, and *he* must have been really convinced that President Johnson, and all others in authority with him, needed the prayers of the Episcopal clergy to bless them and replenish their grace.

The Bishop was not as desirous of praying for the President of the United States as was a young priest after the surrender. He had omitted praying for President Davis since his capture, and had not decided what to do when the Sabbath came; but found relief, when asked by a United States army officer if he had any objection to using the old prayer for the President of the United States, by answering: "No, none whatever; for I know of no one who needs our prayers more than he."

The few incidents of my own experience that I have narrated are to illustrate the condition of the people of the South during the years of reconstruction (annexation), and for preservation for future ages; to show the ills, vexations, humiliations, and indignities so unjustly and designedly imposed upon them as a spiteful punishment for daring to assert their rights and defend their homes. The fifteenth amendment to the Constitution has brought forth bitter fruit to the progress of the freedmen and the peaceful progress of the whole country by offering the negro a dependent support on politics rather than labor. Their votes were generally in the market, and their sale at the presidential nominations for office in the Federal service in the South consolidated the white people against them when harmony would otherwise have existed.

The State of Mississippi was saved from utter ruin by what the North called "the shotgun policy." Seeing nothing but poverty and wretchedness before us, it was determined to rescue the State from the hands of the carpetbaggers and negroes by a compromise with the freedmen. In our county we offered them the offices of congressmen, the sheriff of the county, clerk of the chancery court, clerk of the circuit court, and justice of the peace, but not a member of the Legislature. The educated whites were to redeem the State from perdition in the halls of legislation.

In the hustings absolute protection by arms was pledged to all freedmen who voted the Democratic ticket, and to those who voted the radical ticket, not a hair of their heads should be touched, if order was maintained by them; but under all circumstances *a free election should be held, and peace preserved.* Every one knew that a disturbance imperiled life. The consequence was that a more cheerful, peaceful election never was held. One party had yellow tickets and the other white, open in their hands, and the vote could be counted as well outside as inside at the polls; and furthermore the radical white carpetbaggers were in an unmistakable manner informed that they would be held responsible if peace at the polls was not maintained. Thus was the State redeemed from the hands of the corrupt carpetbaggers and corrupt *followers* of the United States army, and all cried: "Amen!" The joy that followed cannot be realized, and cheerful industry commenced. The suffering, vexations, and agony of mind of the people South during reconstruction years, unless written by those who endured them, will no more be known in history than are the cries for mercy uttered in the chambers of torture in the prisons and baronial castles of Europe during the Middle Ages. And now for all these malicious tortures, for the state debts, for the enfranchising of the negro, and the race problem the harshest condemnation I have known to be expressed by the party which imposed them on us is: "It was a blunder!"

In a statesman "*a blunder is a crime,*" said Napoleon. So by parity of reasoning, you can discover in what class you have placed yourselves. This election is the hegira of misrule and vampirism.

It is difficult to subscribe to the dogma of "an indissoluble union of indestructible States." It is at variance with the foundation of all government; "for governments are founded on superior force that subjects everything to the will of the governor, or it is founded on a compact, express or tacit. . . . When founded on force, resistance is implied. . . . In a government founded on an express agreement, or compact, resistance is unlawful while the ruler maintains his part of the contract. When he violates those rules resistance is legal and justifiable.

Hence in all governments resistance is naturally inherent." (Lord Woodhouselee.)

In the twelfth century, for instance, there "was in Aragon the Justiza, an officer elected by the people, who was the supreme interpreter of the law and protector of the people. . . . This great officer had likewise the privilege of receiving in the *name of the people* the king's oath of coronation, and during the ceremony he held a naked sword pointed at the heart of the sovereign, whom he thus addressed: ' We, your equals, constitute you our sovereign, and we voluntarily engage to obey your mandates on condition that you protect us in the enjoyment of our rights; if otherwise, not.'" Here we find reserved rights of the people, as in our Constitution.

States appear to be destructible. From the Pillars of Hercules, all around the shores of the Mediterranean Sea—where dwelt the people to whom God gave laws amidst the thunders of Horeb and others, whence came language and most of our civilization and religion—are found the ashes of dead empires.

The Confederate States must have been out of the *Union*, unless we admit that the English language is not expressive enough to clearly describe events. To me the act of Congress passed February 17, 1870, to "admit the State of Mississippi," the proclamations to "come back," * to "restore the State," etc., are but a few of the proofs that we were out of the Union; and the declaration of war, the blockade, belligerent rights show that the Confederate States were independent. We were "rebels" (so called) designedly to enable the United States to escape paying Confederate bonds held by foreign powers, and to settle other international questions with them. We were in the Union or out of the Union, as the exigency of the occasion required.

And this reminds me of an incident that occurred in the section room at the United States Military Academy in 1841. Capt. J. A. Thomas was assistant professor of ethics. The subject: "The Constitution of the United States." He there said: "Gentlemen, there are latent powers in this Constitution that will be found to meet every emergency that may arise." And now, behold, since then! "The higher law," "the *extra* constitu-

---

*Lincoln's December proclamation says: "Such States shall be received again into the Union."

tional measures," "the confiscation of property," "greenbacks a legal tender," etc., the wealth of the nation made exempt from taxation by the supreme court, and the trusts, etc. Truly we were a conquered nation, because the United States had to resort to all the constitutional requirements of foreign warfare.

In the platform accepted by Mr. Lincoln is this resolution: "*Resolved*, That we maintain inviolate the rights of the States, and especially the right of each State to order and control its own domestic institutions, according to its own judgment exclusively." And in his inaugural he said: "I have no purpose, directly or indirectly, to interfere with slavery in any of the slaveholding States of the Union."

Then Congress passed, February 11, 1861, the following: "*Resolved*, That neither Congress, nor the people, nor the government of the nonslaveholding States have the right to legislate upon or interfere with slavery in any of the slaveholding States of the Union."

These resolutions and promises were brushed aside like reeds in the path of conquest. Their armies marched on without any check by the act of *habeas corpus*, as it was suspended by article 2 in the President's proclamation of September 22, 1862, which reads: "That the writ of *habeas corpus* is suspended in regard to all persons arrested, or who are now or hereafter during the rebellion shall be imprisoned in any fort, camp, arsenal, military prison, or other place of confinement by any military authority or by sentence of any court-martial or military commission."

I remember a story on the Committee of the French Academy appointed to prepare the "Academy Dictionary." Their definition of a *crab* was "a small, red fish which walks backward." "Gentlemen," said Cuvier, "your definition would be perfect, only for three exceptions: The crab is not a fish, it is not red, and it does not walk backward."

So, if the *Union was indissoluble*, and the States were indestructible, how could they be *reconstructed* and readmitted? It is as erroneous as the definition of the crab.

It may be said, almost literally, that the administration for the expansion of war power deposited the Constitution in the State Department for the use of the supreme court after the war. They now ordained a despotic policy as being more expedient to run the government, because it could be changed, like a vane on a house top, according to the breath of public opinion or the exigency of the times. To confine their troops to the duty of destroying the regular Confederate forces, according to the usages of civilized war, had been tried in vain; but once freed from the restraints of the Constitution and modern rules of war, the work of desolation commenced to the extent that a ruthless general reported that a crow would have to carry its provisions if it crossed the valley he had laid waste. His example was excelled by others. The truth is that if the North had not disregarded the Constitution, IT would have ruined them. It was a government of opportunism.

As regards reconstruction (so called), I will only observe that a conquered people are obliged to accept such terms as the conqueror offers.

In our case the separate or sovereign States that withdrew from the Union were the parties conquered. The negotiators for peace on the one part were the Congressional Committee on Reconstruction, and on the other each one of the sovereign States for itself. The terms offered the States respectively were embodied in the last three amendments to the Constitution. As these were accepted they were admitted into the Union, each a sovereign State. So the thirteenth, fourteenth, and fifteenth articles of the Constitution, when accepted, became virtually a treaty of peace between the North and the South, made State by State. Virginia, Texas, and Mississippi were the last, and they did not accept the terms offered until 1870, when they were admitted into the Union.

As Minerva sprung from the brain of Jupiter, full grown, robed in the panoply of war, and took her seat among the gods, so the Confederate States—born in a day, clothed in all the attributes of government, complete in every department—took her station among the nations of the earth. She exacted from the United States the observance of international law on war and official intercourse. After four years of the most sanguinary war of modern times she fell, white and pure, before the mercenary hosts of the nations arrayed against her. She died for the priceless heritage wrung from tyrants "*that all just powers of government are derived from the consent of the governed.*"

For this inalienable right—a right that has been exercised by almost every nation on earth, and for which millions and millions of lives have been sacrificed—the States seceded, and it will never die.   It was implanted by Providence like religion in the hearts of mankind.   It is an invisible power behind a veil that will break through as certainly as the soul at death lifts the dim veil that hides the life beyond the grave.   It is an occult power pervading the air, and gentle until developed by oppression, whether by bad government or remorseless tyranny incident to aggregated wealth or other causes.   It was not the victories of the Confederate armies; it was not because they gave the world a Lee, a Johnston, a Forrest, and a Stonewall Jackson that won the admiration of the nations; but because over all these the South was true to her convictions of right.   Their achievements were great, but their cause was greater; their deeds are immortal, their cause eternal, and paid for in blood.   It will exist till the leaves of the judgment book unfold.

I must now take my farewell of the good Confederate soldiers with whom I have had the honor to serve.   I know their valor and their worth.   Like the sibylline books, as they diminish in numbers they will increase in value, and with the last veteran the order will end—then silence!   Their valor will be the common heritage of mankind.   Their memory will be revered by their posterity, and linger in the mind as sweetly as the fragrance of flowers.   Their cause let none gainsay; it is the birthright of all the ages.

To you, my children, I have related some of my observations, and given a little of my experience in this wonderful nineteenth century.

In my youth dwellings were lit up with candles; then came gas and kerosene; now electricity illumes cities and streets, cars and ships.   Steam power was known, but it had not been applied to railroads or steamships on the ocean, or to many mechanical purposes.   How well do I remember the many journeys I made over the Alleghany Mountains by stage to Pittsburg, Brownsville, and Wheeling, and how steam power superseded horse power in ferryboats, treadmills, and sailing vessels on the ocean!

I have told you how I went with Prof. Morse to receive what may be deemed the first message of the telegraph; now we send messages around the world.

In 1862 I saw a telephone established from one house to another, distant about fifty yards, by two young ladies in Wilmington, N. C., to communicate with each other. To-day we talk face to face a thousand miles.

The discovery of anæsthetics has alleviated the pain of the surgeon's knife, and with the X ray he looks through the human body, and makes visible the location and cause of pain, etc.

During this century the map of the world has had many changes by the Napoleonic wars, the upheaval of 1840 by Garibaldi, Bismarck, Germany, and France; and all Africa is subjugated. In the Orient—that empire of occult science and mystery, of magic, fakirs, castes, and barbaric wealth; six times invaded from the West through the gates of India by Alexander, Mahmoud, Genghis Khan, Tamerlane, Monguls, and Persians—at last, in this century, with a population of over 300,000,000, has passed into the possession of England, and Queen Victoria is Empress of India! What destiny awaits China, with her 400,000,000 people?

We have witnessed Spain lose possession of all her colonies in South America, Mexico, and her West Indies possessions and the Philippine Islands; the slave trade, conceded to New England, ended only in 1808; imprisonment for debt was in existence when I was young in some of the States—in short, such has been the progress of liberty during this closing century that it has turned the world upside down, and to all oppressors from any cause the spirit of liberty cries:

> "By all ye will or whisper,
> By all ye leave or do,
> The silent sullen people
> Shall weigh your God and you."

APPENDIX.

Some Statistics of the War.

Total enlistment in the United States army.....................2,778,304
Total enlistment in the Confederate States army................ 600,000

FIRST.

NUMBER OF FOREIGNERS IN THE UNITED STATES ARMY.

German...	176,800	
Irish...	144,200	
British Americans....................................	53,500	
English..	45,500	
Other foreigners.....................................	74,900	
Total foreigners....................................		494,900
Whites from the South...............................	276,439	
Negroes from the South..............................	178,975	
Total...		455,414
Grand total...		950,314

Here you will discover a force 350,414 stronger than the whole Confederate army, without enlisting *a native-born citizen* of the North; also that the South furnished the North *455,414* men.

SECOND.

New York troops enlisted.....................................	448,850
Pennsylvania troops enlisted.................................	337,936
Total..	786,786

Here is an army larger than the Confederate States army.

THIRD.

Illinois furnished (men)	259,092
Ohio furnished (men)	313,180
Indiana furnished (men).......................................	196,336
Total	768,608

Here we have a second army larger than the Confederate army.

FOURTH.

The New England States furnished.............................	363,162
The slave States furnished (whites and negroes)..............	455,414
Total..	818,576

23

Here is a third army larger than the Confederate army, and the fourth army came from the excess of numbers in the three preceding ones.

But the most remarkable fact is, that there were in the United States army 950,314 men that should be *called foreigners*, as none belonged to the North by birth.

In connection with the number of foreigners in the United States army, I will remark that Gen. Benjamin F. Butler, of Massachusetts, in his argument before the Tewksbury Almshouse investigating committee, July 15, 1883, said: "Before you go to throwing ridicule on the foreign-born, let me tell you that you had better look into the question of who fought your battles. In the first place, look at the per cent of what birth the inmates in our soldiers' homes were; fifty-eight and one-half per cent of the soldiers in these homes are of *foreign birth.*"

Again he said: "Some of us stayed at home and pressed soft cushions of *skinned paupers* while these foreigners so much sneered at were fighting our battles."

In regard to the tanning of the skins of the dead inmates of the almshouse, Butler quotes from Carlyle (page 354), and goes on to say that at Meudon the skins of the guillotined were turned into good wash leather and made into breeches for paupers. So the paupers in France were dressed in the skins of my lord and lady, "while in Massachusetts it was our aristocrats that wore slippers made from the breasts of women paupers." Matters here are reversed—it is my lord and lady who wear such slippers.

It may be of some interest to quote further from Butler. In contrasting the expenses of the soldiers' home (one of them) he said it took 278 turkeys for their Thanksgiving dinner, and their last "potpie" required 34 sheep, 15½ barrels of potatoes, and 2 barrels of flour. During the year they ate 758 head of cattle, 1,659 head of sheep, 3,714 barrels of flour, 15,744 dozen eggs, 154,932 pounds of butter, 69,289 pounds of coffee, 57,941 pounds of fish, 7,950 pounds of tea, 10,570 cans of tomatoes, 16,431 pounds of rice, 110,440 pounds of sugar, 21,325 pounds of prunes, and other articles too numerous to mention, amounting to the sum of $204,728," hereby establishing that the inmates of the soldiers' home were fed cheaper and better than the paupers of the Tewkesbury almshouse.

I refrain from naming the horrors of this institution in Massachusetts; but the men who are fond of the horrible depravity of mankind, for money, can find their taste gratified in Butler's pamphlet, illustrated by photographs of tanned skins, etc.

Civilization, even among the cultured, is sometimes a diaphanous garment to hide the infernal. "Nature still makes him; and has an infernal in her as well as a celestial."

Well might it be said by an English writer that "the men in the North could, for a moderate sum, engage substitutes to vicariously die for them, while they sipped their wines at the clubs in safety." _____

Percentage Killed and Wounded in Late Wars.

Allies in the Crimea.. 3.2 per cent
Austrians in 1866........... .... 2.6 per cent
Germans in the Franco-German war...................... 3.1 per cent
Federals in the Confederate war.......................... 4.7 per cent
Confederates in the Confederate war,.................... 9.0 per cent

_____

Slave Owners in the Confederate Army.

This question, as far as I am informed, has not been analyzed to separate it from the concrete mass of men that composed the Confederate army. This is desirable to establish what influence they had in deciding the Southern States to secede from the Union, and the solution of it should give the number of slave owners in the army.

The white population of these States was, in 1860, about 8,300,000. There were 346,000 whites who owned slaves. These figures represent and include men of all ages, widows, and minors; also young married women who owned the servant usually given them.

Now divide 8,300,000 by 346,000, and we have $\frac{8,300,000}{346.000} = 24$, which shows that only one person in twenty-four was a slaveholder, and we know not what number in this twenty-four were women, orphans, and old men. If allowance be made for the old men, women, and minors, there would not be over four ablebodied men to the one hundred; hence in a company of one hundred soldiers four would be slave owners. In a regiment of one thousand there would be forty, in ten thousand there would be four hundred, and in the whole Confederate army of six hundred thousand there would be only twenty-four thousand who represented slavery. The remainder (600,000—24,000) would be 576,000 who were not slave owners! This number, however, might be reduced by young men heirs apparent of slaves.

Henceforth, then, let it be known that the Confederate army was not an army of slave owners. To the people of the South it was well known that the slaves were fast becoming the property of the owners of large estates, and on many sugar and cotton plantations there were from one to two hundred negroes employed. The tendency was to consolidate labor, as it was more profitable. Therefore it was that the Confederate army was mainly composed of men as free from interests in slavery as were the men living in sight of Bunker Hill. These men were contending for an object far more dear to them than any arising from slavery. They had seen the accumulated funds of the United States treasury expended in making harbors for towns on the great Northern lakes yearly, and in digging deep-water channels for Eastern cities, and appropriations for little creeks called rivers; while the harbors of the Southern cities were neglected. Then, again, the tariff almost invariably discriminated against the South, even to the extent of nullification, almost thirty years anterior to the war; then the fugitive slave act was nullified by Northern State laws; "underground railroad" was a term used to express how negro slaves were conveyed under cover of the night to the North when enticed from their owners. They openly published that the Constitution was a "compact made with the devil;" and the hatred of the North and the West was so widespread that by a sectional party vote they elected a President antagonistic to the South. These are but a few of the acts that caused secession; and yet he who believes that secession was entertained by more than a mere majority of the people South is mistaken. Genuine love and an abiding fidelity to the Constitution were ever found in the South. Her cause for complaint also was that the people of the North and West, actuated by hatred of the people South, proclaimed that the higher law of *conscience* was superior to the Constitution!

Events came on apace. The Southern people were homogeneous, "to the manner born." Save only in the commercial cities were there any foreigners and but few Northerners. North Carolina did not have quite *one* per cent foreign; the West had about thirty-five per cent. (Census Report.)

When coercion of the South was proclaimed, it was the homogeneousness of her people that solidified both parties at once to a common defense of their homes, and these five hundred and seventy-six thousand soldiers, without interest in slavery, for four years fought for the right of their people to govern themselves in their own way. Their deeds are now a matter of history that will, by them, be recorded, contrary to the past rule, that the conquerors always write history.

Appomattox terminated the war only—it was not a court to adjudicate the *right* of secession—but its sequence established the fact that secession was not treason nor rebellion, and that it yet exists, restrained only by the question of expediency. Wherefore the Union will be maintained mainly by avoiding sectional and class legislation, and remembering always that in the halls of legislation the minority have some rights, and in the minority the *truth* will generally be found.

The charge, then, that the slaveholders, so few in number, forced secession, or that the five hundred and seventy-six thousand nonslaveholders who really constituted the Confederate army were battling to maintain slavery, is a popular error.

The cry at the North that the South was fighting to maintain slavery was proclaimed (as I have elsewhere said) to prejudice the Emperor Napoleon III. and the English Cabinet against forming an alliance with the Confederate States; but the power of public opinion and the press were such that they were obliged to remain neutral; for this constrained neutrality England was *rewarded* by being forced, when the war ended, to pay the United States the sum of fifteen million dollars—the Geneva *award*—for the ships destroyed by Admiral Raphael Semmes, Confederate States Navy; and France was rewarded by obliging Napoleon to withdraw his troops from Mexico, and leave poor Maximilian to his fate—a warning for weak men thirsting for empire.

Prison Deaths and Prisoners.

The number of Confederate prisoners in Northern prisons was 220,000, and the number of Federal prisoners in prisons South was 270,000.

Death rate in Northern prisons...............................12 per cent
Death rate in Southern prisons................................ 9 per cent

See the report of Secretary Stanton, made July 9, 1866; also the report of Surgeon General Barnes, United States Army.

SOME OF THE BRIGADE LOSSES IN PARTICULAR ENGAGEMENTS.

Gettysburg....	Garnett's Brigade	(Va.)	Pickett's Division	65.9	per cent
Gettysburg....	Perry's "	(Fla.)	Anderson's "	65	" "
Antietam.. ...	Wofford's "	(Tex.)	Hood's "	64.1	" "
Franklin......	Cockrell's "	(Mo.)	French's "	60.2	" "
Chickamauga..	Benning's "	(Ga.)	Hood's "	56.6	" "

There are thirteen more brigades with losses, varying in numbers, before the percentage is reduced to forty per cent.

PERCENTAGE OF LOSS IN SOME REGIMENTS IN SINGLE BATTLES.

Gettysburg............	Twenty-First North Carolina	90	per cent
Gettysburg.........	First Missouri	82	" "
Gettysburg...........	Twenty-Sixth North Carolina	88.5	" "
Antietam..............	Twentieth Texas	82.3	" "
Antietam..............	Twelfth Massachusetts	67	" "
Antietam..............	Twenty-First Georgia	76	" "
Antietam..............	One Hundred and First New York	71	" "

And so on. There are over *fifty* regiments in the *Confederate* army before forty per cent is reached. How many there are in the Federal army I do not know. (From "The Confederate Soldier in the Civil War," and other sources.)

The Authority to Tax

is the greatest power a people can give a government, yet it is a necessary measure, but often dangerous; it can be used to impoverish a people, or enrich a comparatively few individuals, or to rob one section of a vast country to build up another. It has caused more distress than droughts or floods; it has caused more insurrections, revolutions, and wars than all other acts of man intrusted with authority. There are many modes of taxation, but the most insidious one is the quiet robbery by a tariff.

This might be demonstrated by the United States pension laws. The pensioners (and I am a Mexican war pensioner) receive as a free gift from the treasury the sum of about one hundred and fifty million dollars annually. It goes to enrich the people of the States where they reside.

If there be no pensioners living in any one State, that State contributes to support the pensioners, but receives nothing in return: so, if all the pensioners were to become citizens of any *one* State, that State would receive in pension money one hundred and fifty million dollars yearly, or in fifteen years the enormous sum of two billion two hundred and fifty million dollars derived by taxation of the people in the other States, less the sum that one State paid and returned to it.

Now, if all the pensioners, from any cause, should migrate to Ohio, or North Carolina, would the other forty-four States be taxed for (say) the benefit of the people of the State of North Carolina in the sum of two billion two hundred and fifty million dollars during the next fifteen years? No, never.

The presumption is that the Southern States pay, under the revenue laws, one-third of the revenue collected. If so, then the South pays the pensioners about fifty million dollars annually, and receives in return only the small sum paid the few pensioners residing within the Southern States; and thus one section of the country is taxed, under the revenue tariff laws, to enrich the other, Q. E. D. ———

Cost of the War.

The total cost of the war between the States was, to June 30, 1879 ....$10,861,929,909
Value of the slaves confiscated and emancipated.......... 3,000,000,000
Destruction of property in the South (estimated).......... 600,000,000

Naval Power of the United States.

The following enumeration of the vessels in the United States service will convey some idea of the power of the North:

Seven hundred vessels were employed in blockading our coast and guarding our rivers.

During the year 1862–63 there were 533 steamers, barges, and coal boats belonging to the United States on the Mississippi river and its tributaries; and at the same time the United States Quartermaster's Department chartered 1,750 steamers and vessels to aid Gen. Grant in his operations against Vicksburg. In short, there were 2,283 vessels, exclusive of iron-clad mortar boats, operating to capture Vicksburg. The actual siege commenced May 18, and ended July 4, 1863, embracing a period of forty-seven days. ———

Names, Rank, and Positions of Officers on My Staff.

Abercrombie, Wiley, Lieutenant, Aid-de-Camp.
Anderson, Archer, Major, Aid-de-Camp.

Archer, C., Lieutenant, Ord. Officer.
Baker, J. A., Captain, Aid-de-Camp.
Baldwin, John M., Captain, Acting Ord. Officer.
Cain, W. H., Captain, Commissary.
Danner, Albert, Captain, Quartermaster.
Daves, Graham, Major, A. A. General.
Drane, N. M., Captain, Quartermaster.
Freeman, E. T., Lieutenant, A. A. I. General.
Haile, Calhoun, Lieutenant, Aid-de-Camp.
Harrison, William B., Major, Chief Surgeon.
Morey, John B., Major, Chief Quartermaster.
Myers, C. D., Lieutenant, Aid-de-Camp.
Overton, M., Captain, Ord. Officer.
Reynolds, F. A., Captain, A. A. General.
Robertson, N. H., Lieutenant, Artillery.
Rogers, H. J., Captain, Engineer.
Sanders, D. W., Major, Adj. General.
Shingleur, James A., Lieutenant, Maj. and A. A. G.
Shumaker, S. M., Major, Chief Artillery.
Storrs, George S., Lieutenant, Maj. and Chief Art.
Venet, John B., Captain, Engineer.
Yerger, James R., Lieutenant, Aid-de-Camp.
Thomas, Grigsby E., Sergeant, Ordnance.

————

Government in Louisiana, 1875–76.

The forces that were developed during the last two years of
the war found a wide field for operation as the Union troops
marched through the South, and induced the troops to plunder,
because there was money in it, and when the war ended this
force entered the wide area of reconstruction, and produced
those cursed scenes witnessed all over the South, because
there was money in it, and yet when the States were admitted into the Union it was natural to suppose that its power
for evil was spent. Not at all; it rallied, and entered the field
of politics; debased by all the license of war, which exempted
them from punishment for all crimes, they sold themselves for
a price, and the *dual* governments commenced: the one established by the property owners and respectable people, the other
by the carpetbaggers, scalawags, and negroes. Here were offices by election and by appointment affording almost unlimited

opportunity to plunder. They had no conscience when they could put money in their pockets.

To illustrate, I will, as briefly as I can, take the State of Louisiana. In 1875 this State had *two* rival courts, *two* opposing Legislatures. One was the radical carpetbaggers, and the other conservative. There were *three* governors; also United States Senators, black and white, and Gen. P. H. Sheridan was military director; and over and above all the United States intermeddling in her affairs. The rival courts were occupied in reversing the decisions of each other, the Legislatures in passing bills that were not valid for the want of a quorum, or obtaining the signature of the right governor, whether of Kellogg, Warmouth, or McEnery (the three governors).

As this threefold government presaged the probability of the radical party not receiving the electoral vote of the State in the coming election for President, something had to be done to ac complish it. Accordingly the President directed the Secretary of War to issue an order directly and secretly to Gen. P. H. Sheridan, who was in Chicago, to proceed to New Orleans, and it was suggested that he should make the journey appear as one undertaken for recreation. So he and some of his staff, and a party of ladies on pleasure bent, sailed down the turbulent Mississippi river to New Orleans, and established headquarters in the St. Charles Hotel.

Sheridan's secret orders, dated December 24, 1874, were sent to him direct from the Secretary of War, and without the knowledge of Gen. Sherman, commanding the army, or of Gen. McDowell, commanding the Department of the South, which embraced Louisiana, with his headquarters in Louisville, Ky.; but he was advised that he might stop and make known to Gen. McDowell the object of his mission if he deemed it proper to do so, but he passed by without seeing McDowell. On arriving in New Orleans he made the State of Louisiana a part of his department, and then issued his decree declaring the people of the state "banditti." This alarmed the President. It was too imperialistic. Sheridan then suggested that Congress be called on to pass an act in a few words making the people banditti. The President declined. Then the chief of the banditti advised the President to issue an order through the War Department declaring the people banditti, and to leave ALL TO HIM, and he would quell them without giving him (the President) any further trouble. In all this there is a thirst for blood and punishment by military authority. But Grant, sitting on the ragged edge of imperialism, declined to support his man-of-all-work on the banditti question. But still undaunted, Sheridan perchance recalled to mind how Cromwell entered the "Praise God Barebone" house of Parliament, and, charging the members to be guilty of dishonorable acts, drove them out of the house by an armed force, locked the door, and put the key in his pocket; or how Napoleon entered the hall of the council of five hundred in Paris, and at the point of the bayonet dissolved the convention—resolved to imitate those great men by taking a company of the United States army, and thrust the members of the conservative Legislature into the street. This he did by sending Gen. De Trobirand to close the legislative hall of a sovereign State in the Union, first ejecting the members.

However much the North was willing to punish the South, they saw in this a usurpation of United States authority which, if unrebuked, might be applied to a "truly loyal" State in the North; and now the Northern press howled, not because it had been done in Louisiana, but for fear their Legislatures might be invaded likewise, and they cried: "Have we also a Cæsar?" And all this was done to secure the vote of Louisiana to the radical party in the coming presidential election.

Pending these events Sherman and McDowell were inflamed with anger that such orders should be issued secretly, and not sent through the proper channel of communication. Such were some of the incidents of the attempt of Sheridan to punish the people of Louisiana who were "to the manner born," who owned the land, and paid nine-tenths of all the taxes, and who intellectually were his equal, and socially and in the amenities of life his superior in many respects.

Time passed on. Election day came, and, had these States been recorded as the people had voted, the election would have been: For Tilden, 203; for Hayes, 166. But the election machinery in most of the Southern States was in Republican hands, and thus by Chandler's orders the States of Florida, Louisiana, and South Carolina could be counted out; and if this was done, R. B. Hayes would have 185 and S. J. Tilden 184. Now "who should count the votes" became the battle ground. For two months scheme

JULIUS L. BROWN

after scheme was proposed and rejected. More than once it was proposed to throw dice, and raffle off the presidency like "a good, fat turkey for Christmas," but this leaked out. One proposition after another again fell through, and at last Hayes won by trickery. Only the great desire for peace, and the marshaling of troops and concentrating naval vessels under the orders of President Grant prevented a clash of arms.

Among the first acts of President Hayes was an order removing the United States troops from New Orleans and Columbia, S. C., as the purpose for which they had been kept there had been accomplished. Those who are fond of reading low villainy can find it written in the chronicles of Louisiana.

Violation of Paroles.

In connection with the violation of paroles I will incidentally mention that Gov. Joseph E. Brown, of Georgia—after the surrender of Gen. R. E. Lee, and when Gen. J. H. Wilson was in Macon on his raid—went to Macon, and surrendered to Gen. Wilson himself and the militia in his command, and obtained his parole; thence he returned to Milledgeville. That same evening Gen. Wilson sent an officer and some troops to the residence of his excellency, took from him by force the parole that he had just given him, arrested him, took him to Macon; then sent him to Washington City, where he was imprisoned with most of the Southern Governors of the Confederate States. This gave rise to a peculiar decision on the validity of his and other paroles. See the following letter from the War Records, Serial No. 104, Page 836:

WASHINGTON, May 19, 1865.

Hon. E. M. Stanton, Secretary of War.

The inclosed makes it appear that Brown, of Georgia, surrendered the militia of that State and himself as commander in chief thereof to Gen. Wilson, and was paroled. If the call for the meeting of the Georgia Legislature was subsequent to the parole, I suppose there can be no doubt but that he stands liable to arrest for the violation of his parole; otherwise, is it not obligatory upon the government to observe *their* part of the contract? I would not advise authorizing him to go back to Georgia now under any circumstances; but I do not think a paroled officer is subject to arrest, so long as he observes his parole, without giving him notice first that he is absolved from further observance of it.

U. S. GRANT, *Lieutenant General.*

The inclosure referred to is probably Wilson to Stanton, May 19, 4:20 P.M. Page 680.

The wording of the parole given the army of Gen. R. E. Lee reads:

The within named, ——, will not be disturbed by the United States authorities so long as he observes his parole and the laws in force where he may reside. (From the War Records, Vol. 46, Part 3, page 853.)

This opinion of Gen. Grant that an officer, who may be in command of an army or of a body of armed men, after the surrender of his men and their arms, can, after "*notice* that he is *absolved* from further observance of it," be arrested is a flagrant breach of faith.

Promise of protection is given to a man with arms in his hand, that if he *will surrender* them he shall have protection as long as he observes his parole. Is it just, right, or honorable after he has given up his arms to notify him that he is released from the *observance* of the parole, unless you first place him in the same condition he was before he surrendered his arms or his command? It is a deception and an outrage. In fact, I am unable to comprehend how a soldier who surrenders himself, his men, and arms on parole can be released from and absolved from observance from it from any act or acts committed prior to its date in order to arrest him. Gov. Brown was denied the rights given him by his parole, and holding him a prisoner and not permitting him to go to his home in Georgia seems to be predicated upon the fear that he might do something in violation of a parole.

The papers showed that the Governor was paroled by Gen. Wilson; then arrested the same day at his home in Milledgeville, and his parole taken from him by force. I presume that his parole was taken from him because some days previous to his surrender he had made a call for the Legislature to assemble.

Joseph M. Brown, to whom I am indebted for much information that he obtained from Union soldiers through years of correspondence relative to the Georgia campaign, is a son of Gov. Joseph E. Brown, and a gentleman of high literary attainments. His elder brother, Julius L. Brown, now a distinguished lawyer in Atlanta, refused to leave the country to be educated in Europe. By a compromise he was sent to a military school in Athens, Ga.

The boys there took up arms, and formed a company to defend Athens. There Brown's first duty was to guard some Yankee prisoners. In 1864 he joined Company A in a battalion of cadets, and rendered good service in defense of Atlanta. Thence his command went to Milledgeville, where, joining with other State forces and Wheeler's cavalry, they fought Sherman's advance at every river he crossed, and otherwise retarded his march to Savannah. His battalion formed a part of the rear guard of Hardee's army on the retreat from Savannah. The last order issued by Confederate authority east of the Mississippi was to this battalion. (War Records, Serial 111, page 420.)

Cassville.

[From "Reminiscences of the War," in the New Orleans *Picayune.*]

The recent appearance of Hughes's "Life of Gen. Joseph E. Johnston," and the announcement of the placing in the hands of the printers of a "Life of Gen. Leonidas Polk," by his son, Dr. William Polk, were the subject of a conversation recently among a few veterans of the Army of Tennessee, and some facts were mentioned that are deemed of sufficient interest to be placed on record through the columns of your valued paper.

To those who participated in the memorable campaign from Dalton to Atlanta under Joe Johnston, the failure to give battle at Cassville is a most fertile source of discussion and regret, and this was the point of conversation on which the group of talkers lingered the longest.

The enthusiasm that swept through the army when the announcement was made that it had reached the chosen battlefield possessed anew the hearts of these veterans; the cheers that went up from each command as "Old Joe's" ringing battle order was read to the troops reverberated again in their ears; the embers of their deep emotions of elation and disgust that so rapidly succeeded each other on that eventful day burned afresh within them for a while. And naturally the oft-debated question of the amount of blame attaching to Gen. Johnston's subordinates for this failure to fight came up as of old, and the measure of it, if any, appertaining to Gen. Polk was stated as follows by one of the group, Maj. Douglas West, who, as adjutant general, attended Gen. Polk on the night of the conference when Johnston felt compelled to forego the battle and retreat across the Etowah river. He said that after Polk's Corps had taken the position assigned to it on the left of Hood's Corps and in the rear of Cassville, Gen. S. G. French, one of the division generals of the corps, sent a message to Gen. Polk that his position was enfiladed, and that he could not hold it.

Gen. Polk thereupon sent his inspector general, Col. Sevier, to ascertain about it. This officer reported back that in his opinion Gen. French was warranted in his apprehension.

Gen. Polk requested Col. Sevier to proceed to Gen. Johnston's headquarters, and place the facts before him, which this officer did.

Gen. Johnston was loath to believe in the impossibility of holding that part of the line; for, though exposed, it could be made tenable by building traverses, and retiring the troops some little to the rear. He instructed Col. Sevier to have Gen. French to build traverses. This general considered them useless, and persisted in his inability to hold his position.

Col. Sevier reporting this back to Gen. Polk, in the absence of Capt. Walter J. Morris, engineer officer of Gen. Polk's Corps (off on some duty), the General sent Maj. Douglas West to the position of Gen. French's Division to have his opinion also, and to have him talk over the situation with this general. When Maj. West reached there, there was no firing from the enemy, and he could not form an opinion in that way. However he conversed with Gen. French on the subject, and returned, reporting Gen. French as highly wrought up about the exposure of his division. Gen. Polk then sent. Maj. West to Gen. Johnston to state the result of his visit to Gen. French's position, and Gen. Johnston reiterated his opinion about the feasibility of holding the position with the use of traverses.

Upon reporting back the remarks of Gen. Johnston, Maj. West found that Capt. Morris had reached Gen. Polk's headquarters, and the captain in turn was sent to French's position to make a thorough survey and report of it. He made a very thorough one, and reported the position as very exposed for the defensive, but as admirable for the offensive. Gen. Polk, since the first report from Gen. French, appeared much annoyed at this unexpected weakness in his line, which, from the pertinacity of Gen. French, was growing into an obstacle to the impending battle, for which Gen. Polk shared the enthusiasm and confidence of the troops.

That evening about sunset Gen. Hood rode up to Gen. Polk's headquarters with Maj. Gen. French, and at his suggestion Gen. Johnston was asked to meet the three lieutenant generals at Polk's headquarters for the purpose of consulting that night on the situation.

At the appointed hour Gens. Johnston, Hood, and Polk met at the latter's headquarters. Gen. Hardee was not present, he not having been found in time, after diligent search. Gen. Hood arrived at the rendezvous accompanied by Gen. French, whose division rested upon his left in the line of battle. Gen. Polk had not asked Gen. French, who was of his corps, to be present at headquarters for the occasion, and Gen. Hood's action in bringing him was altogether gratuitous. Upon arriving with French, Gen. Hood excused his action by stating that he considered the situation so vital to himself and French that he had taken the liberty to ask Gen. French to come with him to the conference. After awaiting Gen. Hardee's arrival for a good while, Gens. Johnston, Polk, and Hood retired to the rough cabin house where Polk had established his headquarters, and Gen. French and the staff officers of the different generals remained outside, beyond earshot.

It was past midnight when the meeting broke up and the generals stepped out and called their escort and attending staff.

Gen. Polk immediately instructed Maj. West to issue orders to his division generals to move as soon as guides would be furnished them. Capt. Morris was ordered to procure these immediately. Gen. Polk communicated detailed instructions, but appeared deeply absorbed. In silence everything was carried out, and the corps had taken up the march and moved some distance before Maj. West was aware that the army was in retreat. He had been by the General's side or close in the rear of him from the moment of the termination of the conference, and the General had not spoken about it. Thus they had ridden a good while. The Major, respecting the General's silent mood, had not thought proper to inquire about the destination of the column. An officer of Gen. Hardee's staff, Capt. Thomas H. Hunt, was the first to inform Maj. West that the army was retreating because Gen. Polk at the conference had insisted that he could not

24

hold his position in the line of battle selected by Johnston. Stung by this statement, Maj. West denied it emphatically, and as his informant insisted on its correctness, Maj. West rode up to Gen. Polk, and asked him where the column was marching to. Gen. Polk said they were retreating to beyond the Etowah river. Maj. West then told him of the report that had reached him, and asked him if he was the cause of the abandonment of the intended battle at Cassville. Gen. Polk asked who had made the statement, and when told that it was a staff officer of Gen. Hardee, who also added that the impression prevailed along the column, and Maj. West asking that he be authorized to deny the report, Gen. Polk was silent for a moment, and then said to Maj. West: "To-morrow everything will be made as clear as day."

Gen. Polk never again spoke of this matter to the Major, although with him day and night during that long and terrible campaign, in which he lost his life at Pine Mountain on the 14th of July, 1864; but the impression left upon his staff officers was that the failure to give battle at Cassville was not due to any representations made by Gen. Polk, but to the objections made by Lieut. Gen. Hood, the left of whose line joined French's Division.

Gen. Polk had so little confidence in the representations of the weakness of the line at the point referred to that he did not go there in person.

But for Gen. Hood's invitation, Maj. Gen. French would not have been called to the conference, and consequently when Gen. Hood urged the untenability of his line, and supported it by bringing one of Polk's division commanders (French) to confirm him, although Polk's other division commanders (Loring and Walthall) offered no objection, and in the absence of Lieut. Gen. Hardee, Gen. Polk could *only* reply upon the report of his chief topographical engineer, Capt. Morris, and Maj. Gen. French, and *sustain* Lieut. Gen. Hood in his opinion that the line could not be held after an attack.

Gen. Polk was too noble and patriotic to care for his personal fame, and made no effort during his life to put himself properly on record for his connection with the abandonment of the line at Cassville, for he was always ready to give battle or to take any responsibilities of his position. He fought for his cause, not for his reputation.

Another of this group of veterans had been of Hardee's Corps on that occasion. He recounted that his battery had been assigned by "Old Joe" to an important post on Hardee's line, the angle at which the left flank deflected back. Vividly he described his position—the knoll upon which his guns were planted, the open fields around, that gave promise of great slaughter of the foe when he undertook to carry the point. This prospect, and the pride arising from the very danger of their post, stimulated the men in their labors of entrenching, which was necessary at this end of the line of battle, where there were none of the natural advantages the troops of Polk and Hood derived from the hills on which they were posted. But all worked with an energy that arose to enthusiasm; for confidence in "Old Joe," confidence in the "Old Reliable," and confidence in themselves inspired the men of this company as it did those of the whole corps. The redoubt was nearly completed when about two o'clock in the morning Capt. Sid Hardee, of Gen. Hardee's staff, rode up and ordered the work to cease and the battery made ready to move. This officer then stated that the intention to fight a battle there was abandoned; that Polk and Hood had insisted that they could not hold their position in the line. He added that Gen. Hardee had objected to the retreat, and had offered to change positions with either of the other corps rather than forego giving battle.

In deep disappointment and disgust Hardee's men moved off, blaming Polk and Hood for compelling the abandonment of a field which seemed to be pregnant with a glorious victory.

The impressions of that night had remained ineffaceable, and the unfought battle had been a deep source of regret during the war, and of deep interest since; so much so since that it had led to a correspondence between one of the officers of the company and Gen. Johnston. ONE OF HARDEE'S CORPS.

REPLY OF GEN. FRENCH TO "REMINISCENCES OF THE WAR."

WINTER PARK, FLA., December 12, 1893.
Editor *Picayune.*

A few days ago a friend sent me a copy of the *Weekly Picayune* of October 26 last, containing an article headed "Reminiscences of the War," that contains a number of errors, which I desire to correct so far as they relate to me, and I will refer to them in the order they are related in the paper. I quote:

1. "After Polk's Corps had taken the position assigned to it on the left of Hood's Corps and in the rear of Cassville, Gen. S. G. French, one of the division generals of the corps, sent a report to Gen. Polk that his position was enfiladed and that he could not hold it."

Any line can be enfiladed if the enemy be permitted, undisturbed, to approach near enough and establish batteries on the prolongation of that line. Therefore before any person can report a line enfiladed, the guns must be near enough to sweep it with shells. To report that a point near the center of a long line of battle cannot be held before the issue is made is mere conjecture, and not justifiable, and I have no recollection of having made such a report, and deem the writer is in error in his statement. A man would not cry out, "Help me, Cassius, or I sink," before entering the water.

2. The next assertion is that Gen. Polk "sent Col. Sevier to ascertain about it, and this officer reported back that, in his opinion, Gen. French was warranted in his apprehension. Gen. Polk thereupon requested Col. Sevier to proceed to Gen. Johnston's headquarters and place the facts before him, which that officer did. Gen. Johnston was loath to believe in the impossibility of holding that part of the line, etc., . . . and instructed Col. Sevier to have Gen. French build traverses. This general considered them useless, and persisted in his inability to hold the position."

In answer to this, I repeat that I have no recollection of having made to any human being the remarks here attributed to me. How, in the name of common sense, could any division officer report, much less persist, as stated? How would he know but that, if necessary during the battle, ample support would be sent him? I had one brigade and a half in reserve at that point of the line. As for traverses, I never heard them mentioned before, in reference to this line. And now, after your writer has sent Col. Sevier to me twice, he sends to me Maj. West, and it was before any firing had taken place, and he (West) could, very properly, "form no opinion unless he could witness the fire of the enemy's guns." West returned to Gen. Polk, reporting Gen. French highly wrought up about the exposure of his division, and Gen. Polk is made to send this officer likewise to hunt up Gen. Johnston, and after "reporting back the remarks of Gen. Johnston, Maj. West found that Capt. Morris had reached Gen. Polk's headquarters," and the Captain in turn "was sent to French's position to make a thorough survey and report of it." He made a very thorough one, and reported the position very exposed for the defensive, but as admirable for the offensive.

I have Capt. Morris's report, but I do not find in it where he reported the line as admirable for the offensive. I will have occasion to refer to this report after a while. I merely wish to remark that when we find Capt. Morris at Col. Polk's headquarters we have something tangible in regard to time.

3. And the article goes on to state that "Gen. Polk, since the first report from Gen. French, appeared much annoyed at this unexpected weakness in his line, which from the pertinacity of Gen. French was growing into an obstacle to the impending battle, for which Gen. Polk shared the enthusiasm and confidence of the troops."

Now, contrast this with what the writer says farther on when he tells us: "Gen. Polk had so little confidence in the representations of the weakness of his line at the point referred to that he did not go there in person."

It is not always safe to divine what is passing through a man's mind from appearances, and, having "little confidence in the representations," the deduction of "annoyance" may not be correct which is attributed to Gen. Polk. Now, inasmuch as Gen. Polk was present (when Gen. F. A. Shoupe "pointed out the fact to Gen. Johnston that his line would be enfiladed before the troops were posted, and suggested a change of position) and strongly supported Shoupe's objections," he must have been early apprised of the general condition of the line before he received the alleged report from me, which the writer explicitly affirms was sustained by Cols. Sevier, West, and Morris; hence the weakness of his line was not unexpected, and should not "have grown into an obstacle to the impending battle." Gen. Shoupe's letter will be found in Hood's book, page 105.

4. In writing about the conference I find the account thus:

"That evening about sunset Gen. Hood arrived at the rendezvous, accompanied by Gen. French, whose division rested on his left in line of battle. Gen. Polk had not asked Gen. French— who was of his corps—to be present for the occasion, and Gen.

Hood's action in bringing him was altogether gratuitous. On arriving with French, Gen. Hood excused his action by stating that he considered the situation so vital to himself and French that he had taken the liberty to ask Gen. French to come with him to the conference."

This shows that Polk and Hood had decided (at a consultation in advance) to hold a conference before I went with Hood to the rendezvous, to which they invited Johnston. About my being there, I have this to say, and the facts are these: The little firing that had taken place almost ceased awhile before dark; so, taking a staff officer with me, we went to our wagon to get dinner, and while returning to my command we met Gen. Hood on his way to Gen. Johnston's. We halted, and while conversing he told me that his line was enfiladed by the batteries of the enemy in position, and that he was going to see Gen. Johnston at Gen. Polk's, and asked me to ride with him to get supper, etc. His meeting me, therefore, was purely accidental, and this place where we met was near by Polk's quarters.

So I went with him, socially, without any special object in view. He said nothing to me about a conference to be held on the situation, called by him and Gen. Polk.

Soon after supper Gens. Johnston, Polk, and Hood went to Gen. Polk's office, and Gen. Johnston asked me to go with them.

The matter presented to the meeting was: "Can we win the battle on the morrow? Can we hold our line?" Hood said he thought not, for if attacked in the morning he would not be able to hold his line, because it was enfiladed by the guns of the enemy, now in position, and that Gen. Polk's line was also enfiladed, and could not be held against a vigorous attack, or words to that effect.

Gen. Polk confirmed Hood's statement in regard to his line. Gen. Johnston maintained the contrary. Of course I took no part in the discussion. When asked, I explained how my line curved, near the end, to the left, sufficient to be enfiladed by one battery on the extreme left of the enemy's line. I have no recollection of being asked if I could hold my part of the line, but had the question been asked me, I am quite sure it would have been suppositively in the affirmative.

As the whole includes all the parts, so, the discussion being on Polk's and Hood's lines in their entirety, the parts were embraced therein, and not specifically referred to, being minor considerations.

Gen. Johnston argued for the maintenance of his plans very firmly. When a silence occurred in the discussion, I arose and asked permission to leave, stating that I wished to go to my line and fortify it. On reaching my division, I set every one to work strengthening the line and getting ready for the impending battle, that I felt sure would begin in the morning. While we were thus busily at work, and at about the hour of 11 P.M., an officer riding along my line stopped and told me that the work would be useless, and "intimated" (that is the word written in my diary) "that the army would be withdrawn or fall back to-night!" Soon after, the order came to move back on the Cartersville road. The receipt of the order was a surprise to me, notwithstanding the intimation that had been made to me.

5. Toward the conclusion of the article it reads:

"Gen. Polk had so little confidence in the representations of the weakness of the line at the point referred to that he did not go there in person. But for Hood's invitation, Gen. French would not have been called to the conference, and, consequently, when Gen. Hood urged the untenability of his line, and supported it by bringing one of Polk's division commanders—French—to confirm him, Gen. Polk could only rely upon the report of his chief engineer—Capt. Morris—and Maj. Gen. French, and *sustain* Lieut. Gen. Hood in his opinion that the line could not be held after an attack."

This paragraph is adroitly constructed, and apparently not intended to be clear. It first accuses Gen. Polk of having little confidence in the representations of Sevier, West, and French, as alleged to have been made to him; but when Gen. Hood brings French to the conference, his testimony is so potent as to make Polk *change his opinions* and *sustain* Hood, who urged the untenability of his (Polk's) line.

This is all wrong. Hood did not take me to the conference. I did not support or confirm Hood in his representations. I have never said I could not hold my part of the line, and it would have been presumption to do so. The commanding general would see that the line at that point was defended.

This paragraph also represents Gen. Polk as going to the conference apparently prepared to defend his line; but when he lis-

tens to Hood's arguments he changes his mind and sustains
Hood; and thus, with two of his corps commanders opposed to
defending their lines, Johnston deemed it better to decline the
impending battle.

6. On page 110 in Hood's book you will find the beginning of
a letter from Capt. W. J. Morris, Gen. Polk's chief engineer,
from which I will make some quotations, abbreviating them as
much as possible.   He says he arrived at Cassville station
about 3:30 or 4 P.M., May 19, 1864.   Col. Gale was there to
meet him and to tell him that Gen. Polk wanted to see him as
soon as he arrived.   He had half a mile to go to Polk's quarters.   He met Gen. Polk at the door.   He says it took him about
half an hour to examine a map that Polk placed before him and
make notes of the General's wishes, and fifteen minutes to ride
from Polk's headquarters to the line that was reported to be enfiladed.   When he left Polk's headquarters he thinks Gen. Hood
was there.   It took him about two hours to examine the lines,
angles, elevations, and positions of the batteries of the enemy
established on their line in front of Hood, and his opinion and
conclusions were:

"(1) That the right of the line of Polk's command could not
be held.   (2) That traverses would be of no avail, etc.   (3) That
it was extremely hazardous for Gen. Polk to advance his line
to make an attack upon the enemy while the batteries held the
positions they then occupied."

"Having made the reconnoissance, he returned to Gen. Polk's
headquarters just after dark.   Gen. Polk immediately sent for
Gen. Johnston.   Gen. Hood was at Gen. Polk's."

You will thus perceive that the conference to be held was determined on between Polk and Hood, before Morris made his
report to Polk, because Hood was already there, for I rode with
him to the "rendezvous."

7. On the 8th of May, 1874, Gen. Hood wrote me a letter to
know what I knew about the "vexed question" of retiring from
Cassville.   He had forgotten that he had met me in the road;
that he had invited me to ride with him to see Gen. Johnston,
or that I was at the conference, and said he "only learned that
I was at the conference from Johnston's narrative," etc.

I answered his letter from New York, where I then was, from
recollection, without reference to my diary.   I have both his

letter and my answer. Gen. Hood and I had talked this matter over at length at the Allegheny Springs, Va., in the summer of 1872, differing, however, about not remaining at Cassville and the defensive strength of the lines.

8. Without endeavoring to recall to mind pictures of scenes through the mist of thirty years in the past, or to revive recollections of words used in the long, long ago, I will refer to my diary, and what was written day by day therein.

After we had formed a line of battle east of Cassville, and maneuvered with Hood with a view to attacking the enemy, our troops began in the afternoon to fall back to a line of hills south of Cassville. Cockrell's Brigade, that was in reserve, had been ordered to a hill there early. The diary says: "I received orders at 4 P.M. to fall back from the line east of Cassville and form behind the division of Gen. Canty and Cockrell's Brigade, which I did. As there was an interval between Hood's line (Hindman) and Canty, I placed there, in position, Hoskins's Battery and the half of Ector's Brigade. This left Sears's Brigade and the half of Ector's in reserve, Cockrell being on Canty's left in line.

"About 5 P.M. our pickets from the extreme front were driven in toward the second line by the enemy's cavalry. Hoskins's Battery opened on them and checked the advance. About 5:30 P.M. the enemy got their batteries in position and opened fire on my line. One battery on my right enfiladed a part of my line." The diary then refers to my going to dinner, meeting Gen. Hood and riding with him over to Gen. Polk's, leaving the conference, believing we would fight, etc.

9. We are now, Mr. Editor, getting beyond the hypothetical, for we have determined certain facts pretty accurately—viz.:

The hour I received the order to fall back from east of Cassville, the time our skirmishers were driven in, and when the firing commenced; also the hour that Capt. Morris arrived.

Capt. Morris declares that he arrived between 3:30 and 4 P.M. If he be correct, I was at that time with my troops east of Cassville, and it is certain no report could have been made by me until after the enemy's artillery commenced firing. Now mark what is declared to have taken place after the alleged report was said to have been received by Gen. Polk.

It would take an officer certainly fifteen minutes to ride from

Polk's headquarters to Hoskins's Battery—a mile and a half distant—examine the lines, the position of the enemy, the effects of the fire, and discuss the situation; then the same length of time to return to Gen. Polk and confer with him. Then it would require the same length of time to go in quest of Gen. Johnston, report to him and explain the situation of affairs minutely; then to return to Gen. Polk and report it to him; then to come to my line a second time, and return to Gen. Polk. These two trips to my line and one to Gen. Johnston would have occupied one hour and a half. Next Maj. West received instructions to go and examine the line, and as there was no firing, he could form no opinion, but only talk with me. Then he went back to Gen. Polk and made his report; thence he too was ordered to go in quest of Gen. Johnston, and found him somewhere, reported to him, and returned. This would have required about one hour. So the line from Polk's to my extreme right was ridden over six times, examined and discussed, and four times from Gen. Polk's to where Gen. Johnston was, consuming not less than two hours and a half. Capt. Morris was not yet at Gen. Polk's quarters when Maj. West went in quest of Gen. Johnston, but he found he had arrived when he returned from Gen. Johnston's.

Now, it is plain that, if my alleged report to Gen. Polk put all this in motion, it must have been received by him at 1:30 P.M., because we know that it terminated soon after the arrival of Capt. Morris at Polk's quarters at 4 P.M. Soon after this Capt. Morris was ordered down to examine the line, which he did, and we have his report.

The question of time may be determined in another way: If I sent a report to Gen. Polk, it was carried a mile and a half to him by courier. Next, consider Col. Sevier and Maj. West in the light of one person. That person must have traveled about thirteen miles, received seven separate sets of instructions from Gens. Polk and Johnston, made five carefully matured reports on the situation, and what was said by me and Gen. Johnston, and made at least two careful examinations of our line, noted the position of the enemy, watched the firing and noted the effect of the same, and it could not physically have been performed under two hours and a half; and yet your published article says that it was all performed during the interval between receiving my report and the departure of Morris to make his survey, which was about 4 P.M.

If I made a report, as stated, it was done after the firing commenced, and hence it must have been dark when Maj. West returned from his interview with Gen. Johnston.

The conclusion, therefore, must be that from the length of time the writer's, or relator's, memory has failed to recall events as they were thirty years ago.

There was only a small part of my line enfiladed, and that was caused by its curving to the left near the ravine, where Hoskins's Battery was.

If Hood's line was enfiladed, I did not discover it, and Capt. Morris's plan, published in the War Records (plate 62), would be faulty, for the enemy's line is nearly parallel with his. To conclude, I have shown that if all this passing to and fro of officers took place between me and Gen. Polk, and between Polk and Johnston, it must have commenced about 1:30 P.M., to have have ended at 4 P.M., which could not be, for I was then east of Cassville. On the other hand, if a report was carried to Gen. Polk about my line being enfiladed, it must have been done after 5:30 P.M.; and this going to and fro, with examinations and discussions, could not have been accomplished before 8 P.M., whereas it is stated to have been done before Capt. Morris left Polk's headquarters, at 4:30 P.M., either of which is incredible.

Very respectfully, S. G. FRENCH.

P. S.—The result of the two hours' shelling of my line in casualties was one officer and nine men wounded—none killed. Horses, three killed. A small matter to create any apprehension, as described in your article. The order placing me in command of *Canty's Division* has no hour date.

Your readers will perceive that it was not I who influenced Gen. Polk in this affair. In fact, I was in reserve and had no troops in line of battle except Cockrell's Brigade—and that was about the center of the line—until I was ordered to take command of Canty's Division. How absurd, then, all this rigmarole about my saying I could not hold my line, and my testimony influencing Gen. Polk. S. G. F.

From the foregoing papers it is evident that I was left alone east of the village of Cassville. After Gen. Johnston had placed

the troops of his right wing in position, an order was sent, and
received by me at 4 P.M., directing me to fall back and form my
troops in the *rear* of Cockrell's Brigade and Canty's Division.
This put my division in *reserve*, except Cockrell's Brigade, which
was on Canty's left. Thus I found myself in *reserve* in rear of the
the line of battle. This could not have been done before 4:30
P.M. Now, could I report that I could not hold my line when I
had none, or only one brigade, and that in the center of a line
of battle several miles in length? However, soon an order was
received (without an hour date) for me to take command of
Canty's Division, and to put or leave Cockrell's Brigade in Loring's Division. I was now in command of two divisions, less one
brigade.

On going to the right of Canty's Division, I found a gap, a dry
water gully, and its approaches unoccupied. From necessity I
had to take a part of a brigade (Ector's), so as to connect with
Hood's left. Then Hoskins's Battery was put in position about
fifty yards in advance on an eminence in front of a gap. Soon
the enemy's cavalry appeared in front of the gap, and were dis-
persed by the fire of Hoskins's guns. The enemy now began to
establish their batteries on the ridge in front of Hood's line, especially near his right, and soon they opened fire on Hoskins's
Battery. About sunset the fire slackened, when Maj. Shingleur,
of my staff, and I went to our wagon in the rear to get our dinner. Up to this time I heard never a word about not holding the
line. I knew nothing about horsemen or couriers or aids dash-
ing about hunting Gens. Johnston and Polk and me on the line,
and I never heard it mentioned until I read it in the newspaper
sent to me one month after it was published, and thirty years
after we left Cassville.

It was perhaps 2 P.M. when Gen. Johnston lost all hope that
Hood, with the two corps as his command, would engage the detached forces of the enemy marching to our right, and crush
them before Sherman could aid them. So no alternative was
left him but to form a line of battle on selected ground, and act
on the defensive. What followed after this has been already
sketched.

I am sorry this article, so replete with errors, was ever published on account of Gen. Polk—a noble, kind-hearted man, ever
practicing the amenities of life--for it makes him appear rather

contumacious in joining Gen. Hood, and making arrangements to invite their commander to meet them at their "rendezvous" to listen to their complaints, and almost dictating what should be done after the failure of the contemplated morning attack. The writer was evidently aware that both Hood and Polk were almost disobedient in their acts at Cassville.

Thirty years had rolled by, and the incidents were almost forgotten, when this writer, to smooth the matter over, maladroitly seizes the fact that I went with Hood to Polk's headquarters, and tries to make it appear that I had influenced Gen. Polk by representations to change his opinion, and join Hood in the statement that their lines were untenable. I never saw Gen. Polk after he left the position east of Cassville until I met him at his quarters where I went to supper, and I do not remember ever sending a message or report to him that day.

He says: "Gen. Polk was too noble and patriotic to care for his personal fame, and made no effort during his life to put himself properly on record for his connection with the abandonment of the line at Cassville, for he was always ready to give battle or take any responsibilities of his position. He fought for his cause, and not for his reputation."

The writer did not even know that I was present at the council of the commanders, and heard both Hood and Polk give their opinions on their side, and Johnston on the other. Therefore, as I differed from both Hood and Polk, I could not have influenced Gen. Polk to "sustain Gen. Hood." Furthermore, in justice to myself and for the truth of history, I desire to correct the many erroneous statements made in the article published. Because a line is enfiladed it does not follow that it cannot be held. During the battle of Atlanta twice I was obliged to hold enfiladed lines nearly an entire day. Gen. Polk did not examine his line of battle after my division arrived. It is the duty of a soldier to obey an order, and not to discuss it, and any soldier who before a battle commences reports that he cannot hold a position when a whole army is drawn up should be relieved from command.

JACKSON, MISS., January 15, 1894.

Gen. S. G. French, Winter Park, Fla.

My Dear General: I have read carefully your letter of the 8th instant; also the newspaper article, "*Vox Populi*," and find your statement in this article perfectly correct. I was the staff officer who accompanied you to Gen. Polk's headquarters. . . . Hood said that he would ride with you to Polk's headquarters, as he was to meet Gen. Johnston there. . . . We rode along leisurely, you and Hood in front, myself and one or two of Hood's staff in the rear. This was possibly an hour after dark. Arriving at Gen. Polk's, we found there, besides Gen. Polk, Gens. Johnston and Hardee. [This is an error. Neither was there when we arrived.—S. G. F.]

Of what happened at the consultation room of course I know nothing. I am sure that you came from the room between 10 and 11 o'clock, followed by Gen. Johnston, who, standing on the steps, told you when you went back to your command to have the word passed through your division that we would fight in the morning, and prepare for it. . . .

About 1 A.M. I was waked up by some one inquiring for Gen. French's headquarters. . . . A courier said that he had an order for you, which we read by making a light. It was the order for us to move, with instructions to leave a few men at the *breastworks* to hammer and make a noise to conceal our retreat. I am sure this order fell upon us like a bombshell.

If you uttered a word about having a position that you could not hold, I never heard of it; and if you had thought so, I am sure that you would have mentioned it to me. On the other hand, I remember clearly that we discussed the situation, and both concluded that we held a very strong position, and could hold it against all odds. . . .

Now all this Cassville affair is as clear to my mind as on the night that it happened. There is no doubt upon my mind that Gen. Hood, and he alone, was responsible for our retreat from Cassville. It is all a mistake about French and all staff officers being sent beyond earshot. . . . When we left Gen. Polk's headquarters you and I went alone. Hood remained. I hope you will be able to put this matter right, and let the responsibility rest where it properly belongs.

Very glad to hear from you. With best wishes. etc.

Yours very truly,

J. A. SHINGLEUR.

SAVANNAH. August 8. 1874.

Gen. S. G. French.

Dear General: Long absence prevented my receiving and acknowledging your very clear and satisfactory reply to my question on the subject of small arms. It is all that I could desire. I wish only to meet such of Hood's assertions as impugn the *truth* of my statements. If he goes on, and I understand that he intends to do so, I shall avail myself of your kind offer.

Can you not sometimes take Savannah in your way from Mississippi to New York, and *vice versâ?* It would be very pleasant to me to see you in my house, where there is always ample room for you and cordial welcome.

Yours truly,

J. E. JOHNSTON.

SAVANNAH, June 13, 1874.

Gen. S. G. French.

Dear General: You may have observed that Gen. Hood has renewed his attacks on me in his report of 1865. His last shot is in the form of a letter signed by poor old Oladowski, the ordnance officer, in which it is asserted that the army lost 19,000 small arms in the part of the campaign in which I commanded. As I have no ordnance returns, I can only refute this calumny by the testimony of the most prominent officers, and in that connection beg you to write me (for publication) about the number of muskets your division lost in the campaign, if any. Certainly the enemy took none, for you never failed to hold the ground intrusted to you. You probably have some idea of the probable losses of arms by your corps, or if it had any losses. And can you say, perhaps, if those losses could have been great enough to correspond with Col. Oladowski's statement? You will oblige me very much by giving me whatever information you can in relation to this matter.

Very truly yours, J. E. JOHNSTON.

Slavery Proclamation and Confiscation Act.

The act of confiscation, and the President's proclamation setting free the slaves in the Confederacy, could not abolish slavery, because it existed under the laws of the *States*. It altered no State law, but it did affect slavery in this way: it caused many slaves to leave their owners, and thus diminished their property and their wealth, but they could buy others under the law.

The President has no legislative power; he cannot declare martial law, for it overthrows the constitution, and his will would become the law; how can the President, an executive officer, nullify laws and condemn and punish at his pleasure?

The great latent power in the constitution is, in Art. I., Sec. 8, to provide for the common defense and general welfare. Under this section almost all the outrages of the war were committed, restrained only by international rules of war; but these were utterly ignored under the plea that this war is only a rebellion, a family affair. Under this article resides the power to imposes *taxes* to any amount for the common defense and public welfare.

The confiscation act of Congress was declared by the United States Supreme Court to be unconstitutional, and, in truth, it was passed as a punishment against the "rebels," without an indictment, trial, or conviction. The constitution declares that the *trial* of all *crimes*, except in cases of impeachment, shall be by *jury.*

As the slave owners were called the only *privileged* class in the United States, it is pertinent to inquire if they did not exist in all the States when the Union was formed, and if the North did not sell their title to be yet a privileged class for a mess of pottage; and then howled at the purchasers for being a privileged people!

Who demanded the continual enlargement of slavery by making it legal to steal or purchase negroes from Africa until the year 1808, to give employment to the six hundred slave ships owned in the North? for the statement is that toward the close of the slave trade there were about that number belonging to New England and New York engaged in that pious enterprise. We know the town of Newport, R. I., had one hundred and seventy ships employed in this money-making trade in the year 1750, and undoubtedly the number increased largely in after years, when made legal; so, on the whole, no doubt six hundred ships were in the trade.

The question here presents itself—and it is a proper one to ask —who first owned these slaves; how did they obtain them; how did they treat them; and to whom did they sell these human beings for money; and then, with the price of blood in their pockets, begin to preach against the sin of slavery? Ye hypocrites! who thank God "we are not slave owners, we got rid of them long ago."

It has been said by a Northern writer that "indirectly, and for ţhe purpose of a more equal distribution of direct taxes, the framers of the constitution tolerated while they condemned slavery; but they tolerated it because they believed it would soon disappear. They even refused to allow the charter of their own liberties to be polluted by the mention of the word *slave;* but take heed, did not this convention give way to the clamor of the owners of slave ships to continue for twenty years the increase of slavery? They could not, consistently with honor or self-respect, transmit to future ages the evidence that some of them had trampled upon the inalienable rights of others."

"Though slavery was thus tolerated by being ignored, we should not dishonor the memory of those who organized the government to suppose that they did intend to bestow upon it the power to maintain its own authority, the right to overthrow or remove slavery or whatever might prove fatal to its permanence or destroy its usefulness."

The answer is: *Yes*, but not by making war and laying waste the country; burning dwellings, public buildings, towns; sinking shipping, blockades; capturing, killing, imprisoning innocent people; nor by creating enormous debts, nor yet by cruel war, but by removing the evil by *compensation* "for the *term of service*" of the slaves to their owners.

The government is under obligation to compensate *parents*, masters of *apprentices*, masters of *slaves* for *loss of service* and labor of their subjects who are enlisted in the army and navy, for the constitution recognizes slaves as "persons held to labor or service."

England compelled the abolition of slavery in her colonies, and she paid in compensation to the slave owners one hundred million dollars. Out of this, the Cape Colony, in Africa, obtained fifteen million dollars, which was about four hundred dollars per slave.

If, then, slavery was believed to be fatal to the permanence of the constitution, it could have been abolished as it was in England, or in some equitable way without the clash of arms.

———

Indenture.

This indenture is here presented for no other purpose than to evidence the mode of manumitting slaves by the Abolition Society in the City of Brotherly Love about four years after the constitution of the United States was framed.

From this instrument of writing it appears that "Betty" was set free (so called) on the 14th of September, 1792, on condition that she should become a bond servant by contract for seven years. Her signature to the indenture (original) is made on the left-hand corner, and not covered by the photograph.

From the wording of her indenture to her master Bordley, it would appear that verily her second condition was worse than her first, and her last worse than all; for in her fifty-seventh year she was to be turned adrift in her old age, possessed of only two suits of apparel—"one of which is to be new"—to struggle with adversity. She was now, however, free to play cards and dice,

25

This Indenture

Witnesseth, That [illegible] ...

... Hath put herself, and by these Presents ... hath voluntarily, and of his own free Will and Accord, put herself Apprentice to the said [illegible] ... of Maryland in the ... after the Manner of an Apprentice to serve ... from the Day of the Date hereof, for, and during ... and Term of [illegible] next ensuing. During all which Term, the said Apprentice her said Master faithfully shall serve, his Secrets keep, his lawful Commands every where readily obey. She shall do no Damage to her said Master ... nor see it to be done by others, without letting or giving Notice thereof to her said Master. She shall not waste her said Master's ... them unlawfully to any. She shall not commit Fornication, nor contract Matrimony within the said Term ... or any other unlawful Game, whereby her said ... damage. With her own Goods ... Goods ... from her said Master ... herself Day nor Night from her said Master's ... Leave. Not haunt ... but in all things ...

... to be taught or instructed ... ... and provide for her sufficient ...

... for the true Performance of all and singular the Covenants and Agreements aforesaid, the said Parties bind themselves each unto the other firmly by these Presents. IN WITNESS whereof, the said Parties have interchangeably set their Hands and Seals hereunto. Dated the [illegible] Day of [illegible] Annoque Domini One Thousand Seven Hundred and [illegible]

Sealed and delivered in }
the Presence of }

Thos. Harrison   Beale Bordley

Hilary Baker, one of the
Aldermen of Philad.

go to alehouses, taverns, and playhouses, and dance and contract marriage, etc.

It would be interesting to know how she passed the remaining years of her life. That is buried in oblivion. Had she remained a slave—"held to a service of labor," which was her first condition—she would have had a home for life. To depend on the benevolence of the Northern people was to be in a worse condition than that of a slave, for the slave did know that he had a friend and a home for life.

How little is known, even at this day, at the North of the general relation between the owner and the slave in the latter days of slavery's existence! and I hope it will not shock the sensibility or puritanical feelings of ye scribes and Pharisees when I state that in the family graveyard near Columbus, Ga., where my wife's father and mother and some of her brothers and sisters rest, there repose the remains of *their* Aunt Betty, who nursed all the children of the family. She was, in name, a slave; in reality, she had all the privileges of a member of the family, and when she died the children declared she should sleep beside them in death, as she had lived with them in life and would rise with them at the resurrection.

I could tell where a slave, after her death, was carried near fifty miles to sleep in the family graveyard, with her master and mistress, who had preceded her to the sacred spot where dust returns to dust. These, and other instances I know, speak of kind feelings, and are significant of the ties that existed between the master and the slave; and this intimacy between master and slave, and almost companionship of children and servant, were more common than any harsh behavior toward them. A man who abused a slave was held in contempt, and was, I suppose, shunned by his neighbors. I had no experience with such men. Once the overseer on our place was going to punish a man for persisting in annoying another. The alleged offender sent for me, and I investigated the case. He was charged with being too gallant with another man's wife, an accusation very prevalent in high society now, when my lady can get a divorce in the morning and marry her admirer in the evening, or the husband do so, as the case may be. No punishment was given the negro in this matter, for the want of evidence; and I here state that no whipping of a negro ever occurred on the plantation.

The difference between the wage earner and the slave is, the *right to change residence.* The former, with his family of wife and children, is too often, for want of means, unable to avail himself of his right, and is therefore practically on a level in this respect with the bondsman, and he becomes reduced to the slavery of wages, which in this age—howling for wealth—becomes a pitiful condition, from which he seeks relief in strikes, so often in vain. He cannot succeed against the money power of the great trusts and monopolies, the power of the State and military interference of the United States forces; so in the end he is only steeped deeper in poverty. From all this the slave was free and happy, if his laughter, song, and dance indicate contentment.

I do dislike egotism, and yet to establish the fact that slaves did possess the power to change masters and homes—and you will admit that practical experience is better than any theory—I will tell you plainly what occurred to me touching this matter.

As administrator of an estate where the land and servants had to be sold, the heads of the families were given notice, months in advance, that they could visit or otherwise see the owners of the neighboring plantations and other persons with whom they would like to live, and induce them to buy the family at the sale; and when the sale was made I think all had selected homes. In this case, at the sales many were informed that they would be bid in by the heirs. I never knew a family to be separated.

I believe it was in the autumn of 1856 I wished to obtain a good cook, and went to New Orleans. Beard & May, cotton brokers, informed me that the German Vice Consul was going home, and had the best cook in the city. I called on Mr. Kock at his office, and he gave me a note to his wife, stating the object of my calling. Madame sent for the cook, and she came into the drawing room and was introduced to me, and my business made known to her. She was a fine-looking woman. She asked me the usual questions—such as "Biddy" in the intelligence office asks persons in quest of a cook—about where I lived, number in the family, if there was a church near by, nearest town, etc. Obtaining the desired information, she told her mistress she did not wish to leave the city, and she was directed to retire. Mrs. Kock said she wished the servant to be satisfied with her new home, etc.

Next Beard & May sent me to a French family. Madame came in, and sent for the cook she wished to sell. This one varied the questions, she asked even as to hot dinners on Sundays, and then she said she would not like to live on a plantation; and so the visit was fruitless. Then Beard & May told me to question the servants they held for sale, and there I found a woman about thirty years old, of fine personal appearance, who was willing to accept a position in the country, and I bought her.

A few days after, Beard & May called on me and said my cook, Maria, wanted to see me; so I went to her, and she then told me she wished I would buy her husband Jim. I expressed my displeasure that she had not told me she was married before I bought her. However, I bought Jim to satisfy her, and took them both home with me. Maria was installed in the kitchen, and proved to be a good cook. Jim had charge of the horses, etc. At the beginning of summer we went North. Jim was put to work in the field. He soon ran away, stayed in the woods by day, came home often at night, and told the overseer that he would come home when I did. When we returned in the autumn, Jim came to see me and explained that he had never worked in the field; so he worked again at the stables and ginhouses. I now learned that Maria and Jim had never been married. When spring came, I told Jim I would take him back to New Orleans, and he was willing to go. I left him with Beard & May to be sold. When we returned in the fall Jim had not been sold. In the winter I visited New Orleans. The steamer arrived during the night. In the morning as I was going on shore I saw a number of fine hacks on the levee awaiting passengers; among them the driver of a fine carriage cried out: "O Master Sam, here is your carriage; ride with me. Don't you know Jim? Mighty glad to see you, Master Sam." He drove me to the St. Charles Hotel. Soon Jim came to see me, and I told him if he did not find a home for himself before I left the city I would have him sold to some one out in the country without consulting him. The result was, Jim got the owner of the livery stable to buy him, and that was the last I saw of Jim. No one would purchase Jim because he told every one who wanted him, "If you buy me, I will run away;" and so he hired himself out for about nine months, at twenty dollars per month, as a hack driver, which supported himself free of expense to me.

B

Indenture

Negress Betty
to
John Beale Bordley Esq.

Term 7 Years

Endorsed 14th Sep. 1799

Philadelphia

Entered Page 34

on the Records of the

Abolition Society kept

by the committee of

Guardians

J. Barker Secy

Entered

And now about Maria: In the spring she got in the habit of having fits, and would foam at the mouth, and the old cook would have to come over. This continued over two weeks.

One morning I saw my neighbor Courtney riding up to my gate rather rapidly. He was excited and said: "Capt. French, I want you to buy my man Parker or sell me Maria." Parker had the main charge of some one hundred and thirty servants on Courtney's place. As I had no use for Parker, I would not entertain buying him, and replied that I would sell him Maria. When he became more composed, he told me that "Parker had become stupid, thoughtless, and could not remember what was told him, and when I called him to account he informed me that he was so much in love with Maria that his mind was all 'upset,' but if I would only buy Maria he would be so happy, and be the best hand on the place if she were his wife." And so Maria became Parker's wife, and never feigned having fits any more. Marriage cured them. Her fits were all "put on" to get a new home at Courtney's.

I was now quite tired and wearied with cooks, but nevertheless, being in New Orleans, I made another venture. Beard & May said they had a good cook. She was a woman of about twenty, with a jolly round face, and said she was a fine cook, and I bought her. Her name was something like Amanda, as I remember it. She was a willing, good-natured creature, but so careless that half the dishes were spoiled; so during the summer I took her to New Orleans and left her with Beard & May (early in the morning), then drove to the hotel. I had finished my breakfast and was smoking in the rotunda, when I saw Amanda approaching, accompanied by a tall, elderly gentleman, to whom I was introduced, naming him "my new master." He was from one of the parishes of the State. He asked me some questions about his new servant, and said he thought her a good cook, and honest, from what she told him. He apologized for the early call, as he had to leave on the morning steamboat. Bidding Amanda good-by, I concluded to abide with our old cook again.

I have briefly sketched these, some of my experiences with slaves, to establish the fact that bondsmen on the Mississippi did have the privilege of selecting very often the persons with whom they wished to live, as well as the place, which is by poverty denied the poor white men when in the iron grip of the rich corporations, where they are held by the relentless "slavery of wages."

A man acting for himself and in the interest of his family must have feelings of humanity for his servants. Their welfare and happiness are indissolubly linked with his, aside from his accountability for his acts to his God. Corporations have no souls, and no God to worship except Mammon. They have no ear for the misfortunes or ills of an employee, no physician for sickness, no priest for the dying, nor coffin for the dead. All these the slave has.

Truly the relentless thirst for gold over the road to wealth crushes to death like a worm the poor laborer beneath its tread. There is no provision in the charter of a trust company for care of life or soul of a laborer, and his condition is disguised in the (unknown to him) glorious privileges of independence, liberty, and freedom. What a mockery are all these human rights to a family perishing in a hut by a coal mine for want of clothing and food, with no ministering hand! And yet all the wealth in the world was obtained from the earth by the miner and farmer.

God in the beginning proclaimed the relations and the obligations between master and bond servant in Holy Writ, and he will judge them by their deeds; but God hath not, nor hath man defined the humanities inseparable between a trust company and its employee, except by injunctions and courts and bayonet rule.

Bad as it is, some may be inclined to believe that Betty, under her indenture, had more privilege and enjoyment than most of the white laborers in the employment of many monopolies.

In connection with this indenture is presented the picture of the Rev. Henry Ward Beecher selling slaves on his theatrical pulpit stage in Plymouth Church, Brooklyn, to raise money, and fire the Northern hearts against the South.

The audience is large, and their countenances express delight at this fine scene of buffoonery, which was then considered *one of the "eight great personal events* of the *nineteenth century,"* and hence worthy of preservation. When passion shall have subsided, and calm judgment presides, it will perhaps be regarded as an act of charlatanry unworthy of so great a man. These great personal events are said to be:

When Jenny Lind sung in Castle Garden.

When Henry Ward Beecher sold slaves in Plymouth pulpit.

When the Prince of Wales was in America.

When Henry Clay bade farewell to the Senate.

When Grant went around the world.

When Lincoln was first inaugurated.

When Kossuth rode up Broadway.

When Mackay struck the great bonanza.

I regarded Mr. Beecher an orator, and have listened to his discourses on theology to his congregation with admiration; but his attacks on slavery were made perhaps with as little knowledge

of the condition of the bondsmen as that distinguished kinswoman of his, Mrs. Harriet Beecher Stowe, has shown in her ideal novel, "Uncle Tom's Cabin." They produced a diseased state of public sentiment, and Demos, turned loose, strained the ties of love and kindred relations that bound the States by the compact, and precipitated secession and war on the South.

If slavery be considered a wrong, and no doubt it was, then, in justice to all concerned in its establishment in the United States and to the condition of the slaves in 1861 and the means resorted to for their liberation, it becomes a matter of impartial consideration, and when that day comes, the South will stand before the world vindicated, and the verdict will be both parties guilty, as will be shown hereafter.

Slavery was only made *possible* by bringing in ships negroes from Africa; and that was mainly done by the people of Old England, New England, and New York City. They were large ship owners. They sent their vessels for slaves, and obtained them by theft, by capturing them in the midnight glare of burning villages, or by purchase. *They owned them all*. They were indeed inhuman slave dealers. They sold some of them to all the thirteen colonies, and to the several States formed of them under the constitution, and they continued this slave trade *legally* until 1808, and illegally until 1862. (See "American Slave Trade," by J. R. Spears.)

In Old England the question of slavery was discussed calmly, with justice and common sense, and they arrived at an equitable decision—viz., that the government should compensate the owners for their property rights in persons held to labor or (in language undisguised) in slaves, and, as I have already stated, $100,000,000 was appropriated to purchase them and set them free, an act of justice to the owners.

In this land of freedom the pious people of the North (I speak plainly) sold their slaves to the planters in the South, and, with the slave money in their pockets, rejoiced that they were not like the people South, and as Pilate did (figuratively) they took water and washed their hands before the people, saying: "We are innocent of the sin of slavery now!"

Next, from causes already stated, like the crusaders to the Holy Land, the fanatical crowd came down South, and took the slaves that they once owned and sold from the purchasers, and forced the States to set them free without compensation. By this act they took over $3,000,000,000 worth of private property from the owners—the greatest robbery ever committed on earth.

In the common courts of the country it has been adjudged, I believe, that the thief is a greater criminal than the receiver of the stolen property; but when the thieves steal the same property a second time, what should the sentence of the court be? Of that crime the North stands convicted.

There is a higher power than any established by man.

"God moves in a mysterious way
His wonders to perform."

In days of old he arraigned nations before his august court, and they lived or perished at his will. The day is not far distant when the South, at his command and in his own way, will arise from their down-trodden condition, to the surprise of their oppressors. Her fields will blossom as the rose, the busy hum of industry will be heard in the land, and the commercial sails of the world will ride on the waters of the Gulf of Mexico and the Caribbean Sea, plying to South America and the Orient through the canal that will connect the two great oceans. What position then will the New England States hold in the general prosperity of the States? Then it will be seen, "Vengeance is mine; I will repay, saith the Lord." And even now along the Atlantic seaboard great steamers go North mainly laden with articles made from wood, lumber, pig iron, cotton goods, fruit, and the great metropolitan hotels and the people generally depend on the fields and gardens of the South for their vegetables half the year; and so it goes on in arithmetical progression of increase.

Leaving out the negroes, the South has a homogeneous population; the solidarity of the nation will rest on her. In 1861 there was less than *one* foreigner to the hundred in the population of North Carolina, while in the West it ranged from *thirty* to *sixty* per cent. (See census reports.) The cities of Chicago and New York contain a population which will be found to be a conglomeration of all the peoples on the face of the earth—with their political ideas, their morality, their vices, their language, and their religion—and on no question will they agree unless purchased for a price, as a business transaction, for money, and "the love of money is the root of all evil," and the history of Rome will be repeated.

Historians estimate the number of slaves carried from Africa to the Americas and the West Indies Islands to have been from eight to twelve millions, out of which number about five hundred thousand died or were killed at sea, and their bodies were thrown overboard. And now let the *sin* of slavery rest on the North or the South, as it will finally be declared by the consensus of public opinion, when investigation discloses and proclaims the horrible cruelty of the Northern slave owners who brought them here, and contrast it with the amelioration of their condition and their advancement in intelligence and morality acquired by the teaching of the best men and women in the South. This opinion will be recorded.

The negro, as sold by his first owner, was a stupid animal speaking a jabbering lingo; he was now taught and trained in civilization until he was adjudged by the North, when set free, capable to perform all the duties pertaining to the high official positions to which the United States government did appoint him or his brother negroes elected him. Yes, under the teachings and training of their owners on the plantations and in the cities, while slaves, they were converted from fetichism to Christianity, and from cannibalism to gentility of living, and their beastly nature curbed by moral surroundings and force of example; and now, to humiliate the Southern people, who were disfranchised, political plans were arranged to have negro Senators elected instead of whites, and from Mississippi two negroes were occupying at different periods seats in the United States Senate chamber. Their names were Revels and Bruce. The latter I have seen riding through my plantation. From Senator he became Register of the Treasury of the United States, a position long held by my friend, Gen. W. S. Rosecrans, United States army.

Out of the three million soldiers that were in the United States army, there were not as many discharged soldiers holding office in the South in 1869 as there were ex-slaves out of the four hundred thousand negro men eligible to office. This indicates either the soldiers' unfitness for office, or that the selection of negroes was made to humiliate the people of the South.

It may be asked: Whence came Christianity among the slaves? Did it come by nature? No, nature is uniform in her laws, and developed no Christianity among the negroes in Africa, or elsewhere when left to themselves: hence it came by teaching, for on Sundays the master and mistress, nurse and children, in the carriage were always escorted to church by the young men on horseback, dressed in their clean and best attire, where all worshiped together in the Lord's house. Also, on many plantations, clergymen were maintained with ample compensation by two or three neighboring planters to preach the gospel to their people.

Whence came qualifications for business, unless taught by their owners? Reading, writing, and arithmetic do not come by birth, and the peasant and the prince alike have to study to comprehend even "the rule of three."

It is not pleasant to refer to the want of information among the common people in the North and West in regard to the real relation of the bondsmen to their owners, or to the ignorance of the masses of the nations of Europe on this question. In Europe they had a foretaste of freedom in 1848; but slavery in the United

States was a sealed letter to them all. For the North there is this excuse: the almost nonintercourse between the North and the South precluded personal observation, and they were taught in the schools, in the lecture room, from the rostrum and the pulpit, by the press in every village, town, and city all over the land, to believe the fabulous accounts of the ills of slavery to be true, and that the slave owners were cruel, illiterate, uncultured, and had "plantation manners," unfit for association with the immaculate people of the North. The populace of the North learned nothing from the utter failure of the advent of John Brown in Virginia, where slaves fled from him with horror and left him to his deserved fate; on the contrary, he was by the North held up as a saint who gave his life for freedom's cause.

Far and wide the abolition and free-soil party preached a crusade against the people of the South to liberate the slaves, and Mr. Beecher's picture shows to what low means they stooped to awaken enthusiasm for their cause. It spread to Europe, and when they commenced the war the illiterate masses there joined in the crusade against the South, as they did to rescue the holy sepulcher from the hands of the infidel, on which occasion, Proctor in his "History of the Crusades" says, "the Welshman forgot his hunting, the Scot his companionship with vermin, the Dane his carouse, and the Norwegian his raw fish," in their fanatical desire to reach Jerusalem; and so again the Welshman, the Scot, the Norwegian, the Dane, the German, and the rest of Europe came over here to enlist as substitutes in the Federal army in its crusade against the institution of slavery which was founded by their ancestors.

Herod the Great, an Idumean, to secure the throne of Jerusalem to the Idumean line of Jews, murdered his wife, the beautiful Mariamne, and his two sons by her. They were handsome, had been educated in Rome, were very accomplished, and beloved by the Jewish people; but as they were, through their mother, of the Asmonean line of Jews, Herod condemned them to death to secure the succession as he desired. When the war between the States ended, the white people of the Confederacy were in the way of the line of succession of the radical party to maintain office: so they were disfranchised, and a new race was made citizens to take their place: they were the late negro slaves, the pets and "wards of the nation!"

Now, when it was told to Augustus Cæsar that Herod had murdered his two sons by Mariamne, he said that "it was better to
be one of Herod's *pigs* than one of his sons;" and so when the
white people of the South were politically murdered, many of
their friends said: "It were better to be a '*ward of the nation*'
than a son of the Confederacy." These cruel proceedings have
been condemned by all the civilized nations of Europe, and will
be condemned by the impartial historians of the North when
passions shall have subsided.

The enslaving of the negro race in the colonies—and which
was largely confined to those called Southern, and almost entirely to them after the ending of the slave trade—placed the white
people of the colonies on a higher and broader plane and released them from the daily struggle after the "almighty dollar."

The busy minds of the Northern people were constantly more
and more given to trade and traffic, while those of the South
turned to the enjoyment of a home life; freed from restraint
and care, they practiced the amenities of social life, with honor,
truth, and charity to all. Strange as it may appear, a civilization—based on slave labor, that was tolerant in religion, that
encouraged freedom of thought, led their minds to the contem-
plation of the rights given man by his Creator when he breathed
the breath of life into his body as he came into this world—resulted in prompting these men to embody their views on this
question of divine right in the Mecklenburg Declaration, made
in Mecklenburg County, N. C., May 20, 1775, and which was
substantially expressed again, July 4, 1776, in the Declaration
of Independence, read in Philadelphia.

And so it was from the thoughtful minds of these quiet slave
owners came these two proclamations: that man was indued, or
born, with certain "inalienable rights" derived from his Maker
—namely, "life, liberty, and the pursuit of happiness." These
were some of the developments of a *civilization* based on slavery.

To secure these rights unto themselves, after the Confedera-
tion, they framed the Constitution of the United States, but unfortunately it was established on a compromise that was left for
futurity to interpret; and disagreement on this matter led to secession as a solution and last resort.

Passing by the particular events of the war between the States,
it may not be unprofitable to inquire what was the difference in

JOSEPH E. BROWN

the developments of the two civilizations that followed the formation and establishment of the Constitution; the North by itself, free, and the South with her peculiar institutions. By their fruits ye must judge them.

There were seventeen Presidents anterior to President Grant, out of which number eleven were Southern born, and six the product of free soil, if we include John Adams. In jurisprudence, the South gave us a Marshall; in the forum they need no mention, as statesmen they have but few peers; among diplomats, John Laurens, of South Carolina, a member of Washington's staff, special Minister to France, stands preëminent; in the darkest hour of our struggle, at the court of Louis XIV., he saved the colonies and turned the tide of war in our favor.

In the field we have Washington, Lee, Stonewall Jackson, and Forrest. For an honest opinion of Gen. Lee and his soldiers, see Theodore Roosevelt's life of T. H. Benton: there he stands *peerless*. Those who desire to learn more about Col. John Laurens may read the December number of *McClure's Magazine* (1899).

Such are some of the fruits of a civilization that has passed away.

When I survey the past, and from it make prophecy of the future, I am as candid in saying I rejoice that slavery is no more as I am in condemning the brutal manner in which it was abolished; and nevertheless I am as sincere in my love of my whole country as I am imbued with dislike to that class of people who out of hatred precipitated that war on the Southern people out of envy because they imagined that the planters were a more favored people than they themselves were.

A Roman consul was never accorded a triumph for a victory in civil war, nor were the spoils of war his. But after this civil war, as it is termed, ended, the emblems of victory have waved in triumph in our faces, and are carefully preserved instead of being hidden away, and the universal looting has enriched the soldiers' homes with the spoils of war. Senator Charles Sumner wanted the captured flags returned.

War is not barbarous, nor is it "hell;" it is just what parties choose to make it. When confined to the enlisted troops it is seldom cruel. Hell is an expression adopted to silence argument on the cruel manner in which the United States government

26

prosecuted the war: when this subject is mentioned we are silenced by the declaration, O well, "war is hell any way."

To cover up his own iniquities, Gen. Sherman said: " *War is hell.*"

During the war with Mexico I was with Gen. Taylor from Corpus Christi to Buena Vista, and during that period heard of but one case of robbery, and that was at Papagallos, on the march to Monterey. There a soldier stole a chicken. Seeing a crowd of officers in the street, I rode up to ascertain the cause.

Gen. Taylor had dismounted. There was the offender; he was severely reprimanded and placed under guard. Turning to the accuser—an old woman—the General gave her some silver coin in payment for her chicken. That war was not hell.

When Richard Cœur de Lion was ill in Palestine the Islam commander, Saladin, "sent him the choicest fruits and refreshment of snow during the burning heat of summer; and at the siege of Jaffa, Saphadan, the Mohammedan chief, observing Richard dismounted, sent him two Arabian horses, on one of which he continued the conflict until nightfall. He further solicited and obtained from Richard the honor of knighthood for his son." This was not much like hell.

Again, Richard promulgated, like Gen. W. T. Sherman, regulations for the government of his troops. "A *thief* was to have his head shaved, to be tarred and feathered." Had Sherman issued and enforced an order like this, the sight of his troops would have frightened all the inhabitants out of Savannah.

Our Unknown Dead.

Extract from an Address of Gen. S. G. French Made to the U. C. V. Camp, No. 54, Orlando, Fla., June 3, 1893.

Comrades: The solemn ceremony of Decoration Day has been performed. The few graves, alike of the Confederate and the Union soldiers that rest in our cemetery, have been decorated with floral offerings, and the cause that so few of the Confederate dead sleep where loving kindred can care for them inclines me to say a few words in regard to the unknown dead.

From Dalton down to Atlanta, and around that city, there was one continuous conflict for one hundred days, and not a day passed without some troops being engaged, and so the dead were left throughout a hundred miles on either side, resting where they fell.

If we turn to the east again, we find that Gen. Grant crossed the Rapidan May 4, 1864, and, taking the direct line to Richmond, immediately the battle of the Wilderness followed, and he announced that he was going "to fight it out on that line if it took all summer." A few days after came the battle of Spottsylvania, and June 1 that of Cold Harbor, where the Federal troops refused to make a second attack.

In these three great and sanguinary battles the commander of the Union forces did not meet with success, and so on the first day of summer he left that line and swung around, as McClellan did, to the James river. After Cold Harbor it seems as if there was no desire for another general engagement, and the hammering away mode of war commenced on Lee. On July 18, 1864, President Lincoln called for five hundred thousand more men, and so the detrition process went on for nine months, mainly on and near the picket line, being in all nearly eleven months and a half that Lee confronted Grant's hosts of men, and over all this extent of country lay the blue and the gray side by side in death. Devastation, as in the Palatinate, had done its work.

Now when the war ended, the Federal government, with commendable zeal, very humanely collected most of its dead and had their remains removed to its beautiful cemeteries, and there keeps green the sod and fresh the flowers on their graves.

There was no Confederate government to collect and care for the remains of the Confederate dead. Along the banks of the "Father of Waters" for more than a thousand miles the inhabitants tread unawares over the unknown graves of those who battled for the South. Along the shores of the Potomac, the Rappahannock, and the James wave the golden harvests on soil enriched by their blood and moldering dust. There the grapes grow more luscious and the wine is redder. From the capes of the Chesapeake adown the stormy Atlantic, and trending around the Gulf, rest thousands of our dead; or go to the heights of Allatoona, to Lookout's lofty peak, or Kennesaw Mountain's top, and you may seek in vain where the dead rest. Time, with the relentless force of the elements, has obliterated all traces of their graves from human eye; they are known only to Him who can tell where Moses sleeps in "a vale in the land of Moab." So the forgotten are not forgot, the Hand that made the thunder's home comes down every spring and paints with bright colors the little wild flowers that grow over their resting places, and they are bright on Decoration Day. The rosy morn announces first to them that the night is gone, and when the day is past and the landscape veiled with evening's shade, high on the mountain top the last ray of the setting sun lovingly lingers longest, loath to leave the lonely place where the bright-eyed children of the Confederacy rest in death.

And wherefore did they die? They fell in defense of their homes, their families, their country, and those civil rights arising from that liberty God gave man as a heritage in the beginning. They furnished to their country much that will be noble in history, wonderful in story, tender in song, and a large share of that glory which will claim the admiration of mankind. We can to-day place no wreaths of immortelles on their unknown graves, yet we can rest assured that the echoes of posterity will render their deeds illustrious.

And now, as I look back on the past and recall to mind your trials and sufferings—which will be forgotten—I am sure the world will not forget that your valor MERITED A SUCCESS which is better now than to have achieved it.